THE HUMANITIES IN THE NINETIES

THE HUMANITIES
IN THE NINETIES

A view from the Netherlands

Edited by

E. Zürcher and T. Langendorff

SWETS & ZEITLINGER B.V. AMSTERDAM / LISSE   PUBLISHERS

Library of Congress Cataloging-in-Publication Data

Humanities in the nineties / edited by E. Zürcher, T. Langendorff
    p. cm.
   Includes bibliographical references.
   ISBN 9026511337
   1. Humanities. 2. Humanities--Philosophy. I. Zürcher, E. (Erik)
II. Langendorff, T. (Ton), 1950-
AZ103.H849 1990
001.3--dc20
                                       90-20548
                                          CIP

CIP-gegevens Koninklijke Bibliotheek, Den Haag

Humanities

Humanities in the nineties / ed. by E. Zürcher, T. Langendorff. – Amsterdam [etc.] :
Swets & Zeitlinger
Met lit. opg.
ISBN 90-265-1133-7 geb.
SISO 002 UDC 009"19" NUGI 606
Trefw.: humaniora ; geschiedenis ; 20e eeuw.

Cover design: Rob Molthoff
Cover printed in the Netherlands by WNO Grafisch Bedrijf Nijmegen
Printed in the Netherlands by Offsetdrukkerij Kanters B.V., Alblasserdam

Copyright © 1990 by Swets & Zeitlinger B.V., Amsterdam/Lisse

ISBN 90 265 1133 7
NUGI 606

CONTENTS

Preface

P. Kramer

Chairman of the Advisory Council for Science Policy,
The Netherlands

The arts and humanities are still in the fortunate position of enjoying avid interest from a wide audience. Numerous professionals – scholars, teachers and students – are active in the field, while many well-informed lay people and amateurs contribute to the arts and humanities or avail themselves of their fruits.

People in fact have always been curious about their own history and that of other cultures and they have never ceased to be amazed at the diversity of languages, religions, philosophies, musical compositions, plays and art and literary works. One can scarcely imagine a world without the arts and humanities. Thus it strikes one as all the more odd that all kinds of lobbying is needed – and fortunately being done – to safeguard the place of the arts and humanities in the ranks of the other disciplines and defend them from being overpowered by economics and technology. As early as 1980 the American Commission on the humanities was vigorously defending teaching and research in the humanities (Report, 1980). In 1988 Lynne V. Cheney, the chairman of the National Endowment for the Humanities, was equally vociferous in his support (Cheney, 1988). Concern is equally being expressed in Europe. In Germany, Rudolf Smend, Vice-President of the Deutsche Forschungsgemeinschaft, has pleaded for a renaissance in the humanities (Smend, 1988). In Switzerland, the Wissenschaftsrat organised a study day on the future of the humanities (SW, 1987). In Sweden, the government has decided to provide additional financial support for the humanities (OECD, 1987). There, too, some fundamental thinking is being done on the place of the humanities in science policy (Elzinga, 1989). In other words, there is no lack of will to do something. The only question is, what and how? A problem arising in answering the question is that many people who are responsible for science policy have little idea of what is going on in the arts and the humanities and what issues are at stake. Such lack of insight is partially attributable to the science background of many of them, but also partially due to the absence of a tradition of regularly publishing state of the arts reviews in the humanities themselves. Thus it seemed to the Advisory Council for Science Policy in the Netherlands a good idea to start a project aiming at gathering information on the academic trends in the humanities. With the publication of this book, the project, which simultaneously produced a survey of the policy problems (Langendorff, 1990), is complete. The Council was so pleasantly surprised by the essays in the book that it deemed it fit to offer them to a wider audience.

I should like to thank Professor Dr. E. Zürcher, member of the Council and editor of the book, Ton Langendorff, staff member of the Council and co-editor, and the authors who have managed to produce a fascinating overview of their disciplines. A word of thanks is also owed to Carla Krassenburg who prepared the text. I should also like to thank the Minister for Education and Science for an additional subsidy which placed us in the position to publish this work.

References

Cheney, Lynne V., 1988. *Humanities in America*. A report to the President, the Congress, and the American People. Washington, D.C.: National Endowment for the Humanities.

Elzinga, Aant, 1989. Humanioras roll i det högteknologiska samhället, In: Thorsten Nybom (red.), *Universitet och samhälle*. Om forskningspolitik och vetenskapens samhälleliga roll, pp. 238-267. Stockholm: Tidens Förlag.

Langendorff, Ton, 1990. De geesteswetenschappen in Nederland: een overzicht van het beleid en het onderzoek. Den Haag: SDU. (Serie RAWB-achtergrondstudies) (*Humanities in the Netherlands:* a survey of the policy and the research. The Hague: SDU (RAWB background studies) (In Dutch).

OECD, 1987. *Reviews of National Science and Technology Policy: Sweden*. Paris: OECD.

Report of the Commission on the Humanities, 1980. *The Humanities in American Life*. London etc.: University of California Press.

Smend, Rudolf, 1988. For a Renaissance of the Humanities. *Interdisciplinary Science Reviews,* (13) 3: 208-210.

SW, Schweizerischer Wissenschaftsrat, 1989. Die Zukunft der Geisteswissenschaften/ L'avenir des sciences humaines. *Wissenschaftspolitik/Politique de la Science,* Beiheft/ Supplément 45.

Introduction

E. Zürcher

This collection of essays provides a fascinating panorama of an area of scientific research that generally receives too little attention. The fact that the essays are being published in English, and so are also aimed at an international public, does not alter the fact that we are here dealing with a view from the Netherlands. The degree to which the specifically Dutch point of view comes to the fore varies for each field of study. In some disciplines, such as linguistics, the study of literature and history, authors could permit themselves to place their subject entirely in an international context; in other contributions, such as the ones on the study of visual arts and on archaeology and prehistory, the international viewpoint is complemented by information on the situation in the Netherlands. However, there are fields of study where the national aspect features conspicuously, or is even dominant, because in these cases the manner in which research is carried out is profoundly influenced by the specifically Dutch situation. This category includes the concept of "area studies", and also theology with its typically Dutch distinction between the "science of religion" and "denominational theology". In spite of the restraints placed on them by this specific context they are of importance to an international public because they are illustrative of the way in which people in this country have attempted to find a solution to problems that people elsewhere are also wrestling with.

The humanities (an outdated term that various authors would like to see replaced by another) comprise a motley collection of dozens of specialist fields ranging from broad disciplines such as linguistics and history to specialized fields of research like Korean literature and Papyrology. From sheer necessity we have restricted our choice to the principal disciplines and to a few large areas of research which are in principle interdisciplinary, e.g. the study of non-western cultures and women's studies. They have been roughly grouped into five main areas which differ from each other in their subjects of research: philosophy and theology, language, the arts (which in this instance also covers Women's Studies because of the emphasis placed in this contribution on "feminine aesthetics"), and the historical sciences.

The volume starts with "hard facts" presented by Ton Langendorff; a statistical survey of the material support given to the humanities in some member countries of the OECD.

The humanities are subsequently approached in two introductory essays from neighbouring disciplines. Goudsblom approaches them from the social sciences, which he combines with the humanities under the common denominator "cultural sciences" – a complex of fields dealing with manifestations of acquired human behaviour, individual and collective. They differ in this from the natural and life sciences, forming a third level of complexity. He poses the question to what extent the present boundaries – notably those between the humanities and the social sciences – are the result of social and ideological factors such as interfaculty rivalry and considerations of status. As a mathematician, Grootendorst takes the opposite path, and presents a "humanistic" view of mathematics as a manifestation of culture. By stressing the role of intuition and ambiguity he makes clear that mathematics is not as "hard" as most people think it is.

In his essay on "Philosophical Research and Philosophizing" Van Dooren describes – and deplores – the isolation and far-going specialization of philosophical research, and the virtual disappearance of philosophizing in academia. He advocates a revival of creative philosophical activity based on research, because in the words of Cournot "philosophy without science is empty and science without philosophy is blind". His argument in favour of a combination of scientific research and the active study of philosophy runs to a certain extent parallel with Wegman's combination of the science of religion (*stricto sensu*) and denominational theology: the study of the phenomenon of religion and the expressing of a personal view on the transcendent. He does so in the context of the specifically Dutch academic situation, the *duplex ordo*, which attempts to maintain an equilibrium between scientific approach and religious formation.

The phenomenon of "language" would appear to be infinitely more complicated than even the linguists thought: this is the essence of Dik's contribution on linguistics. Language has a number of amazing properties by which it defies a full analytic understanding, and so far baffles even the most sophisticated computer. Against this background the author discusses some important trends in general linguistics. His argument is backed up and complemented by Cohen. Taking a branch of phonetics (intonation as a special form of pitch perception) as his starting-point, Cohen discusses the fields in which the humanities could fruitfully be integrated with information science, e.g. computer-aided analysis of complex processes. As a first step the author suggests the study of metaphor.

The arts are represented by five essays, dealing with music, theatre, the visual arts, literature, and "the search for a feminine aesthetics" as a central theme in women's studies. After presenting an overview of the state of the art in the main divisions of musicology (historical musicology, systematic musicology and ethnomusicology), Op de Coul and De Haen review some recent trends in musical research. A striking factor in this is the "communicative approach", with particular attention being paid to the way in which music is experienced and interpreted by the audience. The same emphasis is observed in various other contributions in this section. Schoenmakers lays this emphasis in the field of drama, where the object of study is no longer restricted to the play as such, but where the performance and its reception are expressly involved. We find this new approach in the field of visual arts as well, where "the human eye", both of the artist and the contemporary observer and interpreter, is the centre point. Reception and perception are also central to Fokkema's treatise on the study of literature. After summarizing the succession of theories since World War I, e.g. Russian formalism and the concept of semiotics, he states, as a perspective of the nineties, that "criticism" or hermeneutic understanding can no longer claim to be the only valid method. The empirical study of literature opens the possibility of interdisciplinary collaboration and cross-cultural research. In her essay on women's studies in the nineties, Brügmann gives a critical review of women's studies in the U.S. and Europe, centred around various attempts to identify a feminine aesthetics. As challenges for the future the author mentions, *inter alia*, the reduction of the conflict between rational-conceptual analysis and intuition, and the strengthening of the interdisciplinary character of women's studies.

The section dealing with the historical sciences is opened by Den Boer who, entirely in keeping with the model of the *Annales* school, deals with the developments in the science of history and its practitioners in the long, medium and short term. In particular, he assesses the impact of the *Annales* in European historical research, as well as the most recent reactions against it. Waterbolk opens his contribution on archaeology with a description of the many branches of archaeology, and their relations with other disciplines such as cultural anthropology, geography and biology. A separate section is devoted to the role of archaeology in contemporary society, and much attention is paid to recent technical developments.

"Area studies", treated by Idema, especially refer to studies dealing with regions beyond the limits of western civilization. They are essentially interdisciplinary, as they cover language and literature, history, religion, economic and social aspects, and art and material culture. Area specialists are basically mediators between ourselves and non-western cultures and between the scholarly communities on both sides.

Finally, in a concluding chapter called "Summing up", I have tried to distil some general trends and ideas from this very wide diversity of fields presented, something I did only after a great deal of hesitation. It goes without saying that each contribution gives only an extremely general view, and anyone who generalizes on the basis of generalizations is walking on thin ice.

But I dare say all the authors felt such doubts. Each one of them must have considered it an impossible task to look at the essential developments in his or her field of study, together with the current state of the art, and preferably to look into the future as well, within such narrow confines. All the more reason for me as editor to thank them warmly for their willingness to cooperate. My thanks also go to Ton Langendorff, who is not only responsible for compiling and presenting the quantitative data, but who in many respects did the work of a co-editor.

Part 1

The definiton and place
of the humanities
in modern society

Support for the humanities: some international statistics

Ton Langendorff

In his essay "The idea of the humanities" R.S. Crane tries to grasp the wisdom of those familiar words from Robert Louis Stevenson's *Child Garden's of Verses*:

> The world is so full of a number of things;
> I am sure we should all be as happy as kings. (Crane, 1967: 3)

According to Crane the humanities are most alive when they do *not* move from the diversity and particularity of their observations toward as high a degree of unity, uniformity, simplicity, and necessity as their materials permit but when they reverse this process. The humanities therefore aim, characteristically, at that special kind of happiness suggested by Stevenson's lines, "the happiness that goes with the habitual perception that the world of human experience can never be brought completely under the rule of uniform necessity or compulsion but will always remain – and, if we so will it, increasingly – 'full of a number of things'." (Crane, 1967: 12)

Thus, reading this opening chapter dealing with statistics – figures and tables which reduce the diversity of research activities in the humanities to the highest degree of unity: numbers – must be an unhappy experience indeed. But I am sure hereafter we can all enjoy the diversity the rest of this book brings.

Introduction

Regarding the available statistics on research and development (R&D) there are many sources. Almost every country in the western world produces annual statistical reports, science budgets, and in some cases also special reports on science and technology indicators.[1] But most of these national sources are not suitable for making international comparisons. Thus, international organizations such as UNESCO, OECD, and the European Communities put a lot of effort in achieving one database for their respective purposes.

Although the UNESCO and EC databases allow for a breakdown by some fields of science the humanities can not be made visible. The smallest degree of disaggregation is the field of the humanities and social sciences together. So it seems that we are dependent on OECD data. But .....

1. R&D-expenditures

Although the OECD data on R&D expenditure are the best international figures available, they are limited in their range of uses, and any conclusions based upon them can unfortunately be too easily dismissed as conceptually flawed. First is the lack of comparability of coverage across countries. A second limitation of the OECD R&D statistics is the comparative lack of disaggregation (e.g. for Japan and the USA no statistics on the humanities are available.). A third limitation stems from various technical problems with the methods used to estimate research expenditure. In order to determine the portion of government funds attributable to research (as opposed to teaching and other scientific activities), most countries make use of 'research coefficients'. But the coefficients employed in some countries are of doubtful reliability, in certain cases being based on little more than guesswork.

John Irvine and Ben Martin (Science Policy Research Unit, University of Sussex, England) have attempted to solve the first two problems. (Martin & Irvine, 1990) They selected six countries: USA, Japan, UK, France, Germany and the Netherlands. They obtained data relating to three categories of research funded directly of indirectly from national, state or local government sources:

– academic research financed by general university funds;
– academically related research carried out in laboratories other than those
  at higher education establishments (government-funded work carried

---

[1] See e.g. the latest "Science and Engineering Indicators - 1989" of the National Science Board (1989). Also: Van Heeringen & Langendorff (1989).

out in a variety of research establishments which, although not owned or operated by higher education institutions, are nevertheless so closely linked or so similar in the work they carry out that to omit them would result in unfair comparison being drawn between certain countries);
– academic, separately budgeted research which is financed by government funds specifically earmarked for research.

Irvine and Martin recently published an update of their figures. (Martin, Irvine & Isard, 1990) They show that Japan and The Netherlands spend most government funds on the humanities. Looking at expenditure per capita the differences among the countries are less marked, albeit that expenditure is highest in the smallest country (The Netherlands) and lowest in the biggest country (the USA) (see table 1).

Table 1: Expenditures for academic* and academically related research in the humanities, 1987

	Share in the government budget	Expenditures per capita
United Kingdom	6.3%	$ 3.10
West Germany	6.4%	$ 4.20
France	6.8%	$ 3.90
The Netherlands	8.5%	$ 5.60
United States	2.8%	$ 1.70
Japan	9.6%	$ 2.90

* General University Funds and Separately Budgeted Research
Source: Martin (1990). Population figures from OECD/STIID Data Bank.

In the majority of countries these figures are reasonably stable over time. Japan and the Netherlands are an exception. Expenditure in the Netherlands rose from 1980 onwards with humanities share of total government spending on academic research increasing by more than 1%. Precisely the opposite occurred in Japan.
Subdividing expenditure on the humanities by subdiscipline we see that in all six countries approximately 40% is spent on language and literature

research (see table 2). Table 2 indicates which countries deviate sharply from the average for the other subdisciplines.[2]

Table 2: Percentage share of subdisciplines

% share under mean	six-country mean		% share above mean
UK France Neth.	Creative Arts	23%	US Japan
	Language & Literature	43%	
	History	16%	France
	Archeology, Philosophy &		
	Religious Studies	18%	US France

2. Number of publications

The Arts and Humanities Citation Index (A&HCI) published by the American company Institute for Scientific Information (ISI) contains the names of the authors and titles of their articles published in 1400 journals. The ISI also makes a selection of titles from 5700 other journals, mainly in the social sciences.

The Dutch Advisory Council for Science Policy (RAWB) commissioned a survey of the authors of the articles in the A&HCI from 1980 onwards grouped by country of origin. (Noyons & Nederhof) The address of the author of 175,919 of the 311,484 articles was known (56.5%). The percentage is extraordinarily low compared with the percentage for the Science Citation Index (SCI) and the Social Science Citation Index (SSCI). This means that the figures below must be used with caution. However there is no reason to assume that the statistics display a bias by country of origin.

---

[2] The following calculation was made. An index was worked out first of all for each country for each subdiscipline, called "the relative expenditure priority". This is calculated as follows:

$$\text{REP for subdiscipline A in country X} = \frac{\text{\% share of subdiscipline A in country X}}{\text{\% share of subdiscipline A for all six countries}}$$

A sharp deviation from the average is now defined as a REP of less than 0.75 and a REP of more than 1.25.

Table 3 shows that North America and the European countries (including Eastern Europe and Scandinavia) account for more than 90% of the articles in the A&HCI.

Table 3: Number of publications in the A&HCI (1980-1990)

	number	%
North America	110,540	62.9
West Europe	41,310	23.5
East Europe	8,211	4.7
Australia/New Zealand	5,152	2.9
Africa/Middle East	4,592	2.6
Asia	2,877	1.6
Scandinavia	1,960	1.1
Latin America	1,277	0.7
	175,919	100%

Source: Noyons & Nederhof (1990).

As was to be expected in view of the overrepresentation of English language journals in the A&HCI, authors from the US (98,282 articles or 55.9%), the UK (18,178 articles or 10.3%) and Canada (12,258 articles or 7.0%) dominate; together they produced 73.2% of the articles.
Focusing on a number of European countries (table 4) we see that the number of publications per capita scarcely differs by country. What stands out is that the contributions of the smallest countries (Switzerland and Sweden) deviate sharply; Switzerland makes a relatively high contribution and Sweden a relatively low one.

If one compares the international contributions of the humanities and sciences by country it strikes one that only Sweden and Switzerland make a relatively smaller contribution to the literature on the humanities. The remaining four countries provide (slightly) more for the humanities than to the sciences. I base this statement on a comparison of the A&HCI with the SCI. I have divided the share of a country in the A&HCI (excluding the US, UK and Canada because of their overrepresentation in the A&HCI) by

Table 4: Number of publications in the A&HCI per capita

	number of publications	idem per capita
France	7,299	0.13
West Germany	6,439	0.11
The Netherlands	1,672	0.11
Belgium	1,059	0.11
Switzerland	1,016	0.15
Sweden	629	0.07

Sources: Noyons and Nederhof (1990); population figures (1987) from OECD/ STIID Data Bank.

Table 5: Number of publications in the A&HCI by subdiscipline

	West Europe	North America
General	15%	13%
Archeology	3	2
Arts & Literature	34	43
Classics	5	3
History	16	12
Linguistics	4	3
Philosophy	9	9
Theology	6	6
Other*	8	9
	100%	100%

* "other" includes articles selected by the A&HCI mainly from social science journals.

the share in the SCI (also excluding US, UK and Canada).[3] The ratio for the six European countries from table 4 is 1.64; 1.15; 1.03; 1.29; 0.87 and 0.40.

[3] See Schubert, Glänzel, Braun (1989: 218).
The period for which the articles in the SCI have been counted is not 1980-1990 as is the case with the articles in the A&HCI, but 1981-1985. This may produce a distorted picture.

Subdividing the publications by subdiscipline is only useful for groups of countries for otherwise the figures for the individual countries are too small. This is why table 5 compares only Western Europe and North America.

The differences are not great. The US would seem to publish more in the field of Arts & Literature while Western Europe is geared more to the historical subjects (history, archeology and classics).

References

Crane, R.S., 1967. *The idea of the humanities and other essays critical and historical.* Chicago/London; The University of Chicago Press, 2 Volumes, vol. 1.

Heeringen, A. van & T. Langendorff, 1989. *Science and technology indicators 1988.* The Hague: Advisory Councils for Science Policy.

Martin, B.R. & J. Irvine, 1986. *An international comparison of government funding of academic and academically related research.* Sussex: SPRU.

Martin, B.R., J. Irvine & P. Isard, 1990. *International Trends in Government Funding of Academic and Related Research.* Hampshire, England: Edward Elgar.

National Science Board, 1989. *Science and Engineering Indicators - 1989.* Washington D.C.: U.S. Government Printing Office, (NSB 89-1).

Noyons, E. & A. Nederhof, 1990. *Publication activity in the Arts and Humanities.* Leyden: Centre for Science and Technology Studies (Research Report to the RAWB). Available on request.

Schubert, A., W. Glänzel, T. Braun, 1989. World Flash on Basic Research. *Scientometrics,* 16: 3-478

The humanities
and the social sciences*

J. Goudsblom

Preliminary remark

The task set for me is different from that of most other contributors to this volume. Whereas they have been asked to write about their own particular discipline, my assignment concerns the relationships between the humanities and the social sciences at large. This is a subject of much bigger scope and far more difficult to delimit. In exploring it I have continually been puzzled by the problem of how to mark the boundaries between these two loosely defined intellectual fields. Wolf Lepenies' illuminating book on the 'three cultures' has persuaded me that they are best understood as forming a part of a triangular configuration to which the natural sciences belong as well. (Lepenies, 1988) As sociologists such as Karl Mannheim, Norbert Elias, and Pierre Bourdieu have demonstrated, the substantive or cognitive aspects of any such intellectual configuration cannot be separated from the historical social setting in which it has developed.[1] In order to discuss the division of labour between the humanities and the social sciences ('who are concerned with what?'), it has therefore been necessary also to consider questions to do with solidarity ('who feel akin to whom, and who do

---

[1] See especially Karl Mannheim (1927); Elias (1971); Bourdieu (1988 & 1989).

not?'), and hierarchy ('who look up to whom, who look down upon whom?').
If my paper appears to be written more than most others from an outsider's
perspective, this is partly due to the simple fact that I have not been asked
to report on trends and prospects in my own field, sociology, but to discuss
relationships of a more general nature. Moreover, I think that some tendency towards detachment is inherent in the sociological approach itself.

1. Introduction: the triad of 'new faculties'

Some concepts and ideas sound so self-evident as to make any further
questioning seem improper. A person who shouts 'Long live our fatherland'
does not expect that he will be asked to explain what he means by 'fatherland'.
A similar rhetorical effect is often implied in the term 'humanities'. It
sounds as if a time-honoured tradition of 'humanism' is reverberating in it
– a tradition of apparently unbroken continuity which extends back to the
Italian Renaissance and the universities of medieval Europe and even to
Greco-Roman antiquity.

On closer inspection, however, the word 'humanities' turns out to be
neither as ancient nor as self-evident as its verbal form seems to suggest. It
gained general currency in English only in the nineteenth century. And
even if we include its immediate predecessors in Latin and French, the
history of this small family of words is still relatively brief and far from
unequivocal.

According to the *Oxford English Dictionary*, this chapter in semantic history begins with William Caxton who in 1483 distinguished two kinds of
learning: the study of divinity and the study of humanity. The tenor of the
distinction was obviously programmatic: it was intended to break the monopoly of theology over serious scholarship. In a similarly militant spirit
Francis Bacon proposed some hundred years later that, besides divine
philosophy, there should be room for natural and human philosophy – the
latter being dedicated to the study of humanity.

Caxton and Bacon may have been influential writers, but the sense in
which they used the word 'humanity' does not seem to have entered English usage. In France the term caught on better. As early as the sixteenth
century at French universities, the plural form *les humanités* was used for a
set of subjects which did not fit into the traditional curriculum dominated
by theology. Translated as 'the humanities' this plural became general in
English in the nineteenth century, mainly as the result of a movement in
the United States to reform the universities and, again, to diminish the
predominance of theology.

In some European languages, such as German and Dutch, the word humanities has never become accepted, whether in its Latin or vernacular forms. In the course of the nineteenth and twentieth centuries, however, other words with a different etymology have been introduced into those languages to convey similar meanings. Thus in German the famous term *Geistes-wissenschaften* was coined, while in Dutch first the word 'Letters' (a literal translation of *literae*) and more recently the straight Latin *humaniora* came to serve as equivalents.

The developments in Dutch are interesting because they show that, even in the absence of the word 'humanities', there was a semantic niche becoming visible that needed to be filled. This new need grew out of the expansion and internal re-arrangement of the universities in the course of the nineteenth and twentieth centuries. Essentially, what happened in the Netherlands did not deviate from the general trend over most of the European continent. At the beginning of the nineteenth century, the universities were composed of four faculties: Theology, Law, Medicine, and Philosophy. In the next century and a half, Philosophy was split up into the new faculties of Letters, Natural Sciences, and Social Sciences. Since then, the faculty of Letters has covered most of the area that would be known in English as 'the humanities'.
When today we use the term humanities, its meaning is still to a large extent determined by this configuration of faculties as it has taken shape over the past two hundred years. In order to understand the present position of the humanities, it seems necessary, therefore, to see how this specific configuration developed: how the faculty of Letters related to the other two 'new' faculties, and how the entire group of 'new' faculties related to the old faculties.
These interrelationships have at least two dimensions: organizational and intellectual. The division of disciplines between faculties has been primarily an institutional arrangement; but clearly there is also an epistemological side to it. We shall have to take both aspects into account in our discussion.

For the greater part of the nineteenth century most universities on the European continent continued to be divided into four faculties. The first three of these – Theology, Law, and Medicine – were the most important, since they offered training for specific professions, whereas Philosophy was mainly taught as a general introductory subject. In the course of the century new disciplines emerged, however, which did not fit into the old departmental divisions. Physics and chemistry became too large and too independent still to be counted as branches of philosophy; and a similar growth occurred in the study of history and languages. Thanks to the ex-

pansion of secondary education, all these subjects now also offered their
students the prospect of a professional career. (cf. Ringer, 1979)
The first 'new' faculties to emerge in this process were the Natural or
Physical Sciences, and Philology or 'Letters'. Between them, these two
faculties divided up most of the curriculum of Philosophy, simultaneously
giving it a more empirical twist. As a third newcomer, there were the social
sciences; for want of the *effet civil* of a teacher's career, however, their
institutional position was much weaker. (cf. den Boer, 1987: 224-284) In
many cases only Economics was given the status of a separate faculty;
partly as a result of this relatively early recognition (which was promoted
by strong ties with the world of finance), economists to this day have
continued to stay aloof from the other social sciences. When, after 1945,
most European universities took over the practice already developed in the
United States earlier in the century of setting up separate departments for
the social sciences, economists as a rule maintained their *status aparte.*
In spite of such remaining barriers between related fields, the overall constellation of the three encompassing groups of disciplines became increasingly
manifest. Interestingly, in their mutual division of labour the 'new' faculties continued a pattern already formed by their predecessors. The central
areas of concern for Theology, Medicine, and Law were, so to speak, the
soul, the body, and justice; in the new faculties these were superseded by
culture, nature, and society. The similarities in the direction of interest
make the differences in scope and method stand out even more clearly: the
empirical subject matter of the new faculties is far more extensive, and it is
to a much lesser degree determined by specific professional requirements.

The relationship between the old and the new faculties is, of course, more
complicated than a simple 'succession' with straight lines of 'descent'.
The three new faculties have not simply replaced the old ones; the old
faculties still continue to exist, and all sorts of influences may be traced
across older and newer areas of research and education. The important fact
remains, all the same, that the three new faculties are marked by a broader
field of studies and a weaker tie to specific professional practices. With
their greater freedom from practical restrictions, they have always been
more strongly committed to the idea that the pursuit of knowledge is a
worthwhile value in its own right.
The ideal of knowledge for knowledge's sake was surely not a nineteenth
century novelty. In the preceding centuries, an intellectual culture had
been developing in which literary studies and scientific research took pride
of place. This development had largely occurred outside the universities,

however. It was primarily the work of cultured aristocrats and patricians who not only found diversion in sonatas and sonnets but also in historical and philological investigations and in chemical and physical experiments. Some of them, such as Christiaan Huygens or Edmund Gibbon, could finance research by their own means; others, like Voltaire in his scientific moods, worked with the aid of rich friends (who in his case happened to be female). This long pre-university stage, marked by the founding and flourishing of the Royal Academies in England and France, no doubt contributed to the nineteenth century boom in the 'pure sciences'. Thanks to the patronage of and active participation by members of the highest circles in the preceding era, there was already a great 'prestige by association' attached to the free pursuit of knowledge.

More impulses were given to the culture of pure research as, throughout the nineteenth century, new opportunities arose for experts who could devote their careers entirely to the acquisition and transmission of specialised knowledge. Whatever further social skills these people might have was considered of secondary importance – as illustrated by the abundant jokes about absent-minded professors. By analogy with clerical, military, and governmental hierarchies, a scholarly hierarchy was formed, with knowledge as its main criterion. Especially in secondary schools this criterion became pre-eminent: the efforts of the teachers were primarily aimed at imparting material for the exams, and the students' success was measured by the degree to which they could show they had mastered this material.

2. The relationships between the new faculties: cognitive aspects
What can be noted with most certainty about the threefold division of university disciplines into humanities, natural sciences and social sciences, is that it conforms with generally established institutional arrangements. This having been said, the question arises of whether there is any further, more fundamental rationale underlying it. To what extent are the lines along which the 'new' faculties have been divided also intellectually compelling?
Given their strong emphasis on cognition it is no wonder that the scholars and scientists themselves tend to assume that the tripartition is not primarily due to a social process of institutionalization, but is implied in the nature of reality itself. If pressed for an argument, they will explain that the world they study is in itself heterogeneous, consisting of various levels or aspects which are so divergent that their investigation requires groups of disciplines with very specific methods and techniques.

This train of thought may be found in each of the three areas. As a lucid recent example I take the introduction by the biologist, Richard Dawkins, to his book *The Blind Watchmaker*, one of the avowed purposes of which is to underpin the scientific status of the theory of evolution. (Dawkins, 1986) According to Dawkins, the world studied by scientists is composed of two sorts of things – living and dead. They are distinguished by their varying degrees of complexity. Dead things are relatively simple; their structure and behaviour is determined by relatively few variables. If you throw a non-living object, such as a dead bird, into the air, it will describe a parabola the course of which can be calculated according to the laws of physics. The dead bird is a projectile; if we know with what force it is thrown in a particular direction, we can predict precisely where it will land.

With a living bird things are less simple. You may hold it in your hand and throw it with the same force in the same direction, but it is by no means certain where it will reach the ground again. Of course, the laws of physics remain valid, for the body continues to be subject to the forces of gravity and wind resistance. At the same time, however, there are other principles at play determining the bird's flight. Living things are more complicated than dead things; therefore, Dawkins states, we need a different kind of science to study them. Physics is the science of dead, biology of living things.

For those readers who might wish to object that physics is far from being a simple science, Dawkins has a brief and pithy reply: the science of physics should not be confused with its object. The *science* of physics is a product of the human brain; the human brain is a living thing, and that explains why physics is a complicated subject and not easy to learn.

Dawkins' argument may be read in two ways: as a general and largely disinterested treatise on the theory of science, and as a special plea for his own subject, biology. He takes issue with the hegemonical aspirations of physicists who claim that theirs is the only true science and that all scientific problems can be reduced to problems of physics. Against this one-sided physical reductionism Dawkins puts forward his own model in which there is room for the two sciences of living and of dead matter. He still argues exclusively from the perspective of the natural sciences, however, and he seems to take it for granted that physics and biology together are capable of answering all scientifically relevant questions. The humanities and the social sciences come off very poorly; in so far as the research done in these fields is worthy of the name 'science', it is nothing but a form of applied biology.

Now this opinion clearly challenges the status of the humanities and the social sciences. In meeting that challenge, we may note, first of all, that many physicists today no longer subscribe to the idea that 'the stuff of physics' is characterized by a relatively low degree of complexity. As Ilya Prigogine and Isabelle Stengers put it in the opening sentence of their book *Order out of Chaos*: 'Our view of nature is undergoing a radical change toward the multiple, the temporal, and the complex.' (Prigogine & Stengers, 1984: xxvii) With this statement they are referring to the level of the smallest particles as well as to that of cosmic processes. At both levels it turns out to be possible not only to observe highly complex phenomena but also to make these phenomena accessible to theoretically relevant research. On these grounds Dawkins' argument needs some revision. There is no reason, however, to reject its central point, concerning the hierarchical structure of reality. Even if the lower forms of organization at the level of physics prove to be more complicated than he assumes, we can only conclude that this greater complexity is also present in the living organisms with which biologists are concerned. The complexity of dead things is included in, and only seems to add to, the complexity of living things.

But this does not imply that biologists always have to deal with both levels of complexity. Processes at a higher level may be relatively autonomous with regard to processes at a lower level. It is this principle of *relative autonomy* which enables biologists to describe and explain the behaviour of cells, organisms, and biotopes, without having to expound every detail at the level of physics. The peculiarity of that small part of the universe which happens to be living is not just characterized by greater complexity but also by certain dynamics of its own. Because of these relatively autonomous dynamics of living systems we need not constantly refer to their complexity at the atomic level in order to describe and explain their behaviour at the organic and the social level. If this principle may be applied to make a case for biology, why may it not be equally well applied to the social sciences and the humanities?

It is in this respect that I find Dawkins' attempt to reduce all sciences to either physics or biology untenable. His arguments may be ingenious and they need not even be incompatible with a recognition of the complexity of 'the stuff of physics'. He goes wrong, however, in conceiving of human knowledge in purely biological terms. By maintaining that science is a product of 'the human brain' Dawkins suggests that we are only dealing with separate organs operating independently in each individual. It is far more realistic, however, to regard knowledge as originating in a virtually

endless chain of connections between human brains – a configuration that
is usually referred to as 'culture'.[2]

In a sense, this last idea may even be used to reverse Dawkins's entire
argument. If, indeed, every form of science is a product of culture, it may
be examined as such. Thus, for example, the paleoanthropologist, Misia
Landau, has found that the principles of 'narrative structure' discovered by
Vladimir Propp in the analysis of fairy-tales can me made to apply to
theories about the descent of *Homo sapiens*. (Landau, 1984, and Lewin, 1987:
30-46) As she demonstrates, within Dawkins' own field, the theory of
evolution, models of thought and presentation are employed which show
remarkable structural similarities with folk tales. This observation may
serve to temper the hubris of natural scientists. It is particularly persuasive
since Landau does not lapse into the facile counterpart of scientism – the
equally parochial textism or textualism which reduces all of reality to
texts.

Some practitioners of the humanities indeed appear to think that they can
get the better of the natural scientists by interpreting the latters' work in
terms of 'discourse' or 'idiom'. In doing so, they can refer to a simple
syllogism: all science is expressed in language; language is the domain of
linguistics; therefore a scientific theory of science should be based upon
linguistics. Embroidering on such ideas they may go to the extremes of
pure textualism in which nature only appears as a 'text' which can be
'read' in various ways. This would leave the final say to the linguists, the
reading experts *par excellence*.

Although such scriptural arguments may be logically consistent, their implications are equally as sterile as those of physical reductionism. The
investigation of nature is indeed a mental activity, and those who engage in
it are working in a cultural tradition. It would be nonsensical, however, to
regard these traditions as entirely autonomous constructions, floating freely
over reality. Every culture in itself comprises the experience derived by
people from the real world of which they form a part.

The theory of science which best avoids reductions *ad absurdum* in the
direction of both physics and metaphysics is still, in my view, the one for
which the foundations were laid more than a century and a half ago by the

---

[2] Cf. the definition of culture (still in terms derived from biology) as 'essentially a matter
of each person utilizing the nervous systems of other persons', Johnson (1946: 162-163).

sociologist, Auguste Comte. This theory was later elaborated by Emile Durkheim, and in our own time it has been further articulated by Norbert Elias, among others. We may by now speak of a collective product, although (and this is typical of the state of knowledge in this area) various individual nuances are still discernible. (Durkheim, 1938, and Elias, 1978a)

The sociological theory of the sciences, like Dawkins' theory, may be read in two ways. We may view it purely as an intellectual attempt at indicating, to the best of our knowledge, those properties of the known universe that give the most adequate foundation for the division of labour in the sciences. We may also regard it with more suspicion as the ideology with which a group of professionals, sociologists in this case, try to legitimate their own position. The fact that the theory performs the second function does not necessarily discredit its more general validity. Acknowledging the possible ideological uses of the theory may sharpen our critical sense; but its more general cognitive value can only be assessed on the basis of substantive arguments.

The theory emphasizes in particular that the levels which may be distinguished in reality differ not only according to complexity but also to 'specificity'. All known matter is subject to the laws of physics, but only a specific part of it, the part that happens to be self-reproducing, is also subject to the laws of biology. In an even smaller and still more specific part, other principles again operate – principles which, in turn, exercise some influence upon the lower levels. While thus adding a special emphasis to Dawkins' view, the theory is in full agreement with the elegant opening sentence of *The Blind Watchmaker*: 'We animals are the most complicated things in the known universe'. (Dawkins, 1986: 1) Every human being is a physical body which, when stepping into a bathtub, conforms to Archimedes' law of volume and weight and, when jumping from a springboard, to Newton's laws of gravity. In addition, every human being is a body in a biological sense, an organism with blood circulating in accordance with the principles dis–covered by Harvey. But, then, every human being is also a thinking and talking creature, a member of groups and a carrier of culture.

Naturally Dawkins recognizes these latter qualities, but he fails to accord them a separate place in his model of the sciences. For him, the principle of relative autonomy ceases to be relevant beyond the level of genes and cells. However, if the behaviour of cells cannot fully be explained by the laws of physics, neither can the behaviour of human beings fully be explained by the principles of biology. In living systems,the very behaviour of atoms and molecules happens to be determined to a large extent by the cells of which they form a part, the behaviour of the cells in question by the organisms, and the behaviour of the organisms by the groups to which they belong and by the knowledge they have acquired as group members. Any attempt to ignore these hierarchical relationships, and to account for the higher levels of complexity and specificity represented by human groups and human cultures in terms of cells and genes is not only inefficient, but futile.

If Dawkins' own line of reasoning leads us to recognize that there is more in the world to be studied than physics and biology can cope with, there arises the question of whether his criteria for demarcating biology from physics can also be made to apply to those fields which deal with the higher levels of complexity and specificity in the human world. If there were a straight analogy between the two groups of disciplines, that would enable us to draw up a fourfold scheme, instead of the triad that has actually developed in the institutional structure of the universities. On the one hand, there would be the 'natural' sciences of physics and biology; on the other hand there would be the humanities and the social sciences. The humanities, we might continue, would be primarily concerned with that relatively autonomous aspect of reality known as 'culture', and the social sciences with 'society' as comprising the interrelationships between human beings.

The formulation sounds temptingly neat; but it is highly questionable whether the distinction between 'culture' and 'society' can be made solid enough to sustain such far reaching implications. I shall return to this problem later. First I wish to point to a remarkable fact. Theoretically, the main line of demarcation between physics and biology appears to be rather evident; yet the practitioners of both fields generally consent to being classified together under the common label of the natural sciences. The reverse is true of the relationships between the humanities and the social sciences. Here, there seems to be far more common ground, and the boundaries are much less easily drawn. Nevertheless, many practitioners of these fields continue to set great store by the distinction, and they are certainly not prepared to unite under one banner equivalent to that of the natural sciences.

This peculiar discrepancy calls for an inspection of issues that are of not just an intrinsically theoretical nature. Perhaps it is not only the ordering of reality into levels of varying complexity and specificity that provides the clue to understanding the separation of the humanities and the social sciences. We may have to look at other factors the impact of which is more difficult to pinpoint — factors concerning the hierarchical ordering of society. It is to these issues, which are usually not dealt with in either ontology or methodology, that I shall now turn.

3. The relationships between the three new faculties: social aspects

At several places above I have already made reference to specifically 'social' motives, especially with respect to the hierarchy of disciplines. This could not be avoided. In the actual 'contest of the faculties', arguments put forward as strictly theoretical have repeatedly been mixed with issues relating to the status hierarchy and competition among the practitioners of different fields – both within and beyond the university.[3]

As is to be expected, the very theoretical inconsistencies of the threefold classification reflect longstanding practical arrangements. Not only are physicists and biologists indiscriminately lumped together as 'natural scientists', the triad also simply ignores the 'old' faculties. These, on their part, have not let themselves be incorporated into the new scheme. As a faculty, Medicine has not merged into the natural sciences; nor has Law joined the social sciences; nor even has Theology always surrendered to the humanities. The old faculties have by and large maintained themselves – not by virtue of a splendidly consistent theory of knowledge but because of their firm links with professional training. As long as their graduates found a comfortable social niche awaiting them, there was little reason for trying to justify the curriculum with epistemological arguments.

Right up to today, at every university there are two distinct hierarchies of prestige. One is intrinsically academic, based upon scientific and scholastic accomplishments, with the Nobel Prize as the paramount distinction. The other one is mainly determined by such 'extra-academic' criteria as social background, wealth, and political influence. Pierre Bourdieu and his collaborators have shown that, in France, the newer faculties of the natural sciences and the humanities rank highest on the 'intra-academic' scale, whereas the older faculties of law and medicine are still on top 'extra-academically'. (Bourdieu, 1988)

From the start, the new faculties have tried to legitimate their existence by appealing to a general ideal of knowledge, not directly linked to practical achievements. The old faculties had little use for this ideal of pure knowledge since professional practice dictated what the students had to learn. The only exception was philosophy, the womb out of which the new faculties were to spring. For philosophers objective knowledge was indeed a supreme value; but with their unworldly attitude they occupied the last and lowliest position in the traditional rank-order of the four faculties.

---

[3] The part played by competition in the intellectual community has been emphasized most strongly by Mannheim (1927). See also Bailey (1977).

Indeed, the degree to which the practitioners of an academic discipline can permit themselves to be indifferent towards epistemological problems may well be a measure of the intellectual autonomy and social prestige of that discipline. There is no urgent need for legitimation on theoretical grounds in fields which rank highly in terms of either scientific success or general social status.

The older faculties, generally not given to excessive self-reflection, tended to take as their primary sources of knowledge – to put it in single catch-words – revelation, reason, tradition, and experience. It would, of course, be impossible to attribute the body of knowledge of an entire faculty to any one of these four sources. Yet there were clearly diverging preferences. In theology revelation ranked first, in philosophy reason, in law tradition (rather than experience), and in medicine experience (rather than reason). The new faculties have never recognized revelation; the closest to it that they may accept as a source of knowledge is intuition. The natural sciences rely almost completely on the experimental method, combining experience and reason. In the social sciences there is a strong tendency to follow the same model, but the possibilities for experimentation are severely limited. Respect for tradition is strongest in the humanities; this corresponds to the affinity with theology, philosophy, and law that I noted before.

Something of the hierarchy between the older and the newer faculties resounds in the relationships among the new faculties themselves. Bourdieu's findings for France seem to apply to other European countries as well: the natural sciences tend to be most successful by scientific standards, the humanities in various forms of 'extra-academic' prestige. The social sciences do not score highly on either scale.

In the Netherlands, signs of Bourdieu's dual prestige hierarchy may already be noted at the *gymnasium*, the traditional preparatory school for the universities. Even though the brightest pupils generally choose the 'science' stream of the curriculum, those who are in the 'classics' section may still feel in a certain way superior – by exhibiting an undefinable *je-ne-sais-quoi* which probably has its roots in the culture of the nobility and the high clergy. The humanities at Dutch universities retain many more of the vestiges of this 'higher' culture than any of the other new faculties.

Ever since their very first founding, most universities stood in an ambivalent relation with the church. As indicated by the general use of Latin, ties with the First Estate, the clergy, were initially strong. At quite an early stage, however, the faculties managed to loosen this bond. They were aided by the rise of modern states which soon began encouraging the use of a national vernacular, including its use in the influential Royal Academies. Consequently, the new faculties of the nineteenth century did not have to go to any great lengths to free themselves from bondage to the First Estate. The major relic of such bondage, knowledge of Latin and Greek, as a requirement for university admission, has been abolished almost everywhere. The natural sciences and the social sciences have led the way, and the humanities have followed suit – even if occasionally a note of nostalgia for the traditional language of the First Estate may resound, as in the re-emergence of the word *humaniora* in the Netherlands.

The ideal of knowledge for knowledge's sake has yielded the most lucrative returns in the natural sciences. As in the humanities, graduates could find employment as teachers. The prestige of these disciplines came to depend much more, however, upon the increasingly frequent applications of their findings in industry. Technology and science developed in a process of cross-fertilisation, stimulated by rapidly expanding commercial and military interests. (cf. Willink, 1988)

The efforts made in the social sciences at emulating the natural sciences in this respect have remained of little avail. Economists have done best; their mathematically sophisticated models have become a regular feature in managerial decision making in both private and governmental organizations. All concerned agree, however, that the models are used only for want of anything better; their predictive power is far below that of models in the natural sciences.

The practitioners of the humanities prefer to seek their strength in other qualities such as a command of languages, a sense of history, connoisseurship, and erudition – attributes that are traditionally cultivated in the higher social circles. While in the humanities these qualities continue to be appreciated as signs of cultural competence, their function in the social class structure is seldom openly discussed. Of course, no serious scholar would dream of denying the existence of social class differences as such; but it is another matter to recognize their impact upon one's own cultural values. The general tendency in the humanities is to carry on the tradition of bourgeois intellectuals who, resisting the hegemony of the Second Estate, the nobility, even more than that of the First Estate, have developed an ideal of culture that may best be characterized as 'quasi-classless'. In its universalistic formulations this ideal may seem to be elevated far above all concerns of social class; yet it clearly reflects the social habitus of middle class groups in the process of ascending in the status hierarchy by deploying their intellectual powers.[4]

This habitus still colours the relationship of the humanities vis-à-vis the natural and the social sciences. Although it is rarely said in so many words, the latter in particular are regarded as somewhat *vulgar*. Even if they are no longer suspected of being socialism in disguise, they still seem to represent the even more formidable threat of levelling, standardization, secularization, and 'disenchantment of the world'. Even that branch of the social sciences which has been socially most successful, economics, does not escape from the general disapproval. To many practitioners of the humanities it, too, smacks of the vulgar, if only because of the object which it puts into the centre of attention: money – a plain theme, which is being studied with mathematical models borrowed from the natural sciences and without any attempt at literary elegance.

The differences between the humanities and the social sciences have, from the very first, been marked by both subject matter and point of view. If the social sciences are primarily concerned with the interrelationships among people and the institutions in the context of which these interrelationships occur, the humanities find their themes first of all in the products of the human mind, in culture. Moreover, social scientists have a predilection for tracing and explaining regularities, while students of the humanities set great store by understanding singular events and achievements.
Interestingly, the 'cognitive' and the 'social' differences between the two fields seem here to converge. The purely epistemological issues discussed in the preceding section are subtly fused with other issues which are usually not included in the official academic agenda but which, nevertheless, exert a strong influence upon both choice of subject matter and method. The crucial point at which the two dimensions intersect is the tacit propensity for studying phenomena with a high social and cultural prestige. The priorities of intellectual interest are thus remarkably in correspondence with the hierarchical ordering of society, which also shows a congruence between the singular or the specific on the one hand and the eminent or the powerful on the other. A kingdom consists of one king and many subjects; everyone knows the name of the king, nobody knows the names of all the subjects.

---

[4] For a discussion of the 'quasi-classless' ideal of culture, see Elias (1978b: 1-34); Goudsblom (1980: 156-170). For the concept of habitus, see Bourdieu, 1986.

History books reflect these relationships: they mention the names of the kings, and leave the subjects anonymous.

In societies with an hierarchical structure, people's attention from the bottom to the top is directed toward individual persons, and from the top to the bottom it is directed toward collectives without proper names: peasants, tax payers, recruits. 'For most people are in the dark, and only a few are in the light'. Something of this asymmetry may be recognized in the preoccupations of the humanities and the social sciences. The former are first of all interested in concretely named individuals, works of art, and unique events; the latter in recurrent patterns, underlying structures, and over-all processes. In other words, from a similar position in the middle of the social hierarchy the humanities tend to look *upward*, and the social sciences *downward*.

I realize that this is in itself an example of a highly generalized sociological statement which immediately needs to be modified by individual exceptions. Modern research in the humanities is often substantiated by statistical methods, while some of the most successful work in the social sciences consists of individual case studies. This does not detract from the dominant style of either field, however. The highest esteem in the humanities continues to be accorded to studies whose theme is historically and culturally specific, whereas the most prestigious work in the social sciences is presented in such a fashion as to make it relevant to more general theoretical issues. Summing up, I would conclude that the humanities and the social sciences do indeed exhibit clear differences in subject matter and method. These differences may be explained only in part on purely theoretical grounds, however. The epistemological arguments for a demarcation between the two fields need to be supplemented by an analysis of its sociogenesis. The demarcation line is determined not only by the nature of reality as we know it but also by the hierarchical structure of our societies.

4. Implications

It has been observed that today the problem of classification of disciplines is of interest to librarians only. (Stichweh, 1984: 9) In the daily practice of their work most scholars and scientists do, indeed, have no reason to worry about it. Still, university administrations and research councils continue to find themselves faced with problems of co-ordination – problems that may become particularly pressing now that, under the pressures of continuing specialization, the boundaries of the smaller units formed by disciplines are also becoming increasingly less clear. It would be misguided to deal with the ensuing problems as merely organizational issues without considering the cognitive interrelations among the various disciplines and their potential contributions to each other. The time has not yet come to consider the matter of classification as closed.[5]

Surely any theoretical classification can only be a rationalization in retrospect. As Karl Popper has ingeniously demonstrated in a famous argument, it is impossible to predict the growth of knowledge. (Popper, 1957: v-vi) Both the current state of scientific knowledge at any given moment and the attempts at systematizing it (which aim at the formation of knowledge on a higher level of synthesis) form part of long-term processes the course of which has been neither foreseen nor planned.

Viewed in the broadest possible perspective, the development of human knowledge forms a part of an all-embracing master trend – the gradual expansion of human hegemony over more and more other living species. (cf. Goudsblom, 1990) Step by step, at an accelerating pace, human groups have extended their control over nature. They have been able to do so by developing new means both of social organization, enabling them to operate in increasingly larger groups, and of cultural communication, enabling each generation to hand over some of its own experiences to its successors. Clearly, this entire process has not been guided by any foreknowledge or plan. In retrospect we may look upon it in such a way as to recognize the familiar triad of 'nature', 'society', and 'culture'. Viewed in this light, the distinctions underlying the division into the three 'new' faculties, and adumbrated already in the older faculties, seem to be rooted in the prehistory of human society. But while such a 'paleo-sociological' perspective may reveal a comparable triad of major strands in the general evolution of humanity, an equally evident corollary has to be that these strands always have been interconnected. No control over nature would have been possible without social organization, no social organization without culture.

As long as we keep an eye open for the interconnections it may still make sense to distinguish between natural, social, and cultural phenomena. The distinction refers to an ontological continuum, with a corresponding methodological continuum. Within this continuum we should not expect to find clear demarcations; the lines are blurred, especially those marking the boundaries between the domains of society and culture. Language or music or mathematics may indeed be regarded as cultural phenomena in their own right, with a degree of autonomy which warrants studying them in separate disciplines. At the same time, it is evident that their autonomy is

---

[5] For further discussion of the interplay of organizational and intellectual issues see Whitley, 1984.

relative, and that there is always a social dimension to these phenomena – even to mathematics. Similarly, there is a cultural dimension to the subject-matter of such disciplines as economics or psychology which, in their search for regularities in their own field, tend not to let themselves be diverted by the issue of culture.

Psychology in particular presents us with a case that seems to defy the tripartition of nature, society, and culture. On its broad behaviouristic flanks it leans heavily towards the natural sciences. Yet it also shares with the humanities a concern with understanding the motives of individual action. Not surprisingly, given these somewhat hybrid inclinations, in the institutional structure it is usually grouped together with the social sciences.

Such ambiguities bear witness to the fact that the actual divisions among the three faculties have not been planned according to a preconceived rational scheme. Their internal structure and their mutual relationships continue to reflect their origins at universities in societies with a pervasive hierarchy of prestige and power.

As a result, the institutional arrangements probably exaggerate the differences in styles of research and education that would be necessary for cognitive reasons only. Increasingly, however, these differences of style tend to be reproduced within individual disciplines among both the cultural and the social sciences. Thus in history we find 'cliometricians' along with narrative historians, and even individuals combining both roles. There is, in short, more common ground than meets the eye at first sight. Measured by the extremes, the dominant styles continue to be recognizably different. But when we take a closer look at individual disciplines in the humanities, we often see a remarkable receptivity to concepts and methods from the social or, as in archaeology, even the natural sciences. And in the social sciences, especially in anthropology, there are attempts to enrich the repertory of analysis with such concepts as metaphor and narrative derived from the study of literature.

When Caxton in the fifteenth century first pointed to 'humanity' as a subject of learning, he had no reason whatever to demarcate it from something to be called 'social science'. For him, even the study of nature belonged to 'humanity'. In our time the natural sciences have emancipated themselves almost completely and seem to have left the social and the cultural sciences far behind in their capacity of discovery and application. It is partly due to the sense of losing ground to the natural sciences, I think, that in the faculties of Letters in the Netherlands the urge for a closer affiliation with the old faculties of Theology, Law, and Philosophy has manifested itself.

This trend may also help to explain why the term humanities or, in the absence of a vernacular equivalent, *humaniora*, is becoming fashionable. Not only is 'Letters' a somewhat inappropriate denominator for such fields as numismatics or musicology, it is also unlikely to be fully acceptable to members of the more ancient faculties. The idea of joining the humanities, however, may not sound objectionable to them; the time when this term was first launched as a banner against the theologians and the lawyers is long forgotten.

In so far as closer affiliation between the faculty of Letters and some of the older faculties represents a step toward further integration, not only at the organizational but also at the intellectual level, it is to be applauded. It may also imply a few drawbacks, however. One possible disadvantage is that the ideal of the pursuit of knowledge as something valuable in its own right may be subordinated to technical standards of professional training. The overtures toward Theology and Law may also lead to an alienation from the Social Sciences. As I hope to have shown, however, such a tendency would be unlikely to continue for long.

* Several people have been kind enough to comment upon earlier drafts of this paper. I should like to thank Jan Maarten Bremer, Eric Dunning, Bart van Heerikhuizen, Johan Heilbron, Ton Langendorff, Stephen Mennell, Fred Spier, Ruud Stokvis, Bas Willink, Nico Wilterdink, and Cas Wouters.

References

Bailey, F.G., 1977. *Morality and Expediency. The Folklore of Academic Politics*. Oxford: Basil Blackwell.

Boer, Pim den, 1987. *Geschiedenis als beroep. De professionalisering van de geschiedbeoefening in Frankrijk (1818-1914)*. Nijmegen: SUN.

Bourdieu, Pierre, 1986. *Distinction. A Social Critique of the Judgement of Taste*. Translated by Richard Nice. London: Routledge & Kegan Paul.

Bourdieu, Pierre, 1988. *Homo Academicus*. Translated by Peter Collier. Oxford: Polity Press.

Bourdieu, Pierre, 1989. *La noblesse d'état. Grandes écoles et esprit de corps*. Paris: Minuit.

Dawkins, Richard, 1986. *The Blind Watchmaker*. London: Longman.

Durkheim, Emile, 1938. *The Rules of Sociological Method*. Translated by Sarah A. Solovay and John H. Mueller. Chicago: University of Chicago Press.

Elias, Norbert, 1971. Sociology of Knowledge: New Perspectives. *Sociology*, 5: 149-168, 355-370.

Elias, Norbert, 1978a. *What Is Sociology?* Translated by Stephen Mennell and Grace Morrissey. London: Hutchinson.

Elias, Norbert, 1978b. *The Civilizing Process. 1. The History of Manners*. Translated by Edmund Jephcott. New York: Urizen Books.

Goudsblom, Johan, 1980. *Nihilism and Culture*. Oxford: Basil Blackwell.

Goudsblom, Johan, 1990. The Impact of the Domestication of Fire Upon the Balance of Power Between Human Groups and Other Animals. *Focaal,* 13: 55-65.

Johnson, Wendell, 1946. *People in Quandaries. The Semantics of Human Adjustment.* New York: Harper & Bros.

Landau, Misia, 1984. Human Evolution as Narrative. *American Scientist,* 72: 262-268.

Lepenies, Wolf, 1988. *Between Literature and Science*. Translated from the German by R.J. Hollingdale. Cambridge: Cambridge University Press.

Lewin, Roger, 1987. *Bones of Contention. Controversies in the Search for Human Origins.* New York: Simon and Schuster.

Mannheim, Karl, 1927. Die Bedeutung der Konkurrenz im Gebiete des Geistigen. In *Wissenssoziologie*. Neuwied am Rhein: Luchterhand 1964.

Popper, K.R., 1957. *The Poverty of Historicism*. London: Routledge & Kegan Paul.

Prigogine, Ilya & Isabelle Stengers, 1984. *Order out of Chaos. Man's New Dialogue with Nature*. London: Heinemann.

Ringer, Fritz K., 1979. *Education and Society in Modern Europe*. Bloomington: Indiana University Press.

Stichweh, Rudolf, 1984. *Zur Entstehung des modernen Systems wissenschaftlicher Disziplinen. Physik in Deutschland 1740-1890.* Frankfurt: Suhrkamp.

Whitley, Richard, 1984. *The Intellectual and Social Organization of the Sciences*. Oxford: Clarendon.

Willink, Bastiaan, 1988. *Burgerlijk sciëntisme en wetenschappelijk toponderzoek. Sociale grondslagen van nationale bloeiperioden in de negentiende-eeuwse bèta wetenschappen.* Dissertation University of Amsterdam.

Homo Ludens = α + ß
A plea for more co-operation

---

1. It might be somewhat surprising to find a chapter on mathematics in a book devoted to the humanities in the nineties. One is hardly inclined to include mathematics among the humanities, especially in a period that is often referred to as the 'computer age'. However, the aim of the present essay is to call attention to an aspect of mathematics that was apparent already in classical Antiquity, viz. mathematics as an activity of the mind, based on mental conceptions, embedded in human culture and society. To this I immediately add the question (though not the answer) as to the origins of these ideas. Already Plato and Aristotle held diverging views on this question. According to Plato, mathematical concepts were innate recollections of the World of Ideas. Aristotle, on the other hand, regarded mathematical concepts as abstractions of features of the corporeal world. Furthermore I will sketch some relationships between 'humanities' and 'mathematics' as they are traditionally understood, in order to outline the shape of their interplay.

The dichotomy between humanities on the one hand and science-*cum*-mathematics on the other, was introduced by Wilhelm Dilthey in his "Einleitung in die Geisteswissenschaften" (1883). Later on they became labelled as α- and ß-disciplines respectively. Rather than to dwell on the origin of this designation (over a century old), I want to show some connecting links along which interchange of ideas and competences could be achieved. It is my firm belief that the furtherance of better mutual understanding between 'α' and 'ß' is an important task both for scholars and for scientists (including mathematicians) in the nineties.

2. One may have various reasons for studying mathematics. First of all one may aim at doing research at the front lines: extending and generalizing

existing theories, formulating new ones and clarifying their underlying structures.

Others are primarily interested in applications, elaborating the results of the aforementioned type of mathematicians (though not always with due respect) and applying them to concrete problems. Applied mathematicians also have a different perception of mathematics. Often, when for the pure mathematician a problem is considered to be solved, for the applied mathematician the real problem comes into being. For example: the problem of solving 2 linear equations with 2 unknowns is not fundamentally different from that of solving 100 linear equations in 100 unknowns, and the pure theorist does not worry about the time it costs to get the result on paper or display, nor about the degree of accuracy in concrete situations. The applied mathematician on the other hand is often not interested in details such as exceptional and so-called 'pathological' cases.

A third way of looking at mathematics is what I would call, perhaps somewhat magniloquently: focusing on its cultural value, reflecting on its foundations, its historical development and its social implications in the past, the present and the future.

This 'third way' will play a central part in this essay. At the present day this aspect of mathematics tends to become hard pressed. To put it rather bluntly: there is a real danger that mathematics is more and more going to be considered an auxiliary science or handmaiden of computer science.

In the course of our cultural reflection on mathematics we will touch on the interplay between mathematics and (other) humanities.

3. First of all I will clear up some current misconceptions about mathematics which persist especially among 'alphas'. Outsiders tend to have a false idea of mathematics, owing mostly to the mathematical textbooks themselves: both the way in which they are organized and the way in which they are generally used, give rise to much misunderstanding.

The results as published in a book or article, are regularly presented in the form of a rigid, deductive, linearly ordered chain of arguments. This is misleading insofar as it fails to reveal the struggle with the subject matter that was necessary to achieve the result. It would be a good thing if the author would not only show the 'right' way of arriving at the result, but would also indicate some of the plausible, yet 'false', ways. But this is hardly ever feasible, or as the Dutch mathematician N.G. de Bruijn (1958) put it: "A mathematician cannot possibly publish his waste-paper basket". On the other hand: a mathematical textbook should be 'rewritten' rather than read. This view was poignantly expressed by Dinghas (1979), advising his students: "... ein Buch zu nehmen, dazu viel Papier, einen Bleistift, einen grossen Papierkorb und sehr viel Zeit. So lerne man Mathematik".

A personal experience: I once read a short article which I found very difficult. I worked it out and the result was a considerable amount of paperwork. This I summarized and the result turned out to be nearly the same as the original paper!

In brief: a rigorous deductive proof is always achieved through a process in which intuitions and heuristics lead the way. The history of mathematics offers many examples of this fact.

4. Moreover, it is important to bear in mind that a rigorous proof does not warrant proper understanding of the corresponding theorem.

I give a very simple example (the alphas are kindly requested to hold the line).

Suppose I postulate the following theorem:

$$1 + 3 + 5 + 7 + ... + 99 = 2500,$$

more generally:

$$1 + 3 + 5 + 7 + ... + (2n\text{-}1) = n^2 \qquad (*)$$

There is a quasi automatic way of proving this theorem, the so-called method of complete induction. It runs as follows. First one proves the theorem for $n = 1$ (this is easy: $1 = 1^2$). Next one proves that, if the theorem holds for a certain value of n, it also holds for the subsequent value. Then the problem is solved: the theorem holds for 1 and so – by virtue of the second part of the proof – it holds for 2 and therefore it holds for 3, etc.

However, a great drawback of this method is that it fails to render any insight whatsoever into what the theorem actually means.

This insight we obtain by looking more closely at the left-hand side of (*). Here we find the sum of the first n odd natural numbers and according to the theorem this would be equal to n^2. This is a nice interpretation of the theorem and it leads to an intuitive proof, known already to Pythagoras (ca. 560 B.C. – ca. 480 B.C.) and his disciples. They arranged numbers (of pebbles) in the form of geometric figures (Aristoteles). When one considers figure 1 the theorem becomes obvious, for by counting the dots according to the carpenter's squares we find as their total number the sum of the first *four odd numbers*. On the other hand, we see a square containing *4 x 4* dots. Extrapolating, we may guess that the sum of the first *n odd numbers* equals n x n. Of course this is not a rigorous proof, but it does elucidate the theorem and it does reveal its true meaning.

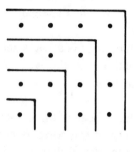

fig. 1

This is a very simple example of the difference between understanding a theorem and proving it rigorously. In mathematics there are many more (and much more complicated) instances of this situation.

In this example we had a proof and a way of elucidating the theorem. However, there are also theorems for which many proofs are known, and yet are not fully understood by any mathematician.

As an example I mention the so-called quadratic reciprocity law. I will not expatiate on this technical theorem; I will mention only the kernel of what is of interest here.

The theorem is about two functions, both dependent on two parameters p and q. The value of these functions is either +1 or -1, depending on the values of p and q. Gauss (1777-1855) solved the problem of how the product of the two functions depends on the values of p and q. It is clear that the product also has either the value +1 or -1 and Gauss found the true answer. This theorem has been proved and even generalized in many ways, but still mathematicians feel that they are lacking in true understanding.

I mentioned this theorem also for another reason. Gauss had found the solution by computing a substantial number of numerical examples and scrutinizing the results. These results suggested to him the relation that he was searching for, and put him in a position to prove it. This is the way in which the discovery and proof of theorems are usually achieved.

One might even call it 'experimental mathematics', and it goes without saying that the growth of computer facilities has opened up a world of new possibilities in this direction.

A final remark on rigorous proofs and proofs by illustration. Rigor has turned out to be a time-dependent notion. Newton, and even Cauchy, heralded as the champion of rigor in his century, often contented themselves with standards of proof that would now be unacceptable.

Even mathematical reasoning is not free from hidden assumptions and logical errors. This has been described masterly by I. Lakatos in his book "Proofs and Refutations" (Lakatos, 1976). In it he demonstrates, on the basis of two well-chosen and extensively worked-out examples, that seemingly simple and generally accepted proofs may still be as leaky as sieves. But we must be glad that mathematicians not always pursued maximum rigor, for that could well have blocked progress. It is for instance generally agreed that, apart from external social factors, pushing the pursuit of rigor to its extremes finally gave the fatal blow to Greek mathematics.

Afterwards, in the 17th and 18th century, most mathematicians were much more audacious. They did not avoid working with concepts that were not yet fully understood. D'Alembert (1717-1783) wrote about negative numbers: "Whatever they may be, the algebraic rules with respect to negative numbers are accepted by everybody, irrespective of the particular interpretation given to these quantities".[1]

This of course entailed that even the great masters of mathematics were prone to make errors. An interesting account of such errors was given by M. Lecat (1935).

5. Before going on discussing current misconceptions about mathematics, I want to resume my previous remark, about alphas and betas studying mathematics jointly. For the moment I restrict myself to only one aspect: knowledge of the original language in which the mathematical texts were written. This may clarify the background of the mathematical concepts involved, for the finer shades are easily lost in translation.

A few examples: as I already mentioned, the Greeks used pebbles to arrange numbers in the form of geometrical figures. This practice reflected itself in their terminology: square numbers (two equal factors, e.g. 25), oblong numbers (heteromèkès, having two different factors e.g. 35; often even only numbers of the form $n(n+1)$), rectilinear numbers (euthugrammikos) for primes (e.g. 2, 3, 5, 7, 11), for one cannot arrange a prime number in the form of a square or other rectangle. Further they distinguished polygonal numbers, e.g. triangular numbers (see fig. 2).

---

[1] Encyclopédie Méthodique, p. 445 (Paris, 1785[2]).

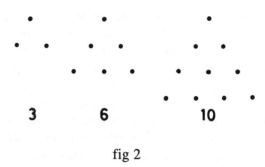

fig 2

As another interesting instance from arithmetic I give the word for root of a number. The Greeks used in that case the word 'pleura', which means: 'side' (namely the side of the square, representing the number). This word reveals the geometrical view of the Greeks on numbers!

An example from geometry: the Greeks distinguished plane curves (straight lines and circles) from solid curves (Greeks: stereos, Lat.: solidus). A solid curve however is not – as one might expect – a space curve, but a plane curve too, generated by intersecting a solid, in this case a cone, and a plane, so a conic section in the literal sense of the word. As one sees, translation is nearly impossible and this example once more illustrates the need of knowledge of the original language. A final example: the non-mathematical point of view of Aristotle on natural sciences, including our 'physics', becomes perfectly clear from the title of his books on this topic, which he called Physika, at least for those who know that 'Physika' is derived from the Greek verb 'phuein' which means 'to grow'.

On the whole, there is in the USA a growing interest in translations of mathematical texts into English (a.o. Arabic, but also French texts), and an imminent shortage of competent translators is not imaginary.
An illustration: A few years ago the translation (from Latin into English) of the famous textbook on number theory "Disquisitiones Arithmeticae" by C.F. Gauss had to be updated. In "The Mathematical Intelligencer" (distributed all over the world) a call was placed for interested translators, versed in Latin as well as in mathematics. No more than ten persons reacted to this call. The chosen three were from Europe, two of them from the Netherlands.

6. After this (first) digression on possible co-operation between mathematicians and 'alphas', I resume my argument as to misunderstandings about

mathematics. Many non-mathematicians will be astounded to hear that even in mathematics there are topics about which no general consensus has been reached, and even more that there are topics which continue to arouse severe controversy.

In the course of its development mathematics has suffered some grave crises. The first occurred in classical Antiquity in the fifth century B.C. when the firm belief in the supremacy and all-pervading importance of the natural numbers (1, 2, 3, ...) was undermined through the discovery of the fact that the side and the diagonal of a square have no common measure. In other words, the ratio of these two quantities cannot be expressed as the ratio of two natural numbers. Tradition has it that the man who first made this discovery public, was drowned! By the way, the first real solution of this problem was given more than 2000 years later, by R. Dedekind in 1887!

This crisis was followed by others. In the first decades of the 19th century mathematicians made the shocking discovery that Euclidean geometry is not the only possible geometry. Several so-called non-euclidean geometries were subsequently conceived.

The most severe crisis, from which the mathematical world has not yet wholly recovered, took place in the first decades of our own century.

First of all, the foundation of set theory, initiated by Georg Cantor (1845-1918), gave rise to serious contradictions, mildly called 'paradoxes'. Although already from classical Antiquity onwards (Zeno, 4th cent. B.C.) people had lived with paradoxes (a.o. the liar paradox (Martin, 1984)), their number grew and they drew more serious attention. Not all of them are so easy to formulate for a layman as is the so-called Russell-paradox: when in a village barber Jones shaves only those men who do not shave themselves, by whom is barber Jones shaved?

Notably many paradoxes and other problems arose from ill-advised use of the notion of 'infinity', a concept which the Greeks had (wisely?) avoided. Their 'horror infiniti' is well-known, and they managed to avoid the infinite in very ingenious ways.

Aristotle distinguished between the actually infinite and the potentially infinite and allowed only the second kind of infinity. An example of the first – forbidden – kind of infinity could be the set of all natural numbers considered as a whole. In fact many paradoxes in set theory from its beginning in the end of the 19th century arose from the use of this kind of infinity.

Aristotle considered the natural numbers (1,2,3,...) to be potentially infinite in the sense that – given a finite set of natural numbers – one always can choose one more, scil. the one following the greatest one of the set.

He expresses himself perfectly clear in Physika III 206b, 33-207a, 2:
"It turns out that what is infinite is the opposite of what people are used to
call infinite. What is infinite is not that which has nothing outside itself,
but that which always has part of itself outside" (scil. outside that which
has been considered up till then).
And Physika III 207b, 28-207b, 29:
"Nor does this account of infinity rob the mathematicians of their study;
for all that it denies is the actual existence of anything so great that you can
never get to the end of it."
This illustrates the remarkable fact that the Greeks not only tackled problems of logic and mathematics which after many centuries proved to be
fundamental, but also avoided concepts which likewise after many centuries proved to be highly elusive.
In this context I want to point out that many examples taken from the
mathematics of classical Antiquity are very appealing to non-mathematicians
too, and that improved mutual understanding between alphas and betas
might well start with jointly studying them. This ought to keep interest in
classical Antiquity alive.

7. Now I will review three main streams in the thinking about the foundations of mathematics, which divided the mathematicians into three (often
hostile) camps. Note that mathematics, often considered as abstract, objective
and serene, can even cause severe, emotional quarrels!
I have in mind the so-called logicists, formalists and intuitionists.
(a) The *logicists* (Russell, Whitehead) held that mathematical concepts can
    be defined purely logically. This implies that mathematics has no spe-
    cific content but only form. Hence Russell's dictum that mathematicians
    do not know what they are talking about, nor know whether what they
    say is true. A great drawback of this view is that it does not explain
    why mathematics is so utterly useful.
(b) The *formalists* (Hilbert) considered mathematics a formal system in
    which the basic concepts enter undefined: their properties are charac-
    terized only implicitly through the axioms. In the formalist view
    mathematics is a purely formal play with symbols deprived of all meaning.
    The various branches of mathematics have their own axiomatic basis.

A great deception for the formalists was Gödel's (Hofstadter, 1980, and
Nagel & Newman, 1956) incompleteness theorem which stated that in
number theory (and in every theory encompassing number theory) there
will always be theorems which are true yet not provable within the axi-

omatic system. To put it simply: there will always remain basically undecidable theorems.

(c) The *intuitionists*. In fact this trend was already going on in Descartes's time (1596-1650). He believed that certain intuitions were implanted by God into the human mind and hence must be true since (as he said) "God is not a deceiver". From these intuitions infallible truths could be derived by mathematical deduction.

The idea of true intuitions was resumed by L. Kronecker in the second half of the 19th century. He expressed himself very clearly: "Die ganzen Zahlen hat der liebe Gott gemacht, alles andere ist Menschenwerk". He thought that the whole numbers existed objectively.
The most influential modern representative of intuitionism is L.E.J. Brouwer (1881-1966). His ideas were directly opposed to logicism: mathematics is an activity of the human mind, independent of the external world, based on clear intuitions, not experiences. Logic can be derived from mathematics, but not mathematics from logic.
Regarding definitions and theorems, Brouwer accepted only such definitions as enable us to construct the object defined in a denumerable number of steps. Regarding logic he did not accept the principle of 'tertii exclusi' (a third possibility is excluded) which means that he accepted three 'truth values': true, not true, undecidable. In his opinion, using the concept of 'infinity' too rashly may easily lead one into errors. This is especially so when statements that are valid for finite sets are carelessly transferred to infinite sets.
One far-reaching consequence of intuitionism is that great parts of an important, fundamental and much applied branch of mathematics, *viz.* analysis, would lose much of their foundation.
A side-note: many intuitionists nevertheless still teach and apply analysis in the old-fashioned classical way!
As a final remark on intuitionism I mention that Brouwer c.s. occupied themselves intensively with the relation between speech and thought.

I dwelled somewhat extensively on these directions in mathematics to stress once more the uncertainties in mathematics with which students are often only confronted in the final stages of their study (if ever). My intention is to emphasize the fact that mathematics is not so unambiguous as is commonly thought, and therefore more akin to the humanities than is usually supposed.

8. Before sketching some fields in which mathematicians and students of the humanities could co-operate fruitfully, I will mention some techniques and ideas that alphas and betas could borrow from one another.

Some of the techniques that mathematicians could borrow from their α-colleagues are practical knowledge of languages (both ancient and modern), facts from history, but also skill in handling archival materials, including palaeography.

The powerful impact of computers on linguistics is well-known. First of all as an aid in composing concordances and dictionaries and in building translation programmes for computers but also – in combination with statistical methods – in detecting the author of a literary text. The role of computers in phonetics is explained in chapter 7 by A. Cohen.

With respect to the 'ideas' which can be exchanged: clearly mathematicians must have sufficient command of (natural) language to develop arguments about concrete, substantive, 'real-world' problems, which do not lend themselves to quantification and for which the rigid and unambiguous language of mathematics is necessarily too poor and inflexible a medium. Alphas on the other hand might take over some concepts from mathematics, in particular structural concepts such as sets, one-to-one-mappings, isomorphisms.

These concepts perhaps need explanation. When, given two sets A and B, it is possible to assign to every element of A one and only one element of B and vice-versa, then we say that we have a one-to-one mapping of A onto B. The sets A and B are then called equipollent.

For example: the set of all integers (negatives included) is equipollent with the set of all even integer numbers (see fig. 3).

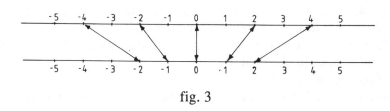

fig. 3

If moreover one can add (or multiply) in A and in B, and if with the sum (or product) of two elements a and b in A corresponds the sum (or product) of their images in B, then A and B are called isomorphic. There are many more instances of 'structural' concepts which might be useful to alphas; especially when they are interested in logic a minimum arsenal of mathematical concepts is indispensable.

9. In the concluding paragraphs I should like to mention some fields in which mathematics – in its widest sense – might be an object of study for those who devote themselves to the humanities, preferably in close co-operation with mathematicians.

First of all: *philology*. In par. 5, I already gave some examples, restricted to Greek and Latin, but of course there are more instances. Especially in the field of Arabic, Chinese and Indian languages there are many manuscripts still waiting to be edited. As to the classical languages: I have always wondered why the mathematical literature which forms such an important and interesting integral part of Greek literature as a whole, is studied by only so few classical scholars. In the exact sciences the Greeks bequeathed us a rich legacy, of which only few people feel a calling to be the stewards.

Secondly: *history* and *sociology*. It is generally recognized that mathematics is by no means an isolated discipline. First of all the demand for the products of mathematics and their applications played an enormous role. Already Archimedes (287-212 B.C.) put his results at the disposal of the military authorities, and this usage has continued up to the present day. The impact of mathematics on science and society is immense.

On the other hand, historical and social processes have exerted considerable influence on the development of mathematics and in this area there are many interesting problems.

When one looks, for example, at a table representing the years of birth and death of leading mathematicians in Europe and the Arabic world, one notices a gap between 200 B.C. and 100 A.D., tremendous gaps in the periods 300 A.D. – 800 A.D. and 1100 A.D. – 1400 A.D. and a nearly exponential increase after about 1600.

Studying the historical and social background of these and other phenomena is highly interesting but demands besides mathematical knowledge also historical and sociological training and skill.

Nowadays in many universities the subject called 'history and social implications of mathematics' is a regular, sometimes even compulsory part of the curriculum. However, finding teachers with the required combination of α and β competences is not always easy.

Obviously, historians and sociologists have a task here, the latter especially when one is interested in the mathematical profession, its place in society and, e.g., the position of women in mathematics.

The aforementioned problems concerning the foundations of mathematics must be of interest to *philosophers* and *psychologists*, for instance the way of thinking of mathematicians and the function of language. For this I refer to the topic stressed above, when I touched upon the role of philology. Now I have the following question in mind: can we think without using language? In the field of Artificial Intelligence, too, the said scientists and scholars may come together.

10. In this essay I have tried to present a small contribution to better understanding of the way in which mathematics works, in order to clear up at least a few misconceptions.

I intended to bring out that for the preservation of mathematics as a cultural legacy, intensified co-operation between alphas and betas is necessary and very well possible. The basis for this cooperation could – and should – be laid already in secondary school. At the moment for many α-pupils mathematics is not a very beloved topic and many of them seem to confirm Luther's saying: "Mathematik macht traurige Leute". They forget however that mathematics is an integrating part of the object of their study: the Greek culture. Moreover it is possible to interest them in mathematics by presenting well chosen interesting topics from Greek mathematics, which are abundantly available.

On the other hand, many ß-pupils look upon classical languages as boring and superfluous, but they forget that the foundations of our mathematics have been laid by the Greeks. I mention only one name: 'Euclid' who brought the mathematics of his time together in his famous "Elements". In English 'Euclid' still stands for geometry in general.

It would be a good thing when the nineties would bring this extension of co-operation.

References

Aristoteles, *Metaphysica*, XIV, 1029 b12.
Bruijn, N.G. de, 1958. *Asymptotic Methods in Analysis*. Amsterdam.
Dinghas, 1979. *Jahresbericht der Deutschen Mathematiker Verein*, 81: 153-176.
Hofstadter, D., 1980. *Gödel, Escher, Bach*. New York.
Lakatos, I., 1976. *Proofs and Refutations*. Cambridge etc.
Lecat, M., 1935. *Erreur de Grands Mathematiciens*. Bruxelles.
Martin, R.L. (ed), 1984. *Recent Essays on Truth and The Liar Paradox*. Oxford.
Nagel, E. & J.R. Newman, 1956. *Gödels Proof*. New York. Dutch: De Stelling van Gödel
        Aula Pocket. Utrecht 1958.
General reading:
Kline, M., 1972. *Mathematical Thought from Ancient to Modern Times*. New York.
Kline, M., 1980. *Mathematics, the Loss of Certainty*. New York.

Part 2

Philosophy and theology

Philosophical research
and philosophizing*

W. van Dooren

"'Forschung' ist einer jener Begriffe, die im Zeitalter der Wissenschaft am häufigsten gebraucht, aber am wenigsten bedacht werden." (Riedel, 1978: 273).

1. The importance and meaning of philosophy
However often we may encounter the word 'philosophy' in modern language usage, that does not mean that is has necessarily become a simple and undisputed concept. There are two extremes: either the word is used very nonchalantly, if no more is intended than a particular meaning which may lie behind something; or it is the indication of a deep wisdom, to which people need to be introduced. Between these two extremes there are numerous variations. We shall consider here only philosophy practised in and around universities. This involves two limitations: everything that does not measure up to the presently accepted scholarly norms is excluded; moreover it is here a question of a European-American affair, so that apart from philosophy exported there, the thought of Asia and Africa is generally left out of consideration.

From time immemorial philosophy has played a great role in culture; philosophy was required to give answers to all kinds of concrete and fundamental problems. A non-specialist point of view was expected, a view for non-philosophers, a reflection on important basic questions. And should this expectation of philosophy not become even stronger as disciplines developed further and specialised even more so that it became even further removed from the 'ordinary' person? Would it not therefore be more obvious to view philosophical research, or rather: philosophy, as being of a totally different kind from scholarly research? Before any answer can be given to questions of the content, direction, goal, desirability of philosophical research, it is necessary to make quite clear in the first place whether there is a particular kind of research that deserves the name 'philosophical'.

Philosophy has formed such an important part of the subjects offered for study by our universities, that it was and is assumed to be natural that in addition to, or even within scholarly research, philosophical research exists.

When we define scholarly research as: the intention to realize systematic and inter-subjectively valid knowledge of a particular field of reality, then philosophy is on the one hand more, since it is not bound to a particular area of reality but covers the whole of reality, and on the other hand less, since it is not so much concerned with inter-subjectively valid knowledge, because a subjective view is often regarded as sufficient.

Now much is happening in the field of philosophy, that is covered by the scholarly definition just mentioned, but the question is the extent to which it can be called specifically philosophical research: the person who deals with ancient philosophers, or the person who interprets texts, is in fact a historian or a philologist; the person who declares a theory about society or sets up a picture of man, is in fact a sociologist or psychologist. If we should exclude all these matters from the practice of university philosophy, or place them under other departments, what would really be left of philosophical research? If there were still any research, should this not then be of a totally different nature than other scholarly research? Can philosophers be measured by standards different from those of other scholars?
Recently this question was explicitly answered in the negative on several occasions and philosophers were placed on a par with other scholars (BUOZ nota 1979; Swart, 1977). The commission appointed by the Dutch minister

of Education to describe philosophical research and to give an opinion concerning expediency and quality, did not come up with a different view (VC Wijsbegeerte, 1987). However, the 'expediency' turned out to form such a problem for this commission, that it did not express an opinion on this matter. In the description of research the path was chosen of mentioning what was being done at that moment at the various faculties, and in order to determine the quality, judgement was passed on the publications. Having regard to the appendices of the report, these were largely theses. They were willing to determine, however, that good research means good education, and they were enthusiastic about specialised research. The attainment of a sufficient public of readers 'can be of importance', but is obviously no criterion of value. Furthermore distinction is still made (with regard to metaphysics) between 'reflection' and 'research'; here a negative implied criterion is used: philosophical reflection is not necessarily research. With this meagre reaction the commission leaves the question thus explicitly unanswered, as to whether there is in fact talk of independent philosophical research: in the report, historical and philological studies are counted as being philosophical without any trouble at all.

Three real problems have now evolved: should philosophical research be specialistic? to what extent should it be aimed at a larger public? must it be of a reflectional character?

Maybe this is the time to put the key question: what do people do at universities – do people practice philosophy, or study it? Or is this the same? Was Themerson right after all when he wrote that philosophy is "what it is all about. And it is about itself." (Themerson, 1979). It was Nietzsche who made such a sharp distinction between the 'Philosoph' and the 'wissenschaftlicher Mensch'. The philosopher must, according to him, have been on the same level as the scholarly researcher, as on so many other levels, but if he is truly learned and a philosopher, then the researchers are his servants (Nietzsche, 1885). At the present time it seems as though this distinction has been forgotten or worse still, it seems as though philosophy itself, particularly insofar as it is distinct from scholarly research, disappears. Heidegger wrote bitterly of it: "Der Gelehrte verschwindet. Er wird abgelöst durch den Forscher, der in Forschungsunternehmungen steht." (Heidegger, 1950). We must realise that it is here not a matter of the difference between philosophy and scholarly research in general, but the difference between scholarly philosophy on the one hand and modern scholarly research practices on the other.

We thus return to the earlier question of what philosophical research should really be, but now as it is distinct from the aforementioned modern research practices. It even seems as though people have tended in the latter case to identify philosophy with this. In order to avoid any misapprehension, it thus seems desirable to make a sharp distinction between philosophical research, that in fact is nothing other than the empirical or historical/philological research of philosophers and their work on the one hand, and the practice of philosophy, reflection and philosophizing on the other.[1]

If people practice philosophy as a 'strict science' (according to the expression of Husserl, 1911), then it intends to be practised on behalf of everyone, it is a reflection on general matters, and it expresses an intuitive vision; philosophy is essentially the knowledge of the first beginnings, of the origins, of the roots of all things.

People may disagree on other grounds with certain elements of Husserl's view of philosophy, nonetheless it is very obvious that philosophy must not be equated with specialised and detailed expert knowledge that is only available to initiated esoteric experts. "Philosophy may not imagine that scholarly theoretical professional work or anything else that claims to be research, must be philosophy," says Adorno; unfortunately he may have to conclude himself, that at present philosophy "in der allgemeinen Situation von Verfachlichung selbst ebenfalls als Spezialfach sich etabliert" (Adorno, 1970). In this way the freedom of spirit is lost. Philosophy stands or falls with creativity, which must be considered on its own and not be measured and judged according to professional-technical standards like publishing quanta. Philosophy is like certain types of art: a painter, a composer or a writer can be just as creative as a philosopher. There is nevertheless a real difference, that is based on the fact that the philosopher, in contrast to the artist, is concerned ex professo with the problems and the results of scholarly research. That is why he has a place within the scholarly research institute, the university. As Popper, for instance, said categorically, philosophy is not to be divorced from other disciplines.

Philosophy is aimed at general reflection and is therefore closely bound up with education. One important task undertaken by philosophy is the analysis

---

[1] This does not mean the exercise of philosophy, the execution of a function or profession as a philosopher, and even less the exercise of 'philosophical practice' as a kind of therapeutic activity.

of specialized scientific education. In this way people learn how to break through their own limitations and are stimulated to "look over the hedge and ask where his science comes, into the general scheme of things" (Smart, quoted by Nittel, 1954). Philosophy is not a technique that people can learn in order to run life, or a means of achieving general development. Philosophy is a basic research and therefore criticism of culture in the broadest sense and self-examination of reason. In another context – and thus with a different meaning – but now correctly, the word 'research' is used for philosophy. It is here a question of critical analysis of the existing society from a commitment to social problems, and of critical research of the instrument with which this is done, reason itself. The real philosopher is responsible for this fundamental critical research.

The essential difference is between those who assume these responsibilities, and those who are only studying those who assume these responsibilities. The first are philosophers, the others are 'scholars'. The first are like the artists: the painters, the composers and the poets, the others are like the art historians, the musicologists and the philologists. The second group is of vital importance, but must not swamp the first. When anywhere in the world philosophy is to be of any importance it is worth cultivating not only these 'philosophologists', but to give the philosophers – in the true sense of the word – complete freedom. Only then can there be justified talk of real philosophizing.

2. The present situation with regard to philosophy
What is the international situation of philosophy at present and which main streams and tendencies are to be seen? To answer these questions we can do no more than to give a global view at the end of the eighties. It is not at all possible to forecast what the situation will be in ten years' time, since the practice of philosophy is highly sensitive to fashion and is very involved in the totally changing present activities, with regard to changes of both a social and scientific nature.
It would be natural to distinguish some main themes in the present practice of philosophy. A good ten years ago this could still be done and words like dialectic philosophy, analytical philosophy, structuralism and phenomenology were used. This is now no longer as obvious because in contrast to the period round 1980, philosophy is no longer as strongly bound to streams that are traditionally determined. Naturally the picture is not completely different, but the accents are not as sharply drawn. The English language philosopher remains largely in a positivist and language analytical orientation,

but the non-English language philosopher in Europe is at present capti-
vated by the 'post modernism' that appeared after 1980, that draws discussions
strongly to itself and pushes older antitheses into the background. A 'post
modernist' attitude means that all 'modern' values like universal reasona-
bleness and humanity, individual freedom and development, emancipation
and progress, are at stake. To some extent there is a continuing line, since
this criticism has been inagurated by dialectic and structuralist philosophers.

In addition it is worthwhile making a distinction between various types of
philosophy, or 'main streams', as Pos once said. He distinguished between
a scientific, a metaphysical and a social-ethical orientated philosophy (Pos,
1954). The metaphysical was strongly emphasised as the attempt to arrive
at a (subjective) total reaction to the world of experience. This was still
distrusted by many, however: the social-ethical was considered to be too
politically coloured, so that then, as the single meagre content, the scientific
remained.

In recent years the meaning of philosophy has still been questioned more
than ever. There is thus a regrouping of schools of thought or trends toward
certain fundamental themes, and for that reason it is now better to discuss
present philosophy on the basis of themes. In this global survey we shall
for the time being not fully limit ourselves to the university philosophy,
since impulses to renewal usually come from outside the universities and
also have their effect outside them. It has now become more difficult to
trace trends, than in the first decade after the Second World War. A possible
coincidental addition is, furthermore, that many great representatives of
particular trends have died in the last fifteen years, like Heidegger (1976),
Bloch (1977), Marcuse (1979), Sartre (1980), Foucault (1984), and Ayer
(1989).

The central theme of the whole of twentieth century philosophy has been
the language; never before has this been so accentuated. This then concerns
both the function and the value of linguistic expressions. The relationship
between language and reality is always being discussed in between the two
most extreme positions, that language can and must give a correct reflection of reality on the one hand and that language itself forms a complete
reality on the other. The problem of reference must be solved in the first
position, whereas in the second it is eliminated. In other words: in the first
case man aims at finding out what is behind the language expression, what

the background meaning may be, whereas in the second case the language expression is looked at on its own. Where a philosophical text is concerned people either ask themselves what the philosopher could have meant by it, or people are not concerned about his meaning, but they only pay attention to the meaning that the text now has for the reader. Some examples from recent philosophy may make this clear.

Both positivist philosophers in the steps of Frege and phenomenological philosophers from Husserl onwards considered the problem of reference; a modern version of it can be seen again in the work of Castañeda. The question is: if we refer to an actually existing something with a word, how can we then identify it? If more than one word refers to the same thing, how do we know that this is indeed 'the same'? For this purpose we shall have to (re)construct something again and again, that meets the content of more and more words. In this manner they can express 'non existent' things in words and attempt to find the corresponding something, but then we come to the problem of whether the square circle exists, and if so, how.

Structuralist and post-modern philosophers avoid this problem by only ascribing reality to the expressions of language itself. What is not said is not, and what is said exists. The whole of reality is nothing other than a story: the more stories the greater the number of realities. The striking thing about these philosophies is the power attributed to language. In addition there is a strong relativity formed by the coexistence of languages or realities. The person who believes in the one reality, whether or not in an absolute manner, repels these philosophers.

In order to get round these problems many philosophers attempt to achieve the clarification of terminology, in such a way that it may appear that the exact definition of language expression or expressions could lead to eventual agreement; in global or detailed manner many philosophers now occupy themselves a great deal with this conceptual analysis. In the extension thereof rationality itself is once again brought into discussion: is there such a thing as pure rationality? are there more forms of rationality which conflict with one another? How far is rationality valid? Is reality itself rationally constructed? In the end it is this question of the relation of thought, language and reality, which dominates much philosophical practice nowadays.

A second theme is society; following the past utopian and philosophical visions which were aimed at society as a whole, the problems now are more specific, like the environment. In many philosophical studies the emphasis comes to lie on honesty and respect for nature instead of on technical control. In this connection the flourishing of the 'technique philosophy' in Germany and the United States may be consider.

As a third theme science may be mentioned, both in its social functioning and in its validity; both are still under discussion, where the general problem of the meaning of rationality is continually posed in this connection and is also perceived in the context of the relationship to myth. Philosophy of science is going through a period of great vigour; this is practised both by optimistic adherents of belief in the progress of research development, as by the pessimistic opponents of unhampered scientific research, since this could be just the thing that could lead to catastrophic results for society as a whole and to unpredictable consequences.

In can be enlightening for the insight into present philosophical situation that people should realise which themes are no (longer) involved. It concerns things that were key matters until a short while ago: God, the soul, human existence. Metaphysical and existential questions live nowadays more particularly on the edge of philosophy, if they are put at all. We thus touch at the same time both the difficult point of the criterium for sensible and worthwhile philosophy and the point what kind of philosophical research may be taken seriously. Should we assume that the university environment is trend-setting and normative for what counts as philosophy, and should we then apply the current scholarly norms now valid in universities? Do we not then finish up in a circle, whereby we exclude in advance particular forms of philosophizing and philosophical research? It will come up again later, when we discuss the criteria of the real practice of philosophy. We can now avoid the circle by concerning ourselves with the description of university philosophy and seeing how the general situation works there.

3. The place of philosophy in university education

Since the existence of universities, that is to say since the late Middle Ages and the Renaissance, philosophy has played an important part in the whole curriculum. It is true that there was no separate faculty for philosophy in addition to the faculties of law, medicine and theology, but in the preparatory study, the faculty of Arts, philosophy was strongly represented. This role differed according to the way how emphasis was given to logic, for example, or natural sciences. It is of great importance to note that philosophy had close contacts on the one hand, within the same faculty, with most of the other and particularly the exact sciences, and on the other was not connected with theology. Attention was paid to philosophy within other faculties from their own disciplines, so that ethics, in particular, could develop as a subject within the theological faculty. Ethics or moral sciences have held a somehow varied position within philosophy: sometimes this subject was included, sometimes it was not.

In the Netherlands since the first university was established in Leyden in 1574, the situation was usually such that there was generally at least a special chair for philosophy. In 1815 the faculty of arts was finally dispensed with and replaced by the new Faculty of Letters and Philosophy, in which there was also at least one chair for philosophy. The connection with the classics was very strong; often the philosophers were classicists. Since the new academic statute of 1876 ethics and philosophy of theology were included as separate subjects within the theological faculty.

This situation was to continue until 1963 when philosophy was placed in a separate faculty, called Centrale Interfaculteit (Central Inter-faculty). This situation was unique in the world and is therefore deserving of some attention. The intention was to allow philosophy to realise its comprehensive position within the university. Extensive discussions had been going on for some time. In the past it had long been a cherished wish of Dutch Philosophers to make philosophy entirely independent within the university and not to allow it to maintain one-sided relationships with any professional subject. In 1931 many professional philosophers were involved in a Dutch congress concerning the meaning of philosophy within higher education. The congress resulted in a number of desiderata and gravamina; philosophy should form its own faculty in addition to which in every other faculty philosophy of that faculty should be taught. The faculty of philosophy should have at least two chairs for philosophy and one or two chairs for psychology (the combination with psychology was still taken for granted at that time). As far as the first is concerned: these chairs need no further specification. On the other hand special lecturers were required to teach the history of philosophy. In addition seminaries were to be founded for research. In 1931 it was considered very urgent that each philosophical teaching task should be altered as soon as possible into: philosophy and its history (Kohnstamm, 1933: 8 sqq). It did not result in anything at all; a little later Pos insisted on the necessity of a central faculty of philosophy (Pos 1940): "Released from its traditional connection with Letters, philosophy should be a faculty which has equal connections with all faculties", since philosophy, which was the 'first undifferentiated science' has now become a 'central science'. In fact this contains the argument for connecting philosophy and 'studium generale' with each other. The Central Interfaculty, which was finally founded in 1963, was to bring all this about. Parts of philosophy which had been included in other faculties were now included in this new 'interfaculty' or organizational contact was made with it. Within the faculty a division was made into three areas: systematic philosophy, history of philosophy and the philosophy of a particular area of science. It was more particularly the parts of the latter which acquired close contacts with other faculties. In 1986 this central position disappeared, when an independent, separate Faculty of Philosophy was founded. The abolition "took place almost in silence" (de Boer, 1988). The main reason must be sought in the fact that the philosophers themselves no longer regard their field in a general manner, but as a specialty next to other subject specialties. In the first part I have already indicated this dangerous and undermining tendency. In spite of this dangerous side, the situation in the Netherlands is still exceptional and offers some perspective, since philosophy has still retained its independence in the new university situation.

When we look at the situation outside the Netherlands at this moment, we see that there has nowhere been talk of such ambitious plans as existed in the Netherlands. It strongly resembles the Dutch situation before 1963, that is to say that philosophy is bound to a particular faculty, mostly that of Letters, but that it remains general without the compulsory extreme specializations. The same applies to all universities in Europe and America. Nevertheless it is a good thing to compare the present university philosophy with that of the near future using the sub-division into subjects, as is specific in the Netherlands but elsewhere at least implicitly present. It will give us a picture of how the practice of philosophy is or is not present, how philosophical problems outside universities can be dealt with and 'investigated'. In this way we get a guideline to unravel the entanglement of philosophical research and the practice of philosophy. The main division is now in historical and systematic philosophy.

A. *History of philosophy*
The history of philosophy is usually divided into three parts: Antiquity, Middle ages, modern period. The connection between these three is nevertheless so great, that it is not unusual for certain areas or themes to bring the whole of history together in one particular respect. Specialization has left its mark here too in the last forty years. If it was normal before that

time that a researcher should first study for instance Kant, then Plato, then a twentieth century philosopher, nowadays one should limit oneself to one's own steadily decreasing area. It all started with the philosophy of Antiquity, which demanded a steadily more specific professionalism. Then medieval philosophy was separated off by specialists; the Renaissance period, everywhere rather badly served for too long, acquired its own researchers, and finally the modern period was then split up into specialist areas. The famous great philosophers of the past and sometimes even of today, all have their own place in their scholarly research arsenal, often internationally, in the relevant societies with official bodies, archives and research institutes. They play an important role in editing activities; philosophers of the past are now for the first time accessible in their original writings. One of the earliest founded societies is the Kant-Gesellschaft, 1904; it was a stimulating force in German philosophical life until the Hitler period. Some other examples: the Internationale Hegel-Vereinigung, an international association for the advancement of Hegelian Studies, 1962, associated with the Hegel-Archiv (Bochum), active in the edition of Hegel's own works; the G.W. Leibniz-Gesellschaft, 1966, associated with a growing number of national Leibniz societies, and stimulating the complete edition of Leibniz works, as yet unfinished. For a budding researcher it is barely possible to find an interesting theme of study in the philosopher that thrills him the most. A final essay of a student on, for example, Kant or Nietzsche is becoming impossible, in view of the need to postulate something new.

Research however can be both philosophical *and* historical. It is only historical in the sense that texts are published critically, commentated and interpreted: the life and work of philosophers are minutely researched and described; subsidiary studies are made on aspects of their philosophy. Besides that it can also be philosophical in the attitude which is assumed with regard to the philosopher or the trend studied. When people actualise this, think it out for themselves or adopt it as a point of departure for their own philosophizing, then the research may be called not only historical but philosophical. It is strange, however, that among the historians of philosophy this attitude generally incites resistance and the reproach of capriciousness. In general, and certainly in the Netherlands, it is eclipsed by pure historic research that takes the same path as if it concerned arbitrary cultural figures or trends outside philosophy.

In addition to the ubiquitous research of the philosophy of Antiquity, the Middle Ages and the Renaissance, the accent in most countries is on the history of their own national philosophy; in the Netherlands this has been a rather neglected area for some long time, but change has been apparent in recent years. Separate trends are also studied, like the dialectic, the analytical and the post modern philosophy. One great activity of all historians of philosophy lies in the expression to a greater public of the results, by means of translations, reprints, paraphrases, introductions etc.

B. *Systematic philosophy*
The official parts of systematic philosophy like philosophical anthropology, social philosophy and political philosophy, the philosophy of language and logic all have very close connections with either the social sciences - like sociology, educational theory, psychology – or with linguistics and with mathematics. Logic can be considered separately, even in the case of the new variation, applied logic. The philosophy of language is closely connected with it too, but with regard to social philosophy and philosophical anthropology it has to be stated that in practice the interrelation is so great that there can be but little genuine 'philosophical' research. Even the rather vague term 'cultural philosophy' which is in use here and there, has little specific content next to sciences like cultural sociology.

Philosophy, apart from the sections mentioned, has also included since ancient times the systematic subjects of metaphysics/ontology, the theory of knowledge, philosophy of science and ethics. A humble place is assigned to aesthetics and the philosophy of language.

a. metaphysics/ontology
These subjects have been strongly neglected, particularly since the influential Neo-Kantianism of the period between the two world wars. Metaphysics was disposed of as an outdated affair. This was also stated by significs and neo-positivist focused philosophy. Even the post 1945 trend-setting existentialism had, on the whole, little need of metaphysics as a too abstract occupation. It remained almost exclusively in a Roman Catholic and theological context.

New stimuli have certainly arisen in the most recent period, and they came from two different directions: Heidegger's Fundamentalontology comes more to the fore and, from the neo-positivist side, more is continually done regarding the fundamentals of the world view, that is to say, ontology.

b. Theory of knowledge and philosophy of science
Recently this subject has acquired a new and additional name: cognitive science, a name which indicates that there is internationally a certain shift

of interest towards the English language area from the former dominant influence of Kant and Neo-Kantianism. Instead of the transcendental question about the value of knowledge, the process of knowledge as it is executed psychologically or linguistically is now at the pivot.

In that way psychology and the philosophy of language are involved in analysis. The problem of artificial intelligence is regarded from all angles and particularly the possible application thereof. Cooperation with technical subjects has even led in the Netherlands (at the University of Utrecht) to a new course of training, i.e. that of 'knowledge engineer'. We are faced with the question of whether we have thus abandoned the field of genuine philosophy.

The traditional content of the subject 'philosophy' of science, that has to be the basis for the method and unity of science, later supplemented with the problem of the social function of science, continues to exist and is reflected in the many publications in university circles. The boundary with ethics can be indicated here, particularly where it concerns questions of the social consequences of a scientific and technical nature, as for example in environmental philosophy.

c. Ethics

In the activities within this subject, account has to be taken recently of a possibly artificial, but in practice much used distinction between theoretical and applied ethics. Maybe the background to this is to be found in the declaration of Schopenhauer, that the founding of morals is difficult, but that the preaching of morals is easy. The attention has indeed shifted in the last decennium from analysis of the bases of essential values to case studies of moral decisions: the 'prisoner's dilemma' always has to be taken into account in the discussions. Even in books about ethics as science, most of the space is given to practical examples.

In the concrete research subjects themselves there has been a slide of political-philosophically tinged questions like work, power, ideology towards medical-technical subjects: test tube fertilization, ovum implants, cases of euthanasia, transplants. In the Netherlands a European society has been founded by the institute of health ethics at the University of Maastricht. When a 'broad social discussion', meanwhile superseded, was set up in the Netherlands concerning the maintenance or extension of the number of nuclear power stations, the ethical fervently joined in the discussion. Now it is the more general environmental questions that play an increasing role in philosophical ethical discussions. A new development moreover, is that within ethics more attention is paid to the nature of the argument than to the fundamental content of the positions; thus applied ethics gets steadily nearer to logic. The question as to the real motives that a person has for his deeds is no longer asked, but rather concerning the 'good reasons', in other words the most plausible arguments. We thus arrive at a normative action theory, that is to say a theory that indicates what the reasons may or may not be for an action.

As an offshoot of the university unrest of the sixties, the demand was also heard within philosophy for socially relevant research; within the framework of new forms of education students were also stimulated to participate in this research. Separate subjects were made of 'philosophy and society'. In practice it appeared that such research was mainly sociological, so that it gradually disappeared again from the philosophy curriculum.

d. Logic and the philosophy of language

The research in logic seems to shift progressively further and further away from subjects with a mathematical or logic basis towards subjects which are associated with the practical application of logical theories. This works in two completely different directions: on the one hand there is the examination of the argumentation theories, which aim at taking more responsible decisions by means of better argumentation; better insights are achieved by the recently developed analysis, as a new branch of logic. On the other hand logic is applied in information-technology. A close connection has thus come about between the cognitive science mentioned above, and logic. In view of the fact that people work with artificial intelligence and artificial languages, linguistics is involved too. There too we perceive a similar phenomenon: instead of reflecting on the basics, the application of language in the philosophy of language is now examined.

e. Aesthetics

This subject, that has long had an inter-disciplinary character due to the fact that it is largely practised from a background of art theory, i.e. by art historians, linguistics and musicologists, has thus mostly had but little contribution from the side of pure philosophy. The original 19th century intention of normative aesthetics has long been abandoned; the present analyses mostly concern the social function of art. Instead of, here again, reflecting on the fundamentals of what is beautiful and ugly, research concerns the reception and communication.

In general one might say that the research being carried out in the Netherlands is not different from what is found elsewhere; people keep in step and treat the same things as in the German and English-speaking areas. There is barely a specifically Dutch contribution. This certainly does not have to be viewed negatively. People can regret that there are few stimuli and initiatives from the Netherlands which fertilize the whole of international research. Using the previously mentioned themes: language, society and science, we can see the inter-weave of Dutch 'researches' with those undertaken abroad.

There is another change that has to be mentioned, which has become noticeable more specifically since the reorganization of the universities at the end of the sixties. This reorganization has also meant that each lecturer became more involved in the contacts within his own faculty and university, but neglected the contacts with other universities or even outside them. Nowadays the contacts are restored, but only between the specialities of the universities in one country, organized in mutual research projects. Before, and even shortly after the Second World War, the research contacts were mainly to be found in scholarly societies, which people decided to join of their own accord or to which people were invited to belong. An example of a society that flourished for many years in the Netherlands was the "Genootschap voor wetenschappelijke filosofie" (society for scholarly philosophy). This association finally led a rather needy existence and was disbanded in 1982. What remained, or were founded anew, were a number of specialist philosophical societies, concerned within a section of philosophy such as logic, philosophy of science, ethics, which mostly also operate in an international context, due to the fact that they are affiliated to a federation or umbrella society. Since 1900 the FISP exists, the International Federation of Philosophical Societies, whose main task is the organisation of a world congress of philosophy every five years. Such a congress (the last one being in Brighton in 1988) is a meeting place for philosophers from all over the world, but is itself again split up into all imaginable specialities. Some successful endeavours are made to break through these barriers and also to reach a broader interested public of non-professional philosophers. Since 1917 the Internationale School voor Wijsbegeerte (International School for Philosophy) had been flourishing at Leusden in the Netherlands. It is an international conference place for all kinds of philosophical discussions; it has contacts with the recently formed "Collège International de Philosophie" in Paris, that is also trying to philosophize in a general way. These institutes are really taking the task of philosophy seriously in their critical approach to human reason and human culture.

4. The task of philosophy and philosophizing

It is at this moment in the discussion that it is highly desirable to eliminate the misunderstanding that an authority called 'philosophy' as an existing instance really exists as such. This misunderstanding thrives abundantly both among those who have expectations of 'philosophy' as among those who expect nothing of it. In both cases people think of an institutionalised authority, which may or may not provide us with appropriate wise pronouncements. The caretakers of this authority are 'the philosophers'. As the official representatives of wisdom on earth they are expected to provide true insight and if this does not materialise, then people are mortally disappointed. It becomes more of a problem if people place 'the philosophers' and 'philosophy' in university institutes and faculties of philosophy, and identify philosophical research with what happens there or should happen there, and then complain that the philosophers among us play such a marginal role in discussion.

We must follow the road in the other direction and first describe or define what should be understood by philosophy and the practice of philosophy, in order then to see whether this actually exists at university institutes and faculties of philosophy, and if not how this should then be stimulated. Only then can we speak in a worthwhile manner of the future of philosophical research.

It was touched on above, when the task of philosophy as the self examination of reason and culture criticism was mentioned. It is a question particularly of the criteria which philosophy has to meet. I mention three: generality, reflection, creativity. The consequence of this activity is increasing awareness, broadening and clarification in the problems tackled. It is assumed that there is a knowledge of the manner in which these problems have been dealt with in the past. Something that is not primarily required is a critical or practical attitude; Horkheimer put this well when he wrote: "Man kann nicht sagen, dass in der Geschichte der Philosophie diejenigen Denker am fortschrittlichsten wirkten, die am meisten zu kritisieren hatten oder die stets mit sogenannten praktischen Programmen bei der Hand waren. So einfach liegen die Dinge nicht." (Horkheimer, 1968: 312).

Now there is an important statement which may certainly not be reversed: the one who meets the given criteria, can be called a philosopher; but: the one who is called a philosopher, for whatever reason, will certainly not always meet these criteria, or even stronger: will not be able to be held responsible that he does not meet the requirements. And people will certainly not have to satisfy the criteria which are generally set a scholarly researcher in order to be called a philosopher. There have to be possibilities and they have to be made, in order to give people the freedom to work in a creative way on the solutions to fundamental problems. For that reason there should be a capacity for philosophy, which is not set apart from the rest of the scholarly behaviour, but simply has this as a premise, as Nietzsche showed. And what is the most necessary condition to be able to arrive at that creativity? it goes without saying that it is the freedom of research; the freedom of spirit which should not be encumbered with all kinds of rules and statutes, or by any authorities or aims whatsoever. And all that can get in the way of the practice of philosophy at this moment is not to be sneezed at. We shall consider it all briefly.

5. Factors which threaten and hinder the practice of philosophy
In the first place we should pose the question, to what extent there can be any talk of useful philosophy. Should willingness to render service be rejected entirely or is this in particular the raison d'être of philosophy? In order to answer the question meaningfully we need first to ask: of service to whom or to what?

From ancient times philosophy was the 'handmaiden of theology' and many cheer that this stage has now passed. The bad thing about it was not so much the serviceability as much as the subservience, whereby philosophy lost its autonomy. Even now philosophy can render good service to theology or even to humanistic professional training, but the danger of subservience is not just a figment of the imagination, especially when philosophy has been brought inside the walls of the training institute, as is the case in theological seminaries and universities, and in the first humanistic university founded, in the Netherlands. The freedom of the practice of philosophy is there under threat.

In another way philosophy can be of service to scientific research, if the practice of philosophy and science appear as equals within the university. In this way Casimir could express his desire in 1931, that philosophy should be made serviceable to the humanities, for only that philosophy can serve well that has an independent life, is convinced of its value, and knows itself to be included in a greater whole. The discussion can naturally also be extended by querying in general the serviceability of the university as a whole. It is certainly so, that the serviceability of the university to society, especially that of a technical-scientific nature, should be seen as an important, if not the most important task of these establishments (Van Bueren, 1985). Then the other main duty of the university is oppressed, namely the cultural function, which includes the assistance of the university in the increase of the cultural level of society. This danger threatens, not least, the practice of philosophy, which can supply even less social value, but which rather distances itself from it by its general and reflective attitude. With regard to the practice of philosophy is valid a fortiori what Van Bueren writes of university scholarship, namely that the historic meaning of it does not lie in the initiating character of the research carried out there, or its revolutionary aspect, but rather in the deepening, commentating and extending aspects, and in the nourishing and supporting role of research in education.

Alas the position is that philosophical research at the university as it now stands, and as it will be ensured in the near future, is aimed at immediate social value. In fact it would still be better to say that it is aimed at the immediate benefit of business life. Contract research is dealt with on philosophical grounds and sponsors are sought. This applies in the first instance to those parts of philosophy which have prefixed themselves 'applied', like applied ethics and applied logic. People there wish to be of service to the computer industry and the pharmaceutical industry. It further applies to those parts of philosophy which are aimed at management and technological development, like cognitive science, argumentation theory and social philosophy. New directions of study are arranged for the philosophy of knowledge, technology and society, which intend to meet the requirements of the authorities and the business world, not only by training people but also more emphatically in the carrying out of research.

There are great dangers that threaten from the side of the meddling of the authorities, from the enticements of the market and from chasing the wind, that is to say in being carried away by fashionable appearances. Moreover the bureaucratic apparatus is also a real threat since it no longer seems to be at the service of the university, but that the situation is rather the reverse. (Sperna Weiland, 1986). Alas on all sides there is a tendency toward adjustment to the demands of a society aimed at productivity, but university systems, which are born of the desire "to dominate the thought of the learned as a controllable material, will produce not only much routine research but also conformity and docility. Meddling with current questions, which is what philosophers have always done, is discouraged, if not punished." (De Boer, 1988). The greatest danger, threatening philosophy, is that the practice thereof is modelled on the example of other 'scholarly research' and is considered to be one of the subject specialties, preferably divided still further into even more specialised parts. Adorno had to ascertain some decades ago that this situation threatened in Germany, and meanwhile it has not ameliorated.

Prophets of doom, like Finkielkraut, now envisage the complete submergence of thought, since 'the thinking life', as practised by philosophers, is no longer considered to be a 'higher life' compared with the life of everyday. Every expression of culture is seen as being equal to every other: thought is of no more value than knitting or an eating habit (Finkielkraut, 1987).

The thing that is really challenged is the practice of philosophy as general reflection. In the university situation, the general as such becomes a specialty and is thus itself lost.

6. Perspective of the future

If we ask ourselves which direction philosophical research will take in the near future, then no meaningful answer can be given. We can state that certain areas of research, which are very extended at present, will remain important, provided the money is not cut off. In the case of the Netherlands this research is in the fields of the history of philosophy and of logic. Research will certainly continue if it is socially relevant and applicable both now and in years to come, like ethical and social-philosophical themes. It here consists of a continuation of existing lines. A certain planning is not impossible in this case. If we also enquire about the future of the practice of philosophy, no meaningful answer can be given. This is so involved in the chance creativity and influence of particular thinkers, and with the attention paid them by the media, that no prognosis is possible, even in the short term. Suddenly certain fashions come about; they can pass just as quickly. In recent years striking examples have been seen in the various fields of the practice of philosophy. When John Rawls published his work "A Theory of Justice" in 1977, he unchained a stream of publications lasting many years, first in the English-speaking world, and following the translations into the relevant languages there too, the most recent being in France two years ago. When T. Kuhn published his book about "The structure of scientific revolutions" in 1963, no one realised how much this book would occupy scholarly philosophers for years. At present Lyotard, with his post-modernist view, dominates discussions in France, recently in the Netherlands and shortly also in Germany. If Foucault had not died too young and if Althusser had not been confined because of a crime, then trend-setting books would doubtless have appeared from these two, and the trend in France would be quite different.

The practice of philosophy depends on the creativity and influence of certain people. This can be neither planned nor organised. Outside the university circuit the influence continues, which can neither be determined or foreseen to the same degree. This practice of philosophy can be encouraged by a free climate, but not at all by suggesting measures for switching to even more specialised specializations, whether they are financed by the authorities or by business. It is obvious that 'philosophical research' in the now valid meaning of specialised scholarly research must not be abandoned, but must continue to exist as 'foundation' and be strengthened where necessary. But there must be more if all of this is to have any meaning. This more is the practice of philosophy itself. According to philosophers of various schools of thought, like Heidegger and Derrida, philosophy in the traditional sense is a thing of the past; Heidegger defended the thesis of 'the end of Philosophy' as belonging to the period of technical scientific rationalization. Instead of that he sees a new task for 'thinking': a thinking, "das nüchtener ist als das unaufhaltsame Rasen der Rationaliserung und das Fortreissende der Kybernetik", that is to be found "ausserhalb der Unterscheidung von rational und irrational" (Heidegger, 1969). The 'thinking' that Derrida pleads, "is characterised by a contravention. The boundary or the framework of that which is permitted within the university is exceeded. At the same time it then becomes obvious of what nature this boundary or that framework is, how it functions within the university establishment and why it is a necessary condition of possibility for this establishment" (IJsseling, 1986). I feel that in this connection the two tasks of philosophy mentioned above, the criticism of culture and the self examination of reason, fit in here.

There is only one condition needed to allow this practice of philosophy, this thought, to occur within the university: an atmosphere of freedom. It then concerns a necessary and not a sufficient reason: this atmosphere of freedom does not guarantee that creative philosophy can actually be realised; without that atmosphere it is not possible at all. Seen from an organizational point of view, we could indicate the situation at most of the European and American universities and hark back to the proposition of the conference of 1931 to call the chairs of philosophy none other than 'philosophy and its history'. The addition of 'and its history' is very essential, because philosophical creativity stands in a great tradition, that must be continually re-thought and brought up to date. Instead of further specialization, philosophy is served by generalization from specialities existing and to be maintained. "Philosophy without science is empty, science without philosophy is blind." (Cournot, quoted by Polak, 1933: 1-8). Everywhere there should thus aimed at having a Central Interfaculty as a general and connecting organization, in which specialised philosophical research can also find its place; in the Netherlands once more, in other countries for the first time. This would be the place for philosophizing, which does not exist before or instead of philosophical research or surround it, but is supported by it and constructs further on it. Only in this way is there any future for philosophy as a whole and thus for society. Philosophy is not problematic, but the world is, and philosophy has to reveal it.

References

Adorno, Th. W., 1970. Wozu noch Philosophie? *Eingriffe* 6: 11-28.

Boer, T. de 1988 De Centrale Interfaculteit, constructie en deconstructie. *Algemeen Nederlands Tijdschrift voor Wijsbegeerte*, 80: 149.

Bueren, H.G. van, 1985. De universiteit als dierbare en dienstbare instelling. *De Gids*, 148: 703.

BUOZ-nota, 1979. *Beleidsnota universitair onderzoek*. Ministerie van Onderwijs.

Casimir, R., 1933. De betekenis van de wijsbegeerte voor de geesteswetenschappen. In: *De wijsbegeerte in haar verhouding tot ons hoger onderwijs*, Haarlem.

Finkielkraut, A., 1987. *La défaite de la pensée*. Paris.

Heidegger, M., 1950. *Holzwege*. Frankfurt.

Heidegger, M., 1969. *Das Ende der Philosophie und die Aufgabe des Denkens*. In: *Zur Sache des Denkens*, Tübingen.

Horkheimer, M., 1968. Die gesellschaftliche Funktion der Philosophie. In *Kritische Theorie II*, Frankfurt.

Husserl, E., 1910/11. Philosophie als strenge Wissenschaft *Logos*, 1: 289.

Kohnstamm, Ph., 1933. *De wijsbegeerte, in: De wijsbegeerte in haar verhouding tot ons hoger onderwijs*. Haarlem.

Nietzsche, F., 1885. *Jenseits von Gut und Böse*.

Nittel, J., 1954. De wijsbegeerte in het hoger onderwijs. *Algemeen Nederlands Tijdschrift voor Wijsbegeerte*, 46: 267.

Polak, L., 1933. Openingsrede, in: *De wijsbegeerte in haar verhouding tot ons hoger onderwijs*. Haarlem.

Pos, H.J., 1940. *Filosofie der wetenschappen*. Arnhem.

* I wish to thank my colleagues Th. de Boer, T. Kuipers, J. Sperna Weiland, for their stimulating discussions and useful criticism on an earlier version of this paper. The translation is made by Veronica Schöfer.

Pos, H.J., 1954. Drie hoofdrichtingen van philosopheren. *Algemeen Nederlands Tijdschrift voor Wijsbegeerte*, 46: 147.

Riedel, M., 1978. Philosophieren nach dem 'Ende der Philosophie'? In: H. Lubbe (Ed.), *Wozu Philosophie?*. Berlin.

Sperna Weiland, J., 1986. Een zelfbewuste universiteit. *Wijsgerig Perspectief*, 26: 117.

Swart, H.A.P., 1977. Onderzoek van onderzoek. *Universiteit en Hogeschool*, 23: 217.

Themerson, S., 1974. *Logic, Labels and Flesh*. London.

VC Wijsbegeerte, 1987. *Rapport van de verkenningscommissie wijsbegeerte*. Den Haag: DOP

IJsseling, S., 1986. Filosofie in de moderne universiteit. *Wijsgerig Perspectief*, 26: 111.

Contingency and transcendence: A proposal for Theological Research in the 1990's

H.A.J. Wegman

At the opening of the University of Leiden in the Netherlands on the 8th of February 1575 during a service of the nearby church of St. Peter a theologician, the city's official minister Caspar Coolhaes (1534-1615), delivered an oration. He gave a summary of the disciplines which ought to be taught in the university: viz. theology, law, medicine, 'philosophies', the other 'artes liberales', Latin, Greek en Hebrew. A conspicuous feature of this list is that theology comes first. The list of required languages, moreover, also points to the study of theology, since Hebrew and Greek are the original languages of the bible that constitutes the foundation of theology. To this very day theology has retained this first place in the state universities of the Netherlands. The situation in France is different. There theology has disappeared from the state universities (except in Strasbourg). In Germany and the Scandinavian countries the situation differs as well. Denominational theological faculties have been set up within the state universities there. The first place given to theology in the list of disciplines in the Dutch universities is, at the very least, remarkable, especially in a

cultural setting characterized as postmodern and secularized and in a country
in which, just as elsewhere, the separation of church and state is legally
established. But it is even more remarkable that a country so profoundly
influenced by Calvinism should boast an arrangement which is characteristic of Roman Catholic universities throughout the world: since the High
Middle Ages the Catholic tradition has persisted in recognizing this first
place for the theological faculty.

The pride of place assigned to theology in a university can certainly be
explained historically. In the Middle Ages Aristotle was a widely read
authority. He places theology under the theoretical disciplines which strive
towards wisdom, insight into the good and the true. Truth and the good are
divine by nature and wisdom is, therefore, the most worthy goal towards
which one may strive and theology is the primary theoretical science.
Since the Reformation, the existing religious denominations, notwithstanding
all their disagreements, have agreed in cherishing the same vision about
theology: the doctrine and science of God is the all-dominant discipline for
the precise reason that the object of reflection is God. The bible which has
been handed down to us is an authoritative document that no other branch
of the sciences can unfold and this bible teaches that God is infinitely pre-
eminent above humankind. This conviction determines the highest place
allotted to theology in the assessment of the value of the sciences. Still a
third reason can be added. Pride of place was allotted to theology because
this discipline provided for the professional training of the ministers of the
church. A servant of the Word, according to this view, is the most important profession and this fact therefore justifies the primary place given to
theology.

But no theologian today would still claim this primary role for theology in
the universities nor insist on its perpetuation. Western society (only the
western?) is, after all, involved in such a profound process of change –
neither a-historic nature nor supernature is normative for humankind but
one is determined by one's contingent project for life – that the place
assigned to normative religious denominations can only be determined
now on the basis of the choice of private persons. The christian churches,
moreover, with their theology are but one instance of a plurality of religions. But, above all, in the constellation of forces in our global society the
churches are no longer the speakers of the first and the last word.

This development affects theology and theological research. This discipline no longer enjoys a matter-of-course acceptance. Modern universities
without theological faculties are not crippled. Branches of science which
were previously considered parts of theology can, according to the judge-

ment of non-theologians, easily be assigned to other faculties. And last but not least, because its normative rules seem to be derived from above or outside, theological research does not appear to measure up to the accepted standards and values of science. Theology as a science, the scientific character of theology, is therefore at stake. My purpose here, however, is not primarily to defend the scientific status of theology. I wish, rather, in the following to attempt to show that a unique organizational framework involving the place of theology and theological research in a university setting – a framework that as far as I know can be found only in the Netherlands – can contribute to guaranteeing the scientific character and warrants of this research. What I am referring to here is the so-called non-denominational theological research for which room has been created by Dutch lawmaking.

1. Organizational options

Unless I am mistaken, there is a variety of options available regarding the place of theology and theological teaching and research in a university. The first option is to exclude theology from the university and to assign its associated disciplines to other faculties. Religion and the churches are not directly or independently included in this kind of university structure. This option results in the university being a-religious. This choice was made in Europe, for example in France and Italy. The antithetical option is the formula of the denominational university, founded and organized on a denominational basis and thereby allowing the theological faculty to play a prominent role. This faculty is then organized according to the principle of the simplex orde: viz., theology is denominational; the manner of practising the various disciplines depends on the denomination in question and research is conducted within the bounds of given frameworks of assumptions and manners of thinking which are determined by the various doctrines and denominations. Such universities organized on a denominational basis can be financed by the state or, alternatively, the relevant church must finance the university or theological faculty out of its own resources. This is the case if the state guarantees freedom of education but refuses to finance any religious denomination on the principle of the separation of church and state. In the countries where the Roman Catholic church has a free hand in this respect, this denominational option is the only one which exists and is recognized and the faculty's theological practice is determined denominationally by Roman Catholic tradition and doctrine. In Germany and the Scandinavian countries, but also to a certain extent in the United Kingdom and the United States, theological faculties are instituted in the state universities and financed by the state, even though these faculties are denominational and linked to specific churches, whether Roman Catholic or Protestant (in a variety of modalities). There is a third option which, however (as already mentioned), is unique, since it has been established by law since 1876 only in the Dutch state universities and has therefore already been put to the test for more than one hundred years. This option is referred to by the term 'duplex ordo'.

The 'duplex ordo' involves the following. The State of the Netherlands founds public theological faculties within the state universities without any form of church interference. In this kind of public faculty research is conducted (and teaching is performed) into the phenomenon of religion and comparative science of religion is practised. According to this option, theology is not a science of a belief of a religious denomination, but a public science of religion. Disciplines such as exegesis of the Jewish and the Christian bible, the history of Christianity, ethics and the philosophy of religion are practised in terms of this perspective, i.e., the optique of the science of religion. Full attention is paid in scientific inquiry to the 'Umwelt'-questions and the Christian religion is placed in the broad religious framework. Appointments of scientific personnel, especially the holders of chairs, come under the competence of the state. This is the primary rule of the 'duplex ordo', that of the decision-making authority of the state.

The second rule orders the decision-making authority of the churches ensuring that these churches are provided with the necessary finances from the state to set up 'ecclesiastical chairs' and to appoint scientific personnel to look after denominational theology, to pay attention to the professional training of the ministers of the churches and to orient their research towards the denominational creed. In this case, one speaks of 'church' or 'faith' disciplines determined by the tradition of the relevant institutional church. The heart of these church disciplines is dogmatic or systematic theology to which is added the theology of the bible and the history of the churches and the history of church doctrine.

In practice, this 'duplex ordo' functions as follows. A particular institutional church can make use of the state faculties to train its theologians and ministers in religious studies and, in that case, the church supplements a neutral basic training with the 'church-theological' disciplines that the denomination considers necessary. This means that theological inquiry is conducted along two paths: 'public', that is, non-denominational theological research directed towards the phenomenon religion, on the one hand,

and church-theology on the other hand. The responsibilities of church and state are separate and, so too, the point of departure and purpose of theological research. This framework of double responsibility has a long tradition and has demonstrated its merits - there is, according to law, separate responsibility and there is, in practice, contact and cooperation between the researchers of the state faculty and the church-related department linked to it. This formula, it seems to me, is a very appropriate guideline for the organizational and substantive realization of theological research in the 1990's because, by means of this option, full account can be taken of the changing position of the churches in society, as described above, and of the desire for the practice of non-denominational theological research associated with the changing position of the churches.

Before going into this more deeply, I would like to draw attention to the fact that the theory of the 'duplex ordo' (let me repeat: a unique Dutch model) has been somewhat watered down during its hundred years of existence; that is to say, without a fuss being made about it, the denominations have nevertheless exerted a noticeable influence on the non-denominational faculties. In theory, the 'duplex ordo' means that the theological faculty of the state university rests on the foundation of the public realm, that, in other words, theology and especially theological research may not be determined by any ecclesial denomination. The practice of the 'duplex ordo', however, indicates deviations from the theory. Since the foundation of the universities by the State of the Netherlands, the influence of the Calvinistic tradition in the upper levels of society has been great. In the course of allowing its ministers to be trained in the state theological faculty, the Calvinistic church tacitly acquired more influence on this faculty than can be justified by the 'duplex ordo'. Biblical exegesis gained a great deal of attention, because this was necessary for future ministers and this exegesis was taught in the perspective of this profession. Research related to the Jewish and Christian bible was largely directed towards writing commentaries which could be used by the ministers. In other words, even though the 'duplex ordo' assumes the separate decision-making authorities of church and state, in practice the influence of ecclesial traditions has managed to work its way through into the state faculty and theological research by introducing denominational traits and preoccupations. A precious phenomenon established by Dutch lawmaking has thereby been relegated into the background in the execution of the law and the Calvinistic denomination has, in opposition to the spirit of the law, unjustifiably co-determined the contours of public theology. The option of the 'duplex ordo' nevertheless remains a unique and important component for the future of theological research, not only in the Netherlands but in the international arena as well. This research, after all, can be set up simultaneously along two lines of approach; the academic and the denominational in mutual contact and cooperation.

2. The organization of research in the 1990's

Under this heading I would like to set to paper some points that could be significant for theological research and could re-enforce its scientific statute. These points may be regarded as part of what I would like to call research management. This is a precarious matter. It appears to be a gross exaggeration of my abilities to describe, out of the limited Dutch situation and with Dutch spectacles on, those issues which might be of importance for theological research beyond the borders of the Netherlands. On the other hand, in my opinion it is worth the effort to wager an attempt at escaping limitations and parochialism.

Internationalization
It seems to me a matter of great importance for theological research to achieve an internationally organized and developed policy. My impression is that theological research lags significantly behind the level of international cooperation already reached in other branches of science. International working associations of theologians who exchange their research indeed exist, but a common policy does not seem to be developing. If I limit myself to Europe (in 1992 a Europe without frontiers), then one is forced to conclude that theologians are not well-informed about what is happening beyond the borders of their countries. They are not sufficiently aware that research is also being conducted elsewhere and appear to assume that every aspect of theological research ought to be promoted in a single country. Theologians have acquired the habit of keeping within the bounds of one's own country and language. One cannot help noticing that in not a few German, French or English scholarly publications, the number of the utilized or cited publications in languages other than its own is significantly lower. This could be the result of the language barrier, but it is also possible that the above mentioned linguistic communities regard themselves as so self-sufficient that setting a foot outside is considered to be unnecessary. It seems to me that this is a shortcoming that militates against a broad knowledge of each other's research and measures to counter-act this state of affairs should be taken. In this respect, it is possible that researchers in smaller linguistic communities than the above mentioned

are perhaps, by necessity, more internationally oriented. But what I primarily have in mind when I refer to a broader and more international (to begin with, a European) orientation of theological research is the beginning of a policy aiming at the allocation of fields of specialization in research. It would seem that a primary requirement for the achievement of such a policy is a general overview of the research that is being conducted in the various regions. This sort of inventory can bring theologians to the realization that it is not necessary for everyone to be at work in every field. A following step can be making attempts to coordinate each others research in theological methodology and in the various disciplinary fields of theology - a sort of clustering of research per country. And finally, such international coordination could be institutionalized. Would it not be an obvious step to take in a united Europe to create an institute for the organization of theological research by means of which this policy can be worked out and guaranteed? Such international coordination of theological research will be beneficial for theology as a science. I see the following positive consequences.

In the first place, the whole field of theology can be more easily covered by means of these international agreements, duplication of research can be avoided and centres or research can enjoy an enhanced outreach and accessibility beyond their national borders. All together, this promotes exchanges and communication between present and future scholars.

Secondly, by means of the international approach to research policy it is also possible to improve the standards of quality and output of theological research. So far we lack a clear policy regarding quality. Acceptance for publication in a journal approved by the scholars is one of the few criteria available to judge research results. I do not wish to underestimate the value of this judgment, but this basis for evaluation is very narrow and the criteria that are applied are not clear. It would benefit each researcher to know ahead of time to which internationally recognized criteria his or her research is expected to measure up.

Thirdly, internationalization of theological research can throw light on the various accents that are placed in the research in each country. On the grounds of this information it can be determined which research on a non-denominational and denominational basis it is most worth pursuing.

Scientific publications
Scientific publications, according to the consensus in the international academic world, are addressed to colleagues at home and abroad who can judge the worth of the research method, the use of the sources, the bibliographic information, the distillation of results and the results themselves

qua composition, style and argumentation. It is, however, important to agree about the definition of the concept 'colleague' and it seems to me that it is particularly important for researchers in an international context to arrive at a sort of definition of the concept. On the basis of a twofold filling in of the concept 'colleague' I arrive at a twofold description of a scientific publication.

'Colleagues' of a researcher are (in my opinion), on the one hand, those who, like the researcher in question, are also working in an academic setting. By means of publication the researcher's new insights, analysis or synthesis is presented tot his or her colleagues for judgment and further development. On the other hand, it seems to me to be legitimate and fruitful to give the concept 'colleague' yet another, broader meaning. A theologian's colleagues or associates in the field of study are also all those who, though professionally active outside the academic world, have qualified themselves through the study of religion or church-theology and still need the publications of theologians for a kind of 'éducation permanente'.

This duality in the concept 'colleague' leads to a twofoldness in the concept of a scientific publication: on the one hand there is a scientific publication sensu stricto (for academic colleagues) and, on the other hand, there is the scientific essay (for colleagues practising a non-academic profession). The difference between both sorts of publications rests above all on their stylistic approach. A scientific publication has the form and argumentative stance of a 'study' and, as such, addresses itself to the first category; an essay is characterized by a personal, elegant and creative digestion of the research evidence in the service of the second category of readers.

In order to flesh out my point of view about the twofold nature of scientific publications, I would like to be so bold as to give an example of both sorts taken from my field of study (the history of Christianity and its rites), namely, two recent publications. Brian Stock's, *The Implications of Literacy* (1983) is, in my opinion, a scientific study, a rereading of the sources which leads to other insights about 'the status of texts' and 'the status of oral discourse'. I consider Peter Brown's remarkable study, *The Body and Society: Men, Women and Sexual Renunciation in Early Christianity* (1988) a successful (and masterly) essay, in which the pluriform vision of sexuality and its perception in early Christianity is described in terms of the known sources. In my judgment both forms of scientific publication are completely legitimate products of theological research and, as such, can contribute to the breadth of the many-facetted field of theology.

The duplex ordo in theological research
In the above I described the Dutch option regarding the position of theology in a public, non-denominational university. In my judgment (attempting to avoid chauvinism as much as possible), this Dutch model also bears an international relevance regarding the status of theological research. I will attempt to develop the substantive aspects of this claim further below; my concern at the moment is its organizational aspect.

I see it in the following manner: in the theological research (but in teaching as well) there should be a clear distinction between non-denominational and denominational, between research into the phenomenon of religion(philological, exegetical, historical and philosophical) on the one hand, and between the ecclesial faith-traditions on the other hand - research into the science of religion, on the one hand, and denominational theory on the other hand. This distinction should be understood in the sense that denominationally oriented theological research is considered to be complementary to non-denominational research. This means, first of all, that non-denominational theological research establishes the basis and that research in Christian theology is considered as a sort of superstructure. Research into the phenomenon of religion is fundamental and research into denominational theology is a necessary supplement deriving from church traditions. Secondly, this application of the 'duplex ordo' in the organization of research should include all of the denominational theological faculties: these faculties ought to make room free for research that is not denominationally determined. Briefly stated: because of their complementarity, denominational theological research cannot expense with non-denominational research, but non-denominational research can.

I have arrived at this point of view because of the following considerations which I incorporated into the title of this study and which, in my opinion, determine the future of theological research.
Post-modern society regards the universalistic pretentions and behaviour of western Christianity (especially in its Roman Catholic form nourished by the claim that its teachings are the only true ones) as convictions and behaviour patterns belonging wholly within the sphere of purely internal Christian belief and neither the public nor other religions pay the least amount of attention to them – let alone accept them. In our society the Christian religion too has become dependent on the principle of supply and demand and can no longer impose itself upon the conscience of peoples, states or individuals. Both in terms of its beginnings as in terms of its

existence in contemporary social structures and in world society, Christianity has become a contingent institution basing itself upon an equally transitory and contingent profile-sketch of God and the divine which, it is true, has developed out of a deeply rooted faith and is supported by a long tradition, but it cannot be automatically assumed that this sketch will hold or that it is the only true one. The Christian religion is one the many religions, perhaps the largest in the world, but qualitatively only one of the offers in the broad spectrum of the religious field.

The theologian, on the other hand, is confronted with an imperishable feeling of transcendence which still, and now even more pregnantly, determines the religious consciousness of many people in contemporary society. The experience of transcendence is one of emptiness, in so far as it feels that the existing systems of thought and living are insufficient, but this experience is at the same time open for that which is not yet in reach and is searching for new words, for new signs of that which is absent. This experience of transcendence is the heart of religious consciousness and allows us to conclude that religion (or the religious question) can still be found in all of the cultures. What is at issue is the meaning of our existence which, it is believed, involves more than what is directly in hand. In whatever form it manifests itself, religion offers people a fundamental meaningfulness of their life. And it is theology which inquires into the fundamental meaning of religion, mapping it out, testing and adjusting or changing it so that its meaning may remain anchored in culture and enrich culture through the experience of transcendence.

This is the most profound reason why I opt for theological research that is organized and conducted in a double order ('duplex ordo'). Non-denominational research undertakes the search for transcendence. Denominational theological research, continually finding new words in the light of the tradition of its belief, can name, test and if necessary change the meaning of transcendence that the church or denomination has given to human existence.

3. Some points of emphasis in theological research
In this part of my study I propose to describe where I would place the points of emphasis in theological research in the 1990's. It is not my intention to provide a detailed account of the developments that will occur in the various disciplines of theology such as exegesis or the history and philosophy of religion. In this era of intensifying specialization, which is also noticeable in theological research, it is impossible to expect those

details from one of those specialized theologians. I will attempt, however, to describe some points of emphasis for theological research in such a manner that allowance is made for the various fields of theological research. This description, obviously, cannot challenge and involve all of these research fields simultaneously or equally cleared. This inevitability, however, is not a sufficient reason to avoid the attempt.

The first point of emphasis that I will describe is related to the concluding remarks of the immediately preceding part of this study. What I there treated as an organizational model will be filled in here substantively, so that the heart of my argumentation can be found in these two parts of this study.

The articles of faith of the people
The term 'articulum fidei' has been used by theologians since the Middle Ages. In this context 'article' means 'part' (member) and has been taken over into the modern languages without translation (article of faith). In classical Latin it is used to indicate a part of an oration or speech (for example, in the works of Cicero). In the Christian tradition the word is related to the so-called apostolic creed or confession of faith which consists of twelve articles and is a confession of the Trinity of God. It is a document of western Christianity dating from the fifth century, but its roots go back to the second century, in particular, to the confession of faith performed by an adult standing in the baptismal fount and being baptized. In the western tradition the creed is a compendium of the truths of faith which a baptized Christian ought to 'hold to' in order to reach or receive the salvation it confesses. The creed is the basis of Christian belief and the other articles of that Christian belief ought to be related to the creed, not in opposition to it. At the same time, the creed is the line of demarcation between belief and unbelief, between the inside and the outside of the church (in a sense even between the churches, since the Byzantines do not recognize this western document and use the creed of the Council of Nicea). The so-called Twelve Articles of the Christian faith form the portals of the church which formulated its truth in this document. This creed is the point of departure and determining factor of denominational theological research.

The Christian churches have used this creed and that of the Council of Nicea internally as a measuring device for the belief of its members, that is, as an instrument by which true belief can be determined and deviations therefrom read off as non-orthodox, not according to the right belief. In the

Roman Catholic church the term onorthodox acquired the meaning of 'in
opposition to the Catholic church', in opposition to the only true teaching
of the only true church. The churches have used the creed externally in
order to express the true beliefs to those who were not yet converted to the
faith in which, exclusively, salvation was said to be found. Both internally
and externally, judgment over the orthodox of belief was reserved for the
overseers, the 'episcopen', the bishops who formulated their judgment
over orthodoxy in their declarations of councils and synods. The result of
this development has been that the determination of orthodoxy came into
the hands of the upper levels of the church, the theologically instructed and
lettered elite. In the course of history, with ups and downs, this elite has
defended and preserved its prerogative, even after the Reformation. In this
respect, thus, a clear distinction has developed between the ministers and
the followers of that belief, although both groups remain united in their
common creed. On the grounds of the universality of the value of this
creed, the Christian churches developed a missionary consciousness which,
in addition, was greatly strengthened by the rise of a colonialist mentality
in the west European states.

The doctrine of the Christian creed, developed by the ecclesiastical elite is
clear and tidy: there is, however, a shadow cast over it and theologians
have become increasingly more conscious of its significance. What I am
referring to here is, first of all, the shadow of contingency. The creed, the
doctrinal document from which the church's leaders derive the content of
true belief and define the true church is, in essence, an accidental document. It is, as it were, an improvisation born with reference to the authenticity of those wishing to be taken up into the congregation by baptism. At
that moment they were asked for the last time about their belief. Confession
of belief, moreover, is not primarily a doctrinal act but a confession in the
original (probably Jewish) meaning of the word: recognition with an un-
dertone of joy. The creed was a song, a hymn. Given the genre of this
confession in faith, its conversion into a doctrinal document is disputable.
The creed does not teach. It brings, rather, in metaphorical language
('fictionally'; I will return to this in the following) the experience of the
transcendent under words; it expresses the experience of God who will fill
the emptiness of the non yet available. The contingency of the creed involves the obligation of viewing it as a document out of a historical era in
which a particular experience of faith was formulated, but which is now
read and spoken out in terms of new experiences. It is not a document in
which once and for all time the truth has been formulated. This has great

consequences for theological inquiry into this confession of faith: this research is directed towards an open, not a closed, text. This research is not adjudicated by that document but derives its criteria from the scientific analysis of that document which, being contingent, is neither timeless nor a-historic but is incrusted in history. This means again that denominational theological research, too, without being bound by the norms and values of church tradition, ought to inquire into the creed in terms of its being a possible profile-sketch of Christian belief.

There is a second shadow cast over the tidy doctrine regarding the creed: its reception by those who sing or recite it. I know of no systematic research aiming at learning how this creed was recited and which religious experiences were thereby expressed. Underlying this issue is the unavoidable question of the depth of the Christianization of society by Christianity, the question of acculturation. Without investigating the matter, we cannot be certain that the experiences of those who recite this religious text are in accordance with the doctrinal views about the content of faith that have been attributed to it by the governing bodies of the churches. If religion is based on the experience of transcendence, as described above, then it is very well possible that these experiences are less articulated, 'emptier', than the churches expect. It is very possible that the word God in religious experience has an 'emptier' or 'different' content than is intended by the ecclesiastical creed in which God is, after all, a clearly described being: one in three persons. It is just as possible that very old mythical experiences lie anchored in the reception of the Christian creed. We find here a new challenge for theological research: inquiry into the reception and influence of the Christian creed in the religious experiences of people belonging to church denominations or who have come to stand outside of one - experiences which are less articulated than one would expect on the basis of the Twelve Articles of faith. Now then, I regard this inquiry as 'basic research' in the sense that I explained above. By that I mean that research into the reception of the Christian articles of faith and, at the same time, into the articles of faith of the people could become a point of emphasis of non-denominational theological research.

To summarize this part of my study I arrive at the following thesis: on the basis of the twofold research model according to the 'duplex ordo', I see the prospect of a substantive point of emphasis for this research. More than has been the case so far, denominational theological research will have to orient itself towards the consequences of the fundamental contingency of the Christian creed and bring it into relation to those of the other religions. Non-denominational theological research could fruitfully direct itself, from the various perspectives of the theological disciplines, towards the meaning of the Christian creed for the religious experience of the people, towards the possibly differently disposed experience of transcendence of the many people who know and hold to these articles. Both research paths can cross each other and, in the end, possibly result in the unmasking of a denominational ideology.

Contextuality and reinterpretation
One of the urgent problems of west European theologians and researchers will increasingly come to lie in his or her stance regarding the acceptability of the social context as the precondition for the reinterpretation of the religious or Christian tradition. One of the most powerful manifestations of contextual theological research, which leads at the same time to the reinterpretation of the sources of the Christina religion, is the so-called liberation theology which was developed in Latin America. It leaves no misunderstanding of its criticism of west European academic theology, a theology which is said to orient itself too much towards maintaining the status quo and attends insufficiently to the social context. Liberation theology takes full account of the social context in its analyses, making it fundamental. In Latin America this means that the most pressing problem, the gap between the wealth of the few and the poverty of the many in part deriving from the social structure set up in the colonial period, is taken into account in theological research and, in terms of this perspective, elements for the reinterpretation of Christian doctrine are then furnished. In an analogous sense, new forms of theology based on 'contextual research' have also emerged in Asia and Africa. This research, which has found its way into challenging publications, has brought about a fundamental shift in the churches, because the faith-documents, the bible and the creed, have acquired a reinterpretation based on the analysis of the social context. This is a result of the fact that these theologians work neither in an armchair nor in a glass house but in the midst of their surrounding world of inhumane human existence and poverty. A new theological project was thereby developed spotlighting, on the one hand, the religious dimension of human freedom and independence and, on the other hand, human solidarity. This engagement with the lot of the poor, moreover, lead those theologians to seek a new interpretation of the bible on the ground of their conviction that the Jewish bible described God as the ally of the poor and oppressed.

Accordingly, among other things, the concrete form of the church changed because of the emergence of the basic communities.

One of the results of this hermeneutic reinterpretation by Latin American theology has been that European theology was rudely confronted with the fact that (mainly because of its lost contact with social revolution in the nineteenth century) it has narrowed down its religious profile to the private chambers of individuals and has not been able to offer any opposition to the privatizing tendencies in this century. This is the case, for example, with respect to the concept of sin of which the macro-dimension, manifesting itself in oppressive structures that victimize people, was replaced by the micro-dimension, the narrowed-down view merely concerning the sins of individuals. Liberation theology also worked out another reading of the bible on the basis of appropriate social and religious experiences, with a quite different feeling of transcendence as the point of departure. This reinterpretation exerted great pressure on west European academic theology to engage in self-evaluation.

In my opinion this contextual reinterpretation of the function of religion and Christianity will also have to characterize west European theology in the near future more than has been the case so far – and this will have to apply to both denominational and non-denominational research. This requires the theologians to change their mentality and to expand their field of research: from the academy to the social context, from internal concerns of the churches to research into external church-related issues. If I am not mistaken, this process is still taking place in the restricted group of critical theologians, but in the 1990's it will be unavoidable for the whole of theological research. Methods will have to be developed to take the social ambience into account in theological analysis and to direct it toward the reinterpretation of doctrine. It is now apparent that, more than in the past, theological research will be dealing with anthropological frameworks, because the reinterpretation of religion and Christianity in western Europe will also have to base itself on humankind and society. Few facets of the Christian profile-sketch that have been handed down to us will escape this contextual reinterpretation which has been born in our midst and has succeeded in gaining an established place. In this respect, theological research enjoys the prospect of wide-open spaces before it: the sources of this research do not only lie in the past.

Another specific and challenging form of reinterpretation, which arose in the 1970's and is now consolidated but which promises to bear its fruit in the 1990's, is *feminist theology*.

Everyone who is at home in the history of Christianity knows that its theology has seldom brought forth thoughts and writings without hostility of women. This conclusion can be drawn from the many known writings of theologians and leading figures in that religion. To begin with the interpretation of the first book of the bible, Genesis, there is a thick dossier available showing the masculine one-sideness of the vision of humankind as the image of God. On the basis of sources studies conducted by women, it has been shown that these sources have been interpreted one-sidedly in terms of a masculine reading-perspectives and that reinterpretation of very many texts of the religion and Christian tradition is necessary. This reinterpretation, too, affects the heart of the religion, because it can be shown on the basis of relevant theological research that many texts contain another message when broken loose from masculine thought-structures. The reinterpretation of the concept of sin, which is said to derive from a woman, is but one example of what has to be done. The reinterpretation of religious texts and claims will affect our manner of speaking about God's likeness to humanity. This is an important aspect of theology and it will have the be wholly refashioned because humanity itself is here at stake, man and woman. This reinterpretation is yet another, no less challenging, task for theological research in the 1990's. I think that the most fruitful climate for this task is present in the non-denominational, public research arena. The denominational arena has not been very receptive for this reinterpretation. Will it be open for it in the 1990's?

Literary theology

This concept is not found in theological jargon but I would like to use it to indicate a new point of emphasis in theological research for both non-denominational and denominational theologians. I am borrowing a concept from literary scholarship to make it the point of departure for research into religious texts and imagery, namely, the concept of *fiction*. The concept is difficult to define. A fictive text or image does not describe the reality in which we exist, but imagines another reality that the reader feels able to recognize. Made up, imaginary relations seem, in the judgment of the reader, to agree with the reality in which the reader lives, notwithstanding the fact that the narrator or writer has made up his or her reality. A fictive text gives no information, does not demonstrate, is not 'referential' but calls a reality into being that goes beyond, transcends, daily life. Fictive texts and imagery add a dimension to everyday existence and accordingly fulfil the needs of people who long for depth and for the secret of life. They bring into imagination what is not yet, call into being that which still lies hidden and idealize everyday reality; and notwithstanding their fictionality they still manage to be linked up with everyday reality. Fiction goes beyond the letter, is not meant literally, is not true in the rational or everyday meaning of the word. One may direct attention to the literal meaning of a text and investigate it philologically, exegetically or hermeneutically; and at the end of the analysis one knows what the outside of the text has to say. But one may also listen further to the text and arrive at the discovery that it has more to tell. One discovers its imaginary, fictive and symbolic power. There is a certain analogy with a concept known to the tradition of bible-reading: one investigates the literal meaning of the texts, but after this research one realizes that he or she is not yet fully at home in the text. It must still be read on a deeper level; one ought to search out its deepest meaning, the spiritual meaning of the text. One searches out the 'sensus spiritualis'. The letters and signs are viewed as bearers of a transcendent secret. The spiritual meaning of a bible text is comparable with that which is called a fictive text. Religious, non-doctrinal texts such as a song and a prayer are, when all is well, fictive: they point to and call into being a hidden dimension.

If we examine the results of theological research, and here I can only mention the fact of its rich variety, then one is struck by the fact that this research bases itself exclusively on texts that are regarded as referential. Bible texts or texts out of the tradition are sometimes identified as literary texts but, instead of being read fictively, only their literal meaning is studied. The same is the case for the creed, as mentioned above: it is frequently viewed as a referential text, as a statement of beliefs. A method has still not been developed in theology to determine if, and to what extent, a religious text can be considered as fiction and what the fictive meaning of such a text is in that case. Did this come about because theologians were of the opinion that seeking the fictive status of a text was incompatible with its literal meaning? Whatever the reason, theologians have almost never read the basic religious texts as fictive, but almost always as referential material. The consequences of this have been great: religious texts are then primarily seen as bearers of truth, not as images of that truth. It was thought that viewing the creed as a fictive text would erase the truth of the creed. According to semiotics a religious text involves an 'interpretant originaire' in which the original experience of an individual or group has been captured. This original experience is appropriated and amplified by the readers of the text with their own experiences which differ in time and space so that a continuing process of reception and renewal of the original interpretative message is generated. Now then, religion is pre-eminently seen as the 'terrain' of the imagination, of fiction; religion calls into being what is not yet but is hoped for and gives this a name: God or the divine. If this is indeed the case, then the obvious conclusion is that theological research should also aim at mapping out religious fictionality in terms of which religious experiences have successively been brought under words, starting with the first interpretations until those of today. I would be very happy to see theological research withdraw from the referential terrain in order to occupy itself, in the 1990's, with the fictiveness of religious statements and with the investigation of the experiences of transcendence that have been heard and captured in those utterences.

Part 3

Language

Linguistics

Simon C. Dik

During the past decades the field of linguistics, the study of human language in all its manifestations and ramifications, has gone through a number of sometimes turbulent developments, which have greatly enriched our understanding of the human linguistic capacity, both in depth and in scope. In depth, since we have gained better insight into the conditions which general linguistic theories and models will have to fulfil if they are to yield explanatory hypotheses concerning the phenomena of language and language use in their manifold variety. In scope, first of all since many more languages of quite different types and genetic provenience have been studied in detail, thus informing our general notion of 'possible human language'. Secondly, because linguistic research has not confined itself to the study of the organization of language as such, but has developed more and more interest in logical, mathematical, philosophical, psychological, sociological, pathological, and other interdisciplinary facets of language and language use.

Continued interest in the basic properties of the human linguistic faculty is well-justified by the central place language takes in human psychological, social, cultural, and political life. Activities ranging from simple everyday jobs such as buying a loaf of bread at the baker's or making an appointment with the dentist, to high-level activities such as writing or reading a literary work of art, thinking about the place of the individual in postmodern society, or convincing a whole nation of the need for economy reform – all such activities would be unthinkable without the human gift of language.

If one thing has become more evident than ever through recent linguistic research, it is the astonishing complexity of that linguistic ability which comes to us so naturally. Two thousand years of research have been unable to unravel this complexity. The complex nature of the human linguistic faculty is also brought home quite painfully in any attempt at the computational simulation of all but the simplest linguistic tasks. As soon as we start thinking about how to devise a computer program which could do only a few of the things with language that children at the age of ten do with remarkable speed and accuracy, and without apparent effort, it is our admiration for the human mind rather than that for the mechanical computer which increases exponentially. This should not be taken to mean that computational linguistic research is all in vain: on the contrary, the rapid development of computational hardware and software provides linguistics with exciting new research tools which will no doubt play a dominant role in the coming decades.

In this paper I first sketch some aspects of the importance of language in human life. Then I discuss some miraculous properties of human language which so far defy a complete analytic understanding. Against this background, I discuss some important trends in recent linguistic research. And in conclusion I sketch some of the problems involved in getting to grips with that intricate phenomenon, the integrated natural language user.

1. Man, the speaking animal

Language plays a central role in most human activities. Let us look in some detail at the role of language in human cognition, in social and cultural behaviour, and in international communication.

1.1 Language and cognition

There is a long-standing discussion on which has priority over the other, whether logically, systematically, or genetically: language or thinking. One influential view, commonly found among philosophers and cognitive psychologists, is that first there is thought, and then there is language as the expression of thought:

"The elements of speech are the symbols of the feelings in the soul", as Aristotle phrased it (*De Interpretatione* 2). Diametrically opposed to this is the view that thought itself to a non-trivial extent consists of 'internalized language': language, on this view, is not the outward carrier of inner cognitive content, but is itself the essence of thought. The very way in which we conceptualize the world would then be strongly determined by the way we talk. And learning to think (as humans do) would depend on the acquisition of language (or some language-equivalent or language-derived symbolism). Which of these views is correct is a question about which philosophers, psychologists, and linguists have made remarkably little headway. Most probably there is an intricate mutual interaction between human cognitive and linguistic abilities, both in the developmental stage and in the full-fledged adult mental system.

What all agree on, however, is this: if man is definable as an *animal rationale*, this is due, to a considerable degree, because he is at the same time an *animal loquens*, a 'speaking animal' (or, less respectfully, an *animal loquax*, a 'talkative animal'). Especially in those higher cognitive functions in which human beings seem to excel: abstract concept formation, logical reasoning, hypothesizing about possible worlds, about future events, or alternative courses of action, human language plays a central role. Language, as Edward Sapir (1949) once formulated it, provides both the boundary and the horizon of thought: we think as we do within the bounds of the linguistic conventions which we have had to take for granted right from the moment we were born into the world, and thus into some linguistic community; at the same time, language allows us to cross the boundaries of convention, create new ideas, hypotheses, theories, and new works of art, just because there is no built-in prohibition on putting it to ever-new tasks, creating new expressions and terminology, and using its combinatory potential in innovating ways.

1.2 Language and social interaction

Language plays a constitutive role in human social life, both at the micro-level of conversation and small-group interaction, and at the macro-level of global societal structure. At the micro-level we establish and re-establish our position in the network of human relations through the art of talking. At this level it is crucial for achieving one's communicative purposes to know, not only what to say, but also how to say it in which circumstances to which interlocutors. What is objectively the same message may, if delivered in different ways, lead to warm sympathy in one, to indignant rejection in another case. This points to the importance of the *pragmatics* of linguistic communication: that aspect which concerns the relations between speakers, their linguistic utterances, and addressees in concrete communicative situations. Language is not just a means of communicating information. It is also an instrument with which we can endanger and threaten, or on the contrary protect and respect the 'face' (the social and psychological identity) of ourselves and our communicative partners.

At the macro-level, as well, there are manifold correlations between ways of talking and more global structures in society. Strictly speaking, no two people speak precisely the same language. There are differences in linguistic competence and performance from individual to individual, from group to group, from place to place, and from time to time. In the interdisciplinary field of *sociolinguistics* this linguistic variation was made a central object of study. It was found that the language variety we speak is strongly determined by the socio-economic group to which we belong, and by the degree of (in)formality of the communicative situation. The relevant differences are typically not a matter of absolute yes-or-no, but rather of statistical more-or-less distribution of so-called 'sociolinguistic variables'. The occurrence of these variables in our speech creates a 'social profile', a finger print of our social group identity and status within society. It was found, furthermore, that such differences in language use are subject to strong attitudes, reactions and evaluations on the part of speakers. Certain forms of talking will be evaluated as prestigious and connected with upward social mobility, others will be stigmatized as vulgar or ridiculous, or even interpreted as a sign of stupidity and lack of logic and reason. Tape recordings of the same person speaking different language varieties may lead to dramatically different evaluations. In one variety he or she may be categorized as an important, sympathetic person capable of leading roles in responsible jobs; in another variety as a person for whom perhaps sweeping the street or cleaning dustbins would be the highest level of attainment.

1.3 Language and culture

Anthropologists agree that in order to really understand the culture of a community it is essential to learn the language of that community. This is not only true in the obvious but superficial sense that cultural values and attitudes are *expressed* in language, but also, and more essentially, in the sense that language, in several ways, is *part of* culture.

One aspect of culture consists in the conventions regulating accepted behaviour in formal and informal situations. This behaviour, again, consists for an important part of linguistic behaviour. An interesting example of this is given by Charles Bird and Timothy Shopen (1979), who compare the interaction between two friends hurrying to their jobs in American and in Maninka (West-African) culture. In American culture, the interchange might take five seconds and consist of no more than:

(1) Tim: Hello Ed!
     Ed: Hi! How are you?
     Tim: Sorry, I'm in a hurry.
     Ed: Yeh, me too.
     Tim: See you on Saturday.

This interchange consists of only five 'turns', the barest minimum for a Greeting ceremony followed by a Leave-taking ceremony. "This dialogue", the authors add, "could be translated into Maninka, but if it ever took place in a Maninka community it would be viewed as unthinkably bad social behaviour."

What happens in comparable circumstances in Maninka culture between two friends in comparable circumstances is a much longer interchange consisting of quite elaborate Greeting and Leave-taking ceremonies, in between which systematic enquiries are made about the well-being of the addressee and his most important family members. In the following exchange Mamodou Diarra meets his friend Sedou Kanté on his way to his job:

(2) MD: Ah Sedou, you and the morning.
     SK: Excellent. You and the morning.
     MD: Did you sleep in peace?
     SK: Only peace.
     MD: Are the people of the household well?
     SK: There is no trouble.
     MD: Are you well?

SK:	Peace, praise Allah. Did you sleep well?
MD:	Praise Allah. You Kanté?
SK:	Excellent. You Diarra?
MD:	Excellent.
SK:	And the family?
MD:	I thank Allah. Is there peace?
SK:	We are here.
MD:	How is your mother?
SK:	No trouble.
MD:	And your cousin Fanta?
SK:	Only peace. And your father?

[etc. for 33 'turns' of conversation]

Being friends, in Maninka culture, is a lot of work! "Not only is it necessary to be able to identify the members of the friend's family, which may
easily involve forty to fifty people, one must also remember all their names;
failure to remember someone's name is understood as a failure to recognize their significance and is therefore a serious social insult."

This is just one example of how ways of behaving linguistically may help
you to get things done or, on the contrary, may cause you to make life-long
enemies. Describing such linguistic habits (in what has been termed the
'ethnography of speaking') is an important part of describing a culture.

In other senses, as well, culture consists *in* language. An important part of
any culture is the body of oral and written songs and texts (whether popular or literary – even that is a matter of cultural attitudes) which one is
supposed to know if one is to be an educated member of the culture. Law
and government likewise are codified in verbal form, whether oral or written. And there is probably no religion which does not derive its identity
from some body of sacred texts, and the cultivation of which does not
consist, to a great extent, of the execution of verbal rituals.

In more than one sense, then, language is much more than an instrument
for transmitting information. It is also a symbol of cultural identity. Recognizing an individual or a group in society strongly depends on recognizing their language and allowing them to use it. From its birth in Ancient
Greek political philosophy, the idea of democracy was closely associated
with *eleutheria* ('freedom') and *parrhesia* ('freedom of speech', the right
to speak one's mind). Indeed, oppressing people has often gone (and still

goes) hand in hand with forbidding them to use their own mother tongue. Take away a person's language, and you take away his culture; take away his culture, and you take away his identity.

1.4 Language and international communication

When visiting an Italian restaurant during your holidays, use only English or French and you will probably have a good meal and a good time. Now learn a few words of Italian and try to order your food in that language. You will now have a splendid time, get special offers not mentioned on the menu, and maybe even a free grappa or sambucca to top off your meal.
When accepting the post of U.S. ambassador in the Netherlands, do your business in English and you will no doubt be a good ambassador. Now try to learn some Dutch and answer your interviewer on Dutch television in that language. You will then be an excellent ambassador and get many more things done than you would have otherwise. This in spite of the fact that many Dutchmen know English so well that visitors sometimes ask whether they have any language of their own!

Recognizing a person's language is recognizing a person's culture; recognizing a person's culture is recognizing his identity, his value as a human being. This holds at all levels of international communication. Just as in face-to-face exchange our communicative partners may take offence at something we say, so whole nations may drift apart, states may get embroiled with one another, through something inadvertently said by one of their representatives. Think of the goodwill that John F. Kennedy created by stammering the four German words "Ich bin ein Berliner"; of how U.S.-Soviet relations were endangered by some 'off-the-record' jokes of president Reagan; of how Bundeskanzler Kohl went astray in using Hitler's name in the wrong connection; or of the more recent event where the people of the DDR shouted "Wir sind das Volk" ("We are the people"), and the same Kohl responded with "Ja, wir sind ein Volk!" ("Yes, we are one people!"): was ever the difference between *das* and *ein* burdened with heavier symbolism?
A high level of foreign language knowledge is of the utmost importance for the international prestige and effectiveness of a country. This especially holds for a country like the Netherlands, beyond whose territory it is easy enough to stray on a Sunday afternoon drive.

Foreign language proficiency in Holland has traditionally been high indeed, and has certainly contributed considerably to the relative success of

Holland Inc. But in this area there is presently more reason for worry than for complacency. The freedom of choice established in secondary education has favoured English at the expense of French and German, so that at the university level competence in these languages can no longer be taken for granted. Other strategic languages such as Spanish, Italian, or Russian have never got a firm footing at the secondary level, not to speak of such vital languages as Arabic, Chinese, and Japanese, which are only known by a handful of specialists. Recent 'no-nonsense' policy, coming down on the universities with budget cuts wrapped in efficiency measures, especially affected the art faculties where language learning and teaching is a major occupation. And the government's media-wide urge to 'choose the exact sciences' has not been qualified by any serious thought about the strategic importance of high-level proficiency in foreign languages.

It is fortunate that the Commission of the EEC shows more insight into the importance of foreign language proficiency for the further development of the European community. Both its programs ERASMUS (for international student exchange) and LINGUA (for language learning and teaching) will be important instruments for furthering cross-European linguistic and cultural understanding, and its program EUROTRA (for automatic translation), even when it will not generate the multilingual translation machine that some optimists expect from it, no doubt contributes to our insights into the intricacies of the translation process.

What is the best way to learn a foreign language? The most adequate (seriously intended) answer once given to this question was: play stowaway in the cradle of a foreign-language speaking mother. The best linguistic curriculum is taught in 'motherese'! The second-best and more practicable answer is: go to the language's country for a year or so, and immerse yourself in the local culture. But even that is not always feasible, so that much of our foreign language learning will be done at school and through courses in our own country. The methods of this kind of language teaching have been greatly enriched through the introduction of audio-visual methods in the language laboratory, and will continue to expand with the rapid development of computer-aided instruction methods. Much research into the fundamental properties of language and language learning is required, however, before we can hope to arrive at an optimalization or a well-founded evaluation of foreign language teaching methodology. Here lies an excellent chance for a government to invest in international cooperation.

2. The miracles of language

Why is a natural language such a complex, intriguing, and in many ways elusive phenomenon? Let us have a look at some of its rather extraordinary properties.

2.1 Complexity

In 1957 the study of language took a revolutionary turn through the publication of Noam Chomsky's *Syntactic structures*. Chomsky's basic idea was to conceptualize a grammar as a system of rules which could automatically enumerate all the well-formed sentences of a language, while excluding the ill-formed ones. The formulation of this ideal, by the way, was a distant echo of the practice of the Indian grammarian Panini who, several centuries BC, had endeavoured to capture the intricacies of Sanskrit word structure in a system of explicit rules or 'sutras' such that, when these rules were applied mechanically and in sequence to a number of abstract underlying forms, the correct derived words would be automatically generated.

Since there is in principle no limit to the length of well-formed sentences, a 'generative' grammar of this type must take the form of a finite set of rules which recursively map a finite set of basic elements onto an infinite variety of sequences of such elements.

Subsequent work has shown how inordinately complex this task is. Far from consisting of simple combinatory principles, the syntax of a language is an intricate network of quite complex rules, monitored by a system of more and more general guiding principles. Writing an actual generative grammar has proved to be a very difficult task indeed. To this day we do not possess a complete generative grammar (in this sense) of any natural language, not even of those languages which have been studied for thousands of years. No wonder, then, that the attention of some linguists has shifted from constructing actual grammars to studying the conditions under which constructing such grammars would, in the long run, be a feasible task.

As a by-product of work in generative grammar, however, we have learned to appreciate the remarkable complexity of natural languages; a complexity which can only be understood in terms of a richly articulated and well-controlled cognitive system which must be assumed to be able to operate in ways largely independent of the actual stimuli that humans receive in the actual communicative situation.

Not only the grammatical intricacy, also the sheer size of the lexical data base which an average adult speaker possesses presents us with various enigmas. It has been estimated that the average speaker has at least passive access to a store of some 50.000 lexical items, which he is able to retrieve at a speed of some 150 per minute. How this enormous data base is acquired, and how such speedy retrieval is possible without leading to continuous traffic jams in the human brain are questions which we are only beginning to get some understanding of.

2.2 Creativity and flexibility

Language, in different ways, allows us to create structures which we have never before encountered. This holds for the man in the street just as well as for the poet: any linguistic behaviour is, in different respects, creative behaviour. Creativity may be rule-governed (as when given rules are applied in novel ways), or rule-changing (as when new rules or rule systems are invented). Linguistic behaviour is creative in both these senses. Consider some examples:

[i] Language users are able to form and interpret ever new sentences and texts which they have never produced or encountered before. Most of the sentences which you are now reading have (I hope) never been read by you before, and yet (I hope) you perfectly understand their content without apparent effort. This form of rule-governed creativity has been especially stressed by Noam Chomsky. He demonstrated that the underlying property of language which makes this creativity possible is its recursive character: the fact that, using a finite set of basic elements, the same rules may be applied again and again, so that they project a virtually infinite variety of linguistic expressions. This has, as Chomsky argued, some important consequences. First, it makes it impossible to describe a language by enumerating its sentences; rather, a grammar must take the form of a finite rule system which projects a finite number of basic elements onto an infinite variety of possible expressions. Second, it has important implications for any theory concerning the acquisition of language. Since most linguistic expressions, in the particular form in which they are perceived, are new to the language learner, language acquisition can never be a matter of rote memorization; rather, it must consist in the creative reconstruction on the part of the learner of the recursive rule system which underlies the actual expressions.

[ii] At the pragmatic level, language users are very creative in adapting their linguistic behaviour to the circumstances in which, the topics about which, and the addressees to whom they talk. As Dell Hymes (1972) put it, we not only have a grammatical, but also a communicative competence. We are not simply sentence-generating robots, we also know what to say when and where to whom in order to achieve our communicative purposes.

Our utterances not only transmit objective information, they also co-signal emotive and relational overtones which, for the final process of understanding, may play an important and sometimes dominant role. Language users are creative, not only in the application of rules of grammar, but also in the implementation of pragmatic conventions of verbal interaction.

[iii] Languages are open structures, catering for the communicative needs of the linguistic community at any point of time. They allow us to talk about anything which can be talked about at all. Should new communicative needs arise, new ways of speaking will develop. When new items or ideas are imported into a culture, new words will be invented (sometimes co-imported) so as to enable speakers to talk about them. Where items or ideas disappear, the corresponding words will sink into oblivion as well. Languages are thus subject to a continuous process of change, where the changes may be internally motivated within the language itself, or occasioned by the many forms of contact between languages either freely arising in intercultural exchange, or imposed through political and military developments.

[iv] Writers and poets exploit the flexibility of language in the creation of works of art, in which the conventional limits of what is grammatically and pragmatically accepted are often transgressed and new forms of expression are created. Directly or indirectly, through the educational system and the mass media, such new forms of expression may work their way into the everyday linguistic behaviour of the community.

These various kinds of linguistic creativity defy any simplistic behaviourist stimulus-response account of human linguistic competence. The (re-)discovery of the recursive and creative nature of human linguistic activity has played an important part in turning psychology and linguistics towards more mentalist, rationalist, and cognitive conceptions of human mental behaviour.

2.3 Cross-cultural variety and uniformity

The great triumph of nineteenth-century linguistics was without doubt the development of a sophisticated theory of how languages may develop through time, and how they may split and ramify into different sub- and sub-sub-languages. This theory of historical-comparative linguistics, however, was largely developed on the basis of the limited empirical domain of one linguistic stock, the Indo-European 'family' of languages. This was also the domain of the Western grammatical tradition since antiquity and, with the exception of biblical Hebrew, the study of non-Indo-European languages had little impact on Western thinking about linguistic phenomena. Note that according to recent estimates there are over 6000 different natural languages spoken in the world, divided into some 20 larger and smaller families, of which Indo-European, with a total of 180 members, is only one.

The arrogant disdain with which the Ancient Greeks had classed all non-Greek speakers as 'barbaroi' (those who speak inarticulate 'br br') persisted through the centuries in the prejudice (which is still influential today) that 'primitive' people speak 'primitive' languages: languages which have only a few hundred words, in which abstract ideas and complex thoughts cannot be expressed, and which are unfit for any form of logical or rational reasoning. While expeditions were sent out to study the tiniest bug and the most insignificant flower in the most remote regions, the only ones who made serious study of indigenous languages were almost without exception missionaries, adventurers, and traders, who in their different ways had purposes and motives beyond the unprejudiced study of the cultural and linguistic communities which they visited.

When anthropologists and linguists in the beginning of this century turned their attention to non-Indo-European languages, they were in for several surprises. First of all, they quickly saw that the notion of a 'primitive' language is a myth: even the (in Western eyes) least developed communities turned out to possess languages which in complexity and expressive capacity could easily rival the languages of 'highly developed' cultures. In the second place, it was found that the indigenous languages could have forms of grammatical organization which could not be adequately described by means of the categories of current Indo-European linguistics. At first sight there was no limit to the variation which could exist across languages. Any next language studied could yield completely new and non-expected grammatical phenomena. In the domains of both culture and language this lead to strong forms of relativism: in an attempt at abolishing the bad habit of measuring non-Western languages by Western standards, these researchers went to the extreme of disclaiming the relevance of *any* general standards in the study of languages.

In the Bloomfieldian period of American linguistics (1933-1957) the popular slogan was that each language should be described in terms of its own structure, and that "the only useful generalizations are inductive generalizations" (Bloomfield, 1933). If this were true, it would be very unfortunate indeed. It would mean, strictly speaking, that for each particular language we would need a particular theory of grammar, that no predictive generalizations across languages are possible, and that, from the study of one language, we cannot learn anything concerning the possible organization of another language. This form of inductivism would turn 'general linguistic theory' into an empty phrase, and would preclude any *general* insight into the nature of language.

Fortunately, subsequent developments have shown that Bloomfield's position was over-cautious. Where two or more languages at first sight appeared to be almost completely different, they could nevertheless often be captured under some higher-level generalization. Natural languages do appear to be built according to a common 'blueprint' which, however, leaves much room for typological variation. Very important for our understanding of the 'universal' aspects underlying language-particular variation was the development of the study of *language typology*, the study of how languages can be classified into different types and of how the parameters which define these types correlate with each other. I return to this subject below.

2.4 The child as an expert linguist

The child learns much of the complex rules and conventions of language and language use within a few years. How is this possible? Is the child endowed with innate linguistic information which is only to be fleshed out by the data offered by experience? Or is the child simply a very intelligent and rapid learner of complex information and behaviour? And why is first language learning so easy, second language learning so difficult?

Most of these questions cannot be answered in any definitive way, although much research into both first and second language acquisition has greatly increased our understanding of the problems involved. Some points seem to be generally agreed on, others are a matter of controversy:

[1] Language is a species-specific property of humans, and languages do not clearly differ in intrinsic difficulty. Any human infant, placed in any human community, will learn the language of that community with comparable ease.

[2] There is certainly an innate component to the human faculty of acquiring a language. What this innate component is, however, is less clear. Some locate it in general purpose capacities such as the capacity for abstracting from the particular to the general, of forming hypotheses and testing these out, and of devising plausible 'theories' which must be assumed to underlie the acquisition and processing of any kind of information. Others believe that the child even brings substantial innate linguistic information, a kind of general linguistic schema, to the task of language learning and uses the external evidence mainly for 'fixing the parameters'

in the schema, which will then generate the kind of grammar required for the language learned.

[3] But it is also true that language learning is aided significantly by the continuous verbal interaction in which children are immersed, willy-nilly, from the moment they are born into the world. Mothers (and caretakers in general) do not speak the adult language to children, they speak a simplified speech register (referred to above as 'motherese'), which is strongly geared to both the concrete everyday situation in which the communication takes place, and the developing linguistic proficiency level of the child. The natural language teacher starts out from the 'here-and-now', and gradually expands the child's world (practically as well as linguistically) to more remote, less concrete, and less situation-bound regions. Some important landmarks on the child's road to linguistic proficiency are his discovery that you can interact with other people, that you can get things done through language, and that you can talk about things even when they are not there, thus conjuring up worlds other than those which meet the senses.

[4] From another point of view, as well, it can be argued that learning things that were not there before must play an important part in language acquisition. As we saw above, the final end-product of the learning process contains some 50.000 lexical items which the speaker can at least receptively understand. Each of these items is unique and particular to the language. No amount of innate endowment will inform a child that a 'horse' is a *horse* in English, a *paard* in Dutch, or a *cheval* in French. But there is more to these words than just the form: words have 'valencies' which define how they can be combined with each other both syntactically and semantically, and they form part of 'semantic networks' by virtue of the meaning relations which obtain between them. That all this is learned is also evident from the fact that children often 'undergeneralize' or 'overgeneralize' the meanings of words during the acquisition process. In the former case, they use 'daddy' only for their particular individual father, and are at a loss when other children use the word for addressing a quite different person. In the latter case, they may use the word for any unsuspecting gentleman passing in the street.

3. Trends in linguistic research

3.1 Theoretical sophistication

As Socrates said: most humans, including philosophers, know little or nothing, but the true philosopher distinguishes himself by realizing how little he knows. When taken in this sense of 'metatheoretical insight into one's own ignorance', the philosophical sophistication of linguists has increased remarkably through the past few decades. The great achievements of the first half of this century lay mainly in the articulation of the fields of *phonology* (the sound structure of linguistic expressions) and *morphology* (the internal grammatical structure of words). The full complexity of the sentence was hardly addressed: De Saussure (1916), who laid the foundations for a general linguistic science, even relegated the construction of sentences to the individual creativity of the speaker, and Bloomfield believed that the methods which were so successful in phonology and morphology could, without too much effort, be transferred to the area of the syntactic structure of sentences.

It was Chomsky who undermined this optimism by placing the syntactic structure of sentences right in the middle of his research program, and proving that the methods of Bloomfieldian and European structuralism were thoroughly unable to account for this structure. His first attempt to remedy this was through the idea that syntactic structures have to be described in two distinct steps, one *formational*, one *transformational*. The formational part would produce a set of rather simple 'deep' or kernel structures for sentences, the transformational part would combine and transform these structures into the manifold variety of 'surface' structures of actual sentences. This had the additional advantage that not only were the sentences generated, but the relations between them were formally accounted for at the same time. It does indeed appear that groups of sentences can be analyzed in terms of a common kernel structure, which is then subjected to different operations which can be combined with each other in different ways. Compare the effect of applying the operations of 'questioning' (Q), 'negating' (N), and 'passivizing' (P) to the kernel structure underlying a simple sentence:

(3) K   John has sold the car.
     Q[K]   Has John sold the car?
     N[K]   John has not sold the car.
     P[K]   The car has been sold by John.
     QN[K]   Has John not sold the car?
     QP[K]   Has the car been sold by John?
     NP[K]   The car has not been sold by John.
     QNP[K]   Has the car not been sold by John?

The research which emanated from these original Chomskyan ideas can be roughly divided into three phases:

[1] 1957-1970. An enormous amount of research was done on the possible transformations which could be formulated for generating the sentences of natural languages, on the formal nature of formational and transformational rules, and on their mutual interaction within the overall grammar of a language.

[2] 1970-1980. Somewhat paradoxically at first sight, it was found that the transformational instrument was less than adequate for arriving at a restrictive theory of natural languages, not because transformations were too weak to do the job they were required to do, but because they were too strong in doing this job: since transformations can in principle transform any structure into any other structure, research shifted to the question of how to limit or constrain the power of this device. In the long run, the constraints or conditions on rules became more important than the rules themselves.

[3] 1980-... This led to a restructuring of Chomskyan theory into the theory of 'Government and Binding': what universal constraints can be imposed on the notion 'grammar of a language', such that from these constraints the actual surface phenomena of languages follow more or less automatically? In using this approach for the construction of a system of 'Universal Grammar' more attention than before was paid to cross-linguistic differences. The idea is that the overall structure of syntactic theory can be divided into a 'core', consisting of universally valid principles, and a 'periphery', monitored by variable parameter settings interacting with the universal principles. Obviously, the fewer the parameter settings that can take care of the actual variation, the more adequate the theory of Universal Grammar.

Whatever one's position with respect to this Chomskyan research program, there can be no doubt that it has greatly enriched our understanding of both universal and language-particular aspects of grammatical organization. It has at the same time set the standards for any attempt at theoretical clarification of natural language grammars, even for those who do not want to accept the rather restrictive metatheoretical constraints which Chomsky has imposed on the notion of 'grammar'. Indeed, certain alternative theoretical developments can be understood as attempts to break away from these restrictive bounds. Let us briefly consider some of these developments.

3.1.1 The formal vs. the functional view
In Chomsky's view a language is an autonomous formal system, geneti-

cally prepared in the human brain. The nature of this system cannot, in his view, be explained in terms of functional constraints pertaining to the ways in which the system is used. The meaning of linguistic expressions and their communicative usage are irrelevant to the nature of the system. The system cannot be learned on the basis of input data: the universal principles underlying the grammar of a language are innate, and have a biological rather than a sociological basis. The human linguistic faculty is like a biological 'organ' which 'grows' in the maturing child just like other innate capacities (such as locomotion, perception, and cognition) 'grow' out of innate propensities. The grammar of a language is thus an abstract formal-mathematical system to which we have access through 'intuition' rather than through sense data or other empirical phenomena. The relevant intuitions consist of judgements on the well-formedness or ill-formedness of sentences. Over against this formal approach to the nature of grammar, we can place the functional view on human language. According to this view, a language is first and foremost an instrument of human communication. Communication consists of forms of symbolic interaction through which human beings influence each other's content of mind, taken in a broad sense, including knowledge, opinions, prejudices, and feelings. If language is an instrument of communication, its nature must be understood as catering for the needs and requirements of communicative interaction. Such interaction consists of communicative acts or speech acts, which constitute the 'pragmatic' component of any semiotic system. In such speech acts, speakers clarify the way in which they wish to affect the content of mind of their communicative partners through proffering meaningful expressions: expressions which can be interpreted in terms of the contextualized information already available to the addressee. The function of the form of these expressions is to transmit meaning. From this functional point of view meaning (semantics) is subservient to use (pragmatics), and form (syntax) is subservient to meaning. There is no way in which linguistic form can be properly understood if it is regarded as autonomous and independent of meaning and use.

3.1.2 Grammatical vs. communicative competence
From this it follows that linguistic theory, from a functional point of view, is not just concerned with the grammatical competence of natural language users: that competence which enables them to judge that *John kicked the ball* is a well-formed sentence of English, and *The kicked John ball* is not. The existence and the relevance of such competence is not denied, but it is regarded as one 'module' within a much wider competence: the 'communi-

cative' competence which enables speakers and addressees to establish meaningful communicative relationships. It is no coincidence that Dell Hymes, who coined the term 'communicative competence', should be an anthropologically oriented linguist. Anthropology is interested in the manifestations of human culture. Human culture is constituted and reconstituted through human communication. And the most versatile instrument of human communication is natural language.

3.1.3 Autonomous vs. semantically interpreted syntax

Chomsky's view on language was co-inspired by certain formalist trends in mathematical logic. Under the influence of positivist thinking logic at some point seemed to reduce the study of human reasoning to the study of uninterpreted formal calculi, consisting of formulae which could be manipulated according to certain mechanical principles. 'Meaning' for some time was not a very popular concept in logical circles. However, modern logic has rather rapidly surpassed this strongly formalist stage. It was realized that formulae, unless interpreted, were no more than possibly pretty ink blots on a sheet of paper. The idea of a 'formal semantics' was envisaged: a formal system which would define how the formulae of a logical calculus can be interpreted. Central to this concern was the idea of 'compositionality': just as linguistic expressions can be compositionally built up from sounds to words, from words to phrases, from phrases to sentences, and from sentences to texts, so it was assumed that the meaning of these expressions could be compositionally construed in a way parallel to the formal build-up of the expression.

One of the most successful attempts in this direction emanating from modern logic, *Montague Grammar*, initiated by Richard Montague (cf. Montague, 1974), is based on a syntactic-semantic correspondence theory: for every rule of syntax, there is a semantic rule to interpret it, and *vice versa*. Every linguistic expression is formally built up through a number of syntactic rules. With each syntactic rule corresponds a convention about how to 'translate' the syntactic structure into a corresponding logical expression. The logical expression, in turn, can be interpreted according to the conventions of 'model-theoretical semantics'. In this form of semantics, a first step is to create a 'world' in which referent entities are assigned to the individual constants of the logical formula; a second step is to define under what conditions the formula is true or false of that world; and a third step is to define inference rules such that, if a given formula F_i is true/false of some world, then inferred formulae F_j, F_k, ... F_n must also be true/false of that world. A formula may be true of one world, false of another. It is thus the full set of 'possible worlds' which must be considered in interpreting an expression. The full set of 'possible worlds' thus provides an interpretation model for the logical formulae.

In recent developments in logical theory, partially in conjunction with artificial intelligence, the notion of semantic interpretation has been undergoing certain modifications, the most important of which are the following:

[a] we may want to consider the interpretation of formulae in a 'partial' model, as if belonging to a mind that has only limited knowledge of 'possible worlds';

[b] the model itself may be dynamically construed as the context builds up: each item of information provided in the context may lead to a modification of the 'universe of interpretation';

[c] we may thus want to set up a 'discourse model', capturing the state of knowledge of an interpreter at a given point in the evolving text.

Through these modifications, each of which in some respect relativizes the notion 'set of possible worlds', we may hope to arrive at a form of logical semantics which more realistically captures what happens to people when they interact with each other in verbal communication.

3.1.4 The variability of language
No two people talk in exactly the same way: there are differences between individual 'idiolects', between groups defined by the place where they live ('dialects') or the socio-economic or cultural circle to which they belong ('sociolects'), and between people talking or writing in different situations, about different topics, and to different addressees ('registers', 'styles'). Chomsky abstracted from such differences in linguistic competence and performance across individuals, groups, social strata, and situations. Over against this, as we saw above, the field of *sociolinguistics* has placed such linguistic variability right in the middle of its attention. In doing so, it has developed new empirical methods for determining 'how people talk', also in a statistical sense (by capturing, in so-called 'variable rules', not only which sociolinguistic variables are used, but also how often and under which conditions these variables are used). This work has not only produced insights into the dynamics of linguistic behaviour across society, but also thrown light on the phenomenon of language change: if everybody talked in exactly the same way, linguistic change would be difficult to understand. But if, at any moment in time, there are different linguistic varieties being used, and if we can indicate factors which favour or disfa-

vour the 'survival' of such varieties across time, then we may hope to get some insight into the process of linguistic change.

3.1.5 Monolingual vs. cross-linguistic research

Chomsky's initial approach to the task of finding the basic elements of 'Universal Grammar' was through the in-depth study of individual languages (in his own case, mainly English), rather than through extensive cross-linguistic comparison. The reasoning behind this could be formulated in the following way: "Grammar is one and the same in its essentials, though there are peripheral variations ... Therefore, whoever understands the grammar of one language understands the grammar of another, as far as the essentials are concerned." Interestingly enough, the preceding quote was formulated by one of the foremen of medieval 'Grammatica Speculativa', Roger Bacon, in the thirteenth century (cf. Robins, 1979, and Reichling, 1947). However, there is a built-in problem in this view: how are we going to sift the 'accidentalia' from the 'essentialia', the 'periphery' from the 'core', except by *comparing* languages with each other? After all, there are about 6000 existing natural languages in the world, and nobody can sensibly pretend to be able to predict beforehand in which respects these may differ from each other.

In the nineteenth century, comparison across languages was established as *the* method for arriving at general insights into the nature of language. Such comparison was mainly used to establish the ways in which languages could change over time (so that even today 'comparative linguistics' is often taken to coincide with 'comparative-historical linguistics'), but in fact the nineteenth century also generated interest in the synchronic comparison of languages according to their 'type', and thus created the beginnings of a 'typology of language'.

This field of *language typology* was revived in a modernized form in the sixties. Language typologists stress the importance of cross-linguistic comparative work in building up a firm data base for underpinning linguistic generalizations. We take a closer look at this field in the next section.

3.2 Extension of empirical knowledge

In 1961, in Dobbs Ferry, New York, a conference was held on *universals of language*: the universal principles underlying linguistic systems. The inspiration behind this conference was the anthropological linguist Joseph H. Greenberg (cf. Greenberg, 1963 & 1978), who contributed theoretical insights and presented comparative linguistic data which have strongly influenced the subsequent study of language universals and language typology.

An important theoretical point was the idea that universal statements may be cast in conditional form, in schemas such as:

(4) For all languages L: if L has property P1, then it has property P2.

Such a conditional statement does formulate a universal law, but it is a law which retains its validity even when there are languages which do not have the property P1. Consider the following example. Some languages have a basic word order Verb-Subject-Object-X (VSOX) in declarative sentences, so that we find constructions such as:

(5) gave the boy the book to the girl.
    "the boy gave the book to the girl"

This order is in fact a minority option: it is found in only about 15% of the world's languages. A seemingly unrelated fact is that some languages have prepositions, such as *to* in *to the boy*, whereas other languages have 'postpositions', as in *the boy to*. One finding of Greenberg's was that these two seemingly unrelated properties have a strong implicational relation, as formulated in the conditional universal:

(6) For all languages L: if L has VSOX order, it has prepositions rather than postpositions.

Conversely, if a language has SOXV order (an option found in about 45% of the world's languages), the following implication holds:

(7) For all languages L: if L has SOXV order, that language has postpositions rather than prepositions.

In SOXV languages, in other words, we will expect structures of the following form:

(8) the boy the book the girl to gave
    "the boy gave the book to the girl"

We thus find that the choice on the parameter preposition/postposition depends on the antecedent choice on the parameter initial verb position /

final verb position. Apparently, relational markers such as prepositions/postpositions orient themselves to the basic position of the verb.

This is only one example of the many implicational relationships which have been discovered either by Greenberg or through the research which he inspired. Such universal (or statistically dominant) relations serve to restrict the number of possible language types: (5) and (6) exclude languages with VSOX order but no prepositions, and languages with SOXV order but no postpositions. At the same time, these statements allow us to predict language properties on the basis of other, given properties: once we know a language has VSOX order, we may expect it to have prepositions as well. In the third place, universal statements of this type can be used in delimiting the possible changes a language may undergo in time. On the assumption that no language develops into a type which is excluded by universal principles, certain forms of change which would be logically possible may be empirically excluded. Further, in theoretically reconstructing the ancestral 'proto-language' of a given language family, we had better remain within the limits of what counts as a 'possible language' by universal principles.

Note that while universal statements such as (5) or (6) 'explain' certain lower-level phenomena, they themselves in turn ask for explanation in terms of higher-level principles: *why* do implications such as (5) and (6) hold universally for human languages? Several attempts have been made to reduce the recurrent typological patterning of natural languages to general principles of psychological and cognitive information processing. Even though these attempts have not yet met with complete success, they certainly advance our understanding of the underlying factors which delimit the notion 'possible human language'.

Another important research instrument which developed out of this implicational formulation of universals was the 'typological hierarchy', which can be understood as a sequential connection of universal implications. Let us illustrate this with a simple, but rather significant example, the Basic Colour Name Hierarchy discovered by Brent Berlin and Paul Kay (1969).

Colour naming had been structuralism's paradigm example for illustrating the 'arbitrariness' of the linguistic sign, the haphazard way in which languages impose 'form' on 'substance'. Every language, it was argued, articulates the colour spectrum in its own, individual way. What Berlin and Kay found on the basis of a typological study of some 100 languages, however, was something quite different. It is true that languages differ in what colour terms they possess, but it was also found that there is a clear and quite regular pattern to this variation.

First of all, implicational universals could be formulated, such as:

(9) If a language has a distinct word for 'blue', it also has a distinct word for 'red'.

Secondly, it was found that these universals could be partially ordered in a sequential ordering, a 'typological hierarchy' of the following form:

(10) black > red > green > blue > brown > purple
    white   yellow   pink
                                              orange
                                              grey

This hierarchy was further specified by the following rules:
(i)   all languages have colour terms for 'black' and 'white' or 'dark' and 'light';
(ii)   if a language has a colour term later in (10), it also has all the preceding colour terms;
(iii) no language has more than the eleven basic colour terms listed in (10).

Hierarchies such as (10) epitomize in compact form the typological organization of a certain sub-domain of the language system. They are powerful tools for capturing the underlying cross-linguistic pattern, while at the same time providing a systematic specification of how languages may differ from each other in the relevant sub-domain.

Again, the hierarchy has a two-face character: it explains a great number of regularities, but it also asks for explanation in terms of higher-order principles. Some have sought an explanation in the perceptual 'saliency' of the different colours. This is possibly one constitutive factor. Another factor might be a functional one, based on the working hypothesis that it is more expedient to have a distinct word for referring to something, the more often we want to refer to it (here the reader may think of the rich vocabulary for 'snow' and 'ice' in Eskimo). It is remarkable that the text frequency of the Dutch equivalents of the colour names in (10) does decrease in almost linear fashion by about 90% as we pass through the hierarchy from left to right.

Language typology is an excellent instrument for bridging the gap between
the 'universal' and the 'particular' in natural languages: on the one hand, it
tries to formulate universal principles underlying the articulation of individual languages. On the other hand, these universal principles not only
codify those properties which all languages have in common, but also
provide the means for understanding how languages can differ from each
other in systematic and predictable ways. An excellent survey of modern
typology is given in Comrie (1981).

3.3 Linguistics and the Computer
The rapid developments in computational hardware and software are having and will continue to have an enormous impact on research and practical
applications in the field of linguistics. Nevertheless, a warning should be
voiced here: don't interpret recurrent news items in the media about 'speaking
machines', 'machine translation', and the like as indications that the problem posed by the computational modelling of linguistic behaviour is all but
solved. Better listen to one of the top experts in this field, Terry Winograd
(himself the creator of one of the best 'language understanding' programs
to date): "It will be a long time, if ever, before we can create programs that
understand and produce language as people do" (Winograd, 1987). Indeed,
there are no computer programs that even remotely approach the ability of
human language users to produce, interpret, and translate linguistic expressions in such varied communicative situations and in such natural
ways that it is at all difficult to tell them apart from human speakers.
At the same time, however, a great number of attempts at modelling particular bits and pieces of the overall human linguistic faculty have enormously
advanced our insights into the intricacies of linguistic behaviour, and will
no doubt continue to do so in the coming decades. Also, these efforts have
already produced some very useful practical tools which are of great help
in various areas where language plays an essential role.
We have also learned *why* it is so difficult adequately to model human
linguistic behaviour. Apart from the intrinsic complexity of linguistic systems as such, the main factor here is without doubt the fact that a language
is not a closed system which carries all its information on its back, so to
speak, but rather an open-ended instrument which is used by people who
already have an enormous amount of knowledge to support their interpretation of linguistic data. Linguistic expressions are used in context, and all
of the contextual knowledge built up through a text helps in interpreting
them. They are used in concrete situations in which language users get a
great deal of non-verbal information to support their interpretations. This

situational information includes knowledge and assumptions about the person that we are talking to or who is talking to us. Furthermore, speakers and addressees have an enormous amount of 'knowledge of the world', much of which is shared between them in terms of common assumptions about the world around us and about the actual topic of conversation. Thus, only a small part of what is eventually transmitted *through* the linguistic expression is actually contained in the *meaning* of that expression as such. Much comes in through the interaction of that meaning with the rest of our knowledge, which helps us select or create the correct interpretation of the expression in the given circumstances.

This contextualized nature of linguistic behaviour has certain important implications. First, it explains why natural language expressions may be vague, ambiguous, sometimes even seemingly contradictory, without these properties leading to misunderstanding or lack of communication. Consider the following three examples:

Example 1.

(11) (person in a shop):
      This one, please.

(11) is utterly vague, and totally dependent on situational (and gestural) support for its correct interpretation. Nevertheless, it is more effective than something like:

(12) I should like to have the blackish hammer with the steel head which, as measured on the distance between me and you, the one I am speaking to right now, is closer to me than to you...

and even *that* would be uninterpretable without situational support.

Example 2.

(13) (at the table):
      Can you pass the beans?

Here, due to the ambiguity of both the words and the expression as a whole, interpretations might range from anything like "Could you bring the green string-like vegetables into my possession", through "Are you able to hand me the money" to "Could you be so kind as to drive beyond the beans factory", but situational support will, without us even noticing it, steer us to the correct interpretation. (13) is also an example of an 'indirect speech act' in which we 'do not say what we mean': literally we inquire about the ability of our addressee to carry out a certain act, while in fact we want him to carry out the act. Much of our daily talk is indirect in this way, especially when human interrelations are at stake (in some sense, direct speech 'hurts'). All this is much to the distress of the computer.

Example 3.

(14) (mother to child who just broke a plate):
      You're a great help!

Here we have a case of irony, where we actually say the contrary of what we mean: so strong is the force of situational support, that the correct interpretation may be the exact opposite of what we actually say. Poor computer!

Logicians have sometimes regarded this situational dependency as a 'flaw' of natural languages, which should be remedied in fully explicit artificial or logical codes which would then, once and for all, establish complete rationality in mankind. From a linguistic point of view, however, this is a serious mistake: it is, in fact, the 'open-endedness' of language which greatly enhances its efficiency and effectiveness, and explains how it is possible to talk about an infinite variety of things with only finite means. Rather than trying to emulate natural language we should do our best to understand how it actually works.

4. The integrated natural language user

At several points in the preceding sections we have touched upon interdisciplinary aspects of linguistic research. Indeed, the last few decades have generated a rather considerable articulation into subfields and sub-subfields, especially in the various borderline regions between linguistics 'proper' and adjoining disciplines. At the same time, the internal articulation of linguistics proper has proceeded to a point where one may be an excellent specialist in phonology or morphology, without even trying to keep abreast of the developments in other related fields. The many disciplinary and interdisciplinary ramifications of the linguistic sciences create a constant tension between specialization and integration. On the one hand, each of the many subfields is a subject in itself and puts high requirements on those who attempt to contribute to it beyond already established limits. It is thus necessary for there to be specialists in the semantic component of language acquisition, in the morphology of the verb, or in the linguistic articulation of temporal relations. On the other hand, such specialization creates a danger of mutual lack of communication between the subfields, and indeed one sometimes gets the impression that each of the branches of linguistics has an object of its own, rather than studying one particular aspect of a unified phenomenon.

For such reasons as these there is great need for more integrated approaches to language, approaches in which system and usage, rules and applications, language and language users are not regarded as distinct or even opposing or irreconcilable entities, but rather as complementary entries into a unified and integrated human cognitive and communicative system. One of the most impressive attempts at such integration was recently contributed by the Dutch psycholinguist Willem Levelt (1989).

The central question for such an integrated approach would be how it is that speakers and addressees succeed in communicating with each other through the use of natural language: how do natural language users 'work'? How is it possible for them to make themselves understood, to influence each other's content of mind, and ultimately each other's practical behaviour, through the use of linguistic expressions?
A constructivist way of formulating this basic question is: How could we build a model (in the theoretical sense of functional modelling) of the natural language user? What sorts of modules would have to be built into such a model, what sorts of relations would have to be established between these modules, and what kinds of processing strategies would be required to approximate the communicative performance of human natural language users?
This question, again, can be operationalized within the 'computational paradigm' of scientific thinking: How could we build a computational version of a model of the natural language user? We saw that the final answer to this question can only be expected in the distant future, if ever. But computer modelling can be used for other purposes than solving short-term practical problems; it can also be used in thought experiments aimed at long-term clarification of deep and ultimately philosophical questions concerning the structure and the operation of the human mind. It is in the latter sense that I believe devising a computational model of the natural language user is a useful thinking tool for the theoretical linguist.

Thinking about and working on the implementation of an integrated computational model of the natural language user (C*M*NLU) is more and more becoming a meeting ground for students of philosophy, logic, cognitive psychology, cognitive science, artificial intelligence, and linguistics (including phonetics and speech and language technology). Let us briefly consider some of the many capacities which will have to be built into C*M*NLU if it is to provide an interesting analogue to the communicative competence of human natural language users:

[a] C*M*NLU must be able to perceive the incoming speech signal and decode it into some standardized internal phonetic representation. This is the problem of 'automatic speech recognition' which, due to the variability of speech sounds across speakers, contexts, and situations, has so far proved very difficult indeed to solve in an adequate way.

[b] C*M*NLU must also be able to 'read' written input. If this is typed or written text, this is manageable. Automatic recognition of handwriting, however, is almost as difficult as recognizing speech.

[c] Once it has formed an internal phonetic representation, C*M*NLU must be able to assign a grammatical structure to the utterance: it must be able to 'parse' the linguistic expression onto some kind of syntactic representation. For this it needs a model of the grammar of the language, plus an algorithm for reconstructing the grammatical structure underlying the utterance. Especially where the utterance can be grammatically analyzed in different ways (is 'syntactically ambiguous') this 'parsing' task may be quite difficult.

[d] C*M*NLU must be able to assign a semantic interpretation to the reconstructed grammatical structure. For this, it needs (at least) a lexicon which defines the possible meanings of the basic items of the utterance, plus a compositional algorithm for building up the meaning of the whole utterance from the meanings of its component parts. It also needs higher-level information, however, since the same words may mean different things in different contexts, and we wish the model to come up with a correct interpretation in the given context rather than with a list of all the possible things that the utterance might mean when considered in isolation.

[e] C*M*NLU must be able to reconstruct the communicative intention of its communicative partner: it is not sufficient for it to understand what the speaker says, it must also grasp what the speaker wants the addressee to do: just store the information, answer a question, execute an action, etc. The field of 'speech act theory' is an important partner in tackling this problem of determining the speech act value of an utterance.

[f] C*M*NLU must be able to relate the information contained in the interpreted utterance to its knowledge base, which contains all the contextual, situational, or general encyclopedic information which may be relevant to performing a linguistic task. This poses the questions of 'knowledge representation' (how can knowledge be coded in the system) and 'knowledge utilization' (how can that knowledge be retrieved, updated, managed, and brought to bear on the ongoing communicative process). The importance of the knowledge base is perhaps most evident when a question is posed to the system: when it has understood *that* a question is posed and *what information* it is supposed to deliver, it will have to search its knowledge base for the information required to construct an appropriate answer.

[g] 'What we know' can be defined as 'what information our knowledge base contains' *plus* whatever we can derive from that knowledge by rules and principles of logical and probabilistic reasoning. C*M*NLU will have to contain a logical component or 'inference machine' if it is to properly simulate this inferential capacity of natural language users.

[h] Much of our knowledge is derived from the verbal information we receive. But another important source of knowledge is perception through the senses. It makes a lot of difference, for example, whether or not we can see our communicative partner and his or her mimicry and gestures within the concrete situation in which the interaction takes place. C*M*NLU will thus need an analogue to the perceptual capacities of human beings, plus the ability to derive knowledge from perception, to code non-verbal information either in 'images' or in the form of some verbal description, and use that information both in interpreting and appropriately responding to utterances.

[i] If the communicative initiative is on the side of C*M*NLU, it must be able to generate some communicative intention appropriate to its communicative partner, the situation, and the current point in the interaction. It must be able to then formulate its intention in a semantic and syntactic structure which has a good chance of evoking, in the addressee, the intended communicative response.

[j] C*M*NLU must then have the capacity to map that abstract structure onto some appropriate phonetic representation and

[k] output that representation through the equivalent of its 'articulatory organs', or map it into written form.

It will be clear from this description that constructing a C*M*NLU even remotely approximating the 'real' natural language user is a formidable task, and sceptics will be quick to remark that this whole program is doomed to failure. Such scepticism is out of place, however, for several reasons. First of all, remarkable advances have been made in all of the task components [a]-[k] over the past few decades, even though the insights gained do not yet add up to a consistent and integrated over-all system (see, for example, Winograd, 1983). In the second place, let us suppose for a moment that it is intrinsically impossible to simulate fully the competence and performance of the natural language user. Then there will be some limit L, such that up to L computational simulation is possible, but beyond L this is impossible. Under these assumptions, it will also be clear that we can only find out where L lies by pushing forward the computational simulation! So that in order to find out whether computational modelling of the natural language user is possible at all, we have to embark on a program of computational modelling.

References

Berlin, Brent, & Paul KAY, 1969. *Basic color terms; their universality and evolution*. Berkeley: University of California Press.

Bird, Charles & Timothy Shopen, 1979. Maninka, in: Shopen (1979: 59-111).

Bloomfield, Leonard, 1933 *Language*. New York: Holt.

Chomsky, Noam, 1957. *Syntactic structures*. The Hague: Mouton.

Comrie, Bernard, 1981. *Language univerals and linguistic typology*. Oxford: Blackwell.

Greenberg, Joseph H., ed., 1963. *Universals of language*. Cambridge, Mass.: MIT Press.

Greenberg, Joseph H., ed., 1978. *Universals of human language*. 4 volumes. Stanford: University Press.

Hymes, Dell, 1972. On communicative competence. In: J.B. Pride and J. Holmes eds., *Sociolinguistics*: 269-293. Harmondsworth: Penguin.

Levelt, Willem J.M., 1989. *Speaking; from intention to articulation*. Cambridge, Mass.: MIT Press.

Montague, Richard, 1974. *Formal philosophy*. Selected papers of Richard Montague (ed. R.H. Thomason). New Haven: Yale University Press.

Reichling, Anton J.B.N., 1947. *Wat is algemene taalwetenschap?* Groningen: Wolters.

Robins, R.H., 1979. *A short history of linguistics*. London: Longman.

Sapir, Edward, 1949. *Selected writings in language, culture, and personality* (ed. D.G. Mandelbaum). Berkeley: University of California Press.

Saussure, Ferdinand de, 1916. *Cours de linguistique Générale*. Paris: Payot.

Shopen, Timothy, ed., 1979. *Languages and their speakers*. Cambridge, Mass.: Winthrop.

Winograd, Terry, 1983. *Language as a cognitive process*, vol 1: Syntax. Reading, Mass.: Addison-Wesley.

Winograd, Terry, 1987. Natural language: the continuing challenge. *AI Expert* 2: 5.

Homo ex machina; reflections on the relation between the sciences and the arts

A. Cohen

We are prone to think in opposites, although we know that, ultimately, all is one and originally all was one. To declare my interests right from the start, this is not going to be another attempt to advocate some hazy holistic scheme to view the world. What I do like to emphasize from the outset is that there is a danger involved in taking apparent distinctions too readily for granted. Too easily our mind, as Wordsworth warned, supplies us with

"...some false secondary powers, by which,
In weakness, we create distinctions, then
Deem that our puny boundaries are things
Which we perceive, and not which we have made."

(quoted by Minsky, 1985)

Such a stubborn division has plagued the realm of scientific endeavours, leading in 1959 to the publication of C.P. Snow's influential lecture on "The two cultures and the scientific revolution".

In this he forcefully argued that people devoting their lives to studying the natural sciences were living in a world of their own, apart from that inhabited by students of the humanities. The polemics to which this publication gave rise were enthusiastically taken up in this country, recently culminating in a collection of essays under the same Dutch title: "De twee culturen" (Mijnhardt & Theunissen, 1988). The reason why Snow's assumption of the gap between the arts and the sciences was given so much attention in this country is that our educational system has been permeated for a long time with a division into what are called *alpha*, arts, and *bèta*, exact sciences. This superordinate labelling in terms of innocent looking abstract symbols has had an obscuring effect on its users rather than an enlightening one.

Although it is an intriguing question to find out how this division of the mind(s) has come about, I shall try to resist this temptation by concentrating on the present situation and on what lies in store for the near future, rather than making excursions into the past.

Taking a pragmatic stance, based on a realistic view of the present scene, we can observe that developments in the natural sciences, all the more so in recent technology, have led to a wider acceptance of the fruits of the so-called exact sciences in their impact on society than anything accruing from the humanities.

This is mainly due to the fact that results in the natural sciences generally lend themselves more directly to applications which can influence our daily lives. In a way, the sciences attempt to control the phenomena of the natural world, whereas in the humanities, scholars, often working as individuals, try to understand and describe human affairs.

Recently our traditional splitting up of the subjects to be taught at universities into alpha and bèta was extended to a threefold division so as to accommodate the rapidly expanding research activities in the social sciences, for which the term *gamma* was coined.

Special attention to the relation of this stream of studies to that of the humanities will be given in a special chapter in this book. I will here restrict myself to the observation that this recent contender for the attention of the scientific world was based on the conviction that it was, after all, feasible to apply some of the methods that were so obviously responsible for the success of the natural sciences to the field of studies involving human affairs, notably the study of man in society. In this respect the social sciences can be seen as a link between the erstwhile disconnected areas of the study of nature and that of man. In my opinion this in itself hopeful attempt at building a bridge across the alleged gap between the human and the natural world is not necessarily the most successful means of showing how the link between the natural sciences and the humanities can be best established.

In order to do this I would like to suggest that there is more to be gained from an effort to look at the humanities from the perspective made possible by recent developments in the computer sciences rather than the introduction of statistics and experimental techniques borrowed from the natural sciences into the work of those doing research in the social sciences.

1. The impact of chaos studies

In this respect there appears more to be learned from the efforts of those engaged in the study of phenomena within the most recently created field of collected studies in the physical sciences that go under the name of chaos studies. In this new branch, which is highly interdisciplinary in character, phenomena are studied, such as weather conditions, for which deterministic physical laws of the linear kind are not really valid. An admirable exposition of the importance and intrinsic interest to a number of sciences of this new approach, made possible by sophisticated and creative computer programming, is to be found in James Gleick's book: "Chaos, making a new science" (1987).

In order to understand the possible impact of this new approach it should be emphasized that in the past, the natural sciences, in their attempts to explain the world of nature, have largely confined themselves to studying natural phenomena of a highly ordered character, stripped of everything that might interfere with the strict workings of physical systems in an idealized world of abstract, causal laws. In fact experimental physicists normally create their own manipulated world of laboratory settings to test their hypotheses about the quintessential forces dominating the natural world. They resort, of necessity, to reducing the enormously complicated reality to its bare essentials. The classical world of physics was rather a static one, to which the study of chaos has added the hope of enabling its vanguard to undertake tackling dynamic processes of a highly intricate nature and to account for the seemingly unstructured patterns underlying them.

2. Common aspects of all research

Before going to discuss the possible influence of computer techniques on the study of the humanities I will strive to point at some of the features which any of the disciplines, either of the arts or the sciences, have in common when it comes to doing research. No scientific endeavour starts from mere observation impinging on a tabula rasa. If we want to explore any topic in whatever field of study we have already some heuristic device which helps us on our way to circumscribe a small area to which we want to draw our attention. We will always have to artificially isolate some well marked out subfield in which we will confine our research activities.

For argument's sake I will indulge in giving a subjective account of my own experiences as a linguist by training. With my interest in speech I felt I could not profit from studying language in the abstract but phonetics as such was too large an area to cover and I decided to concentrate on the phenomenon of intonation, speech melody, the study of pitch inflections in natural speech. Since pitch is primarily a perceptual phenomenon, I chose a perceptual approach taking intonation to be a special form of pitch perception. This decision made it necessary to embed my research activities within a larger domain of pitch studies as presented by the field of psychoacoustics. All the while I was aware of the fact that intonation has everything to do with what speakers intend to do in communication. Working in a set-up with good research and instrumental facilities I was then able to apply tools which helped me in analyzing the various factors that were involved in the production of fundamental frequency, the quasi-periodical acoustic correlate of the vibrating vocal cords.

The details that can be established by means of an acoustic recording are so overwhelming that one is in danger of no longer being able to see the wood for the trees. It is therefore necessary to try to reduce the details by looking for overall patterns in an effort to abstract from accidentals and to focus on those features that can be assumed to play an essential role in the workings of the pitch mechanism. These patterns eventually seemed to emerge on the basis of a correspondence between some salient pitch movements and the assumed intentions of a speaker. In order to test this hypothesis it was fortunate that it became possible to simulate the apparently capricious movements of the vibrating vocal cords by stylizing the underlying hypothesized pitch patterns by synthesizing them on the computer. This technique, which can be called analysis by synthesis, proved to be very fruitful in producing hypotheses about possible pitch contours in any new speech material and allowing for subsequent checking by ear whether the stylized contours, from which apparently irrelevant details had been removed, were indeed indistinguishable from the pitch in the naturally spoken sample.

This example, taken from my own field of interest, phonetics, which to my mind securely belongs to the domain of the humanities, is in no way intrinsically different from the approach used in the field of the natural sciences. But my claim for the sake of a contribution to the possible status of the humanities in the nineties goes much further. I will maintain the claim that a machine like approach to studying other disciplines traditionally belonging to the humanities stands much to gain from applying recently developed techniques in the computer sciences.

3. Computer simulation as a research technique: analysis by synthesis
One may object that the example chosen from phonetics, intonation, being so closely related, as an acoustic phenomenon, to the natural sciences is rather exceptional in the humanities. I will therefore stick out my neck by extending my claims about the feasibility of introducing computer techniques to the field of language studies of a much wider scope. Here we enter the domain of computer sciences that are closely related to that of cognitive studies encompassing the processing of natural languages. Most of the initial claims of solving this problem by constructing suitable computer programs have come to nothing, since those engaged in it were most of the time naively ignorant of the way human beings handle language. Nevertheless, the unsuccessful attempts at simulating natural language by means of computer programs, even for such elementary tasks as instructing a machine to handle a restricted world of building blocks, has taught workers in this field some of the essentials of operating with human language that had hitherto been overlooked.

Contrary to what is commonly valid for artificial languages as used in mathematics or in formulas expressing relations between well known entities, such as physical terms, chemical symbols, where the notions referred to are explicit and well defined, there is no such neatness when it comes to expressions in ordinary language. There are the much studied cases of ambiguity of a syntactic nature, which have formed a favourite hunting ground for linguists in testing alternative models in syntactic analysis, e.g. *they are flying planes*. But there is also morphological ambiguity, e.g. in the conjugation of many strong verbs, e.g. *said* as past tense or participle, whereas the biggest headache seems to be caused by the frequency of occurrence of ambiguity on the lexical level, e.g. in the guise of homonyms like *bank*, where there is no association of meaning between the financial world and that of natural scenery. The case of polysemy is a much more interesting one, since it provides a challenge to look for some more systematic way of indicating the various categories of meaning involved than is customary in ordinary dictionaries.

Another trap for the unwary worker in the field of what has come to be known by the name of artificial intelligence is the occurrence of anaphora comprising grammatical means by which reference can be made to words, phrases or even sentences somewhere in the context or the situation: *he, it, this, v.v.*

Much of the bane of life for workers in the field of automatic translation is due to the phenomenon of ambiguity. Another pitfall in this area of research is constituted by the incidence of metaphor, the figurative use of words prevailing in all forms of natural language. In a later section the near ubiquity of this phenomenon will be singled out for special attention in an effort to indicate a possible concerted research program for the nineties, in which this theme may be chosen as a specific focus for bringing together workers in different disciplines.

Coming back to the experience that analysis by synthesis has proved to be fruitful in the study of intonation, I would like to take up the wider theme of speech synthesis and speech recognition by machine. Large amounts of money and research efforts have been invested in this so-called field of language technology.

4. Speech synthesis by machine

In order to be able to design a full fledged system for the automatic conversion of written texts into acceptable synthetic speech one needs knowledge about the strategies a human language user brings to the task of reading aloud a passage of prose.

As in the case of automatic translation the machine has got to be knowledgeable about the many open ends that a written text presents to the reader, not only in the shape of obvious linguistic ambiguities but also, even more insidiously, in the interpretation of the way the author of the text has intended to convey his intentions. Here we are in direct contact with the factor 'mind', the mysterious basis of all our conscious and even subconscious human actions. These involve such seemingly intractable features as motives, idiosyncrasies, having to do with a person's previous history, his memory, his momentary feelings, all eluding so far our capacity to account for them adequately.

As long as the prose passage is restricted to neutral language, as used in technical publications which are mainly intended for silent reading, no great harm is involved in automatic conversion by means of synthetic speech. (One may wonder, by the way, whether any good can come of such a laborious undertaking with texts that were never meant to be spoken in the first place.) When texts are involved of a general, informative nature, like those adopted in spoken news bulletins, a wide knowledge of worldly affairs is implicitly taken for granted. This may affect among other things the decision as to which words will have to be accented. In an item referring to George Bush' recent visit to this country, it would not make sense, after having identified him by name, to go on by accenting the word *president* in a following sentence beginning: "The president concluded his visit with a speech at Leyden", since the audience is supposed to know that Mr. Bush and the president of the U.S. are one and the same person. Yet, errors of this nature are frequently made, even by professional news readers.

When we look at matters of a more artistic kind of prose, as in dramatic dialogue, it is evident that a far more complex and subtle knowledge is required for an oral rendering, involving suitable timing and putting the right emphasis to create a maximum effect on the audience, all in the spirit of the character that is being portrayed.

5. Machine recognition of speech

In the realm of automatic speech recognition we encounter a host of new problems that are even more severe than those involved in speech synthesis. As was the case with automatic translation, most of the earlier efforts in this field were exerted by investigators who knew little about speech or language, but all the more about acoustic analysis and computation.

In the carefree days of the fifties, with the introduction of computers in the speech laboratories and hence the rise of a new dawn according to the optimists, the problem of converting speech into some form of written language was simply seen as one of acoustic speech analysis. Waveform recordings of spoken utterances seemed to lend themselves readily to segmentation corresponding to the phonemes and words of the language at issue. In the sixties, when knowledge about the intricate nature involved in the special character of speech sounds had accumulated, the term 'speech analysis' was quietly dropped and replaced by 'speech recognition'. Now the word 'recognition', as so often happens in science, was borrowed straight from ordinary language with all the implicit associations with what human beings are capable of. Moreover, it so happened that at that time sophisticated algorithms had become available for a technique called pattern recognition. Human beings are highly adept at recognizing patterns and it was the silent hope of the acoustic engineers that, somehow or other, the refractory speech waves would lend themselves to this technique by which they were compared with prerecorded, stored frames, preferably from the speaker whose voice output had to be recognized. But again, as in the case of simple speech analysis, the results were by no means very impressive. Isolated words of a restricted set, such as the names of digits and simple command words like add, subtract, etc., used in connection with cash registers, selected with an obvious eye on the market, could successfully be recognized in this manner. However, as soon as it came to uninhibited flowing utterances of speech an utterly unexpected problem had to be faced, i.e. the unfortunate habit of speakers of running their words together without making the kind of pauses that naive workers in this field had hoped to encounter on the basis of their being used to finding them as convenient spaces between the words in writing. This 'discovery' about the special character of human word recognition in running speech has led to a new topic of research within the discipline called psycholinguistics, viz. that of auditory word recognition, after a long history of studies in visual tasks. From this area of studies the notions of bottom-up and top-down strategies have been adopted in the field of machine recognition. A similar distinction is nowadays being made into data driven and knowledge based with reference to information processing in general.

It will come as no surprise to notice that in recent times, in the area of automatic speech recognition, the newest systems of a more sophisticated kind are designated as 'speech understanding' systems.

Now the introduction of the term 'understanding' most blatantly involves an implicit appeal to the world of man's mind, to which those working within the framework of a mere acoustic approach were of necessity driven. With this observation the wheel has come full circle, to the effect that, in wishing to tackle the facts of natural language, workers whose bent is for a physical and computational approach are in need of knowledge to be obtained from those whose specialty is in the field of the humanities. The latter might therefore be well advised to contribute their expertise to this challenging new research front created by the clamour for language technology. More than that, it may also be seen as an incentive towards basic research to investigators who are intent on testing out their models in connection with the problems revolving round the theme of natural language processing.

6. Comparing research in the sciences and the arts

A number of observations can be made, following from the above account, about the relations between the sciences and the arts. So far we have not yet hit upon any essential differences between the two approaches as far as the overall aim of doing research is concerned. Researchers in any field stake out their claims for studying a limited area in which they have reason to believe that they will make progress. By and by they may wish to extend their scope so as to encompass phenomena met on the way. It may turn out that the traditional methods with which they are familiar will not suffice to handle the problems they encounter in their efforts at extending their knowledge. This deficiency may be overcome by looking beyond the frontiers of their own discipline and by borrowing methods developed in a not necessarily related field of studies. This line of thinking made me decide as a linguist, through my interest in speech, to seek inspiration from the domain of acoustics. It will have become clear by now, on account of the above, that such an excursion into another discipline need not be one-way traffic. Investigators in the acoustics world stand as much to gain from contributions by linguists when dealing with speech as v.v.

This observation naturally leads to another, to the effect that what we can learn, in the humanities, from a confrontation with the other sciences, is the rather fluid coupling of basic and applied research. The engineers in the speech laboratories had a very strong idea, based on their solid knowledge of acoustic phenomena, that their expertise might be profitably applied by concentrating on a special case of sound, viz. speech. A similar case can be seen in the efforts of computer scientists, having a solid knowledge of artificial, programming languages who were eager to take up the challenge presented by natural language which they regarded to offer a special case of a system obeying linguistic rules, reminiscent of their own algorithms. Their experiences were largely analogous to those of their colleagues in the speech laboratories; in the case of automatic translation they were equally forced to admit that their original framework was much too narrow and that contributions from investigators with a different background and expertise would have been highly welcome.

7. Basic and applied research

At this juncture I would like to expand a little on the relation between basic research and its applications in general. There was a time when this distinction between pure and applied science was almost one of social standing; those engaged in basic research were held in higher esteem than their fellows in the so-called applied sciences. In our own country, until the beginning of this century, engineers were not qualified to take a doctor's degree. The largest national body for funding research, sponsored by the government, went by the name, in full,: "The Netherlands Organization for the Advancement of Pure Research" (Z.W.O.) and was renamed, only a couple of years ago "National Organization for Scientific Research" (N.W.O.), thereby nominally removing the previously existing barrier between pure and applied research. Ironically enough, its administrators never held this separation to be operative for the humanities; it was merely meant to distinguish itself from a similar government body set up for the purpose of supporting research in technology.

The elitist view of the difference between pure and applied research, imprinting a rather stern image on Z.W.O., as organization for Pure Research, may have had a negative effect on the humanities in finding its way towards working together in an organized manner in writing proposals for research funding, which was mostly left to the enterprising individual. In the seventies this backlog was gradually being removed, partly on the initiative of workers in the various disciplines, and partly through strong encouragement from the organization itself. Nowadays it can be said that the humanities managed to get themselves organized and sorted out into a number of subsidiary research foundations under N.W.O. corresponding to the various disciplines.

Now the main reason why workers in the natural sciences were so far in advance of their colleagues in the arts in getting themselves organized with a view to getting research funds was that they had been used to working in teams, often around large instruments. The main body of research within the humanities was carried out by individuals, working in isolation in their own studies, with books of their own as their main research tools. The development of the past decades has shown that this situation has been drastically changed and in this respect one may observe that the humanities, either voluntarily or not, have taken their cue from the experiences in the world of the other sciences and are now willing to accept responsibilities for carrying out research within a much wider context, involving more workers around a larger theme.

In spite of this healthy awakening towards the advantage of undertaking research tasks in a programmed, organized way, there is still a widespread resistance against the underlying idea that such a planning and implementation of research is always feasible within the humanities.

To quite a few senior researchers in this field doing research, as one of them remarked, is still the most individual expression of the most individual emotion, thereby consciously referring to one of our national poets who claimed this for the act of writing poetry.

I admit readily that there is a lot more to doing research than working in teams and jockeying for better positions towards the acquisition of grants by playing at politics in well organized research foundations set up for this purpose. To me, in the words of Medawar, science is indeed the art of the soluble. To devise tactics to make any problem within the realm of research at all manageable will always remain largely an individual activity. I would like to emphasize in this context that, far from constituting a threat, the pressure of the outside world for applied research can be taken up as an incentive to keeping an open eye for possible applications, thus making a virtue out of necessity. Such an attitude of openness towards a possible exploitation of knowledge need not be seen in the narrow sense of being directly determined by the demands made by the outside world.

8. The study of mind as a focal theme

I believe that the position of the arts as less worthy of respect due to the greater contribution by the natural sciences to the welfare of the world is a rather defensive one. This unfair, and to the arts highly unfavourable, comparison on this score is of a fairly recent date. When not so long ago the world's administrators were to set up an international organization as a subsidiary to the United Nations, it was first called UNECO, C standing for culture in its broadest sense, to which later the S of scientific was added, almost as an afterthought. This historical incident illustrates the contemporary situation following upon W.W.II, after which the natural sciences have fought a winning battle for the regard of the world. A reasonable conclusion might be that the humanities have lost the initiative after having led for so long a rather protected and sheltered life under the roof of the prestigious term 'culture'. In this context the appearance of Snow's study of the two cultures can be seen in a different light. To him it was mandatory to claim that the natural sciences had every right to be taken as seriously as the humanities, in spite of the supercilious attitude taken by some of the scholars he met as representatives of the arts world. In this context I cannot refrain from quoting a telling remark, made quite recently by a staunch defender of the humanities, Alan Bloom (1987: 356) lamenting: "All that is human, all that is of concern to us, lies outside of natural science".

My point would be that studies in the humanities, far from getting adulterated in the vicinity of the natural sciences, have much to offer in conjunction with the information sciences which open up entirely new areas of research in which the study of the human mind is receiving attention from many quarters. In the interdisciplinary teams set up for this purpose the humanistic contribution should no longer be absent.

Before setting myself to the task of sketching a wider perspective for the humanities within the coming decade I would like to expatiate a little on the role of the human mind in science in general. By the way, the restriction of the word 'scientist' to a professional investigator of the natural sciences is of a fairly recent date. It is attributed to the methodologist Whewell who coined the term in his book "The philosophy of the inductive sciences" (1837). The notion of induction as the only way to extend one's knowledge has been largely abandoned by now. Nevertheless, too often (natural) science is seen as the accumulation of facts in the eyes of students of the humanities who see themselves as dealing with ideas. This narrow view of science is flatly contradicted by the growing awareness of scientists that mental constructs (metaphors, analogies, personal philosophies, imaginative leaps)-not empirical discoveries are what bring about scientific advance. It may not be accidental that such a statement to be found on the score of a biologists' work should look admirably fitted to apply to what goes on in the humanities.[1] It would not be the first time in history that the study of biology, dealing with the life sciences, seems to offer prospects in relation with the humanities, whose focus is on the products of the mind of human beings. This certainly holds good for linguistics, where in the previous century the idea of growth was borrowed from biology, leading to the adoption of notions as decay and survival to account in terms of evolution for the history of language changes.

To illustrate this point the following quotation may suffice: "Languages are considered to be organic natural bodies, which are formed according to fixed laws, develop as possessing an inner principle of life, and gradually die out because they do not understand themselves any longer, and therefore cast off or mutilate their members or forms, which were at first significant, but gradually became more of an extrinsic mass."[2] Considerations like these ultimately led to the claim by the founders of what came to be known as the comparative method in linguistics that it was to be reckoned as one of the natural sciences.

Use of metaphor in science

We find numerous examples of this process whereby terms designed origi-

---

[1] New York Review of Books, May 28, 1987, p.37
[2] F. Bopp, as quoted by O. Jespersen, *Language 10*. London 1954.

nally for use within a specific discipline came to be borrowed and taken over wholesale as descriptive devices pertinent to a different set of analogical phenomena in another discipline. What often started as a deliberate adoption of a figurative, expository style came to constitute the dominating frame of reference in which the data studied were to be seen in a new light.

It is by no means certain that in all instances this crossing of the borders between the sciences has always led to profitable results. In this century the rise of the so-called theory of communication was bodily taken over as a conceptual framework by psychologists. The original theory was devised for the specific purpose of establishing a quantitative criterion for the transmission of messages as signals along a communication line, acoustic waves for speech or dots for T.V. pictures. Psychologists hoped to have found a way in which to measure the capacity of the human mind in terms of bits of information, the ultimate unit devised by the communication engineers. This hope was founded on a false analogy in the mistaken belief that what the theory amounted to was a measurement of meaningful information. The mistake originated in the literal interpretation of the metaphorical use of the term 'to carry meaning', as if communication of meaning is like carrying passengers in a train. As a matter of fact, Information theory, as it later came to be called, is all about the statistics of signals and the upper limits of the transmitting capacity of a communication channel but says nothing about meaning. Nevertheless, since the notion of meaning, however incorrectly, came to be associated with this new theory it was also hopefully incorporated into the field of linguistics. Here, as in experimental psychology, the high strung expectations were never fulfilled and the idea that meaning as such could be readily measured was quietly dropped. It is only in certain heavily constrained situations that the human mind appears to act along lines that have any resemblance to the limitations constraining technical channels of communication. In the latter the capacity is defined in terms of expectancy of which signals are transmitted out of a possible set and it is therefore economical to devise a method to estimate how best use can be made of a limited capacity. Thus it pays, once the set of possible messages is known, to code them as efficiently as possible in order to send them at the lowest cost. A good example of such inexpensive transmission is the code used for the transmission of greetings as used by telegraph offices. Thus such a message as "To the most wonderful daddy in the whole wide world – for his birthday" can be telegraphed through transmission of a simple code, D,3. In ordinary circumstances we are entirely free to choose whatever words we like and therefore the amount of information or meaning does not lend itself to be readily measured as is the capacity of a technical communication channel.

The few examples given so far pertain to the less successful transference of ideas from one field of study to another, based on false analogies and captured in terms of figurative language, or metaphors.

But the use of metaphorical language is all pervasive, in all branches of study, as indeed in all human language. As such it can also be put to good usage as long as one is aware of its sometimes illusory power of persuasion. Nowadays in the methodology of science ample room is provided by what are called theory constructive metaphors. They can be relied on to give us the power to represent one strategy for the accommodation of language to as yet undiscovered causal features of the world, in the words of one of the methodologists (Boyd, 1979).

9. Machines as metaphors

The most powerful metaphor within the realm of the sciences is constituted by the idea of a machine-like operation in otherwise human processes. The notion of the working of man's body as some kind of machine became very popular in the 18th century through the influential book "L'Homme machine" by La Mettrie, in which the human body is seen as an engine that winds up its own springs. The most productive metaphorical portraying in machine terms in those days was that of the clock mechanism. It was advocated both by deists and the more materialistically inclined atheists to reach a better understanding of the macrocosm, the universe, as well as the microcosm of man. It gave rise to the actual construction of machines that were supposed to imitate human arts, such as ingenious boxes for performing music.

Although it would be tempting to include a survey of the various attempts at portraying human faculties by means of the construction of machines I will refrain from doing so and prefer to concentrate on the more general issues at stake in any kind of engine keeping in mind the contemporary passion for the computer as the ultimate machine of our own days.

The notion of man as a machine may be an abhorrent one to most of us in the humanities. Being an artificial device it seems to stand out from anything natural. Yet machines do obey natural laws. The word 'machine' derives from the Greek mechane, which we came to know forcefully through its Latin cognate in the expression 'deus ex machina', a stage contraption allowing the gods to enter the scene of a dramatic performance and to interfere with human actions on the stage.

Machines are always built for some intended purpose, but whose? The ready answer is its designer, but we always have to allow for the contingency that even simple tools such as a knife, whose alleged purpose is to cut, can also be used in an emergency for quite a different purpose, e.g. to wriggle underneath the cap of a drawing pin in order to remove it. It was not meant to fulfil this particular purpose, but it can nevertheless be given this specific function by a user. Although in principle the designer of a machine knows the causal relations through which his device is able to operate he does not necessarily have to be aware of all the functions to which it can be put. Looked at it in this way the modern digital computer can be seen as a general purpose engine which can be put to any kind of use, dependent on the demands made upon it by its users. Joseph Weizenbaum, much to his regret, came to learn that the program Eliza that he had set up to expose the naivety of the psycho-analytic approach was taken seriously by the same professional workers in the field whom he meant to ridicule. This ironic incident can also be interpreted in a wider perspective, to the extent that machines built by man can come to exert an influence on man's life far beyond anything that could be foreseen by their devisers. It can lead to changes in human behaviour. Clocks, which were originally seen as models of the planetary system assumed the role of time keepers and as such came to control the regulation of man's daily life.

According to Weizenbaum (1976) "The feeling of hunger was rejected as a stimulus for eating; instead one ate when an abstract model had achieved a certain state, i.e. when the hands of a clock pointed to certain marks on the clock's face (the anthropomorphism here is highly significant too), and similarly for signals for sleep, rising, and so on."

It has become a truism to observe that the modern computer has come to influence our daily lives in many respects. For our purposes it is convenient to focus our attention on those aspects that can serve to increase our knowledge. Thus we will look at its role in our scientific pursuits particularly from the point of view of the humanities. From this vantage point its powerful attraction does not lie merely in its capacity to process large amounts of data, but rather that it seems to be able to deal with tasks that are normally reckoned to be human actions. Such a view had led students of human behaviour to see it as a suitable metaphor for human intelligence. On this belief was founded the notion of artificial intelligence within the computer sciences, which purportedly would lead to better insights into the working of the human brain, since both were processing information by means of language. Computers were fed by algorithms along the rules of specially designed programming languages each with their own syntax and semantics, resembling analogous subsystems used in the descriptions of formalized grammars of generative linguistics, supposedly the language of the brain.

10. Memory as metaphor

Most of the terms employed in talking about computers and their functioning is rife with borrowing from their alleged human counterparts. Among these memory is probably the most powerful one. As such it is nothing but a metaphor, derived from what was taken to be the prime function of human memory, to store and classify data we have assimilated in our experience. But it is indeed a very impoverished view of our faculty of memory which was incorporated in the terminology of computer studies. It is only recently that psychologists have started serious research in order to explore its mysterious powers of handling information. They are nowhere near to knowing anything about its implementation in the brain.

Human memory in any case is bound up with an individual's biological and psychological life and cannot be separated from his consciousness, his personal identity. Compared to this machine 'memory' is of a different kind, static rather than dynamic as is the case of human memory. Nevertheless there is no intrinsic reason why in the end computers cannot be empowered with better ways of fulfilling memory tasks more in line with what humans do. I believe with Gregory (1981) that 'technological innovations typically come before conceptual bases by which they are understood; as understanding grows, principles can be described with increasing generalization to allow deeper analogies'.

If we want to know how human memory works we must also know how the brain is organized to accommodate the functioning of memory or indeed any of our mental faculties. The computer models of the early years were deficient for carrying out the tasks set to them, like natural language processing. Of late, however, optimists in this branch of studies have been given a new lease of life by the more sophisticated models based on an analogy with neutral networks as found in the human brain. The emphasis is shifted in this approach, called connectionism, from following strict rules, which have to be run off by a sequential program of rules, to some form of parallel processing.

11. The brain as a machine

Once more it is the powerful metaphor of the computer as a kind of neural network that has been the inspiration to the connectionist approach. However, in comparing the brain to a computer large differences are apparent. There are about 10^{11} to 10^{12} neurons, each having hundreds of thousand of synapses to other neurons. The speed by which information is transmitted is vastly slower than in electronic circuits. The reason why the brain nevertheless works so efficiently must be looked for in its massive parallelism, involving huge numbers of neurons working simultaneously. Not all of them need to function faultlessly since there are vast built-in tolerances; in fact many neurons die out every day. The modern idea is that the neural functioning of the brain is not strictly localized but rather distributed over large parts of it. This idea was picked up by the machine model makers, hence the term now in vogue to indicate this type of simulation: parallel distributed processing, P.D.P. Working along P.D.P. lines involves concentrating on a level of information processing below that of the serial arrangements of programmes of the earlier type used in A.I. In this symbols were manipulated that were direct representations e.g. of the words of natural languages.

It is important to notice that the new technique in modelling supposed functions of the brain has learnt from past mistakes. It is once more the method of analysis by synthesis that can be seen to lie at the basis of computer simulation. But in order to simulate successfully, the analysis of the phenomena under investigation has got to be made explicit enough to merit being tested. It is only feasible to model complex systems when there is reason to believe that they can be reduced to a few simple components interacting according to simple rules to the effect that computer modelling must use a simpler programma than the system that is being modelled. This strategy is in line with the tenet of all reductionist attempts at finding scientific explanations of complex reality, in this case expressed in the language of computer modelling, i.e. the program, not the data. However, it is the very capacity of the computer to handle vast quantities of data that affords hope for sciences other than physics or chemistry in which deep theories can be tested. No such deep theories as yet exist in either the humanities or the behavioral sciences, but working with so-called phenomenological models to account for the data, in quantitative descriptive way, can lead to better understanding. This approach has already proved fruitful in the biological sciences, e.g. in capturing the essential features of ecosystem organization.

Nowadays there is a great interest in the sciences of complexity in which mathematicians have opened up a new area of study, called complexity theory, as a subdiscipline of the wider field of chaos studies.

In this approach complexity is seen as a quantitative measure assignable to a physical system or computation, midway between simple order and chaos. This new perspective offered by the study of chaos phenomena within the physical and mathematical sciences might provide a suitable analogy for work in the humanities. Metaphorically speaking the products of the human mind, which in essence are the objects of study within the humanities, can be seen to hover between the realms of order and chaos.

12. A new perspective for the humanities

In the previous sections the main object has been to explore the possible relations between research activities in such diverse fields as the natural sciences and the arts. We are used to a strong proliferation of disciplines within a single university faculty. What we see now in other fields is a development towards a concerted approach attracting workers from apparently highly diverse disciplines, assembled round large research themes such as those constituted by the new field of chaos studies. It can be seen as a logical development in any scientific undertaking that researchers open themselves to new possibilities when their traditional methods and techniques are incapable of dealing with phenomena that are of obvious interest. The ultimate hope for any science apart from being able to describe or even to explain the data under investigation is to get a grip on them, controlling nature as it were.

Humanistic studies have far too long struggled with a handicap in comparison with those in the natural sciences. They have been pushed on the defensive since none of them can be said to have exerted an influence on the outside world coming anywhere near to that brought about by the natural sciences. Yet even so, it need not always be through a direct connection with profitable results that a scientific discipline gains respect. Astronomy e.g. has always exerted an obvious appeal to the imagination of people and its efforts in exploring the world of the macrocosm were rewarded by large fundings without the expectation of getting quick results. In this context the words of the humanist philosopher Vico, living more than two centuries ago come to mind "...the world of civil society has certainly been made by men, and its principles are therefore to be found within the modifications of our own human mind. Whoever reflects on this cannot but marvel that the philosophers should have bent all their energies to the study of the world of nature, which since God made it, He alone knows; and that they should have neglected the study of the world of nations or civil world, which, since men had made it, men could come to know." (as quoted by Pagels, 1988: 214)

This, in essence, is a formulation based on the traditional dualism between the world of matter and mind, nature and man, going back to Descartes.

Now that through the power of computation the world of civil affairs and even that of man's mind seem to be accessible for advanced research it is time for the humanities to present themselves with some self-assurance to take a legitimate share in this challenging endeavour by drawing attention on their own pursuits. The battle for the conquering of man's mind, as a research enterprise, should not be left to be engaged in by cognitive psychologists and computer scientists.

13. The force of interdisciplinary research

Thanks to the newly established research area of complexity, in which scientists of various persuasions take part, all sharing the conviction that the ordinary causal laws of nature cannot be relied on to solve the problems involved in the study of complex systems, it becomes possible to cherish some hope that eventually the phenomena that form the hunting grounds within the humanities lend themselves to a similar, interdisciplinary effort. It would require a rather dramatic shake-up of the traditional divisions that have reigned between the various disciplines.

On the basis of my personal experience I can vouch for the great advantage that can result from a conscious effort to cross the lines, as it were, and to take up the challenge of doing work of an interdisciplinary nature. We should be prepared to acknowledge the situation that we are all, in our several ways, engaged in an effort to understand the workings and products of the human mind. From my own perspective, as a linguist, the moment of joining those in the field of cognitive studies round the computer has come already. This is apparent in developments, mainly in the U.S., where trained linguists take a large share in the study of simulation of the processing of natural language.

There is, indeed, in the outside world a vast interest in what is called language technology. Recently this cry for the creation of such a new field of studies has been taken up by the scientific division of the E.E.C.

I believe that there is more at stake than the possible fruits of application in this area. On the basis of theoretical insights into the abysses of ignorance of the actual functioning of language, not so much in the hypothesized system of abstract rules of grammar, but in the daily handling of information by language users, there is much to be discovered. Seen from the point of view of how human beings actually communicate by means of speech and language there is scope for workers outside the field of linguistics proper, viz. historians, students of literature, anthropologists, cognitive psychologists, philosophers.

14. The role of metaphor
As mentioned in several places in the above the role of metaphor seems to lend itself very well for adoption within a larger framework entailing the services of researchers traditionally belonging to different disciplines, philosophy, literature, history as well as the fine arts. Within the latter the subdiscipline of iconology has come to fruition under its ow steam.

I believe that a concerted effort to study the role of metaphor can be a leaven to the study of the humanities within a larger framework of a study of communicative behaviour.

It requires the study of complex mental processes to explain the use of figurative language in general. Exploring its use by human beings in different areas may create an opening towards the way our mind works in associating data from seemingly diverse areas on the basis of analogy in both our communicative intentions and our scientific thinking.

There is nowadays a very widespread interest in the study of the use of metaphor in scientific research. As such it can supply a lever for activities within the research community of the humanities to take part in such proceedings. As a very attractive possible spin-off it will force those willing to take up this challenge to gain a better insight into what is actually going on in branches of research that are at face value far removed from their own, beyond their ken. They are bound to find out that there is lot more of mind involved in the practice of research than seems to meet their eyes, even in the natural sciences.

If research in the humanities is to be taken seriously within the next decade its participants might do well by looking beyond the borders of their own disciplines and accept the challenge that what they are dealing with has everything to do with products of the human mind. On this score they will find ready acceptance by those working on similar lines outside the humanities proper.

The most obvious meeting ground for such an enterprise would have to be found in the places where people's preoccupation revolves round the question of what man does with language, more generally with meaning, and in particular with figurative language.

15. Summary and conclusions
The title I have chosen has been devised on the score of reflections on the possible links between research activities within the natural sciences and the humanities. The problem as such is indeed too vast and too difficult for any person to handle by himself. Inevitably I have had to fall back on my

own subjective experiences as a member of the humanities community in whose research an interdisciplinary approach has proved to be a fruitful pursuit.

The technique of analysis by synthesis has certainly helped me in tackling problems within a limited subfield of research, that of intonation or speech melody. Although legitimately belonging to the wider field of linguistics, it proved to be amenable to be handled within the context of acoustics, one of the physical sciences. This effort was highly facilitated by the technical means made available in laboratory setting including computer means. The main object was to obtain a better understanding of the phenomenon from a theoretical point of view. It appeared, however, that use of the results could be applied in improving the quality of synthetic speech. This in itself, the generation of synthetic speech, has come about as a byproduct of computer technology and constitutes one of the major efforts in language technology. In this way a link could be established between basic and applied research. However, this does not imply that all problems have been solved; on the contrary, this link has helped to indicate some possible new research aims to reduce our ignorance about such matters as the factors underlying our behaviour in determining the actual patterns we use in natural speech. This kind of feedback or cross fertilization between basic and applied research, due to the technique of analysis by synthesis, has induced me to choose the title of this essay.

It was mainly the negative findings of workers in the cognitive sciences in the field of simulating the processing of natural language by machine, which has prompted the idea that there is an opportunity for those whose own research revolves round products of the human mind, within the humanities, to take their share in such pursuits.

In order to strengthen my case I have found it necessary to emphasize that, by and large, there is no essential difference about the way research is carried out in the seemingly opposite fields of the natural sciences and the arts. However there can be no doubt about the real existence of differences when it comes to questions of respectability and public esteem, not to mention government and administrative concern.

To reduce this disadvantage on the part of the humanities the members of this community might benefit from the lessons provided by the natural sciences. They would do well to show their willingness to take a proportional share in the field of studies of the human mind, to whose better understanding the humanities are at least nominally committed.

As a possible research strategy I feel inclined to advocate a less defensive role and a more outward going attitude towards developments outside the present domain of the humanities. These take place most promisingly, from our point of view, in the study of complex processes, in which new computer techniques have led to the opening of new perspectives, primarily within the natural sciences, but eventually even for the humanities.

As a tactical start I suggest the study of metaphor, since it lends itself to the possible coordination of research efforts within the arts community. Moreover, it is certainly a relevant theme since metaphors can be seen as vital mental instruments being used, either wittingly or unwittingly, by workers in all domains of knowledge, irrespective of their own disciplines. Presently it constitutes a topic which is being hotly discussed in highly diverse fields and, therefore, a contribution from the humanities is bound to fall in fertile ground. Moreover, to study metaphor in its own right might well help in an indirect way to learn more about the way in which man's mind, in using language, seems to operate.

By his fruits man shall be known and it is maybe not stretching things too far to claim that the study of the products of the human mind falls within the legitimate scope of the humanities. If it cannot be done directly then indirectly by means of computer simulation.

References

Bloom, A., 1987. *The closing of the American mind*. New York, Simon and Schuster.
Boyd, R., 1979. Metaphor and theory change: what is metaphor a metaphor for? In: Ortony, A. (ed.) *Metaphor and Thought*, p. 356-408. Cambridge, C.U.P.
Gleick, J., 1987. *Chaos, making a new science*. New York, Viking.
Gregory, R.L., 1981. *Mind in science*. London, Weidenfeld and Nicolson.
Minsky, M., 1985. *The society of mind*. New York, Simon and Schuster.
Mijnhardt, W.W. & B. Theunissen (eds.), 1988. *De twee culturen*. Amsterdam, Rodopi.
Pagels, H.R., 1988. *The dreams of reason: the computer and the rise of the sciences of complexity*. New York, Bantam Books.
Weizenbaum, J., 1976. *Computer power and human reason*. San Fransisco, W.H. Freeman.

Part 4

The Arts

Musicology in the 1990's

Paul Op de Coul and Frits de Haen

Introduction

In recent years musicology has undergone considerable international growth. Not only are trained musicologists active in the many sectors of society where music plays a significant role; research has also expanded rapidly, as the countless publications in the form of journals, series, monographs and editions testify. The aim of this essay is to indicate certain trends in musicology and to articulate our view of the ways in which the discipline could develop in the years ahead. The following topics will be dealt with:

- the historical development of musicology;
- the various subdisciplines (historical musicology, systematic musicology and ethnomusicology); recent issues and developments;
- the relation between scholarship and musical practice - how could this be improved?
- a number of recent developments: the role of modern technology (computer science) in research and teaching; the systematic study of art policies and management; research into the role women play and have played in the musical world; the RIPIM and the RIdIM projects.

1. The musicological tradition

Musicology can be defined as "a field of knowledge having as its object the investigation of the art of music as a physical, psychological, aesthetic and cultural phenomenon." This definition, formulated by a commission of the American Musicological Society (1955), covers a very broad area which necessarily draws on several auxiliary disciplines. In practice, however, a strong historical tradition seems dominant. Many musicologists interpret music as a phenomenon of cultural history and study it with historical-philological methods (palaeography, text editions, comparison of sources). In view of the history of the discipline this approach is very understandable. Although music has been studied for centuries, and although the Greeks already investigated the philosophical and physical aspects of music (to say nothing of the oriental tradition in this field), the study of music as a scholarly discipline is of fairly recent date. While it is true that music was taught at a few universities in the Middle Ages and that even today a great deal of study is devoted to the work of Aristoxenos, Pythagoras, Plato and their Christian successors Boethius, Odo of Cluny and Guido of Arezzo, this tradition still differs distinctly from that of present-day scholars. The theorists mentioned above were primarily concerned with musical ethos and viewed musical studies as a part of the quadrivium, in other words as a mathematical discipline.

Contemporary musical studies, on the other hand, grew out of a historical orientation; musicology can be viewed as the child of nineteenth-century historicism. A historical approach can be found in a few writers of the seventeenth century, but it is generally accepted that it was not until the eighteenth century that scholars like Charles Burney and John Hawkins attempted to write a history starting with the ancients and continuing right up to their own time.

The great interest of the nineteenth century in the musical past found two main forms of expression. In the first place a start was made in studying and performing older music. A tangible result of this was the publication of the complete works of important composers: in 1850 the Bach-Gesellschaft was founded, and the publication of the works of Bach by this organization was followed by the works of Händel, Palestrina, Beethoven, Mendelssohn, Mozart, etc. In addition it was felt that a forum was needed for the exchange of research findings. This led to the first musicological periodicals: Friedrich Chrysander founded the *Jahrbuch für musikalische Wissenschaft* in 1863, and Guido Adler the *Vierteljahrsschrift für Musikwissenschaft* in 1885. In an article setting forth his convictions, Adler maintained that the primary goal of musicology is to shed light on the theoretical and aesthetic principles of the art form in various stages of its history. (Adler, 1885) In his *Methode der Musikgeschichte* (Leipzig 1919) Adler expanded this article and provided a foundation for the discipline which is still influential today.

But alongside this historical approach there was for centuries also interest in the mathematical, Pythagorean tradition mentioned above. This line of study was pursued not only in the Middle Ages, but also in the eighteenth century by mathematicians like Joseph Saveur and Leonhard Euler. They devoted a great deal of attention to the acoustic aspects of music. In the nineteenth century their work was taken over by scholars such as Herman von Helmholtz and Friedrich Carl Stumpf, who were especially interested in the psychology of hearing. Since Adler these researchers have been classified as 'systematic' musicologists.

Nineteenth-century interest in a scientific and scholarly study of music resulted in the founding of university chairs for musicology. Germany led the way with the appointment of a special professor in Bonn in 1826. From then until the end of the first quarter of the twentieth century, Germany and Austria remained the most important centres for musicological research. Vienna followed the German example already in 1870, inaugurating the renowned musical critic Eduard Hanslick as professor of music and aesthetics. In other countries the importance of a scholarly study of music was recognized only in this century. The first chair at the Sorbonne dates from 1904, while the Anglo-Saxon countries introduced musicological research and teaching at an even later date. In the United States the first chair was established in 1930 (Cornell), while British university research gained momentum only after the Second World War. Although England had an uninterrupted tradition of university chairs since the Middle Ages, the curriculum was geared to techniques of composition rather than to systematic scholarship. English students were taught the craft which composition students in the Netherlands learn at a conservatory.

Of prime importance for Dutch musicology was the competition sponsored in 1826 by the Royal Dutch Institute for Science, Literature and the Fine Arts, on the topic: "What are the achievements of Netherlands music, particularly in the 14th, 15th and 16th centuries, and to what extent can Netherlands artists who went to Italy at that time have influenced the Italian Music Schools which sprang up in Italy shortly thereafter?" Two of the essays submitted were awarded prizes. They were not, however, written by Dutch scholars. An Austrian, Raphael Georg Kiesewetter, won first prize, and the second prize went to a Belgian, François-Joseph Fétis. What became unmistakably clear from these publications was that Netherlands music history included a great deal of uncharted territory. This may explain the need that was felt to stimulate further research, which led to the founding in 1868 of the *Vereniging voor Nederlandse Muziekgeschiedenis* (Society for Netherlands Music History, the oldest association for music history in the world) as a subsidiary organization of the *Maatschappij tot Bevordering der Toonkunst* (Society for the Promotion of Music), established in 1829. Starting in 1869 the *Vereniging voor Nederlandse Muziekgeschiedenis* prepared musical editions; the first yearbook, *Bouwsteenen* (Building Blocks) was published in 1872, and the *Tijdschrift van de Vereniging voor Noord-Nederlandse Muziekgeschiedenis* (Journal of the Society for North-Netherlands Music History) was first issued in 1882. For the preparation of musical editions the association had to rely on foreign scholars. Robert Eitner and Max Seiffert edited the works of Sweelinck (1894-1902), and Johannes Wolf the works of Obrecht (1908-1921). The first Dutchman solicited for the task of editing was Albert Smijers. In 1919 he was asked to take charge of editing the works of Josquin des Prez. Smijers worked on this project until his death in 1957.

Since musicology was not represented at any Dutch university, Smijers was forced to pursue his studies abroad. He earned his doctoral degree from the University of Vienna in 1917 with a dissertation under Adler. Although the *Maatschappij tot Bevordering der Toonkunst* had requested the government to include "higher education in the history of the fine arts, particularly music," in the curriculum of universities as early as 1875, musicology did not make its appearance in Dutch universities until 1929. In that year a Royal Dutch Decree enabled the *Vereniging* to set up a special chair for the theory and history of music in the Humanities and Philosophy Faculty of the University of Utrecht; Smijers was appointed to this chair. It is not surprising that both teaching and research stressed the historical dimension of musicology, particularly the acquisition of philological skills for conducting historical research and editing older music. Accordingly, the transcription of Renaissance music from so-called mensural notation to modern notation constituted an important part of the curriculum.

In Amsterdam, too, attempts were made to set up a course of study in musicology. K.Ph. Kempers, who was awarded his doctoral degree in 1926, was appointed unsalaried lecturer at the Municipal University of Amsterdam in 1929; in 1937 he was promoted to lecturer and in 1946 to associate professor. As in Utrecht, historical studies were predominant here, although 1912 brought the appointment of Jaap Kunst as unsalaried lecturer in ethnomusicology.

2. Three musicologies?

Already in the nineteenth century musicology was subdivided into historical musicology, systematic musicology and ethnomusicology. The question arises as to whether this kind of rigid classification does justice to the respective areas. Perhaps the differences are more a matter of emphasis than of substance. The label 'systematic musicology', for example, is often used as a catchall for a wide range of disciplines which do not have a predominantly historical orientation: acoustics, psychology of music, music theory, aesthetics of music and sociology of music. As a consequence the borders of this subdivision are much less clearly defined than those of historical musicology. In addition there is some overlap between the disciplines. The musicologist who wants to give an interpretation of Beethoven's piano sonata opus 111 will have to devote as much attention to historical as to systematic considerations. Another area of overlap can be found in analysis, a field which makes important contributions to all of the subdisciplines. Nor is it difficult to see how ethnomusicology is linked to the other areas. In this specialty, which has a decisively anthropological orientation, traditional historical research can play an important role, for the cultures dealt with by ethnomusicology also have written sources. If, on the other hand, ethnomusicology is defined as the study of music and culture, as the study which tries to determine the reciprocal influence of music and ideas, behaviour, organization and other structures of a given group of people, cultures and/or subcultures, then the borders separating this field from both historical and systematic musicology become blurred. Our adherence to the traditional tripartite approach in this essay is primarily for reasons of clarity: a greater interweaving of historical musicology, systematic musicology and ethnomusicology (the development of an 'interdisciplinary musicology') could well be one of the challenges for the 1990's. In German language areas, which have a long tradition of musicology, this idea also seems to be taking root, witness recent publications on the topic (*Neues Handbuch der Musikwissenschaft*, vol. X). The following paragraphs will discuss some recent developments in each of the subdisciplines.

Historical musicology
In view of the historically oriented origins of musicology, it is not at all surprising that historical musicology has achieved a position of well-defined prominence. In the Netherlands great stress was laid on the study of Renaissance music; the Dutch production of scholarly work in this area is still second only to that of America. The music of Sweelinck and his contemporaries can be singled out as another area of special interest in the Netherlands. Only recently has more attention been paid to the music of the eighteenth and nineteenth centuries, with scholars attempting to relativize the 'decline' of Netherlands music after the death of Sweelinck (1562-1621).
Because Smijers was more an editor than an author, his students were trained mainly in editing techniques, with the result that several editions were produced. What stands out here are a few larger projects which will be completed in the 1990's. An *editio altera* of the works of Sweelinck, Obrecht and Josquin is presently being prepared. New editions were considered necessary in view of the growing number of accessible sources, new ideas about transcription and present-day criteria for critical commentary. This is part of an international trend: works of Bach, Mozart and Liszt (to mention just a few examples) are being published in new editions involving a team of editors. In contrast to earlier practices, there seems to be a consensus that a task of such magnitude should not rest on the shoulders of one enthusiastic devotee, but ought to be entrusted to several scholars, each of whom has specialized skills or knowledge. This kind of cooperative project is both international and interdisciplinary.

The New Josquin Edition is a prime example of international cooperation. The first of the thirty planned volumes of music and critical commentary appeared in 1988, and the project is expected to be finished around the year 2000. This is the first time that an edition is published under the auspices of three institutions: the International Musicological Society, the American Musicological Society and the *Vereniging voor Nederlandse Muziekgeschiedenis*; chairmanship is in the hands of a Dutchman.
This international approach has parallels elsewhere, as the editions of Bach (1954-), Mozart (1955-) and Beethoven (1961-) testify. These editions also bear the names of musicologists from various countries.

Large-scale projects like these are highly suitable for interdisciplinary approaches. Work on the New Josquin Edition, for example, includes a role for the disciplines of late medieval Latin and French literature. The preparation of the editions is having wide-ranging effects on research: studies on smaller and related topics not only follow in the wake of the new edition but form part of the preliminary work as well. An example of this for Josquin is the problem of attribution, which became the topic of an international symposium held in 1986. Also, the problems of transcribing old music require specialized research.

An interdisciplinary approach appears to be a *conditio sine qua non* for arriving at a definition of a certain period. Fortunately this insight is steadily gaining ground. One of the many Dutch examples is the project "Performance practice of Medieval Music" included in the research program in Medieval Studies at Utrecht University. This project explores the interplay of scriptural, oral and visual forms of cultural transmission in the Middle Ages and shares much common ground with other disciplines such as literature, art history and semiotics of music, as well as liturgical and book studies. A prime example of the possibilities offered by this type of approach are the contributions made by textual and iconological studies. In past decades sources were generally interpreted as a reflection of medieval musical practice, whereas in the 1980's it became increasingly clear that a straightforward approach of this kind misses the real significance of the sources. Symbolism, topoi, reality and fiction must be taken into account before one can make sound statements about musical reality. On the other hand, not every research project lends itself to an interdisciplinary approach; there must always be room for monodisciplinary research as well.

In addition to the large (new) editions of works by great composers, there is also increased interest in lesser known masters and genres. Even in Renaissance research, with all the attention paid to composers from the Low Countries, a clear picture of composers on the Netherlands scene has not yet emerged. In point of fact nearly all the composers from the so-called Netherlands schools of the 15th and 16th centuries came from outside the national borders as we know them today, and a large number of them lived and worked at Italian courts. Now that scholars are realizing how much of Netherlands music history still needs to be written, research into typically Netherlands features of musical life in the Renaissance is enjoying greater attention. Topics of research in this area are street musicians, musical instruments (information in archives), government and music, as well as repertoire studies of, for example, the Dutch song. This last area overlaps considerably with the fields of Netherlands literature, (social) history and folklore. Research of this kind is carried out not only at universities but also by institutions like the P.J. Meertens Institute in Amsterdam.

Other periods will also benefit from the deepening and broadening of source research. Until now music history has been written largely in terms of works by the great masters. For insight into a given period which goes beyond the oeuvre of the greats, however, works by 'lesser gods' have to be investigated as well. Musical life outside the great artistic institutions will also have to be studied. Relatively little is known, for example, about the *Volksconcerten* ('Popular Concerts') organized in the Netherlands during the nineteenth and the first half of the twentieth century. This approach requires that research goals be formulated in such a way as to leave room for questions in the area of social developments; for example: what role was played by the social organizations and by the government in providing for culture? Research of this kind, supplemented by studies of light music, will provide a fuller picture than earlier studies when it comes to describing 'everyday musical culture' of individual periods.

An attempt will have to be made to construct a theoretical model which places music in a total cultural context with sociological, aesthetic, philosophical, economic, religious and political dimensions. The idea of a coherent totality ('Zeitgeist') suggested by this approach should be subjected to close scrutiny, and the alternative possibility, namely that there is little or no coherence among the various cultural dimensions, must also be entertained. Particularly concepts borrowed from other disciplines should be carefully tested for their applicability (Baroque, Rococo, Sturm und Drang, Classicism, Biedermeier, Jugendstil and Impressionism, to name just a few). The reluctance to use such labels is clearly evident in the *Neues Handbuch der Musikwissenschaft*; here the period previously known as 'Baroque' is called "Music of the 17th Century" and "Music of the 18th Century".

A very remarkable development is the concentration of musicological activity on nineteenth and twentieth-century research topics. In Germany this trend has been visible since the late 1960's. Evidence can be found in the series "Studien zur Musikgeschichte des neunzehnten Jahrhunderts" (Studies in Nineteenth-Century Music History), an impressive sixty volumes of which have appeared since 1965. Editions of the complete works of Richard

Wagner (1970-), Arnold Schönberg (1966-) and Paul Hindemith (1975-) presently in preparation are also indicative of this growth in interest. In America this trend resulted in the journal *19th-Century Music*, first issued in 1977.

By way of conclusion a few words should also be devoted to instrument studies. The original concern of this research area was the conservation of historical instruments. Now that an increasing number of old instruments (or authentic reconstructions of them) can be heard in concert halls, the importance of this research should not be underestimated. Dutch organ studies benefited greatly from the internationally recognized chair for this discipline at Utrecht University. In this case research produced tangible results, since grateful use was made of research findings in the restoration of Dutch organs.

Besides continuing these activities, the field of instrument studies is spawning new ideas. Now the objects of study are not only traditional instruments but also the newer electric and electronic instruments (in the Music Section of the Municipal Museum of The Hague, for example). There is also interest in the restoration and study of mechanical instruments, not in the last place because of the insights this can yield for performance practice. The conservation of mechanical instruments has given rise to a new field of musicological research.

Systematic musicology
Despite the historical roots of musicology, the discipline has long shown interest in more areas relating to music than history alone. Already in 1885 Guido Adler, in the article cited above ("Umfang, Methode und Ziel der Musikwissenschaft") mentioned systematic research, a term which for him functioned like a kind of catchall for all non-historical approaches. The specialties he assigned to this category included aesthetics, psychology of music, music pedagogy and 'Musikologie'. This last discipline (as distinct from 'Musikwissenschaft' - for him the more general field of music studies) was explicitly concerned with ethnography and folklore, and thus corresponds to what is often understood by the term ethnomusicology. Systematic (or theoretical) research has gained a place at German universities in particular; there is less interest in this field in the Netherlands.

Systematic musicology can be described by analogy to rhetoric. To use the words of Jos Kunst: just as rhetoric studies the persuasive power of language, systematic musicology investigates "the way in which music possesses 'persuasive power'". (Kunst, 1988: 24)

It was the American musicologist Joseph Kerman who in 1985 made a plea for the expansion of what he labelled "musical criticism". It was not the journalistic domain of music criticism that he had in mind but an academic activity comparable to that of literary scholarship. This approach concentrates on the complex response, both emotional and intellectual, which music evokes in the listener. An important feature of these studies is that the analysis is not separated from the person who hears and interprets the piece. Considering the present lack of tools for implementing this approach, one of the challenges for the 1990's could be the development of appropriate methods and tools; this would entail the evaluation of historical, analytic and ethnic information.

This new approach to analysis also calls into question the dominance of what has traditionally been the subject of musicology, namely classical, written 'art music' as preserved in manuscripts and printed editions. For musicology would then have to undertake much more than the investigation of this music; it would also have to make statements about the function of diverse types of music in various social contexts. What comes to mind here is the role played by popular music as well as so-called 'muzak', the background music which is increasing all around us without our requesting it, and which so aptly illustrates Kant's dictum that music is an 'obtrusive art'. What is the influence of muzak, and is there any truth to the assertions of its defenders (and interested parties) when they praise muzak as a panacea which helps increase production, improve atmosphere and raise morale? The investigation of unwritten music will also influence musicological methods: the primacy of the score, of the written notes, and the belief that that is what music *is*, must be greatly relativized. Against the background of an increasing number of sound sources, it is only a matter of time before musicology will begin to orient itself more to sound than to text, as was already remarked years ago at an international congress of the International Musicological Society. (Kerman, 1987)
The traditional working concept can especially be questioned in the study of twentieth-century music. Improvisation and indeterminacy (the practice of leaving open, to a greater or lesser degree, one or more aspects of the musical structure) have become such important elements that a score is no longer a definitive version but simply a stage in the creative process. Instead of concentrating solely on the score, analysis will be largely determined by performed interpretations.
These were not the only considerations which made traditional analysis the subject of debate in musicology over the past decade. Voices from various

quarters urged that the discipline, developed as a foothold for conservatory students, had little merit as a scientific discipline and should be expanded on the basis of sound scholarly and scientific principles. The criticism consisted of two main points: first, that a written record of a work constitutes no more than an approximation of the sounds as intended by the composer, and secondly, that an approach which concentrates on the written record fails to take into account the way in which music is perceived by a listener (or by various listeners with diverse backgrounds and degrees of familiarity with the style). Theorists in particular were reproached for arbitrariness and for their inability to test for repeatable phenomena.

Solutions to these problems were sought in various quarters, with two options predominating: the linguistic and the cybernetic approach. Scholars attempted to apply a linguistic analytical model to music by using semiotics, the study and theory of signs. (Nattiez, 1972) The problem with this approach, however, is that the analogy between language and music is debatable: what, for example, is the musical equivalent of a word? Other researchers looking for help from linguists explored the possibilities of transformational grammar, but there, too, the analogy broke down; linguistic correctness is not the same as musical correctness. What did prove possible, however, was to apply the concept 'good' (as used by transformational linguists) to stylistic purity, with the result that analysts were able to generate compositions resembling chorale melodies by J.S. Bach. (Baroni & Jacoboni, 1970) F. Lehrdahl and R. Jackendoff also draw on linguistic methods. With their attempt "to develop a formal musical grammar that models the listener's connection between the presented musical surface and the organization or organizations he attributes to the music", (Jackendoff & Lehrdahl, 1981) they are also creating a link with the psychology of music. Their approach tries to incorporate linguistic categories into music theory, as well as to expand music theory by adding concepts from psychology. Their hypotheses will have to be supported by empirical research.

Other scholars have also tried to embed the analysis of music in disciplines concerned with communication. This approach includes a role for the psychology of music, with its investigations into how music 'works'. One of the challenges in the years ahead will be to bring the psychology of music (and especially perception research) up to a higher level. Researchers will have to try to arrive at a theory which says something about the effect of, for example, a symphony by Mahler. Also, the resources of the social sciences can very likely be tapped, particularly for their views on communication and convention.

Whatever new perspectives these approaches may yield, they in any case make it clear that dissatisfaction about traditional analytical practice is widespread; analysis focused exclusively on the internal structure of a work is too limited. The autonomous structure is merely one element among many which must play a role in research. In addition to the initiatives mentioned above, results can also be expected from combinations of analysis with historical reception studies aimed at tracking down lost presuppositions which could be relevant to the analysis and interpretation of music.

The limitations of analysis become most palpable in dealing with the written scores of avant-garde music. For lack of theoretical models, scholars are only too eager to make use of explanations given by living composers, who are of course somewhat easier to consult than masters who have already died. It is extremely doubtful, however, whether statements made by composers have scientific value or whether they can actually explain how their music 'works'. (There can be no question that such statements deserve scholarly attention, but more as objects of research than as research tools.) It looks very much as if the means for interpreting musical phenomena must be sought outside traditional musicology. Particularly in the area of developing adequate models for interpretation, disciplines which deal with the social and personal perception of music will have to be consulted. One point of departure could be theories of behaviour which view music as a part of a culture and as interaction among members of a specific cultural group. This would make it possible to bridge the gap between theory formation on the one hand and practical analysis on the other, and to describe the interaction of the musical structure and the listener. If an approach of this kind is to be worthwhile, however, it will have to be interdisciplinary, otherwise it runs the risk of stranding in dilettantism. The social and psychological aspects of this research are such that any attempt to conduct it within the limits of one discipline is inconceivable.

In order to arrive at a theory which says something about the effects of music, it is necessary to make a critical evaluation of the various views of music, its structure and the perception of musical phenomena. The consequences of such an evaluation are dealt with in section 3. For the time being it is difficult to ignore the claim made by systematic musicology, namely that musicology must in the final analysis make statements which are verifiable or falsifiable and which explain musical processes – statements, in other words, which have predictive value.

Ethnomusicology

Ethnomusicology can be defined very broadly as the discipline which deals with the question of what people do with music. Traditionally the emphasis was on oral musical tradition from non-western cultures. Because of the obvious overlap with anthropological studies, it has proved difficult to give a conclusive definition of the discipline. Whereas anthropologically oriented scholars characterize ethnomusicology as the study of the place occupied by music in the culture, those who focus more on the musical aspects define ethnomusicology as the study of traditional music, meaning music which is unwritten and passed down by oral tradition. In the broadest sense, however, ethnomusicology can be viewed as the discipline which tries to determine the reciprocal influence between music and the thought, behaviour, organization and other structures of a given group of people, cultures, and/or subcultures. In addition, the findings for one group are compared, either in part or in their totality, with findings for other groups. If this last definition is adhered to, the distinction between ethnomusicology and the sociology of music as a subcategory of the systematic musicology disappears completely, making even more apparent the debatable nature of the traditional subdivisions of musicology.

The research methods generally used by ethnomusicologists are: field work with participant observation and direct interaction with members of the informant culture (including use of audio-lingual techniques and in some cases computer support), and, in combination with the field work, a study of literature and archives.

The growing interest in the music of other cultures is manifest in the increased number of teaching and research positions in ethnomusicology; there is also an ever-expanding scholarly interest in music in the context of pluralistic societies and in the rise of 'urban ethnomusicology'. In this respect Dutch practice is in step with international trends. One development in the last decade has been the adoption of models from adjacent disciplines such as linguistics and anthropology for ethnomusicological research. Of equally recent date are the attempts to construct a local theory of music. One way of going about this is to talk with persons who belong to the culture in question. Dutch ethnomusicology, which gained international acclaim in the person of Jaap Kunst, has concentrated on Dutch folk music (particularly the narrative song) and music from Indonesia, Surinam and the Antilles. In addition a great deal of research is devoted to music from India, Japan, Turkey, Peru, North Africa and sub-Saharan Africa. A large project now underway is the preparation of a bibliography for the entire field. Important contributions can also be expected from studies devoted to the music of Dutch subcultures and ethnic minorities, as well as to popular music and the Dutch folk movement.

Research into the music of ethnic minority groups is closely related to the attempts in ethnomusicology to take account of social developments. The central question is therefore: to what extent are music and dance means for emphasizing cultural distinctiveness, and to what extent can the social emancipation of ethnic minorities, particularly of the second generation, be fostered by knowledge of the history and variety of their own musical traditions. The interdisciplinary nature of this question implies that other fields such as anthropology, history, languages and psychology, play an important role in research of this kind.

3. Scholarly research and musical practice

Musicology and conservatories

In many countries the educational system makes a distinction between the theoretically oriented field of musicology and the more practically oriented applied music programs. Up to now the two disciplines have developed along parallel but - more importantly - separate lines. Some disadvantages result from this separation, as various opportunities remain unexploited. University music departments and conservatories are, after all, concerned with the same subject, each from their own perspective. On the one hand musicologists cannot do without musicians, dependent as they are on the acoustic realization of the objects of their study. On the other hand, musical practice is supported by the research of musicologists and by the material which they supply to musicians; thus musicians cannot get along without musicologists either. Greater cooperation between universities and conservatories, possibly leading to the eventual integration of the two disciplines in one department, would therefore be a welcome development. Integration of this kind would conform to the situation in a number of Anglo-Saxon countries.

Extensive cooperation would require a consensus on one important aspect which separates university and conservatory, namely the entrance examination. Whereas universities admit all students with a VWO diploma[1], Dutch education in the arts requires an entrance examination which tests the quality and potential of each student with regard to performance technique and auditory skills. In this way, aspiring students with inadequate skills or

---

[1] High school diploma, university preparatory stream.

ability for these specific subjects can be advised against studying music. In our opinion university departments for arts subjects would do well to introduce similar tests. An entrance examination for musicology would not, of course, have to test practical performance skills, but it could determine whether or not the student is adequately equipped to pursue the course of study, both in terms of auditory ability and familiarity with notation. The study of music in secondary school cannot be made an entrance requirement since, regrettably, few of them offer music as an examination subject; a good high-school test in the areas of solfeggio and analysis could take the place of an entrance examination. In this connection it would also be advisable to regularly subject the entrance examinations themselves to systematic scrutiny in order to insure and increase their long-term reliability.

The advantages of more extensive cooperation between universities and conservatories are obvious. Musicologists can test the material they bring to light more rapidly in high-level performances; they can more readily take into account current issues of musical practice when deciding on their research area; their studies of performance practice could take actual practice as their point of departure, and thus immediately bear fruit for future performance practice. For further discussion of this topic, see the paragraph on performance practice.

In recent years cautious attempts have been made in the Netherlands to set up a cooperative program between university music departments and conservatories, but in practice the integration goes no further than offering students from each institution the opportunity to enrol in courses taught at the other. Nevertheless, the two institutions are moving closer together, and the possibility of a new educational program is being explored which would combine the (as yet separate) activities of musicological and conservatory training. However, in view of the demanding level envisioned for this program, it would be suitable for only a few extremely talented students and would therefore not offer a structural solution for the fundamental dichotomy characteristic of Dutch musical life. The unsatisfactory relation between musicology and musical practice is forcefully illustrated by the status enjoyed by the discipline music theory.

The position of the discipline music theory
Today the term music theory refers primarily to the craft of music and is thus a discipline concerned with the 'poetics' of music in the Aristotelian sense. In this context the most important components are melody, rhythm,

counterpoint, harmony and form. In practice, however, these elements are so intertwined that it is pointless to make rigid divisions between them. Traditionally music theory has played an important role in musicological research and teaching. Historically oriented research in particular often makes use of the field of analysis to gain insight into historical developments and to adequately describe and distinguish works from various stylistic periods.

In contrast to the relatively young field of musicology, music theory can boast a venerable tradition. Descriptions of western musical practices go back to the first centuries of the Christian era, while theoretical treatises on Chinese, Indian and Greek music date from before the birth of Christ.

Although the history of music theory belongs to the domain of the musicologist, the subject has, paradoxically enough, gained a place in the curriculum of Dutch conservatories, where the stress is on musical practice. In fact, the only official program in the Netherlands for training music theorists is that offered by conservatories. The orientation of this program is a very practical one, with an emphasis on acquiring a number of different skills. This means that the theory of music as a scholarly discipline which attempts to explain, for example, how a series of sounds constitutes music, hardly exists in the Netherlands. A consequence of this lack of a scholarly component is that theorists are generally not trained in the tradition of scholarly publishing. Because there is no 'literary infrastructure', Dutch music theorists seldom take part in scholarly discussions. As a result, new questions, opinions and research findings in this sector become known very late, if at all. In addition, the lack of a research component means that the task of a theorist affiliated with a conservatory is strictly limited to teaching, and this in turn will stand in the way of further development of the field. If a theorist at some point conducts research for the sake of his teaching, the results will never be noticed outside the classroom; there is absolutely no inventory of current topics and projects. The existence of German and American periodicals for music theory (for example *Journal of Music Theory, Music Analysis, Zeitschrift für Musiktheorie*) indicates that the situation is different in other countries.

Performance practice
Research into performance practice is enjoying a great deal of international interest. Pioneering work in this area was done in England and the Netherlands. Contrary to what the word 'research' suggests, however, these studies are not conducted solely by musicologists. Most of the results have, in fact, been achieved by people like those who did the ground-

breaking work in this field: musicians with a great interest - and in some cases training as well - in musicological issues. This combination of theory and practice illustrates the importance of integrating the work of universities and conservatories, as advocated above. The role which musicology can play in collecting information about a certain performance practice is evident. It can formulate and attempt to answer questions such as: in what context, in what way, by whom and for whom was music played and sung in a given period? While it is true that in the final analysis musicians make many of their choices on the basis of intuition, an essential requirement for high-level concert practice is that performing artists are acquainted with the relevant principles of performance. Whether they wish to apply this knowledge in practice is, of course, a totally different question. This means that musicology will not only have to continue collecting relevant information from written records, pictures, eye-witnesses, and old instruments; it will also have to supplement the publication of reliable scores with facsimile editions of the sources.

Contact with musical practice can also take the form of symposia and other meetings devoted to specific topics or problems. A good example of this is the collaboration between the Music Department of Utrecht University and the Holland Festival Oude Muziek (Early Music). As a follow-up to the Lute Symposium of 1986, these institutions decided to organize an annual symposium, featuring a different instrument each year. The symposia devoted to Mahler can also be mentioned here (*Mahler X*, Utrecht; *Mahler VII*, Amsterdam), for the way they successfully combined theory and practice. Cooperative projects of this kind take place in various countries; one of the many examples is the workshop organized in England under the auspices of The London Classical Players and their artistic director Roger Norrington. In the last few years each workshop has focused on one composer, and has included a number of lectures on the composer as well as concerts demonstrating the most recent insights into his works.

A research topic which has recently received a great deal of international attention is tempo: how fast should music of the eighteenth and nineteenth century be played? Several scholars are questioning the generally accepted interpretation of metronome figures from nineteenth-century sources. Some of these tempi, they maintain, are realized much too fast today. Further research in the years ahead should determine whether premises like these are viable and practicable. Important progress has also been made recently in the area of Gregorian performance practice. The deciphering and exact interpretation of the neumatic notations by means of semiotic methods has gained momentum and is making an impact on rhythm.

The study of performance practice is expanding its research domain by progressing through the historical periods. Attention is gradually being given to music from the middle of the nineteenth century, and it will not be long before auditory sources start to play a role. The question, "How were Mahler's works performed by his contemporaries?" can, after all, be partly answered by phonographic material. Also, information obtained directly from musicians and musicologists who knew the composer will start to play a greater role. This is the point of departure used by the Schönberg Quartet, for example. The members of this ensemble sought advice from Eugene Lehner, violist of the former Kolisch Quartet, which was greatly admired by Schönberg.[2]

4. Recent developments

Musicology and computers
Like scholars in so many other disciplines, musicologists have not failed to take note of the rise of computer technology. Aside from the very obvious use of word processing in reporting scholarly research, a few developments deserve mention.

Already in section 2 reference was made to the efforts made by adherents of transformational grammar to inventory stylistic rules in such a way that new melodies could be made 'in the style of....'. For this kind of research computers have, up to now, been used to process data. The great advantage offered by the new technology is that the computer has heuristic potential which a traditional research tool, like the card file, lacks. This general development can find a specific application in musicological research. Patterns of encoded music, for example, can be detected with no effort whatsoever.

A second application of new technology can be found in 'score processing'. The writing out and copying of music has always been extremely time-consuming work; now, however, it can be done nearly perfectly and in much less time. Further improvements can be expected in this area.

---

[2] Divergent views of others who had close contact with Schönberg (Robert Tusler, for example) show how problematic this attempt to achieve authenticity can be. See on this point Knödler (p. 109).

The computer also offers more possibilities besides those of storing and processing information used in research. Programs for writing music can, for example, be linked to sound generators, making it possible to transpose computer codes into sound without human intervention. Conversely, sound can be digitalized, and the information stored in this way can be modified; this can be put to practical use in the notation of improvised music in particular. This kind of computer application can be of great consequence for the study of popular music and ethnomusicology.

Finally, the computer can also be used in teaching. Particularly when it comes to the training of skills, the computer can be an important source of practice material. Solfeggio courses come to mind here, for which experiments with computers are already underway at various institutions.

Art policies and art management
Musical life owes its existence partially to the government which advocates and implements a specific policy. Systematic research into policies relating to art and culture is in many countries, including the Netherlands, still in its infancy. An expansion of research in this area seems desirable. The social role played by music cannot be adequately described if the material relating to musical life, musical infrastructure, offerings, distribution and sales is ignored. What comes to mind here is the investigation of historical sources to determine the origins of musical policy, as well as a critical comparison of the literature on topics relating to the infrastructure as it has developed. As yet too little research has been done on the artistic policy and management of music institutions. Also, the problem of the segmentation of the public deserves more study. The ramifications of this type of research are not of a purely scholarly nature; it can lead to increased versatility among musicologists. Many graduates eventually hold some kind of public office, but their training does not adequately prepare them for the specific demands of the music world, which has over the past years become much more businesslike. If musicologists with these ambitions are to benefit from the opportunities available, some courses in management will have to be included in the curriculum.

Women and musicology
In choosing topics for study, the musicologist is often guided by personal or culturally determined preferences. This is especially true of the subject "Women and Musicology". Historical works currently in use depict the role of women in music history as secondary or even negligible. This picture, however, is determined by the availability of material from the

past. If certain scores, letters by composers and theoretical treatises can either not be consulted at all or only with great difficulty, this will influence the way scholars portray the history of music.

An example of this problem can be found in Fanny Mendelssohn (1805-1847), one of the most interesting women composers of German romanticism. She wrote more than five hundred works, including three hundred songs, which is comparable to the number produced by famous nineteenth-century song composers like Robert Schumann and Johannes Brahms. In spite of this she is rarely mentioned in books on music history. The question is whether this can be explained in terms of the quality of her work. It is possible that she has not been noticed up to now because the majority of her works were never published, since publishing was not in keeping with the conventions of her surroundings. Her family advised her against entering a harsh world in which she would be called upon to prove herself: they felt that this would be at odds with her womanly nature. The result was that almost none of her works were published (with the exception of a few songs, but then under the name of her brother Felix), and her oeuvre is still hardly accessible.

Bringing to light this kind of neglected repertoire therefore constitutes an important task for musicology in the years ahead. This is only a first step, however. Only when these works are accessible will it be possible to fully evaluate them and, if necessary, to adjust our view of music history. Another area requiring investigation is the background for excluding women composers.

Research into the position of women in music will have to be undertaken in a broad framework. If music is considered a type of cultural behaviour in various societies and periods, the role of women will constitute an important part of the study area. This approach has already gained ground in both the United States and West Germany; it is also on the increase in ethnomusicological research. Concrete questions like the following could be asked: Which circumstances in which countries were (un)favourable to women in music and why? What forces are active and how do they influence selection procedures for men and women in present-day institutions such as orchestras, impresario agencies, record companies, conducting functions, management and teaching positions at conservatories and universities? How does the proportion of women compare to that of other artistic fields and other countries? Why were or are certain tasks specifically reserved for women, such as salon music in the nineteenth century, the playing of certain instruments, teaching at lower levels.

Opening up sources

Quite recently two projects were started which will be of great significance for future musicological research and which for this reason deserve mention: RIPM and RIdIM. In analogy to *Répertoire International des Sources Musicales* (RISM) and *Répertoire International de Littérature Musicale* (RILM), the aim of *Répertoire International de la Presse Musicale* (RIPM) is to compile a bibliography of English, French, German, Italian and Dutch music periodicals for the period extending from the end of the eighteenth to the beginning of the twentieth century. *Répertoire International d'Iconographie Musicale* (RIdIM) makes an inventory of visual material which is relevant for musicology. Both projects were initiated by the International Association of Music Libraries and the International Musicological Society. The importance of these projects extends beyond the field of musicology; RIPM and RIdIM will also open up many sources for other disciplines that deal with the cultural history of that period.

It would also be very important to make the popular illustrated magazines of the nineteenth and early twentieth centuries more accessible. Periodicals like these often give a strikingly accurate picture of musical life of that time. For the history of Dutch opera, for instance, they are a gold mine of largely undiscovered iconographic material.

Afterword

Looking into the future is difficult. On the one hand it is impossible to predict how things will develop, on the other the choice of topics to be dealt with is necessarily a subjective one. Nor does joint authorship eliminate this problem. Although colleagues have been consulted and their remarks incorporated into this report, the subjective element remains. This sketch therefore represents no more than an attempt to catch a fleeting glimpse of the 1990's.

We want to express our gratitude to those who, at our request, put their ideas in writing: Willem Elders, Cees Vellekoop, Louis Grijp, Kwee Him Yong, Florian Diepenbrock and Rudolf Rasch of Utrecht University; Ernst Heins, Leo Plenckers, Jan Eijzermans and Helen Metzelaar of the University of Amsterdam; Konrad Boehmer and Frans de Ruiter of the Royal Conservatory of The Hague. Of course, the fact that we mention them here does not make them responsible for the final text. We also want to express our indebtedness to those whose publications we have consulted; the names of some of them can be found in the bibliography.

References

Adler, G., 1885. Umfang, Methode und Ziel der Musikwissenschaft. *Vierteljahrsschrift für Musikwissenschaft* 1.

American Musicological Society, 1955. *Journal of the American Musicological Society* 8.

Baroni, M. & C. Jacoboni, 1970. *Proposal for a Grammar of Melody: The Bach Chorales.* Montreal.

Brook B. & D. Bain, 1985. Music in the Life of Man: Theoretical and Practical Foundations for a World History. *Acta Musicologica* 57.

Jackendoff, R. & F. Lehrdahl, 1981. On the Theory of Grouping and Meter. *Musical Quarterly* 67: 46.

Kerman, J., 1985. *Musicology.* London.

Kerman, J., 1987. Round Table VIII: Analysis and Interpretation in Musical Criticism. *Acta Musicologica 59.*

Knödler, L. Rekenmeesters in muziek. In: Theo Stokkink, Ed. *De cultuur elite van Nederland.*

Kunst, J., 1988. *Filosofie van de muziekwetenschap.* Leiden.

Nattiez, J.-J., 1972. Is a Descriptive Semiotics of Music Possible? *Language Sciences* 23.

Nettle, B., 1986. World Music in the Twentieth Century: A Survey of Research on Western Influence. *Acta Musicologica* 58.

Nowak, A., 1980. Von Zusammenhang der Forschungszweige in der Musikwissenschaft. Bericht über eine Diskussion. *Die Musikforschung* 33.

Schneider, A & U. Seifert, 1986. Zu einigen Ansätzen und Verfahren in neueren musiktheoretischen Konzepten. *Acta Musicologica* 58.

Siedel, W., 1987. *Werk und Werkbegriff in der Musikgeschichte.* Darmstadt.

Veen, J. van der, 1988. *Timaeus en de marktwaarde.* Farewell lecture of December 13, Leiden.

Between reasonless passion and passionless reason theatre studies in the nineties

H. Schoenmakers

1. Introduction

On the coast of Holland, there are beautiful sandy beaches leading up to
the dunes. These beaches get very crowded in nice weather. When, on a
summer's day, a woman lets her children bury her up to her waist or neck
in a mound of sand, we do not care. In fact we hardly notice. It is just one
of the games people play at the seaside. At the very most, someone may
worry whether her children will excavate her before night falls.

If a similar thing were to happen in a park in Amsterdam, Athens or New
York, and that same woman was to be found buried in a mound of sand, we
would consider it very strange, perhaps even think the woman mad. In a
modern, civilized country it is possible that the police would come to take

her away. People watching her would not form profound thoughts about the possible intentions lying behind her actions.

When in a performance of Beckett's "Happy Days" a woman is seen sitting up to her waist – and later to her neck – in a mound, spectators would not think this woman mad, but would ponder deeply on the possible meanings of such a situation. After a recent performance of this play in Holland we could read that it portrayed symbolically the diminishing freedom of human beings from their birth till death.

These versions of the woman in the mound can be used to illustrate some of the characteristics and problems of theatre studies such as shifts in focus and subject, the problems of defining the essentials and characteristics of theatrical arts and media, the approaches within the study of theatrical arts and media, and some related epistemological problems.

2. Focuses of theatrical scholarship

In our Western culture the study of theatrical phenomena is nearly as old as these phenomena themselves. At first it was orientated on practical problems such as the art of scenography about which – as early as in the fifth century – Agatarchos of Samos seems to have written a book. Plato and Aristotle started fundamental discussions, which shall be topics of discussion for centuries in the work of philosophers, church fathers, and scholars in the field of theatre studies; questions such as the positive or negative effects of the theatrical arts. Barish presents in his book "The Anti-theatrical Prejudice" a survey of the antipathies and arguments – even of major philosophers – against theatrical arts. Especially since the development of audiovisual mass media, questions about the negative effects of theatrical works are again hot topics for scholars; and not only for them. However, the rhetorical attacks on television by, for instance, Jerry Mander and Neil Postman are put in a too generalizing way, as if they have chosen to look at the wrong television programs. They suggest that one answer is possible, and that the same answer is possible in every culture, for every social group, and for every theatrical work.

Historically, the most important theory in the field of theatrical arts is, of course, Aristotle's "Poetics". Not only because it is the first theory dealing with the definition of dramaturgical terms and with the essential problems of theatrical communication such as 'the pleasure of tragic emotions' spectators may experience while looking at a theatrical work of art, but also because of the influence of his theory on form and content of theatrical arts has had over the centuries. It is a pity, however, that in the centuries of thinking about theatrical arts, Aristotle has been seen mainly as an authority, and not as a first step of a journey of discovery trying to shed some light onto the unexplored domains of one of human competencies: to communicate with 'as if' actions; a journey of discovery trying to understand, for instance, the phenomenon that spectators – knowing that they are looking at 'as if' actions, and in fact looking at non-existent characters – may experience intense emotions such as sorrow, pity and fear. The main concern in drama theories has been the elaboration and application of Aristotelian concepts in a normative way. An emphasis has been laid not on the question of what theatrical communication is, but on the drama text itself, on its construction principles and on the question of whether the drama text under investigation can be considered a good drama text, applying norms as the Aristotelian unities and concepts as 'bienséance', 'vraisemblance', 'verisimilitude' and so on. To use the example of the woman in the mound anachronistically: scholars were looking – as though they were schoolmasters – at whether Beckett's play fitted with the norms of drama theories. They did not see it as their aim to describe and explain reality, drama, and theatre as they appeared, but rather to proclaim how this drama and theatre should look like. These normative approaches have been overruled by the activities of dramatists and theatre makers who made plays and produced performances not fitting with the normative statements in drama theories and not fitting with the limited number of dramatic genres which were expected to exist with their own specific laws and characteristics. In fact, the theorists were running after new phenomena devised by playwrights and theatre makers who wrote and performed innovative plays, such as "Happy Days", which do not realize the traditional ideas in drama theories. Theorists were running after the new phenomena like – in the twentieth century – futurist theatre, epic theatre, absurd theatre, and post-modern theatre, trying to generalize some essentials of theatre by looking at the characteristics of the new phenomena, or by condemning them as exceptions to the rules.

The institutionalization of theatre studies as a university discipline in the beginning of this century was the result of a shift in focus from drama to theatre. Already in 1846, Th. Wund at the Berlin University was lecturing about theatrical arts, about performances instead of about drama texts. And around the turn of the last century at several European universities professors of Aesthetics and of Literature were lecturing on theatrical arts: W. Creizenach in Cracow, B. Litzmann in Kiel, Jena, and Bonn, A. von Weilen in Vienna, G. Lanson and E. Lintilhac in Paris, and G. Pierce Baker at Harvard University. They lectured on the history of performances. The shift in focus from drama to theatre stimulated interest in the collection of theatrical sources. An important exhibition of such sources took place in 1892 at the Internationale Ausstellung für Musik- und Theaterwesen in Vienna. An example of the problems the new university discipline met with was that dissertations on theatrical arts supervised by M. Herrmann, one of the founding fathers of German theatre studies, were not accepted at his own Berlin University. They had to be defended at universities which had a more sympathetic attitude to theatre studies.

The shift in focus from drama text to theatrical performance does not mean that words such as 'Theatre Studies' or 'Theaterwissenschaft' covered the study of identical subjects and from the same approaches. In fact, the use of these words illustrates very well how the relation between words (symbols) and what words are referring to are subject to change. The words 'Theaterwissenschaft' or 'Theatre Studies' are not only related to different subjects of study, different ideas about scholarship and about education programs in the same period, but are subject to change over the course of time too.

'Theatre Studies' or 'Theaterwissenschaft' used at the end of last century emphasized that the study of theatre was independent from the study of literature and of drama texts. The first decades of this new discipline were characterized by an opposing attitude against the study of literature from which theatre studies divorced itself. The autonomy of theatre studies as an independent university discipline was not only sought in the performances, but also in the basic passion of mankind to express himself in role playing and in a competence or ability to imitate (Kutscher, 1931 & Niessen, 1956). That explains the interest both in the development from ritual to theatre (Murray, 1912) and the interest in the so-called non-literary theatre, as in the Commedia dell'arte (Mic, 1927 & Appollonio, 1930). The main focus, however, was – and remains – on drama in performance. Theatrical dance got relatively little attention. The musical theatre as opera received divided attention from theatre studies and musicology.

At the end of the sixties and the beginning of the seventies of this century, a discussion arose whether the subject of theatre studies should be enlarged with those other media in which people communicate using 'as if' actions. This meant the study of film and television drama too. Some universities saw the study of film and television as part of the study of literature (see Knilli & Reinecke, 1988); and sometimes as part of more general Media Studies; other saw the study of film and television – because of the similarity in which 'as if' actions are presented – as part of a more general study of theatrical arts and media (Birbaumer, 1972). A number of institutes for theatre studies in Western Europe enlarged their fields of study. Some named their institutes otherwise, for instance 'Medienforschung' or Institut für Theatre-, Film- und Fernsehforschung (Cologne). Others kept the name Theaterwissenschaft or Theatre Studies, and interpreted the word 'theater' as an indication for all phenomena where people played 'as if' actions or communicated with 'as if' actions (Vienna). In a recent book by Martin Esslin (1987), the word 'drama' is used in such a way, indicating theatre, film and television.

The central focus in the enlarged as well as in the limited meaning of 'theatre' – in other words, with or without film and television drama – as on the theatrical work of art itself, on the actions shown on stage or on screen even when the spokesman for orthodox theatre studies, Kindermann, mentioned (1966) the public, the critics, and the sociology of the actors as points of interest for theatre studies.

It was also in the seventies that – influenced by developments in the study of literature – a shift in focus took place from the theatrical work itself to the process of theatrical communication by means of the theatrical work, the process of communication between theatre, film or television makers on the one hand and the audience watching these theatrical products on the other. The advocates of this shift stated that theatrical works 'only' present the sign vehicles by which artists try to communicate with the spectators. A consequence of this shift is, or should be, that scholars analyzing theatrical arts and media should no longer look for the one and only meaning of the performance, film or television play, as if this meaning were included in the sign vehicle itself. In this new opinion, meanings are attached to the sign vehicles by the audience because of their knowledge and frames of reference. Interest arose in the possibility that different people may attach different meanings to and may experience different effects from looking at the same works of art. It resulted in interest in research methods and theories enabling the analysis of the reception by spectators. Psychological methods and theories were introduced in theatre studies (Schälzky, Tinchon). An Institut für Publikumsforschung was founded in Vienna in the seventies.

A consequence of such a communicative approach is related to the definition problems of theatrical arts and media. It makes no sense to try to
define theatre, film or television drama and its genres or subgenres by
looking at characteristics of only these theatrical works. The new definitions
focus on process characteristics (Paul, 1971). It is not possible to define
what theatre 'really' is by looking at characteristics of the productions
alone, as many theorists have tried, and as the examples of the woman in
the mound illustrates. Of course, in theatre history it has been an exception
that stage images have been presented in such a realistic way that images
on stage and in reality were – or could be – identical. But in principle they
can, as realistic and naturalistic theatre has made clear. The chickens walking
around in the performance in the Théâtre Antoine of Zolas "La Terre"
(1902) were real chickens. In many films and television plays such a realism convention has been dominant, and was even seen by many theorists –
including such authoritative ones as Kracauer and Bazin – as a necessary
condition for these genres. Developments – especially in theatre, film and
television practice – make clear how limited most approaches in the field
of theatre studies are which look only at the theatrical phenomena themselves and not at the conditions under which theatrical phenomena take
place. Exactly the same woman in a mound can be represented on stage, in
a fiction film and in a documentary. The context – and often, but not
necessarily, information contained in the product itself – is decisive for
what the spectator believes he is seeing. A concept of theatrical frame
(Goffmann, 1975) or convention (Schmidt, 1980) can be used to explain
that people, with the knowledge that they are watching theatrical phenomena,
process the actions in a way different from that which they would use if
they saw the same actions in a non-theatrical situation. In a performance or
in a fiction film with a woman in the mound we believe we see an actor and
a character. This is not the case in a documentary.

A last shift in the subject of theatre studies is an extension of such a
communicative approach. Instead of paying exclusive attention to the process
of communication between artists and spectators by means of the work of
art, the structures within which theatrical arts and media take place also are
paid attention to. This approach can be seen as a sociological one. It de-
parts from the idea that to be able to present a woman in a mound on stage
many kinds of decision processes in institutions have taken place, especially
when so much money is involved in the production of theatre, film, and
television drama. It is these decision processes which are in fact responsible – or co-responsible – for the question of what theatrical works we as

spectators are able to see at a special place and at a special time. And in fact it is the norms and values of the persons in the institutions within the theatre system which decide which kind of innovation may take place and which may not. The theatrical works we are able to see are the only the tip of the iceberg of theatrical works devised and dreamed of by artists. Most of them did not get the money from the decision makers in the theatrical systems to realize their ideas; they had to keep their ambitions frozen in the frustrated knowledge that nobody would ever be able to watch their ideas.

This short survey of shifts in the definition of the subject of theatre studies and of the approaches to theatrical arts and media, discussed theatre studies in its meaning of scientific discipline or of research institution. The word 'Theatre Studies' does not only refer to research institutes, but also – in fact, in most cases – to education institutes. The aims of education institutes and of research institutes may be different and may influence each other. Different aims and the interaction between research and education has brought about significant differences in the development of institutes for theatre studies.

3. The relation between theatrical scholarship and theatrical practice

The aims, activities and possibilities of institutes for theatre studies as education institutes are defined by the structures of higher education in the respective countries. From the foundation of theatre studies as a university discipline we are therefore able to see differences in the aims and organization of the education programs especially between the English speaking countries and the countries on the European continent. G.P. Baker, the 'father' of American Theatre Studies, also taught play writing, first at Radcliffe in 1905, then at Harvard and the Yale School of Drama. His book "Dramatic Technique" (1919) is one of the results of these activities. The kind of education program developed in the English speaking countries has to be divided on the continent into two different educational subsystems: the university institutes in theatre studies and the higher acting- and directing-schools. Most continental institutes function in a system of higher education in which universities provide education programs for research and theoretical studies, whereas specialized schools or colleges provide practical training programs for functions in theatrical practice. In the English speaking countries these two kinds of activities can be combined at the universities. This does not mean that the continental university institutes do not prepare students for functions in theatre or media practice. They restrict themselves – or, better, have to restrict themselves – to the theoretical functions in these practices as there are dramaturges (literary advisers for theatre groups), critics, cultural managers and so on. In English speaking countries, the theatre departments also offer education programs for actors, directors, and scenographers. A recent report (Rea, 1989) makes clear how important the British University Drama Departments are for the professional training of directors.

A problem for the university drama departments on the continent, however, is that the students themselves often opt for an orientation on theatrical practice. An enquiry in 1982 at the Institut für Theater-, Film- und Fernsehwissenschaft at the University of Köln made clear that two-thirds of the students wanted to study something other than 'Theaterwissenschaft'. Most of them wanted a professional education and training at film, television, or theatre schools. An enquiry in Munich in 1986/87 indicated that 52% of the students aimed at a praxis-orientated education too (Schälzky, 1989).

One of the consequences of the orientation towards theatre and media practice which the institutes for theatre studies pursue to a greater or lesser extent, is that they try to obtain the preconditions and facilities necessary to realize such a practical orientation in their courses. The institutes tried to obtain their own theatre spaces and – since the enlargement of the subject to film and television – their studios and montage facilities. Many American and English theatre departments own several theatres of different sizes. As early as 1968 the Amsterdam Theatre Department opened a multifunctional theatre. The Utrecht Theatre Department obtained a theatre in 1988. Departments on the continent need these facilities to provide students with elementary experience in the production processes of theatrical arts and media, in the processes from text or idea to performance, or from script to film. In the English speaking countries these facilities are necessary to provide professional training for the functions in the practices mentioned above. Experience in theatre, film and/or television practice is seen as important by all the departments – including the theoretical ones – since graduates may find a job in situations where works of art in collective working-processes are made. In this respect, education in the field of theatre, film and television (and music) has to be different from education programs in the field of literature or arts where graduates will not take part in the production of these works of art.

The twofold orientation – towards science or scholarship on the one hand and towards theatrical practice on the other – means that the different

demands of scholarship and of practice are not always clearly differenti-
ated. Norms and values in respect to the theatrical arts and media themselves
and those towards scientific work are often mixed up. Many epistemological and methodological problems in theatre studies are the result of a lack
of distinction between the education function and the research function of
the department. This mix-up of education for theatrical practices and for
research, and the inadequate way in which the different demands are made
explicit, has its repercussions for the characteristics and quality of research
in theatre studies. Elementary demands of scientific work such as
intersubjectivity and well-foundedness – which already offer interpretation
problems for the scholars who agree on these demands – are not seen by all
scholars as necessary qualities for research within theatre studies. That is
why a rigid definition of 'theory' – in the sense of a logical system of
related concepts and verifiable hypotheses – may occur beside a conception
of 'theory' in which the individual norms and ideas of the researcher about
his subject of study are manifest. That is also why we meet historical
research in which the interpretations and evaluations of the researcher of
the work of art under study dominate. Other historical researchers investigate
the intentions, interpretations, and evaluations of the theatre makers and
spectators, based on analyses of sources which provide insight into these
different aspects of theatrical communication. In the first case it is the
framework of reference of the researcher himself, and his passions, norms
and values which colour the results. In the second case the researcher tries
to describe and explain the subjective passions, norms and values of the
partners in the theatrical communication in an intersubjective way. In the
first case the researcher would analyze, interpret and evaluate the play or
performance "Happy Days" himself. In the second case the researcher
analyses the intentions and interpretation of the theatre makers and the
interpretation, emotional effect, and evaluation of the spectators. The researcher in this latter position lays a strong emphasis on methods which
may help to provide the information he is looking for in a controllable way.
According to these researchers the passion of the more subjective researchers
for their object of study is interfering with the demands of the intersubjective-
rationality scientific work is asking for.

The passion for theatrical arts and media is, of course, a common basis for
every scholar in the field of theatre study. But scholars working at research
institutes should also try to understand and explain what is going on in
human societies, and not only what is going on in their own minds, although this may be an important starting point for the building of hypoth-

eses about what is going on in the minds and bodies of other people making or watching theatrical arts and media.

I propose an accentuation of the difference between criticism and scientific work. Not because one is better than the other, but because two different aims are followed. The scholar as critic is taking a role in the theatrical system. Such roles are important in our complex societies to guide possible spectators to the performances and to stimulate the discourse on theatrical aesthetics and its norms and values. The scholar as researcher is trying to understand and explain aspects of our reality, in this case that part of reality in which fictional worlds activate real interpretational and emotional processes. He chooses a way of communicative action in which the highest norms with respect to intersubjectivity and controllability are aimed at. When we wonder what university institutes in their functions of research institutes should pursue, I think this second position is the most necessary, especially since a professionalization and specialization of the roles of critics within the theatre and film systems (many critics have university degrees) has taken place. There are no other institutes which will carry out fundamental historical and theoretical research within the fields of theatrical arts and media.

Since – as we stressed before – the university institutes are not only research institutes, we may wonder what else university institutes as education institutes should pursue. I think the professional training for the field of criticism is also necessary as well for the other roles and functions the institutes are allowed to provide an education for. Here we meet the Janusface of the institutes for theatre studies: one face is looking at theatre practice; the other at theatrical scientific scholarship. The two faces should not be reduced to one. The research task and the education task have their different aims for which different specialization courses are necessary. Both faces, however, have a common body: the elementary basis for a practical as well a scientific orientation is knowledge of the history of theatrical arts and media, of the theories in these fields, and of the basic tools to analyze theatrical works. It is this common body which makes it meaningful to combine both orientations in these institutes or departments.

4. Discussions about the foundations of theatre studies as scientific discipline

We mentioned that the development of theatre studies as an independent university discipline is characterized by an opposing attitude to the study of literature. Theatre studies had to divorce itself from this discipline. In spite of this opposing attitude the epistemological and methodological basis has for decades been basically the same as that for the study of literature and arts. That is why hermeneutics is the dominant epistemological approach. Systematic reflection upon the foundations of the discipline and its epistemology was very rare and was mainly concerned with discussing the historical approach and the consequences of the transitory characteristic of its object, the theatre performance. As recently as 1967, a special edition of the Dutch literary journal "Forum der Letteren" discussed the same topics that were being discussed at the beginning of the century. A summary of the development and aims of traditional theatre studies up to the sixties is provided by Kindermann in his article "Theaterwissenschaft" (1966). Since that time a tendency – inspired by developments in the study of literature – to take more interest in theory, methods, and reflection about the foundations of the discipline can be seen. Semiotic approaches and the communicative approach stimulated discussions about theories and methods and the kind of knowledge scholars in this field should aim at. A lively debate arose at the beginning of the seventies, reacting to the subjective hermeneutics of the generation of founding fathers such as Kindermann and Niessen. H. Zielske (1970), N. Schöll and J.W. Kleindiek (1970), D. Steinbeck (1970), M. Dietrich (1971) and A. Paul (1971 & 1972) were among others active in this debate. The work of Steinbeck (1970) and Paul (1971) stimulated the communicative approach, interdisciplinary collaboration, and a more rigid scientific attitude. Schöll und Kleindiek proposed an attitude in along the lines of the critical theory. In 1971, Dietrich proposed an integrated, fundamental research in a multidisciplinary way, focusing not only on theatre but also on the theatrical media. Historians, sociologists, and psychologists should become partners in such an integrated approach. From these disciplines, theories and methods are borrowed which are supposed to be helpful in the investigation of questions about the production and reception of theatrical arts and media. It was at the beginning of the seventies that the discussion about the enlargement of the subject with film and television studies took place. It was at that time too that researchers – because of the discussion about the kind of knowledge they were looking for – had to choose the more or less rigid scientific attitude.

Typical of this less rigid attitude is that passion for the theatrical arts and media or ideological ideas about society functions as an excuse to not accept the demands of scientific work or – more positively stated – to attach very specific demands to research focusing on the arts.

This more rigid attitude aims at an interpretation of 'science' or 'scholar-ship' in which the elementary demands of scientific research – such as intersubjectivity, well-founded and logical reasoning – also play important roles in the study of art disciplines. In the first attitude, the question "Is Happy Days a good play?" is seen as a sensible question and as one which can be answered scientifically. In the second attitude, such a question is not seen as one which can be answered scientifically. Such a question would be reformulated in a question like: "How do spectators or critics judge the play or performance of "Happy Days", and why?"

In the first attitude, the interpretation and evaluation of drama texts, thea-tre performances, films, and television dramas is seen as an important goal. All kinds of interpretative frameworks are used to interpret and analyze the theatrical works under investigation. Bordewijk presents in her disserta-tion (1988) "Pinter Appeal" an interesting overview of the results of inter-pretative frameworks which function as lenses through which the observation of the data – the drama texts and performances – becomes coloured. She describes how biographical approaches see a connection between Pinter's childhood experiences in the aggressive East End of London and the ag-gression in his early plays (M. Esslin) or a relation between his Jewish background and the nature of the conflicts in his plays (Baker & Tabachnik). The psychoanalytic approach turns Pinter's "The Room" into a play about the latent Oedipal wish to kill the father. From a anthropological approach, Stanley in "Birthday Party", Ben and Gus in "The Dumbwaiter", and Edward in "A Slight Ache" function as the scapegoat or the victim/conqueror; Ruth in "The Homecoming" as the goddess of fertility. From an feministic-anthropological approach, Ruth in "The Homecoming" visits London to celebrate the Eleusian Mysteries; in this vision the play is about the sus-pending of the patriarchal order. From an existentialistic point of view, Pinter's work is about people's fear in the course of their everyday lives. The different interpretations related to different frameworks illustrate how we see what we want to see or have learned to see. It illustrates, too, how prudent we should be when we aim at intersubjectivity in scientific work. Even when interpretation is not the central goal, interpretation may colour the results. Observation without interpretation is, in fact, impossible. The consequences of a normative approach in which interpretation and evalua-tion are seen as central goals are far-reaching for historical as well as theoretical research.

For historical research, it meant that the main interest was focused on theatrical works which are part of the corpus of highly-esteemed ones.

That is, highly-esteemed by connoisseurs. Mostly no attention is paid to the question of how the spectators in the historical situation reacted to the theatrical work. Only since reception aesthetics were introduced have such questions been accepted as a legitimate task for researchers to take seriously. In respect to theatrical works which have not become part of the corpus it is not asked if and why many of these works were liked so much by the spectators at that time. Such an attitude is very obvious in, for instance the respect paid to the many adaptations of plays by the classical Greek dramatists or other classical playwrights such as Shakespeare (an interesting, recent example is Leek, 1988). The scholar seems to know what authentic performances should look like and that adaptation is a violation of the work of art. He forgets in his argument that a lot of the works of classical dramatists – such as Shakespeare, Sophocles, Euripides – are themselves adaptations.

It is from such an attitude that a scholar like Antony Price lists the "distortions" in his performance history of Shakespeare's "A Midsummer Night's Dream". He writes, for instance: "In recent years the Royal Shakespeare Company has introduced its own distortion. Charles Laughton in 1959 reduced the ass's head to a pair of furry ears and hooves, which certainly allowed the audience to see his face, but made him look less like an ass than a rabbit. He was in part followed by David Waller in Peter Brook's production in 1970: this time Bottom's face was bare apart from a black rubber nose and points on his ears, which gave him the appearance, not of an ass, but of a circus clown". And he continues gloomily: "yet even this has been defended" (Price, 1983: 20).

Scholars with such an attitude would criticize the description of the 'woman in the mound' in the introduction. They would say that Beckett wrote: "Expanse of scorched grass rising centre to low mound". "Where is the grass?" – they would ask. They forget, however, that even an exact reproduction of a stage image will not reproduce the framework of reference of the spectators necessary for the decoding of the intended meanings and effects. For spectators of another time and culture the meanings attached to the same sign vehicles will be different. An exact reproduction of the witches in "Macbeth" will evoke quite other meanings and effects for an audience who only believe in the existence of Walt Disney witches in fictional worlds.

Typical is how scholars react to innovations. They react as if – thanks to their interpretation and evaluation – it is finally possible to see the real values of the work of art in question; they show an attitude that spectators in the historical situation were too shortsighted to see these values and they feel pity for these poor theatre-goers. We find a typical reaction in an article by E. Istel on the first performance of Carmen in 1875. He does not want to pay serious attention to the first reactions to this opera which is such a popular one nowadays, but which frustrated critics and spectators in the eighteen seventies. He states (Istel, 1984: 190) that it is a waste of paper to print again all the nonsense the Parisian press wrote about the first performance of Carmen. Another attitude arises when the scholar takes also these reactions seriously and tries to explain why such a pattern of refusal and frustration of critics and spectators so often takes place at the time of the first presentations of theatrical works. We may suspect that the scholars themselves are subject to these kinds of reactions to the works in their own time and that in fact, we often are reacting in the same way as the supposedly shortsighted or naive spectators in their time.

When we depart from such ideas, a shift will occur from an emphasis on immanent characteristics and the so-called eternal values of works of art to the historical interaction between the frameworks of reference of spectators and the possibilities of works of art to evoke (new) meanings and effects. Other consequences are the attention given to the functioning of theatrical systems, which means attention to the institutions and persons deciding which theatrical works are worthy of being presented, as well to the characteristics of the spectators visiting the different kinds of theatrical works. Instead of a strong emphasis on the interpretation and evaluation of the theatrical works, a strong emphasis is laid on the interpretation of the sources which provide insight into the aspects of theatrical communication: the intentions of artists, and the interpretation, emotions, and evaluations on the part of the spectators. Such an approach can be followed in historical as well in theoretical research.

In theoretical research, the epistemological position which laid emphasis on the interpretation, analysis, and evaluation of the work itself was often combined with an approach in which the scholars in these works under investigation thought to find the essentials of the theatrical arts. These essentials were described in normative theories – as are the poetics. These kinds of theories functioned, in fact, as instruments propagating traditional ideas about theatrical arts and media, limiting the freedom of the artist, who had to defend himself, as Corneille did when he deviated from the prescriptions of the theories. The way of thinking behind the normative theories is, in fact, an illogical one often combined with an appeal to authorities (the Classics). The argument is that since highly-esteemed works of art have specific characteristics, then new works of art, in order to be estimated very highly, should display the same characteristics. One point not dealt with in such an argument is that other, quite different characteristics may result in highly-esteemed works of art – as the history of theatrical arts and media has proven. That is why developments such as epic theatre, the theatre of the absurd, or animation film had to be considered as exceptions to the rules of the theories. That is why normative theories never last very long. Human freedom of action makes it possible for artists to produce theatrical works with characteristics other than the ones mentioned in theatre, film, or television theories. A film like Fellini's "E la nave va" does not conform to the ideas of classical film theory. The work of Dennis Potter, for instance his "The Singing Detective", does not conform to the realism conventions in traditional television theory.

A serious problem in the theories about theatrical arts and media – beside the hostility of many researchers towards theory – is the lack of communication between researchers. They presented new theories without first having discussed critically former contributions in the same field of study. This can be partly explained by the existence of a Babylonic wall between not only English, French and German on the one hand and the more exotic languages (such as – for Western scholars – Eastern European languages in which the contributions of Czech, Polish and Russian structuralists and formalists were written) on the other, but also between these languages themselves. In the thirties, Mukarovsky and his colleagues of the Prague school were already focusing on the relationship between an aesthetic object and its observer. Until the seventies it was exceptional for these approaches to be mentioned in the bibliographies of theatrical theories. In French bibliographies of theoretical literature it was an exception when English or German studies were mentioned. Therefore, the publication of studies in which literature from several languages was discussed: has been of great importance to the development of an international theoretical discussion for instance Pfister's "Das Drama", Pavis' "Dictionnaire du Théâtre" and Fischer-Lichte's "Semiotik des Theaters".

Since from the sixties onwards there has been less hostility towards theory and methods, we can see attempts at a more scientific analysis of theatrical works of arts, especially with the help of semiotic and communicative approaches. Just as Mr. Jourdain in Moliere's "Le Bourgeois Gentilhomme" discovered that he had been speaking in prose for years without knowing it, so many theorists discovered that they had been semioticians – since they were always analyzing signs – for years without knowing it. The attention given to semiotic theories, which was especially stimulated by Kowzan's "Littérature et Spectacle" (1975), contributed to the development of a technical terminology necessary for more intersubjectivity in the analysis of theatrical products. Many semioticians in the field of theatre studies classified theatrical signs; many forgot, however, that classification is not the same as explanation. Typologies of signs can be useful in characterizing theatrical works of theatre makers, or of periods or trends. However, it does not provide information on its impact and effects. There was a quest for the specific characteristics of theatrical signs. However, neither the classification categories of Kowzan (1975) or Pfister (1977), nor the analysis of the specificity of theatrical signs in terms of – for instance, the 'sign of sign' character – are typical of theatrical signs – as Fischer Lichte (1983) made clear. The drawing of Magritte "Ceci n'est pas une pipe" (about which Foucault wrote his essay with the same title) may illustrate the problem of theatrical signs. Magritte's drawing shows a picture of a pipe. He wrote under it: "This is not a pipe". The drawing emphasizes that a picture or a representation of an object is not the object itself. Although this may be true for the visual arts, in the theatrical arts representations of objects are often shown by presenting the object itself. A pipe in the theatre or on screen can be represented by the pipe itself. This, as Erica Fischer Lichte made clear (1983), may be the most typical of theatrical signs. An extreme example is the play "Minetti" by Thomas Bernard in which the actor Minetti should play the leading part, the character Minetti. He actually did. We may state the paradox: Typical of theatrical arts and media is that no sign has to be typically theatrical. Though, when the observer believes he is seeing a sign in a theatrical situation, another process of information processing is already taking place – as the examples of 'the woman in the mound' in the introduction showed. In fact, everything from reality can become a theatrical sign, not because of the qualities of the sign or object itself, but because of the activation of a theatrical frame by the observer. It is this frame that makes the signs theatrical. At some moment during our socialization process – probably somewhere in the 6th century before Christ – it was discovered that theatrical communication is possible, and that the activation of a specific frame causes us to see not only the object but its representations too. We believe we see worlds which do not actually exist. The fact that theatrical sign and the object it represents may be – or may look – identical, may mean that in the information processing and in the emotional experiences we react, though very momentarily, as in reality – but then immediately regulate these reactions. That is why we do not jump onto the stage to prevent the awful actions which take place in so many tragedies. However, in theatre history spectators sometimes reacted to the actors who played the villain as if he actually were the villain: the actor got a thrashing which was intended for the character he portrayed. The character – the 'real' villain – did not feel anything at all.

Approaches in the field of theatrical theory in the seventies and eighties vary markedly between passion and reason. They range from subjective theories in the line of the "Dynamics of theatre" (Beckerman, 1970) to intersubjective mathematical linguistic analysis of drama texts (Marcus, 1973) or quantitative historical film analyses (Salt, 1983), and from interpretative analysis of depth structures focusing on the dramatic functions in theatrical works in the line of Souriau (1950) to empirical analysis of spectator reactions with quantitative methods (Schälzky, 1980).

In film theory, semiotic approaches became dominant after the classical ones. Of note was Christian Metz' "Language et Cinéma" (1971), which stimulated the semiotics of film, focusing on its supposed specific grammatical and syntactical system. In the second half of the seventies, the focus shifted from analysis of the film itself to its effects on spectators. But very different theoretical frameworks were chosen. French film-semiotics analyzed the (unconscious) effects of film by introducing psychoanalysis into film theory (Metz, 1977). Freud, Althusser and Lacan offered influential frameworks. Separate from these psychoanalytic developments, a semiotic approach developed in the German speaking countries which Kanzog indicates as 'film philology'. Here also an orientation towards the spectator is increasing (Kanzog, 1988). American developments in film theory choose cognitive psychological frameworks to design a spectator-orientated film theory (Bordwell: Narration in the fiction film, 1985). From this side of the Atlantic, several film scholars – like Andrew (1984) and Carroll (1988) – attack heavily the French semiotic contributions on the other side of the ocean. They criticize its metaphorical language, its lack of intersubjectivity, and its lack of verifiable informative value about what is going on during reception processes of real spectators.

Consequences for the theories of theatrical arts of the problems discussed here are far-reaching. From a scientific point of view it makes no sense to develop the normative theories which, by definition, will be of a short-lived nature. Nor does it makes sense to build theories in the field of theatrical arts and media on only the characteristics of the products. It is not there that we will find the essentials of these arts and media. It is necessary to pay attention to the theatrical processes, to the relationship between the product characteristics and the ways spectators are dealing with them. This does not mean, however, that the normative theories are useless. They provide important information on the historical norms and values which are applied to the information processing of theatrical works. There an interesting research program is possible: what are the characteristics and consequences of the theatrical frames? Do these remain the same over the course of time? Are these the same for the different subgenres in the field of theatrical arts and media, and are these the same for different groups of spectators and in different cultures?

The developments in the field of performance analysis, and film and theatre semiotics provide – as I pointed out – important contributions to a technical terminology and to tools analyzing theatrical works. We have to forget both the normative connotations which accompany these analyses and the fact that we are dealing with essential characteristics. Most theatrical works are constructed around conflicts between characters. But even this most used characteristic is not essential, as a play like "Happy Days", or an Opera such as "Einstein on the Beach", or a film like "Koyanisquatsi" show. An approach as presented here leads to a more strict differentiation between theories and methods of analysis. The theories consist of hypotheses which are verifiable or falsifiable. The methods of analysis play important roles in the process of transformation from the theoretical language to the natural language and systematic observations. The theories which try to be of a non-normative nature will be rather abstract, with open concepts such as 'innovation', 'complexity', 'similarity', and so on. These concepts have to be open to be able to focus on the relation between the characteristics of the works and characteristics of the spectators. Innovation is not a characteristic of a work of art, but is a result of the relationship between the work of art and the frames of reference of the spectator. The same is true for the experience of complexity or similarity. Somebody may feel similar to a fictional character, but not everybody will feel the same similarity, with different processes of identification as a result (Schoenmakers, 1988). It is the characteristics of the spectator in relation to the characteristics of the work of art which is decisive for these experiences.

Only from such a theoretical approach is it possible to do justice to the freedom of artists and to the dynamics and innovations in the development of theatrical arts and media since characteristics in the products are no longer prescribed. The researcher does not state that identification with fictional characters is necessary. But he is wondering why and under which circumstances spectators identify themselves with a fictional character.

From such an approach it is possible to explain that the same theatrical works of art can be experienced as new by some spectators, but not by others. Also that characteristics of theatrical innovations in the twenties, such as Bauhaus or Russian futurism, can still be experienced as new and innovative, since the dominant tradition which is decisive for the framework of reference is still a more realistic kind of theatrical work.

5. Western theatre and non-Western theatre
At the recent world conference of the International Federation for Theatre Research (Stockholm 1989) scholars from the so-called third world had severe problems with the term 'Ethnic Studies' as an indication for the study of theatrical arts in South America, Asia, and Africa. They stated that, in fact, every study of theatrical phenomena can be seen as a kind of ethnic study when the functioning of theatrical arts in societies is studied. They thought it typical of the dominance of Western theatrical norms in the study of theatrical phenomena. An example in drama of biases projected onto other cultures is given in David Henry Hwang's traditional Western play "M. Butterfly". In respect to the plot of the opera "Madame Butterfly", a Chinese singer said: "Consider it this way: what would you say if a blond homecoming queen fell in love with a short Japanese businessman? He treats her cruelly, then goes home for three years, during which time she prays to his picture and turns down marriage from a young Kennedy. Then, when she learns he has remarried, she kills herself. Now, I believe you would consider this girl to be a deranged idiot, correct? But because it's an Oriental who kills herself for a Westerner – ah! – you find it beautiful. (...) I will never do Butterfly again (...). If you wish to see some real theatre, come to the Peking Opera sometime. Expand your mind."
Referring to the statements about the way scholars in the field of theatre studies were studying the essentials of theatre by looking at the dominant and highly esteemed theatrical works, it is understandable that the same frame of reference is active when looking at theatrical arts in other cultures. The result is, or can be, that only those phenomena which show the external Western theatrical features are recognized as theatrical. We see the same attitude from theatre makers. At the end of the sixties and in the seventies of this century many theatre makers (such as Peter Brook, Richard Schechner, Eugenio Barba) had an urgent need to search for the roots of theatre preferably in cultures where non-institutionalized forms of theatre exist.The quest for the roots of theatre was motivated by the idea that perhaps the solution could be found to the problem of Western culture in which the theatre has lost its essential function. Also, there arises the

question of what reason there is to recognize actions as theatrical ones. Often the idea that people play roles is the reason for such an interpretation. But, as Schechner's work makes clear, such a broad concept of role playing is used that, in fact, the sociological concept of role playing as metaphor for daily-life behaviour patterns is applied. It mixes up the concept of role playing on the one hand and theatrical phenomena as aesthetic phenomena on the other. We can also state here that it is impossible to recognize whether we are dealing with theatre by looking only at the external characteristics of the actions. When we put a ritual from a far culture on a Western stage, the Western spectators will see theatre. In a theatre space in Amsterdam a few years ago all the actions of Holy Mass were presented, but for the observers – in spite of the precise imitations of the actions – it was not a Holy Mass which was taking place, but rather something theatrical, in the sense of imitation of an action. This example is typical of the problems which arise when we look only at the outside characteristics of the actions. Defining theatrical phenomena in terms of the function of performers and spectators is the only possible way to solve the problem.

In our culture – as well as in others' – we have to realize that the word 'theatrical' is only a word. Words refer to objects or concepts because of conventions. The meaning – and thus the relation between the word and what that word is referring to – may be subject to change. The characteristics of the concept activated by the word 'theatre' and the related norms and values about good theatre are also subject to change – as is becoming clear from the many moments in the history of theatre when spectators were screaming "This is not theatre anymore". Often after some years the same phenomenon is functioning not only as theatre but as typical theatre. The researcher has to be careful not to end up like the snake biting his own tail. Is he analyzing the meanings of the words? Or is he analyzing phenomena in society, such as role playing, which sometimes – under specific conditions and in specific situations – is attributed words such as 'theatrical'?

6. Epilogue
On the basis of this personal sketch, what perspectives do we get of the situation of theatre studies and of the problems involved?

Theatrical work, theatrical process, theatrical system
In the first place, the plea for a focus of the studies of theatrical arts and media on the theatrical work itself – a plea which in fact was already being

made a century ago – may be repeated. This is necessary because scholars of literature are still being appointed to European chairs in theatre studies. The result is that too often the drama text is still seen as the centre of theatre studies, and that too often the words of drama texts are analyzed instead of being seen as possible sources of performances. Another result is that linguistic points of departure or analogies are often applied to the objects in which actions and behaviour, not language, are the central sign vehicles. The moving images on stage or screen, and the ways these images are presented, should be the focus of interest of the researcher.

Scholars focusing on the performance itself may make important contributions to the knowledge of the theatrical arts, as is shown by, for instance, the well-edited series "Les Voies de la Création théâtrale" of the French Centre National du Recherche Scientifique edited by D. Bablet and J. Jacquot.

Related to the focus on the performance is the focus on the senders and receivers in the theatrical communication process, the theatre makers and spectators. Compared to film, attention on theatre directors in theatre is much more rare. In the eighties this seems to change with important projects such as the series "Directors in Perspective" edited by Christopher Innes for the Cambridge University Press. Books on famous directors – such as Antoine, Bergman, Blin, Brecht, Brook, Chaikin, Copeau, Craig, Guthrie, Meyerhold, Mnouchkine, Prince, Reinhardt, Stanislavski, Stein, Strehler, and Wajda – are, or will, be published. Continuation of such projects combined with more documentation and analyses of production processes and theatrical works should be a central element in the tasks of theatre studies during the next decade.

Compared to the recent attention given to theatre makers, the focus on the reception side of theatrical communication has been even more limited. In 1990 the theory of (historical) reception is still mentioned as an 'extremist' approach in Casetti's book "D'un regard l'autre; Le film et son spectateur." (Casetti, 1990: 37). But even more than reception aesthetics a (theoretical) empirical approach of a sociological as well of a psychological nature focusing on the spectators is very incidental. The Institut für Publikumsforschung in Vienna, founded in the seventies to stimulate scientific analysis of the spectators, was suspended in the eighties before it had got – compared to traditional approaches – enough time to conquer the theoretical and methodological problems in this new field of study. The suspicion – and sometimes hostility – met with when approaches are focused on the spectators can be explained by the fact that methods other than the ones traditionally used within theatre studies have to be used, for instance methods from the social sciences. The International Committee of Audience and Reception Research (ICRAR), the World Congresses of Sociology of Theatre (1986 Rome; 1989 Bevagna), and the Institut de Sociologie du Théâtre (Brussel) try to stimulate research in this field and to promote an exchange of information on methods, theories, and results. The sociological approach, investigating who is going to which theatrical works and why, and the psychological approach, investigating what the spectators are experiencing when they watch theatrical works, should complement each other.

The psychoanalytical approach, which was especially popular in film studies as an answer to questions about a focus on the spectators, seems to be in a crisis, especially since the attacks of Noël Caroll (1988). Does this approach resemble the new clothes of the emperor? Does it – contrary to theoretical empirical approaches – contain all the problems of hermeneutics in disguise? These questions – and the question of whether a cognitive orientation in the field of theory of theatrical arts and media offers an acceptable alternative – have to be answered in the nineties. Also, the question of whether an empirical testing of propositions in theories about theatrical arts and media will become a normal procedure in theatrical scholarship.

The communicative approach applied to historical research in the field of theatre studies implies more interest not only for documents giving insight into the stage images of performances of the past, but also into the intentions of the makers of theatrical works as regards the interpretation and emotional impact and effect on the part of the spectators. More critical editions of sources of performances are necessary, relating both to the stage images themselves, and to the theatre makers and the spectators. When we look critically at, for instance, the standard works of Trendall and Webster on the visual sources of Greek drama, it is amazing how improbable it is that the sources under discussion are really sources of performances. More critical editions of sources of performances and of the aspects of theatrical communication could, therefore, be a very important international research project. Critical, in the sense of Ronald Vince's proposals to avoid a quasi-positivistic approach.
The point here is not to think of this or that approach or focus as concurrent, but rather as complementary ones. Such an attitude could stimulate an

integrative approach of a multidisciplinary and interdisciplinary nature. Using the example of the woman in the mound again, we can point at some different general theoretical frameworks to illustrate the complementariness of approaches. We need a general theory of systems to describe and explain that in our societies institutions, and decision and financing structures have been developed which make it possible that people in specific institutions do or do not decide that at a special moment and at a special place freedom will be given to theatre makers in order to present stage images of a woman in a mound. Action theory may be used to describe the actions of the people involved in these systems, as well as the needs, wishes, and intentions of the decision makers, theatre makers and spectators. It helps to answer questions such as why do some theatre makers think it is an efficient and interesting way of communication to present a woman in a mound; or why grown-ups should visit places to look at somebody imitating somebody else sitting up to her waist in a mound. It stimulates research into the characteristics, intentions, and needs of these makers of theatrical works and of the spectators watching them. And it makes it possible to compare these results with those of other countries, cultures, theatrical (sub)genres, groups of spectators, popular theatrical culture, and so on.

Semiotics and communication theory are necessary to describe and explain that the actions the observers are looking at are seen as communicative actions. Watching the woman in the mound, the spectators are looking for possible intentions of the theatre makers and of the author, who they see as responsible for the presentation and construction of these images. They are interpreting the actions and objects they watch as intended signs – that it to say, as signals. The question has to be answered whether all spectators always and in all times and cultures have the same information processing characteristics when watching theatrical products.
Aesthetics or art theory is necessary as a general framework to describe and explain why the spectators have specific demands, and why they activate specific norms and values while watching the signals they interpret as theatrical. They want and expect that the woman in the mound is sitting there in an interesting or pleasant way: something they would not care about – at least not in the same way – if they saw the same actions in one of the non-theatrical situations described in the introduction. Here the analysis of differences between interpretation of actions in theatrical situations and outside such situations may lead to better knowledge about what is essential for theatre than the approaches looking at theatrical works has brought forward.

These approaches and questions all have theoretical and historical implications. More collaboration between theoreticians and historians is necessary. For theoreticians it is important to realize that a lot of generalizations cannot be made since many results in theoretical theatre studies are only true for a limited number of theatrical works, or for some periods, some cultures or some groups of spectators. For historians, collaboration with theoreticians is important for them to become more attentive towards their own norms, values and implicit ideologies which colour their interpretations of historical theatrical events.

Given the incredible number of performances, the question may arise of what kind of selection and on what ground an integrated historical and theoretical approach could make to gain an insight in changing theatrical systems and communication processes. Intersubjective criteria for selection could be: clashes between the political and the theatrical systems as acts of censorship; and clashes between theatre makers and spectators where spectators could not understand the theatrical images or theatrical structures, or even where they experienced the theatrical images as interrupting their own aesthetic of social norms and values. Using such selection criteria, a history of theatrical arts and media is possible informing us of changes in conventions, norms and values applied to theatrical works. It forces us to describe and analyze the dominant traditions and its innovations. It also forces us to not choose as a point of departure those literary canons of drama texts which have become classic ones.

Even less attention has been paid to the system aspects of theatre, film, and television than has been paid to the reception side of theatrical communication. These system aspects, however, provide the conditions under which the theatrical products are produced. The explanation as to why so many more Swedish spectators visit theatrical performances in their country than Dutch spectators do in their country cannot be found by looking only at the qualities of the theatrical works. Performances which attract so much attention in Stockholm would not do the same in Amsterdam. A comparative analysis of the financing structures, of the status which one may obtain by going to the theatre, of the alternatives for social contacts, and so on, provide a possible basis for such explanations.

Media comparison
An important result of the broadened scope of some departments of theatre studies is that the attention paid to film and television stimulates a comparison of theatrical arts and media. This is important since the theories in

the field of theatre, film and television developed quite separately without paying much attention to developments in the neighbouring disciplines. Many concepts such as identification, catharsis, focalization, and so on, are alike or could use the same kind of general theories. Definition of these concepts in a general theory, afterwards specifying to the different subgenres seems nearly self-evident. Also, when the theatrical disciplines focus on different problem areas an inter-exchange is fruitful. For a long time, the film theories have had a psychological orientation – for instance, the work of Munsterberg (1916) or Arnheim (1957) – and have paid attention to what was seen as the most filmic elements: montage and the point of view of the camera. Little attention was paid to analyses of the staged world. This, however, is what the theatre theories used to focus on – the ways the theatrical world is staged and presented. These different orientations can be seen as complementary. In the seventies, Thomas Kuchenbuch combined the orientations in his "Filmanalyse" (...). Especially in these times when theatre, film, and television makers like to work in different theatrical genres and even break down conventions of the subgenres – such as between dance and theatre, or between mime and theatre – scholars should not stick to old opinions about supposed essential characteristics of these genres which, in fact, are no more than historical norms, conventions, or appearances. It would stimulate research into new theatrical genres, or genres with theatrical aspects such as video-clips, computer-animation, and so on. It would also stimulate an analysis of different competencies, expectations, and reception strategies spectators activate when they interpret theatrical actions as belonging to one of the subgenres. A woman in a mound seen as an element in absurd theatre, in a television play, or in a happening or video-clip, will have consequences for differences in interpretations and evaluations. Doubt over which aesthetic norms should be applied was caused by a recent performance of Euripides Bacchae directed by a famous Dutch director Gerardjan Rijnders and performed by members of a dance company. The daily papers did not know whether to send the theatre critic or the dance critic to the performance. Some papers sent both, and each looked at quite different aspects of the same performance as though they had seen different performances: this is because they looked at it from totally different frameworks of reference with different norms and values. That the interest for such a comparative approach is increasing is shown by books such as Martin Esslin's "The Field of Drama" (1987), or by principal articles like Hickethier's "Film- und Fernsehanalyse in der Theaterwissenschaft" (1988), who also pleads for an analysis of acting aspects in the field of film and television studies.

A dissertation discussing the fundamental problems of media comparison departing from a theory of communicative action is in preparation (Kattenbelt in prep.)

Theoretical theatre studies
A consequence of the sketch of the situation of theory in theatre studies is not that – as Caroll (1988: 234) puts it in his very critical analysis of the state of the art in film theory – "We must start again". Too many interesting observations, careful analyses, and statements with a more or less explanative value could be thrown away too easily. A critical attitude should guarantee that we do not throw out the fictitious babies with the fictitious bath-water. We have to wonder what epistemological status the propositions within theatre studies have, or are aiming at. We have to be very critical to the external validity of the propositions. As many semiotical analyses are no more than hermeneutics in disguise, informing us more about what the scholar has seen than about the subject he is investigating, so many results of empirical analysis are formulated in general statements that do not pay attention to the question of which of the characteristics in the theatrical work that have activated some variables on the part of the spectator correlate with specific reactions. Sometimes variables such as sex, age, education, and so on correlate with differences in reactions; sometimes not. Before drawing too general conclusions, the researcher should ask for which theatrical works, which social groups, which cultural areas, and for which periods he wants to generalize his results – and why. In this respect, a critical attitude towards a lot of empirical research is correct because often attention is not paid to these kinds of generalization problems. It is not the number of figures behind the decimal point that makes the results trustworthy, but rather the attention paid to the generalization problem and to the ways in which hypotheses are operationalized in methods.

Intercultural research
Just as media comparison may be of great help in looking at the different theatrical genres with a more expanded mind, so too intercultural research into theatrical arts and media could be of great help. More aesthetics are possible in theatrical arts and media than the ones developed under the influence of dominant Western traditions – as theatrical forms in other cultures show. But here the attitude of the researcher should not be the attitude of a holiday maker impressed by the colourful and – to his eyes – exotic images and actions he meets. He has to be critical towards his

observations and should realize that he in fact sees what he has learned to see and what he wants to see. His observations are guided by his own framework of reference. To investigate whether supposed theatrical activities are indeed theatrical, and what function and meaning these actions have, is only possible by analyses of the system in which these actions take place, and by analyzing the meanings and effects on performers and onlookers. These meanings can be different for an outsider – which, per definition, the researcher from another culture is.

Dutch theatre studies
What role can Dutch theatre studies play in theatre research? That an emphasis on theoretical reflection has been made right from the beginning of theatre studies in Holland is made clear by the external university lectureships of Balthasar Verhagen and of Willy Pos. Verhagen wrote "Dramaturgie" (Dramaturgy) in 1927, and Pos re-edited it in 1963. Since the chairs for Theatre Studies in Utrecht and Amsterdam were founded in the sixties, historical theatre studies have been paid attention to in the work of professors Hans de Leeuwe and Benjamin Hunningher. Hunningher's book "The Origin of the Theatre" even stimulated an international discussion. In the seventies and eighties, a more theoretical orientation again became clear in the work of the new professors Hogendoorn (Amsterdam) and Schoenmakers (Utrecht) with contributions to theatre semiotics, performance analysis, and reception research.

The Dutch theatre itself received relatively little attention from the university institutes (exceptions were the dissertations from Pos on Defresne, and from De Jong on Heijermans). The main contribution to the history of Dutch Theatre came from an outsider, Ben Albach, who was awarded an honourary degree for his scientific work.

A more systematic approach in Dutch historical theatre studies is necessary to delve into the many sources which provide information on performances, theatre makers, audiences, and theatre systems. Here the same selection criteria as mentioned above could be applied. It means that research should not restrict itself to the performances of drama texts which have become part of the literary canons, or been labelled 'classic', but also – and especially – to those kinds of performances which give insight into the changes in theatrical conventions, norms, and values. Beside such criteria, the importance of national developments for international theatre history could also be an important selection criterion. Unique material such as the Abele Spelen, or many Rederijkersperformances, the Amsterdamse Schouwburg, or the acting ideas of, for instance, Jelgerhuis, should be presented in international editions.

Beside this historical research focusing on Dutch sources, a continuation of the theoretical orientation seems fruitful. Active participation in international discussion is necessary. It was a pity that the work of Verhagen (Dramaturgy) and of Van der Kun (Handelingsaspecten in het drama) were never topics in international discussion: it was not because of the quality of these works, but because the books were not written in an international language. Institutions in those countries which have similar problems should pay more attention to the translation of scientific work.

Is there a solution to the problem of the tension between passion and reason which was seen as a current causing theatrical studies to drift between theatrical practice and scholarship? In fact, two solutions are mentioned. The first is to define clearly the forum the scholar is writing for: Does he want to inform the general public of his opinions and his analyses of theatrical arts, or does he want to contribute something to scientific knowledge about aspects of theatrical processes in societies? In the second case, the passions for the subject of study may play a role in the context of discovery. In the context of justification, all agreements on the question of what transforms knowledge into scientific knowledge should be followed. This solution distinguishes between activities within the theatre system and those within a scientific system. A second solution is to apply the same distinction to the departments for theatre studies. It means distinguishing between theatre studies as a research institution and theatre studies as an educational institution, each with their different demands. In preparing students for functions in theatrical practices it is also essential to train them in interpretation and evaluation of theatrical works; that means reflecting and writing about their passions for the theatrical arts and media and about the norms and values which, for them, are at issue. In preparing students for scientific work in the rigid sense we have to realize that not only methods necessary to answer the scholarly purposes of intersubjective communication should be learned, but that we also have to stimulate the students to reflect upon their astonishment at theatrical communication. Scholars who have many rational methods at their disposal, but who have no real passionate astonishment at human activities and competencies will never be able to formulate the relevant questions. It is not the method itself which will result in interesting research, but rather it is the statement of the problem in relation to the effectiveness of the methods chosen that will do so. Perhaps here we scholars can learn something from a practitioner like Brecht who stated at the beginning of his play "The Exception and the Rule":

"Find it estranging even if not very strange
Hard to explain even if it is the custom
Hard to understand even if it is the rule..."

References

Albach, B., J. Punt en M. Corver, 1946. *Nederlandsch toneelleven in de 18e eeuw.* Amsterdam.
Albach, B., 1965. *Duizend jaar toneel in Nederland.* Bussum.
Arnheim, R., 1957. *Film as Art.* Berkeley - Los Angeles.
Appollonio, M., 1930. *Storia della Commedia dell'arte.* Rome/Milano.
Andrew, D., 1984. *Concepts in Film Theory.* Oxford: Oxford University Press.
Arnott, K., 1981. An introduction to Theatrical Scholarship. *Theatre Quarterly* (X) 39: 29-42.
Bablet, D., J. Jaquot (eds.), 1970. *Les Voies de la Création Théâtrale.* Paris
Barish, J., 1985. *The Anti-theatrical Prejudice.* Berkeley, Los Angeles, London.
Baker, G.P., 1919. *Dramatic Technique.* Boston
Bauer, L., Elfriede Ledig & Michael Schaudig, 1987. *Strategien der Filmanalyse.* Zehn Jahre Münchener Filmphilologie Prof.dr. Klaus Kanzog zum 60. Geburtstag. München. (Diskurs Film Band 1).
Bazin, A., 1959. *Qu'est-ce que le cinéma?* Paris.
Beckerman, B., 1970. *Dynamics of Drama: Theory and Method of Analysis.* New York.
Berg, J., 1987. *Bestandsaufnahme Film- und Fernsehwissenschaft in der Bundesrepublik Deutschland. Dokumente einer Tagung.* Münster.
Birbaumer, U., 1972. Spielformen im Fernsehen. Medienwissenschaftlicher Ansatz zur Untersuchung der Mikrostrukturen. *Maske und Kothurn* (18) 3.
Bordewijk, C., 1988. *Pinter Appeal. A Comparative Study of Response to the Homecoming.* (dissertation). University of Amsterdam.
Bordwell, D., 1985. *Narration in the Fiction Film.* London: Methuen.
Caroll, N., 1988. *Mystifying Movies: Fads & Fallacies in Contemporary Film Theory.* New York: Columbia University Press.
Caroll, N., 1988. *Philosophical Problem of Classical Film Theory.* Princeton: Princeton University Press.
Casetti, F., 1990. *D'un regard l'autre. Le film et son spectateur.* Lyon.
Dietrich, M., 1971. Sinn und Notwendigeit von integrativwissenschaftlich koordinierter Grundlagenforschung in ihrer Beziehung zur Theaterwissenschaft. *Maske und Kothurn,* (17) 275-284.
Esslin, M., 1987. *The Field of Drama.* London & New York: Methuen.
Fischer Lichte, E., 1983. *Semiotik des Theaters.* Tübingen (3 Bde)
Foucault, M., 1988. *Dit is geen pijp.* Amsterdam.
Goffman, E., 1975. *Frame Analysis.* Harmondsworth.
Hunningher, B., 1961. *The Origin of the Theater, an Essay.* New York.
Hwang, D.H., 1988. *M. Butterfly.* Harmondsworth.
Istel, E., 1984. Die Uraufführung, die Pariser Presse, die Galli-Marié und der Tod Bizets.

In: A. Csampai & D. Holland (hrsg.): *Georges Bizet Carmen. Texte, Materialien, Kommentare*, 186-195. Reinbek bei Hamburg: Rowohlt.

Jarvie, I., 1987. *Philosphy of the Film. Epistemology, ontology, aesthetics*. New York and London.

Jong, E. de, 1967. *Herman Heijermans en de vernieuwing van het Europese drama*. (diss. Utrecht) Groningen.

Kanzog, K., 1988. Konstruktivistische Probleme der Filmwahrnehmung und Filmproto-kollierung. *In*: H. Korte & W. Faulstich (1988: 20-30).

Kesteren, A. & H. Schmid (hrsg.). *Moderne Dramentheorie*. Kronberg: Scriptor.

Klier, H. (hrsg.), 1981. *Theaterwissenschaft im deutschsprachigen Raum: Texte zum Selbstverständnis*. Darmstadt: Wissenschaftliche Buchgesellschaft.

Kindermann, H., 1966. Theaterwissenschaft. In: M. Hürlimann, *Das Atlantisbuch des Theaters*, 414-433. Zürich.

Knilli, F. & S. Reinecke, 1988. Filmanalyse aus medienwissenschaftlicher Sicht: Zur Praxis an der TU Berlin. *In*: H. Korte & W. Faulstich (1988: 31-39).

Knudsen, H., 1971. *Methodik der Theaterwissenschaft*. Stuttgart, Berlin, Köln, Mainz.

Korte, H. & W. Faulstich (Hrsg.), 1988. *Filmanalyse interdisziplinär*. Göttingen: Vandenhoeck & Ruprecht. (Zeitschrift für Literaturwissenschaft und Linguistik (Lili Beiheft 15)).

Kowzan, T., 1975. *Littérature et spectacle*. La Haye - Paris: Mouton.

Kracauer, S., 1960. *Theory of Film. The Redemption of Physical Reality*. New York.

Kreuzer, H., 1980. *Fernsehforschung und Fernsehkritik*. Göttingen: Vandenhoeck & Ruprecht. (Zeitschrift für Literaturwissenschaft und Linguistik Beiheft 11).

Kuchenbuch, T., 1978. *Filmanalyse. Theorien, Modelle, Kritik*. Köln.

Kun, J.I.M. van der, 1938. *Handelingsaspecten in het drama*. Nijmegen.

Kutscher, A., 1949 .*Grundriss der Theaterwissenschaft*. 2. überarb. Aufl. München. (1st pr. 1931/36).

Langsted, J., 1989. Towards Modern Theatre Research. Nordic Theatre Studies. *Yearbook for Theatre Research in Scandinavia*, 2/3: 174-181.

Leek, R., 1988. *Shakespeare in Nederland*. Kroniek van vier eeuwen Shakespeare in Nederlandse vertalingen en op het Nederlands toneel. Zutphen.

Mander, J., 1978. *Four arguments for the elimination of television*. New York.

Marcus, S., 1973. *Mathematische Poetik*. Boekarest, Frankfurt am Main.

Metz, C., 1971. *Langage et Cinéma*. Paris.

Metz, C., 1977. *Le signifiant imaginaire. Psychanalyse et Cinéma*. Union Générale d'éditions.

Metz, C., 1982. *Psychoanalysis and Cinema. The Imaginery Signifier*. Houndsmill: The Macmillan Press.

Mic, C., 1927. *La commedia dell' arte ou, le théâtre des comediens italiens des XVIe, XVIIe et XVIIIe siècles*. Paris.

Munsterberg, H., 1916. *The Film: A psychological Study*. New York (reprint 1970).

Murray, G., 1912. Excursus on the Ritual Forms preserved in Greek Tragedy. In: J.E. Harrison: *Themis. A Study of the social origins of Greek religion*. Cambridge.

Niessen, C., 1956. Theaterwissenschaft. In: *Aufgaben deutscher Forschung*. Bd. 1. 2. Aufl. Köln, Opladen.

Paul, A., 1971. Theaterwissenschaft als Lehre vom theatralischen Handeln. *Kölner Zeitschrift für Soziologie und Sozialpsychologie* (23) 1.

Paul, A., 1972. Theater als Kommunikationsprocess. *Diskurs*, 1: 33

Pavis, P., 1980. *Dictionnaire du Théâtre*. Paris: Editions Sociales. (New Enlarged Edition 1987)

Pfister, M., 1977. *Das Drama. Theorie und Analyse*. München.

Pos, W., 1971. *De toneelkunstenaar August Defresne*. Amsterdam.

Price, A. (ed.), 1983. *Shakespeare: A Midsummer Night's Dream. A Casebook*. London and Basingstoke.

Postman, N., 1986. *Amusing Ourselves to Death*. London, New York.
Rea, K., 1989. *A Better Direction. A national enquiry into the training of director for theatre, film and television*. London.
Salt, B., 1983. *Film Style and Technology: History and Analysis*. London: Starword.
Schälzky, H., 1980. *Empirisch-quantitative Methoden in der Theaterwissenchaft*. München: Kitzinger. (Münchener Beiträge zur Theaterwissenchaft 7).
Schälzky, H., 1989. Studenten der Theaterwissenschaft. Ergebnisse einer Studentenbefragung am Institut für Theaterwissenschaft der Universität München im Wintersemester 1986/87. In: *Symposium: Der Wert des Studiums der Theaterwissenschaft für die Theaterpraxis*. Köln (Schriftenreihe des Deutschen Bühnenvereins Band IV.2.)
Schmidt, S.J., 1980. *Grundriss der empirischen Literaturwissenschaft*. Bd.1: Der gesellschaftlichten Handlungsbereich Literatur. Braunschweig/Wiesbaden.
Schoenmakers, H., 1988. To be, wanting to be, forced to be. Identification processes in theatrical situations. In: W. Sauter (ed.) *New Directions in Audience Research*. Utrecht (Icrar Publication 2).
Schoenmakers, H., 1989. *The Spectator in the Leading Role*. Lecture at the plenary meeting of the XIth World Congress of the International Federation for Theatre Research "New Directions in Theatre Research" Stockholm 29 May - 4 June.
Schöll, N. & J. Kleindiek, 1970. Braucht das Theater eigene Wissenschaft? In: *Klier*: 171-178.
Souriau, E., 1950. *Les deux cent mille situations dramatiques*. Paris: Flammarion.
Steinbeck, D., 1970. *Einleitung in die Theorie und Systematik der Theaterwissenschaft*. Berlin.
Tinchon, H.-J., 1972. *Untersuchung der Objektivierung von Zuschauerreaktionen auf theatralischen Spielsendungen im Fernsehen unter Anwendung elektrophysiologischer Methoden* (diss.) Wien.
Trendall A.D. & T.B.L. Webster, 1971. *Illustrations of Greek Drama*. London
Verhagen, B., 1963. *Dramaturgie*. Amsterdam. 2e dr. bezorgd door W.Ph. Pos.
Vince, R.W., 1989. *Issues in Theatre Historiography*. Lecture at the plenary meeting of the XIth World Congress of the International Federation for Theatre Research "New Directions in Theatre Research" Stockholm 29 May - 4 June
Webster, T.B.L, 1962. Monuments Illustrating Tragedy and Satyr Plays. In: *Bulletin of the Institute of Classical Studies of the University of London*. London
Zielske, H., 1970. Theatergeschichte oder praktisches Theater? Bemerkungen über den Gegenstand der Theaterwissenschaft. In: *Klier*; 164-170.

The continuing future of the present in the visual arts[*]

A.W. Reinink

Investigations in the field of art history are always concerned with the wonder of life. Nor will it be otherwise in the coming decade. They will focus on the miracle of the ability of the human eye in confrontation with natural objects and artefacts. They will refer to the observations of millions and millions of people – people who once looked, are looking, or will look during what, in the nineties as well, will be called the past, the present or the future.

The human eye, be it that of artists, their audience and researchers of art history, has its physiological and cultural limitations. This is, and will probably remain, the chief fascination of the study of the visual arts. One of its main tasks will continue to be to open up new ways to adequately support our visual memory, and to clear up the misunderstandings surrounding the appreciation of works of art. By doing so, the study of the visual arts has performed, and will continue to perform, a wholesome and hygienic function, all the more so because the creators of those works of art – the artists – are continually engaged in the exploration of the physiological and cultural limits of our visual abilities *in general*. They record *and* manipulate our visual traditions. If we consider this fact properly, we cannot avoid the conclusion that this field of study has a broad impact. The importance of the discipline indeed banishes the futile question of its 'social relevance'.

It might seem that I am underrating the investigation of the physical properties of the works of art and architecture by stressing the study of 'ways of seeing'. Of course it will be necessary to develop our know-how in the field of preservation. It will be of vital importance, in the nineties too, to increase our expertise of techniques of preservation and restoration. We do want to pass on our inheritance in as perfect a condition as possible to the generations of the twenty-first century and beyond, and we are confident that much work will be done and much progress will be made towards achieving this goal. We also know that the study of art is entirely dependent on the physical presence of the work of art or architecture. Still, the guardianship of this part of our field of study will continue to remain the somewhat restricted domain of experts.

Experts speak the language of specialists. Their jargon is often of fundamental importance. This is especially true, for instance, in the field of medicine. The layman, for whose benefit and health that discipline is continuously advancing, is unable to understand the specialist literature. Still he can be confident – and rightly so – that specialists ultimately communicate with each other for the common good.

The same should be true within the discipline of art history, not only between specialists in preservation, but also between those who make inventories of works of art and architecture or those who interpret those works. This means – and it applies equally to the nineties – that art historians should always bear in mind, as a moral duty, the central aim of their discipline: to work for the eventual benefit of the community at large, which can only be achieved by the commitment of the historians of art. They are obliged to inform the public about the issues that matter, the issues that are of existential value. Otherwise, the discipline will only be devoted to the lifeless rather than the life-enhancing.

In this perspective I would like to dwell upon the special position of art history among the various disciplines of the humanities (one which it partly shares with archaeology). The history of art is a historical discipline for which the artefact – the work of art or architecture – is the be-all and end-all. As a result, those artefacts occupy an entirely different position from, say, the illustrations of a narrative account. For art historians, the presence of the work of art is *the* central issue. This means that their field of study is more closely concerned with the present than is the case with most other historical disciplines. This constitutes the background to the title of this essay.

The fascinating thing about this discipline is that the art object is here, in the 'now'. It has been given to us, in most cases by former generations. It carries the traces of their activities. What we have is not those activities themselves, but a configuration of materials of this earth and nothing else. The activities of our kinsmen, the traces of which we can observe on the object – however altered and aged they may be by the passage of time – can be taken as the results of their planning of the future. All human reasoning aimed at action can be considered as such. This is especially true of architecture: it is not just that buildings are raised for use in the future, but every action leading to their completion has this orientation. Thus we can regard every work of art – not just architecture – as the material traces of the planning of the future by its creator or creators.

However, no one can tell the full story of the underlying reasoning. Even the artist himself cannot fully explain what considerations led him to the final result, because nobody's memory is infallible. Every artefact is thus enigmatic by definition. This is the challenge facing the art historian, and this is the reason why every generation feels the need to develop new interpretations: the continuing future of the present.

1. The state of the art

The image of this present is indeed very diverse. Even if one omits the history of non-Western art (within Europe, a traditional limitation which should be abolished before long), the discipline is extremely rich in scope, and often in quality. Very many intelligent people are producing good, even excellent work.

It is virtually impossible to give a complete overview of this multicoloured image. One only has to consult the programmes of the giant Annual Meetings of the College Art Association of America of the past few years. About two thousand members (artists included) now attend these meetings, which are held in places like the New York or San Francisco Hilton hotels. The programmes include a wide variety of sessions, ranging from 'Recent Discoveries' (from the whole world), 'The Middle Ages and Renaissance in Northern Europe: The Psychical Context' or 'Americanism: The Old World Discovers the New' to 'Garden History: Where Did It Come From? Where Is It Going?', 'Japanese Art and Culture in Transition: Personality and Patronage in the Twelfth and Thirteenth Centuries' and 'French Art During The Reign of Louis XIV (1643-1715)'. (Here I am simply quoting the first six announced for the San Francisco Meeting held in February 1989.)

Quite clearly, no one could produce an introductory survey of such a market, with hundreds of people presenting their papers. This is not only because today one can expect a range of methods of hitherto unknown diversity. One could almost say: 'Anything goes'. We are living in an age in which everybody can believe that his or her approach is the standard. Thus we can expect to find semiotic, deconstructivist, Marxist and feminist approaches alongside more traditional ones like style criticism or iconology. Moreover, the new media applied in modern art blur the boundaries of both the existing methods and the criteria of art itself.

So today we are witnessing an eclectic carousel of methods which some people have chosen to designate as post-modern. The whole scene can also be characterized as being devoid of oppositions or clashes between schools of thought and of method. There is virtually no *Kunsthistorikerstreit*.[1] The post-modern lack of norms has induced people to characterize the situation as a crisis in the history of art. One could ask, when was there no crisis? I prefer to regard the contemporary scene as a ferment of new ideas born of a deep curiosity. The thousands and thousands of students who enter the universities in the Western world every year are evidence of that desire to enquire.

Not only at the College Art Association of America, but also at national associations of art historians in countries like Austria, West Germany and Great Britain can we find evidence of enormous inventiveness and energy. In the programmes of their annual or bi-annual meetings there is a happy tendency to group certain issues under a theme. Thus the *Österreichischer Kunsthistorikerverband* (an association established only seven years ago, which is remarkable in a country with an old tradition in the discipline) has held an admirable series of meetings with themes such as: 'The History of Art as an Institution', 'Art History and General History', or 'Art and Art History'. The last conference (in September 1989) was devoted to the theme 'Art History amidst Changing Values' (*Kunstgeschichte im*

---

[1] The scene is dominated by a sort of unbearable tolerance, with perhaps one exception, that being the row about Svetlana Alpers's book, *The Art of Describing* (1983) which had the effect of a stone thrown into a pond. The author attempts to demonstrate that Dutch seventeenth-century painting was largely inspired by a desire to represent reality with great optical precision, leaving little room for inner allegorical meanings or other *sous-entendres*. I have never seen so many scholars so infuriated. I even heard one distinguished art historian complain that too many people were reading the book. Why make such a fuss over a supposedly bad and irrelevant work?

Wertewandel), during which the main facets of the community (universities, museums, architectural heritage and the independent professions) were discussed in a consistent way and at a very high level. Of course, not all of this dealt with research on art history, but it is a fact that all the main participants on the floor were competent researchers in the field. They demonstrated their liveliness of mind and a keen awareness of their predicament amidst the *Wertewandel*.

The existence of the various national associations of art historians also draws attention to the issue of interdisciplinarity. I am not sure whether the participation of both artists and art historians in the College Art Association of America has a mutually beneficial effect or not. The British Association of Art Historians, however, seems to benefit from its open attitude to other disciplines. The wide range of interdisciplinary themes presented at its 1989 annual conference was a convincing example of how the history of art can have a real impact on essential issues of the day. Thus, by treating specific themes related to 'Landscape Painting' as part of the general subject 'The Landscape' and all its dimensions (ecological, literary, sociological, etc.), the discipline can make an authentic contribution to the thinking on fundamental matters which affect society at large.

On the subject of society, I should like to say something about the effect of finance on research. Money entails competition, also between disciplines. Indeed, Wolf Lepenies' *Drei Kulturen* (1985) are all three engaged in the field of the study of art and architecture. Science is involved in the development of identification, preservation and restoration techniques. Here, we have recently witnessed not only competition between experts, but also fortunately, some examples of good cooperation between them, as shown by the impressive Rembrandt Research Project. What used to be two different cultures in the approach to ancient buildings by technologists (e.g. experts in the building trade or dendrochronology) and by architectural historians are showing a gratifying tendency towards cooperation or even personal union.

But people involved in the 'third culture', the sociologists, psychologists and social geographers, have also widened their field of study, and have occupied themselves with the visual arts, historical towns and architecture. In the 1970's we witnessed the almost suicidal efforts of architectural historians to question their own discipline's right to exist. "(Is) Architectural History a Social Science?" was the daring title of an international symposium in May 1977. Inquiring scholars like Pierre Bourdieu did extremely important work in investigating the sociological and psychological foundations of taste and the art market.

Strangely enough, people from neighbouring fields of study in the humanities are often the ones with the greatest misconceptions when it comes to the use and interpretation of images from the past. Time and again one finds general historians illustrating their books with reproductions of pictures, drawings or prints without realizing how these age-old images respond to specific historical laws of representation. Hilarious blunders abound.

2. To sum up

How should we sum up the present 'State of the Art'? It is not feasible in an essay of this size to give an adequate impression of the 3,000 different subjects listed in the eighth world compilation of *Sponsored Research in the History of Art X*, covering the academic years 1987-1988 and 1988-1989, issued by the Center for Advanced Study in the Visual Arts in Washington (1989), nor of those featured in the programme of the Twenty-Seventh International Congress for the History of Art in Strasbourg (September 1989), under the title *L'Art et les Révolutions*.

I am not sure if all the 543 American PhD dissertations included in a recent list from a bookseller in New York State meet the qualification of the first sentence of this essay, or the moral obligation I dared to refer to as I discussed the use of jargon. Most of the titles deal with Italian art and architecture. Although one cannot say that the list shows a bias towards certain major themes, it is undoubtedly the case that there is a lack of truly new subjects. Most of the titles seem to follow the well-beaten track.

It has even been argued recently that research into the history of art is showing an increasing tendency to produce more publications on fewer subjects. This proposition was put forward by a distinguished art historian (one of the 2,500 employed in the German Federal Republic) who counted the number of articles published in the main periodicals over the last thirty years. He reached the conclusion that one can speak of a world hierarchy of 'champion'-artists, with Picasso at the top and descending by way of Dürer, Rubens and so on. There may be some truth in this observation, but it is certainly not the only valid conclusion.

What matters here is the fact that there are monopolistic tendencies at work. Researchers concentrating on the top of the hierarchy tend to lay an exclusive claim to subjects. Outbursts of research activity are prompted by the cash which suddenly begins to flow on the occasion of the anniversary of the deaths or births of famous artists. Such coincidences are very rarely connected with the intrinsic value of the art, or to the relative necessity of new research on that particular artist. Groups of scholars appear to act like small firms, occasionally handing out commissions to smaller groups or individuals. The outcome is the thick exhibition catalogue which is too heavy to carry.

One wonders indeed whether money is not corrupting the independent eye that can no longer find its way as easily to the watchtower that will give it a view over the monopolistic walls. Money of course *can* do a lot of good, but we must be aware of its negative effects. It certainly *does* do a lot of good, as has recently been shown by the support of the J. Paul Getty Trust for infrastructural research projects such as bibliographical systems, for current projects and many other things. But we have also recently been confronted with a phenomenon that was unknown before: archives and architectural drawings can become commodities. Strange new powers are at work, even in the central domain of research itself.

The discipline of art history has accomplished many things since it came into existence in around 1750. It has compiled vast inventories of buildings and collections in the western hemisphere, and has made a start in doing so for the rest of the world. It has developed sophisticated methods of identification and attribution. It has known impressive schools of interpretation of individual buildings and works of art, ranging from theories of a purely materialistic and technical determinism to a view of a total dependence on the 'spirit' of contemporary culture. It has often risen to great heights in order to gain a bird's-eye view of the history of art and its various stages, thereby developing idealistic theories according to which the unfolding art tends to a final goal on the one hand, or ascribing the differences between styles to a historicist notion like the 'will to form' (*Kunstwollen*) on the other. Heroic efforts have been undertaken to construct a systematic 'science of the arts' (*Kunstwissenschaft*). One of the jewels in the crown has been the rise of iconology within the circle of scholars associated with the Warburg Library (founded in Hamburg, now in London), a super-discipline that endeavours to uncover (often subconscious) deeper meanings in works of art. This school, founded by Aby Warburg (1866-1929), has systematically opened up the history of art to other fields of study, thus paving the way for the development of a concept of the world of all artefacts as a system of visual communication in which psychology not infrequently plays a prominent role.

More than two hundred years' work by the discipline had generated whole libraries of books and periodicals and countless categorizations of buildings and art collections when, at the end of the 1960's, the movement of the critical art history made its appearance. It had a salubrious effect both

internally and externally. The main clash between the old establishment
and the young critical scholars took place at a meeting of the German
Association of Art Historians in Cologne in 1970. The discipline was shocked
by Marxist analyses of the background to art and architecture. The whole
issue of the sacrosanct autonomy of the individual work of art was openly
challenged. What had seemed exclusively aesthetic motives which gave
rise to the beauty of the porticoed villas of the sixteenth-century architect
Palladio were now analyzed as a set of half-conscious intentions meant to
express the self-evident domination of the common people by the Venetian
gentry. Here, too, the Marxist notion of 'false consciousness' (*falsches
Bewusstsein*) was introduced. The object was to demonstrate that all the
altruistic and ethical motives the landed gentry ascribed to themselves
when they built their villas in that particular form, were in reality egoisti-
cal, and served the sole purpose of perpetuating their domination.
Thus the concept of substructure and superstructure (*Basis und Überbau*) was
introduced into the field of art history. Scholars became aware of the
impact of economic and social circumstances on cultural phenomena. As a
result, even non-Marxist scholars returned to the archives and embarked
on varieties of research that concentrated more on the daily predicaments
of artists than on the details of the individual commissions they received.
One can argue that the critical movement of the late sixties and seventies
has left a legacy to the whole discipline. Even the most conservative of
scholars now encourages or engages in research on broad subjects such as
the history of all the houses in one street or of all the buildings on a country
estate, not excluding the living quarters of the poor. But there is more to
the legacy than this. It has paved the way for all those approaches we
classified above as 'Anything goes'. However, they have their origin not
only in this general liberating critical movement, but also in a fundamental
way in the influential writings of E.H. Gombrich. In his main work, *Art and
Illusion* (1960), the psychology of perception, often in connection with
everyday and banal images, is introduced in a way that has become almost
inescapable for whole generations of art historians. It is here that the main
foundation was laid for what was described above as a conception of the
world of all artefacts as one system of communication.
In the post-war decades another scholar, H. van de Waal (1910-1972),
who, like Gombrich followed the Warburg tradition, designed a method
for the consistent ordering of such a system. With his *Iconclass*, which has
been introduced into computer software, we now have an easy, quick and
universal method of accessing iconographical data. Alongside the
infrastructural provisions for other fields of study, such as international

bibliographies and catalogues of collections, the computer has also entered the world of art history. Its full deployment is only a matter of time.

3. The future: reassessments and new techniques

The computer, naturally, will have an increasing impact on research in the history of art. In many respects this process will be connected with ongoing projects such as inventories. One of the basic tasks of art historians will continue to be the registration of our architectural heritage and public collections of art objects. There have always been arrears in these activities and there will always be new art and architecture which demand stocktaking. What the computer can do is make these inventories more accessible and easier to consult. However, it will not alter the discipline in any fundamental way. We will return to this point later.

There is no reason to doubt that a number of other traditional activities will continue during the nineties. Monographs on artists, architects, architectural *ensembles*, *catalogues raisonnés* and the like will still be written and published, but there will probably be a shift of focus. I would not be surprised if more attention were paid to the traditionalist currents in twentieth-century art. Further, a renewed interest in Northern European art from around 1600 has already emerged, and will certainly be an important topic in the coming years.

Another shift of attention is already affecting the relationship between metropolitan and local art. The next annual meeting of the British Association of Art Historians, to be held in Dublin in March 1990, will be entirely devoted to this theme. What we have witnessed up to now is the appreciation of local or 'provincial' arts by the standards and from the point of view of the great art centres from which they are considered to be derived. Monsieur Pierre, holding his exhibition in a gallery at Avignon, is delighted when critics compare his work to Picasso's. Equally pleased is the owner of the gallery, who has done his best to nurture this reputation. It is fine that every small town now has three galleries, but they should not make constant references to 'great' art. This description of a fictitious provincial situation may also reflect a trend in art scholarship, which still has too great a tendency to compare local artists to famous ones.

We may well witness another shift of focus. A country like Spain is now coming increasingly to the fore, and we should not be surprised to see a boom in the study of its art. In addition, other European countries whose presence on the continent had been all but forgotten will feature more in the general scene of art history. All this will be related to the emergence of a new European identity in the coming decade.

Reassessments

However, the reformulation and redefinition of some notions and methods also seem necessary. Do we still know what we mean by 'influence' when we use this word in our discussions? What exactly do we mean when we say that two figurations are comparable? There has been renewed interest in the connoisseur methods of Giovanni Morelli (1816-91). Even the computer has been enlisted in order to implement the typical Morellian way of comparing two works of art by concentrating on seemingly unimportant details like earlobes or fingernails, a reduction by which the painter can be, so to speak, surprised in the act. The computer should here function as an instrument for quicker and more objective diagnosis. Given the problems, described below with the computer's recognition of figurations, this would seem to be a very courageous effort.

It may also be necessary to develop new definitions in the field of architectural history and the resulting theories concerning the stewardship of our architectural heritage. The traditional notion of a 'monument' has been evolving since the European Heritage Year of 1975. I consider this a positive development. It means that we cannot forever go on applying the traditional notions which are still commonly held by those responsible for our cultural heritage. In my view, there is an alarming cultural gulf between those who know everything about old building techniques and materials on the one hand, and those who are interested in what motivates young artists and architects on the other. The official theoreticians and the responsible people, I fear, always have a hidden ideal in their heads: that the world will once again look the way it did in the Middle Ages. Of course am I exaggerating, reality will also enter into their thinking. But it will not altogether dispel the dream. We must find new definitions (and look to thinkers from former generations) with which we can work in a frank and up-to-date manner. Terms like replica, monument, document, ruin, *Denkmal*, authenticity, historicity and others should be redefined as much as the relationship between notions like 'companionship with history' and the experience of beauty *hic et nunc*.

As in previous decades, the art historian wil be continuesly concerned with reassessing his function in society at large. The history of the profession will be the subject of new studies, perhaps with more stress on the circumstances under which representatives of the discipline have worked. For instance, how was the functioning of a man like Franz Kugler (1808-58) influenced by the composite nature of his professional career? (He was a civil servant in the Prussian Ministry of Culture, a university professor and a museum curator, as well as being a poet and draughtsman.)

Finally, it is likely that more scope will be creatd for psychoanalysis in the history of art. It could possibly make a breakthrough in the coming decade. Psychoanalysis should gradually become a self-evident part not only of scholarly but also of political and even daily life. Our discipline does not possess a wide and workable platform for serious psychoanalytical debate. Let us hope that recent discussions of the work of the great art historians, like Warburg and Riegl, are indications of a future flowering of such a much-needed development.

New techniques
Now we may return to the issue of automation. However much work has been devoted to it, we are as yet unable to fully assess the future role of the computer. There is no doubt that, next to airlines, libraries today boast one of the most successfully shared databases. This is also of great benefit to libraries of art history. We have already mentioned the role the computer has come to play in activities such as the compilation of inventories, bibliographies and the consistent iconographical database called *Iconclass*.
One of the specific problems in the history of art, when it comes to automation, consists in the difficulty of linking art objects and art information. Most information systems, including those used for art, are basically verbal in nature or, at any rate retrieval methods depend upon the word. This could be considered an anomaly. There is no natural connection between words and objects. This central problem has not yet been resolved satisfactorily, let alone that we will soon be in possession of a universally compatible system.[2]

Some people may have great expectations of computer developments in the history of art. There will of course be some results by the year 2000, but they are not likely to be very significant. We will witness the increased use of compact disks (often sold by museums) on which large collections of images can be recorded. Up to now, though, the quality of these images has generally been very poor, due to the low resolution of the VDU (large dots, no details visible). Some recent methods of digitalized image storage and display have reached such a high pitch of perfection that the art historian can use them in his research. The equipment which produces these large, high-quality images on the screen is very expensive. A broad application

---

[2] The ambitious J. Paul Getty Trust project, set up to inventory the needs of art historians in this field, has resulted in the publication *The Art Historian at Work* (1988). In spite of its great documentary value, the book can hardly be said to contain guidelines for the future.

of it would of course bring the price down. Such a trend seems improbable, however, because this kind of digitalized image storage requires a very large amount of computer memory. Moreover, the collections which are in the process of being computerized are not compatible with these high-quality techniques.

Computers and art history do not make a happy marriage. This is due to the limitations of existing software in recognizing figurations. If we want to compile an anthology of poems about autumn, and we already have a poetry database, we can search for words like fall, October, November, etc. This yields a choice of poetic words quite quickly. One can even obtain a sharper focus, for instance by searching for words like mushroom or boletus. With images, however, we have no comparable retrieval system. Suppose we have introduced all the pictures by Monsieur Pierre (whose exhibition at Avignon we visited above) by scanning them into bitmaps (pictures on the computer screen consisting of many small, coloured dots). Now, if we ask the computer to show us all the pictures by Monsieur Pierre in which mushrooms are depicted, the screen will remain blank, let alone tell us why the critics compare his style to Picasso's.

If we had introduced titles and descriptions in words of Monsieur Pierre's works it would of course be different. And if we had the luck that the word mushroom (but probably not boletus) was in the thesaurus, we would succeed in obtaining the desired selection. The screen would show us the word mushroom, alongside the images. But here we have not searched among the visual material itself, but *only* in the database, which consists of words. This means that one is entirely dependent on the verbal selection we or others have made when analyzing and describing works of art.

Thus, in the autumn of this century it is still not possible for a computer to analyze and recognize figurations of a certain degree of complexity. (In the medical sciences, on the other hand, it now seems possible to have the computer analyze, by image-processing techniques, digital microscope images and make a distinction between circular and lancet-shaped microbes.) It seems improbable that the nineties will produce software that can be of real service to the art historian. His or her marvellous and sophisticated instrument will remain the human eye, whose vital importance I stressed at the beginning of this essay. Here we could perhaps add – like what Professor Dik exclaims in his chapter on linguistics – 'Poor computer!'.

Significant progress will probably be made with another sort of image processing: computer-aided drawing. Here we have images consisting of geometrically describable 'primitives', such as straight lines and circle segments. This digital technique uses 'vectorization', and was developed in the aircraft and automobile industry where it is known as CAD (Computer-Aided Design). Its main purpose is to represent three dimensions on a two-dimensional screen, especially of aerodynamic shapes. The great advantage of the computer is its ability to change the drawing continuously without having to redraw the elements which do not require alteration. (The reader who uses a word processor will understand immediately what the advantages are.) The importance of 'vectorization' for the art historian lies in the fact it can enable him to work with images of artefacts that are reduced to linear configurations. Such a reduction of course means a certain loss of information compared to the original. This drawback, however, is least apparent in drawing techniques which are based on well-established conventions for rendering the artefacts. This is the case with architectural drawings. In fact, many architects' offices already design with CAD. But the architectural historian can also profit from computer-aided drawing when he or she wants to reconstruct alternatives to a plan. Without having to redraw all the other elements the architectural historian can display on the screen (and have plotted on paper) the consequences of alternative details, not only of designs of individual buildings but also of physical town planning. The computer can perform this service both with two-dimensional drawings like plans or elevations, and with perspective representations. Thus it would be possible to create an almost cinematographic representation of the consequences of Nicholas Hawksmoor's proposals for streets and squares in Cambridge (1714). On the basis of his drawings one could walk through the town, as it were, thanks to a new technique which replaces years of work on the drawing board.

Another new tool, which will probably be increasingly applied and further developed, is so-called neutron activation autoradiography. To my knowledge this has so far only been used experimentally in two places, the New York Metropolitan Museum and the Staatsgalerie in Berlin-Dahlem. With this technique, paintings are made radioactive. The radiation is then registered on X-ray films. The main feature of this method is its ability to yield a variegated range of information. The radiation lasts about three months. During this period, every element (in the sense of the periodic system) becomes prominent in turn. As a result, one can obtain a far greater amount of data, which are also of greater variety than those available from ordinary X-ray photographs. This neutron activation autoradiography method has some disadvantages to which we will return in the final section of this essay.

The application of science in research into art objects will definitely not stop. On the contrary, it will be even more widely applied in the nineties. This tendency is linked to a trend that does not essentially involve science in a technical sense. It is a renewed interest in the work of art as an individual artefact. If inventive researchers are provided with favourable and relaxed circumstances (which will require liberal financial policies, among other things), many people will discover many unexpected things and reach the conclusion that research into the individual artefact has barely begun. If one really dares to look at the object in an unbiased way, and casts aside the filter that 200 years of art history have put between us and the work of art, new ideas could perhaps enter one's mind.

This could also be of importance for the already growing impact that art historians have on the preservation of works of art. Such a trend was observed at a session of preservation experts at the Annual Meeting of the College Art Association in Los Angeles in January 1989. They are more willing to merge their views with those of art historians. This implies that, on the one hand, art historians are enjoying preservation experts' confidence more then they used to, but that also, on the other hand, they should continue to develop a detached and objective eye – one that is not fettered by what it was once taught in the lecture room. What it has learnt in the classroom may be a way of looking at pictures with the knowledge of art treatises at the back of one's mind. A future learning process could be the development of a new awareness: the awareness that the reality of daily studio practice is barely touched upon in art treatise. The tradition of the main elements of that practice, namely the actual transmission of the culture of making and rendering, has always been passed on by non-verbal, practical instruction. By developing a fresh look at the artefacts, art historians can learn to formulate hypotheses that can be corroborated by what is, in fact, written between the lines of the treatise. In doing so they might possibly be able to reconstruct a 'studio language' of a certain school.

In the 1990's we will almost certainly witness a trend which appears to oppose the one I have just described, but which runs virtually parallel to it. Computer-aided techniques of digesting finds in archives enable us to gain a clearer view of the relationship between the individual work of art and the surrounding contemporary world. This is a necessary complement to the fresh look at the artefact itself.

4. The Netherlands

"Let us hope that soon young minds will set to work again who will exercise their eyes to the fullest. The present trials of Holland may have inter-

rupted many labours, but some day the enthusiasm, based on a sound tradition, is bound to revive". These are the final sentences of an essay, written by the famous Dutch connoisseur Frits Lugt during wartime in America. It appeared as one of the twenty chapters of a remarkable book: *The Contribution of Holland to the Sciences* (edited by A.J. Barnouw and B. Landheer, New York 1943).
The main trend of Lugt's essay is his bias against art history as an academic discipline. As a man who did not attend university and who had become a connoisseur by practical experience, he states with satisfaction that notions like the German *Kunstwissenschaft* or *Kunstgelehrter* barely have an equivalent in Dutch. This is not due to the anti-German feelings prevalent at the time, but is an expression of Lugt's deep conviction that the essence of the history of art lies in expertise and that this cannot be taught at a university.

The cry from afar that Frits Lugt sent out over the ocean to the postwar future was overheard barely three years later by the then 36-year-old H. van de Waal (1910-1972). In his inaugural lecture, *Traditie en bezieling* (Tradition and Inspiration; Leiden 1946), Van de Waal confirmed what Lugt had said in New York: Dutch art historians are generally wary of theoretical speculation because of their practical disposition. 'Our art historians have mainly been connoisseurs whose thorough knowledge has traced, attributed, dated and localized the material'.
These activities were indeed to be largely resumed after the War, both by those who had seen their labours interrupted and, as Lugt put it, by the 'young minds (...) who (would) exercise their eyes to the fullest'. In this context, Lugt rightly prophesied a great future for the now world-famous Rijksbureau voor Kunsthistorische Documentatie (Netherlands Institute for Art History). This national centre for those researching the history of art, where everything in the way of books, catalogues, notes and reproductions is available, had been founded in The Hague by the Dutch Government in 1931. Its foundation was due to the generous bequest of C. Hofstede de Groot, consisting of about 200,000 reproductions of Dutch and Flemish art, around 40,000 old sale catalogues (the richest series after Paris) and vast files of handwritten notes.
Those postwar years were generally a favourable time for all Dutch art historians. It was as if an empty freeway had been opened to them. Those were the years of the great exhibitions from abroad, especially from the recently defeated countries, from which masterpieces could easily be borrowed. In 1952, Amsterdam hosted the Seventeenth International Congress

of the History of Art. Research in the Netherlands was generally of a high
standard, but it mainly followed traditional lines.

Van de Waal was the only future postwar professor who was not mentioned by Lugt. He was not primarily a connoisseur. In his inaugural address,
Van de Waal pleads for an iconological approach. He is wise enough to
stress that iconology is not the answer to all the problems of art history: it
can only be regarded as a phase in the development of the science of art
(*kunstwetenschap*). His two-volume *Drie eeuwen vaderlandse geschied-
uitbeelding 1500-1800. Een iconologische studie* (Dutch Portrayal of History 1500-1800: an Iconological Study) had been completely typeset and
was ready to be printed in 1942, when the plates, which were hidden in St
Martin's church tower in Zaltbommel, were found and destroyed by the
German occupiers. (It was eventually published in 1952.) This book is an
original and eloquent demonstration of the iconological method as applied
in the Netherlands. Van de Waal compared sixteenth to eighteenth-century
representations of historical events that had mainly taken place before the
sixteenth century. In doing so he established an Archimedean point from
which he was able to map out the differences between the ways of representation characteristic of a period in the history of art. This enabled him to
develop a theory of the complicated process of creating of images and their
tradition within a culture. This fundamental masterpiece was not reviewed
till much later. It was the late Polish art historian, Jan Biaostocki, who,
shortly before Van de Waal's death, honoured it by a long appreciative
review in *The Art Bulletin* (1971), almost twenty years after its appearance
(and almost thirty years after its completion).

Although Van de Waal's *Geschied-uitbeelding* contained a summary in
English of more than sixty pages, one of the reasons for its relative obscurity
was the fact that the main text is in Dutch. We are rightly proud of our own
language. We should use it wherever we can. Most foreign art historians
who have specialized in Dutch art have a passive knowledge of it. But
when it comes to views of a more theoretical nature the specialists are
generally less interested and the scholars to whom they are addressed have
no knowledge of Dutch.

This is why the other truly brilliant Dutch art historian of the postwar
decades, J.A. Emmens (1924-1971), has also remained relative unknown.
In his *Rembrandt en de regels van de kunst* (Rembrandt and the Rules of
Art; 1968) he enters a brand new field which was unknown to Dutch art
historians: the comparative theory of art. Here the traditional image of
Rembrandt as a rebellious genius is challenged by peeling off the reputation
he had acquired in the nineteenth and twentieth centuries. Emmens then

endeavours to develop a more authentic image of Rembrandt by concentrating on contemporary theories of art. The author, who later became professor of iconology and art theory at the University of Utrecht, was not only a great art historian but also one of our most original and gifted poets. It was a great loss for Dutch culture and for the whole community of art historians when he died at a far too early age.

Thus, in discussing the origins of the postwar studies of the visual arts in the Netherlands, we can roughly distinguish between the category of connoisseurship and the 'schools' of Van de Waal and Emmens. I hasten to add, however, that there are no longer any clear methodical boundaries between them, although there are still distinctions in a social sense.

In the realm of connoisseurship today, we find very few purely stylistic analysts. Nearly everybody has been affected by the wave of contextualisms described earlier in this essay. So one will seldom come across a publication which merely proposes a new attribution of a work of art to an artist. One could perhaps even speak of a lack of connoisseurship, not only in our country, but in the rest of the western world as well. Frits Lugt would have been very concerned.

Moreover, new, non-Dutch fields of the visual arts have been conquered by Dutch historians of art. One could speak of a new school of researchers of Italian art. Whereas the work in this field by the Dutch art historians Raymond van Marle and F.H. Fokker during the 1930's was never integrated in the national scene, this new and broad category of investigators has gained support both in our own universities and abroad. This field has a promising future.

Another remarkable broadening of the postwar scope of Dutch art historians has taken place with the host of young colleagues who specialize in modern art. Here, the great initiator and model was H.L.C. Jaffé, who had fled Germany in 1933 and who was the first to hold a chair (at the University of Amsterdam) of Modern Art. Research into this branch of study is now very popular. In my view this can be, but is not necessarily always, a fortunate development. Really fundamental investigations into the character and impact of phenomena in the visual arts of this century are too few in number. There is a trend towards 'safe' research into subjects of minor importance.

However, this trend is not restricted to modern art. Studies of medieval art are also menaced by a certain provincialism. Young researchers have often shown a shyness when it comes to subjects which imply knowledge of palaeography and of the traditional modern and classical languages. Some colleagues even speak of a certain indolence among the young. This is a relatively recent phenomenon that is related to the changed standards in secondary school education.

Research into the history of art is mainly done in or under the auspices of the universities. In museums, however, there is not only a great dearth of basic research, but also of inventories which meet the simplest scholarly standards. A survey recently commissioned by the Dutch Association of Art Historians revealed a backlog in this field of 200 man-years! There are however a few museums – the Rijksmuseum in Amsterdam is one of them – which produce interesting scholarly publications. Moreover, a recent trend has become noticeable: exhibitions and catalogues which are the fruit of cooperation between museums and universities. This is a very healthy development indeed, especially because there always used to be a gulf between the activities of the two kinds of institution, not entirely foreign to Lugt's biased impression of olden times. Great prospects lie ahead, and they deserve wholehearted encouragement.

This would seem to be a good point at which to mention an early and very special result of this kind of cooperation: the Rembrandt Research Project, which is now known throughout the world. In this pilot project, which was started about twenty years ago, art historians and scientists are working together to produce a new *catalogue raisonné* of Rembrandt's *oeuvre*. This kind of research, in which the Dutch have gained a great deal of expertise, surely has a great future. It will also have interesting spin-offs which will be reflected in future events such as 'The Arts and Machines' (*Alfa's en apparaten*), a symposium to be held in Amsterdam in 1991. The most fascinating by-product of this project is the fundamental revival of concentration on the individual artefact, combined with new techniques in archive research, mentioned earlier in this essay.

There we also touched on the new technique of neutron activation autoradiography. It is doubtful whether this will be applied in our country in the coming decade. There will surely be a demand for it, but much will depend on the economic situation, because it is an expensive process. Moreover, there are practical drawbacks. If one wants to inspect a picture using this technique, it has to be removed from the gallery for three months. Larger paintings would be excluded, because they are simply too big for the reactor. Last but not least, this kind of research will have to be restricted to paintings on canvas. Wooden panels would suffer too much, not only from the physical conditions in the reactor, but also from the vacuum application of X-ray films on the paint layer.

Concentration on the individual artefact and all its physical aspects has also been characteristic of much of the best work done by architectural historians. Here we can state that the Dutch have acquired and developed an up-to-date expertise. This is absolutely essential for the future maintenance of our architectural heritage. Some of them are also gaining experience with computer-aided drawing, a method described earlier in this essay, and seem to have acquired an international reputation. It will be worth sounding out to the full both the potential and limits of this new technique for studies of the history of architecture and physical planning.

When speaking of this field of study, it should be observed that it has experienced a very lively period recently, especially with regard to the history of modern architecture. Since the early seventies, the latest theories and methods from abroad have been introduced rapidly. Almost too rapidly, one might say, because in their enthusiasm young architectural historians have shown a tendency to absorb the vocabulary of undigested doctrines from the Faculty of Architecture in Venice or from difficult texts in books by philosophers like Nietzsche or Foucault. There is now a tendency among some architectural historians who no longer grant primacy to the eye to proceed from the widest possible context of socio-economic factors, via the history of land-use planning to physical planning, ending with the designed and built architecture. Some years ago, one of the representatives of this trend even held up the miserable figure of Oedipus, who blinded himself, as the personification of the development of architectural history. He ended with a rhetorical question: Is this ill-fated blind man only able to unite with Mother Science when he has demolished the precepts of Father Art History?

One other field on which perhaps insufficient light has been shed, both nationally and internationally, is the study of fundamental theories of the visual arts. It is here, at the end of this essay, that we return to the legacies, first of H. van de Waal and then of J.A. Emmens.

In the previous pages we have met Van de Waal as the author of the *Geschied-uitbeelding* and as the *auctor intellectualis* of *Iconclass*. Outside the narrow circle of his pupils, however, it is a little known fact that his conception of iconology comprised a fundamental doctrine of all visual communication which he revealed in his lectures and seminars with great imagination. Some of his pupils, their respective pupils, and various others have thoughtfully developed it further, concentrating on issues like information theory, the relation between language and image, the contribution which the works of anthropologists like C. Lévi-Strauss have made to this field of study, and its potential for creating a better understanding of modern

art. This fundamental kind of iconology (*beeldleer* in Dutch) has been un-
derexposed up to now. It fully deserves more attention being devoted to it,
preferably by publications in other languages in addition to Dutch.

As for what we have called the legacy of Emmens, publicity in other
languages has been a less pressing problem. Iconological studies of seventeenth-century Dutch painting, in particular, have enjoyed a great renown
and certainly will continue to do so.

Before finishing this essay, I would like to make a few final remarks.
When asked about their knowledge of the activities of art historians in the
Netherlands, most of our foreign colleagues find nothing to say. This is
unjustified, unnecessary and most unwelcome. In the foregoing I have not
made the slightest attempt to conceal provincial traits which are indeed
menacing, and are sometimes very definitely present. However, the sound
kernel of research into the history of art in our country is of an absolutely
adequate level, and promises good and new perspectives. Moreover, the
sober-minded and commonsense attitude that characterizes Dutch research
could perhaps counterbalance a trend which nowadays is often all too
successful. I am referring to the trend whereby a researcher distils a new
concept that he or she then develops as an intellectualistic construct, and in
which he or she ends up by using reproductions of works of art as if they
belonged to the file of a barrister charged with the case for the defence.
Poor works of art!

The last International Congress of the History of Art at Strasbourg (1989)
was opened by the French Minister of Culture, Jack Lang, with a speech in
which he gave his full and generous support to French research into art
history. Let us hope that, at the opening in September 1996, of the XXIXth
International Congress in Amsterdam, there will not only be a Dutch minister
who is wholeheartedly prepared to support research in the Netherlands, but
that the congress itself will give a wide and convincing demonstration of
the vitality of the discipline in our country.

* During the preparation of this essay I received help and advice from the
following people: Jochen Becker, Horst Bredekamp, Madeline Caviness,
Ida Clermont, Heinrich Dilly, Natascha Drabbe, Thomas W. Gaehtgens,
Géza Hajós, Klaus Herding, Michael Hoyle, Joop Joosten, Martin J. Kemp,
Irving Lavin, J.L. Locher, James Marrow, Sergiusz Michalski, Henry Millon,
Harald Olbrich, Paul Op de Coul, Henk W. van Os, Dominique Ponnau,
Merel Reinink, Artur Rosenauer, R.W. Scheller, Merilyn Schmitt, Henri
Schoenmakers, Ronald Stenvert, Victor Stoichita, Jeroen Stumpel, Pierre
Vaisse and Ernst van de Wetering.

The study of literature

Douwe Fokkema

1. Introduction

In this century the study of literature has gone through an extraordinary development, and – what is even more remarkable – this can be said of most disciplines in the humanities, from linguistics to history. A solid consensus backs this view, so much so that the statement itself has become a platitude. Let me try to describe the situation in less general and perhaps more controversial terms.

The turbulent (at times confusing) development in literary studies has much to do with their uneasy and ambivalent relation to theory – a term which has been used to signify a wide range of different things, from concept or model to falsifiable hypothesis, and from scientific approach to critical tradition. Moreover, while some researchers in the field of literature have been under the spell of the persistent but mistaken belief that they should engage in literary criticism and express value judgements, others have rejected evaluative activities and aimed at finding general theoretical statements that can be tested. The existence of these two opposite positions favoured a lively discussion of fundamental issues.

Slightly varying Wellek's position in his article "Literary Theory, Criticism, and History" (1960), I would argue that literary studies consist of research, criticism and historiography. The roles of researcher, critic and historian, however, (and here I depart from Wellek completely) should be clearly distinguished, if a fruitful discussion of the position of the discipline – the study of literature – is to follow. The distinction and separation of these three roles is one of the prime conditions for the further development of literary studies.

Historiography is important in most of the humanities, but much less so in the natural and the social sciences. However, the distinction between research and criticism, or research and application, seems to apply not only in the humanities, but also in the social and the natural sciences. This is a reason to subscribe to the idea of the *unity* of method in research – i.e. the empirical method of trial and error-elimination – as a result of which the distinction between the humanities, social sciences and natural sciences becomes a relative one (Popper, 1973: 185), justified only by a difference in object of research, or, more accurately, in clusters of problems. This conclusion runs counter to Dilthey's distinction between *Natur-* and *Geisteswissenschaften* on the basis of a difference in *method* (Dilthey, 1900: 317-338), defended by Hans-Georg Gadamer and others participating in the hermeneutic tradition, and invoked recently in some of the contributions to the colloquium *Neue Technologien und die Herausforderung an die Geisteswissenschaften* (1987). Indeed, ninety years after it was first phrased, Dilthey's claim of a special position for the humanities no longer applies, mainly because his scapegoat – the reductionist positivism of Auguste Comte and Hippolyte Taine – no longer plays a serious role in scientific discussions, having been superseded by other, more sophisticated philosophies of science.

The denial of Dilthey's distinction is still rather unpopular in the German context and to some extent elsewhere. Thus the case for a special position for the humanities was reiterated in France by Ricoeur (1969) and in the Anglo-Saxon world by the New Critics (cf. Wellek, 1978).

However, a broad shift of research goals in literary studies, from an exclusive focus on the text to an emphasis on the communication situation, has brought the discipline close to the social sciences. Indeed, the increasingly important sociology and psychology of literature not only belong to literary studies or *Literaturwissenschaft* but also to sociology and psychology respectively. Advanced research methods in the field of literary communication have made Dilthey's position out-of-date.

I propose, then, to replace the trichotomy of humanities, social sciences and natural sciences by the dichotomy of research and criticism (historiography has a somewhat hybrid position between research and criticism). When the barriers between the natural sciences, the social sciences and the humanities have been razed, the prospects for interdisciplinary research appear bright indeed.

These introductory remarks merely serve to indicate the line of my argument, which, of course, needs further elaboration. Many questions have remained unanswered, or were not even posed, such as the well-known problem of whether the humanities should focus on the particular, on the concrete, on the unique, rather than on general problems. A discipline has its own history, its own tradition and social context. These need to be sketched as well, if we wish to understand its major issues and potential development. Although, in principle, the boundaries between research in literature and in the social sciences are permeable, academic institutions have legitimized a division of labour which has proved satisfactory for decades. The borderline between the humanities and the social sciences cannot easily be crossed; but is this situation indeed still satisfactory?

2. Major issues in the history of the study of literature since World War I

There is a broad consensus that the beginnings of the modern study of literature are to be sought in Russian Formalism (c. 1915-1930). The Russian Formalists distinguished themselves from their predecessors by openly arguing for a *scientific* study of literature, and their view of scientificity was certainly a modern one. Like Popper would argue at a later stage, one of their major spokesmen, Boris Ejchenbaum pointed out: "The vitality of a science is not measured by its establishing truths but by its overcoming errors" (1926: 3-4).

The Formalists proceeded by providing precise descriptions of their object of research and introduced a number of well-defined concepts. For them, literature consisted of texts which were capable of inducing an aesthetic experience among their readers. They hinted at the possibility of a psychological study of readers' reactions, but their interest in the readers' perception led primarily to a close examination of textual devices, such as "the device of making things strange" and "the device of the impeded form." In their conception of literature, exposure to the same stimuli was bound to lead to habituation while the devices of literature were supposed to break through habitual perception. The evolution of literature, therefore, could be described in terms of a gradual familiarization calling for a sudden de-familiarization provoked by new artistic means. The notion of surprise was highly valued. Or, as Viktor Šklovskij wrote: "The aim of art is to convey the immediate experience of a thing as if it is seen instead of recognized" (trans. from Šklovskij, 1916: 14).

These views were stimulating and rather original, though in part a continuation of German idealist thought. However, throughout the period that the Formalists could publish their work in the Soviet Union (up to the late 1920s), they did not disentangle psychological and textual factors, which were lumped together in the writings of Šklovskij, Tynjanov, Jakobson and others. This made them vulnerable to criticism; it also prevented their theories being tested.

The Russian Formalists were prolific in introducing new concepts. When they came to the conclusion that literary devices should not be studied in isolation but rather in their mutual relationship, the concepts of 'structure' and 'system' appeared in their writings, but the epistemological status of these terms remained unclear. Was the structure of a text inherent to the text? Would it be possible to find one and the same structure as a result of repeated analysis by different observers? Or was a structure imposed on a text by the reader or researcher? The same questions could be asked with respect to the concept of system.

The Russian Formalists were so much committed to establishing a science (*nauka*) of literature as an independent discipline that they were not inclined to be led astray by psychological or sociological problems. To a considerable extent their views were determined by a polemical attitude against a reductionist positivism which had overemphasized the importance of social conditions and biographical detail. This may have been the reason why they refrained from delving into sociology and psychology, although the direction of their argument brought them close to these disciplines. Two instances may exemplify this.

In 1921 Roman Jakobson argued that poetry is "an utterance with a set towards the expression," with the result that the 'communicative function' which predominates in practical language is reduced to a minimum (trans. from Jakobson, 1921: 30). 'Set' is here the translation of *ustanovka*, which is usually rendered in German as 'Einstellung'. The question to be asked here is, of course: can an utterance have a 'set'? Or did Jakobson, in fact, want to suggest that the *reader* or *listener* would be induced by the text to focus on (the particular form of) the expression? In his later phrasing of 1960, Jakobson argued that "the set (*Einstellung*) toward the message as such, focus on the message for its own sake, is the poetic function of language" (Jakobson, 1960: 356). Here, too, the same question can be asked: who actually is supposed to focus? Jakobson's definitions inevitably point to some action by a recipient, motivated (but not determined) by the text. Yet, he was never explicit on such reader's reactions.

The other example can be taken from the well-known article by Jurij Tynjanov, "The Literary Fact." Here, Tynjanov defines literature as a "language construction which is experienced as a construction: i.e. literature is a dynamic language construction" (Tynjanov, 1924: 406-408). In this context, the word 'dynamic' implies that the text should not be regarded as an isolated, static thing, but rather as part of a changing tradition, as an element in a communicative process. The passive form in Tynjanov's definition conceals the question of *who* is supposed to experience a particular language construction as a construction. Will *everyone* see that particular text as a 'constructed' (aesthetic) text? Or will there be different answers among different groups of people as to whether a particular text is a 'constructed' text? And will one and the same person, having once considered a text a 'constructed' text, always subscribe to that same judgement? Not only the question of *who* recognizes a text as being literary is important; also the question *why* certain people read literature, and to what effect, is a relevant one. The Russian Formalists stopped short of asking these questions. Their major contribution was in the field of conceptualization and many of their precise distinctions are still respected in present discussions.

These distinctions did not include a differentiation of the roles of researcher, critic and historian. Working in a context of Futurism, revolution and emigration, they never came to the point of presenting a systematic account of their views. However, their work is often characterized by a commitment to the avant-garde in literature and the arts, by an acute political awareness, and at times a streak of genius.

In scientific research, the introduction and precise definition of concepts is of great importance. How would it be possible to describe the grammar of a language without a set of grammatical categories? Likewise, in both the synchronic and the diachronic study of literature, technical terms and their precise definitions are indispensable. Without the names of particular genres, periods, movements, codes and conventions it is almost impossible to write the history of literature; and without terms such as meter, rhythm, stanza, *fabula* and narrative structure (*sjužet*), interior monologue and dialogue, direct, indirect and free indirect speech no analysis of texts would be possible. It is precisely young disciplines, such as the study of literature, which devote much time and energy to the definition of analytical terms, so much so that it is sometimes forgotten that their usefulness will only appear when these terms enable us to make precise and testable observations. That moment, however, did not arrive soon and it has hardly arrived even now. Are we still in the stage of overcoming the errors of the past (which Ejchenbaum considered a sign of vitality)?

Some progress in the direction of precise and testable observations was made in the 1930s by the Polish scholar Roman Ingarden and the Czech Jan Mukařovský; or rather, their different conceptions of the literary work made further explorations into the nature of reading and interpretation possible. One of the crucial problems in literary studies is to what extent a text can be considered an observable fact; and if it is not directly accessible to observation, in what way can it be made accessible to rational analysis supported by testable observations? Philology, which primarily focused on text edition and explanatory commentary and which had its roots in nineteenth-century positivism and earlier methods, had always avoided this question. Philologists had to proceed on the assumption that what they saw was there, and indeed the ink on a page is an observable, physical phenomenon. But are the words shaped by that ink relevant as a literary fact? Do they, interrelated as they are, add up to a literary fact?

Ingarden and Mukařovský provided different answers to this question. Though using a slightly different terminology, they both distinguished between the material artefact (the ink constituting words on the page) and the aesthetic object (the concretization or realization of the work of art in the mind of the recipient). Mukařovský devoted much attention to the aesthetic object which, as an individual or collective concretization, was assumed to differ among different readers or populations of readers in different times and social contexts. In this respect, Mukařovský continued the tradition of the Russian Formalists, of Šklovskij and Tynjanov. Ingarden, however, based his approach on the materiality of the work of art and only hesitantly subscribed to the view that one artefact may give rise to different concretizations. Throughout his life, he continued to look for the theoretical possibility of the one plausible or adequate interpretation to which the reading of a work of art should lead (cf. Fokkema & Ibsch, 1978: 30-38). Undoubtedly, Mukařovský and Ingarden were aware of each other's work and knew that they differed, but there is very little direct polemics in their work. Yet, the difference between their positions is paradigmatic for the discussion concerning the problem of interpretation since the 1930s. Much of that discussion, of course, was carried on quite independently of their writings, which for linguistic and political reasons began to play a role in the international debate only after World War II. Ingarden had published

Das literarische Kunstwerk in 1931 in Germany, and his ideas were as-similated earlier than those of Mukařovský, whose work was translated into German only after the war. However, the translation of Ingarden's books into English materialized with considerable delay in the United States in the 1970s, whereupon his views became rather popular and were absorbed in other parts of the world, leading to such anachronisms as a paper on Ingarden and Chinese traditional Kunqu opera, read by a Chinese scholar at the 12th Congress of the International Comparative Literature Association in Munich in 1988.

Mukařovský's position is well-known in the German context, but much less so in the Anglo-Saxon world, although part of his writings appeared in English translation in the United States in the late 1970s.

The international debate in literary studies has been seriously handicapped by the anachronistic reception of these sources. The findings of the Russian Formalists, too, were introduced to the Western world with a considerable delay, by Victor Erlich (in English, 1955), Tzvetan Todorov (in French, 1965), Jurij Striedter (in German, 1969), Matejka and Pomorska (in English, 1971). The role of expatriates in the distribution of knowledge is both undeniable and disquieting. To what extent is the scientific debate dependent on the non-scientific context, the outcome of wars, narrow escapes, and immigration policies? What would have happened if in the early 1940s Roman Jakobson had not been admitted to the United States (which almost was the case) and had not come into contact with Claude Lévi-Strauss who, after his escape from France, taught for some years at the New School of Social Research in New York?

These musings lead to the conclusion that scientific progress, notably in the humanities, is incompatible with totalitarian rule. Research in the humanities needs the backing of democratic institutions, the continuity of academic traditions, well-stocked libraries, proficiency in several languages, and – as the present situation in Europe teaches us – non-interference by bureaucratic directives.

Insufficient knowledge of foreign languages conditioned the rise of a 'French' and a 'Czech' structuralism, as well as the popularity of the French branch in Spain, Portugal and Latin America. The late and hesitant discovery of the work of Roland Barthes and Lévi-Strauss in Germany is partly due to a lack of knowledge of the French language and French research traditions in Germany. From the opposite perspective, it became possible in France to discover Nietzsche as a contemporary of the 1970s (as interpreted by Gilles Deleuze, Jacques Derrida, Michel Foucault and others), to construct a 'French' Nietzsche, and to export this selective image of Nietzsche to the

United States where it was received extremely well for various reasons – one of which was a lack of knowledge of the writings of Nietzsche in the original language and of the reception of Nietzsche in Germany. Heidegger has followed a similar trajectory; he, too, has recently received much attention in North America, uninhibited by knowledge of the German language and of the political conditions in Europe in the 1930s. That these remarks are more than speculation may appear from the fact that neither the 'French' Nietzsche, nor the cult of Heidegger has made any impression in Germany itself, or in Holland or the Scandinavian countries, where there is still a historical awareness of the dangers of combining a philosophical aporia and political blindness.

We cannot deny that there is an element of coincidence in the history of the study of literature. The reliance on translations and the ignorance of the political and academic conditions under which much work was done (and interrupted) are part of the context of our discipline. It would be foolish to ignore this, but it would be equally absurd to acquiesce in it. The scholars who have resisted this Procrustes-bed have contributed much to the development of our discipline.

Here mention should be made of René Wellek, who in his *Theory of Literature* (1949), written together with Austin Warren, summarized, not uncritically, the findings of the Russian Formalists, the ideas of Ingarden and Mukařovský, and the insights of New Criticism and T.S. Eliot. Wellek, who was born in Czechoslovakia and did research in England before moving to the United States where he became a professor of Comparative Literature at Yale, was well qualified to write the greater part of this stock-taking book. On the issue of the interpretation of literary works, he seems closer to Ingarden than to Mukařovský. Wellek insisted that analysis cannot be separated from the appreciation of a literary work. His statement that "evaluation grows out of understanding; correct evaluation out of correct understanding" (Wellek, 1963: 18) comes very close to Ingarden indeed.

For various reasons I would not subscribe to this statement, but in this historical sketch it should be recalled that Wellek is probably polemicizing here against two tendencies he rigorously rejected and hated. One is the depersonalized (in the pejorative, not Eliot's sense of the word) aspect of German historicism, which allows for an interpretation of the historical phenomena of a certain period (including texts), on the basis of the norms and in relation to the other historical phenomena of that period. This historicism enabled scholars to construct self-contained historical contexts and to exclude present conditions and their own value judgement from their consideration, isolating their research from contemporary political conditions. The other tendency he rejected was the depersonalized aspect of a structuralism, as propounded by Jan Mukařovský, which reduced the work of art to "an assembly of extra-aesthetic values and nothing but such an assembly" and aesthetic value to a "designation for the dynamic totality of its mutual relations" (quoted in Wellek, 1970: 291), thus leaving no space whatsoever for the individual judgement. Both views, historicism as well as structuralism, detracted from the individual's responsibility whether in aesthetics or – if the conjecture is warranted, since Wellek was never explicit about it in writing – politics. In any case, political conditions were very much present in the background. In the case of German historicism this is evident; but it is equally so in the case of Mukařovský, who after the war refashioned his thinking in a materialist way (Mukařovský, 1947: 7-8) and became rector of Prague University under the Stalinist regime.

In his views on the indissoluble unity of interpretation and evaluation, Wellek did not stand alone. His position was shared in the United States by Cleanth Brooks and other New Critics, and in Europe by Wolfgang Kayser, Emil Staiger and Hans Teesing, teaching respectively in Germany, Switzerland and the Netherlands.

Scholars in the field of literature have often combined their analytical interests with criticism and creative writing, and many did not resist the temptation to write for the daily or weekly press. Several of the Russian Formalists were also critics or creative writers. In some instances the other interest was dictated by economic necessity, in other cases it resulted from individual choice. Umberto Eco, who began his career as a journalist, became a professor of semiotics at Bologna, and finally combined journalism, scholarship and creative writing, is the most well-known example, but is far from being the only one. Roland Barthes was famous for a highly individualized style of writing that is partly essay, partly scholarly analysis, aiming at both an academic and a wider audience. Malcolm Bradbury and David Lodge in England, Serge Doubrovsky in France, István Sötér in Hungary, Ton Anbeek in the Netherlands, Yvette Centeno in Portugal, are respected both as scholars and as writers of fiction. Many writers in the United States are affiliated with a University and teach literature.

These entanglements with creative writing and literary criticism very much determine the social and cultural embedding of literary studies and correspond to certain expectations of the general public. However, these connections with the production and criticism of literature also obscure the goals of literary research. One can hardly expect clarity about the various functions of analysis, interpretation and evaluation, if literary scholars engage in all three without explicitly distinguishing between them (Eco is a favourable exception here), in essays which address themselves to a general public rather than to the community of researchers. We are bound to conclude that the emancipation of research in the field of literature is not only an intellectual problem, but also a social one.

In spite of the presence of literary criticism as an adjoining and sometimes rivalling activity, research in the field of literary communication has made progress, notably in the last twenty or thirty years. To conclude this section, we will briefly refer to the remarkable development of semiotics as applied to literature. In this field, it is again Russian scholars such as Jurij Lotman, Vjač. Vs. Ivanov, V.N. Toporov, who took the lead, continuing the tradition of Russian Formalism but combining it at the same time with new insights from in information theory and cybernetics (for which they heavily relied on American publications). The publications of the Russian semioticians were more promptly and more completely translated into Italian than into any other language. This may explain why Italian scholars were the first to support the semiotic approach (Umberto Eco, Cesare Segre, Tullio de Mauro, Maria Corti and others). Significantly, the first congress of the International Association of Semiotic Studies was held in Milan in 1974, and although the Association gradually expanded its field to almost any human (and even animal) activity, it has remained one of the international forums where the state of the art in literary studies is discussed, in addition to the International Comparative Literature Association (founded in 1955) and the various international associations which bring scholars working in the field of one specific language and literature together and which belong to the International Federation of Modern Languages and Literatures.

More clearly than reception aesthetics, which – notably through the efforts of Hans Robert Jauss – was gradually absorbed into the hermeneutic tradition, semiotics drew attention to the necessity to distinguish between the role of critic and researcher. A number of precise concepts were introduced: not only signifier (form) and signified (meaning) were distinguished, but also different types of sign. Most important probably was the notion of code: the system of conventions regulating the attribution of meaning to particular signs, thus connecting signifier and signified. This new concept was elucidated clearly and convincingly by both Lotman (1970, 1977) and Eco (1976), but it was also criticized from various points of view. As I have argued elsewhere, I am convinced that the concept of code is useful and will remain a central element in the study of literature (Fokkema, 1985).

We cannot elaborate here on the many stimulating ideas in Lotman's work, but must draw attention to Eco's attempt to show how signs, in particular new signs, are *produced*. Partly elaborating on the work of Saussure, Peirce and Jakobson, Eco clearly distinguished between the role of sender and recipient, between intended and non-intended (i.e. attributed) meaning. He also showed how codes are established (and renewed) and in doing so he was bound to distinguish between participation in a particular communication situation and the examination of that communication situation from an outside point of view, between criticism and analysis.

These semiotic studies – which were followed by valuable publications in other countries, notably Germany (Roland Posner) – increased both the quantity and the quality of the analytical terms available to literary research. Moreover, the elaborate semiotic methodology has put the study of literature firmly on a road different from that of literary criticism. Semiotics, which may be taken to include narratology (Claude Bremond, Gérard Genette, A.J. Greimas, Dorrit Cohn, Gerald Prince, Mieke Bal, Shlomith Rimmon-Kenan), has provided a substantial and crucial contribution to the study of literature, by designing and defining the concepts it still needed before it could be considered a full-fledged discipline, well-equipped for empirical research. In short, semiotics was instrumental in establishing the theoretical tradition of a metalanguage, and it contributed very much to its actual creation. After Lotman and Eco, a return to hermeneutics had become impossible, but the step towards empirical research was made only hesitantly.

3. The present situation: An analysis of major trends
The two principal conditions which restrict the development of literary studies – on the one hand, the social and political context and, on the other hand, the rivalling activities in the field of literary criticism in the media – are still playing a crucial role.

Of course, the social and political context means different things in different parts of the world. In the Soviet Union, the government did not favour the development of semiotics which was assumed to be either hostile or indifferent to Marxism; official circles tried to promote a Marxist semiotics instead. In China, where since the late 1970s foreign literature was a preferred topic of research, the study of comparative literature was institutionalized, but in 1989 the open-door policy in cultural matters was interrupted for an indefinite period of time. In the European Community the social and political context is being felt in terms of budgetary restrictions. Good scholars have been forced to accept early or part-time retirement, which has seriously affected the continuity and climate of research, notably in England but also elsewhere. The result has been that a considerable number of scholars in the field of literary studies have accepted positions at American universities. This must be considered a serious loss, especially in those cases where research traditions in Europe differ from those in North America, so that those who 'change places' cannot continue their research in the line of their own expertise.

The cultural context in which literary studies must survive and develop is also different from country to country. In Japan the discipline is generally conceived as being close to criticism and creative writing, as needing no theory, and as a vehicle for emphasizing traditional aesthetic and moral values. The same description applies to much work done at American universities, although other trends are also visible there which have found expression in journals such as *Diacritics* and *New Literary History* – the first favouring a trend in criticism which has become known as Deconstruction, the second providing an outlet for theoretical reflection concerning literary history. Neither Deconstruction, nor literary historiography has been discussed so far, and it is appropriate to do that now, as both are vital trends in the contemporary scholarly discussion. We will also have to devote some space to the empirical study of literature, which is a promising new trend. However, it is necessary to keep in mind that the cultural context in which literary studies develop in Europe, as well as in North and South America, is literary criticism and the teaching of literature (including discussions about the canon). From a distance, critics and teachers are carefully watching the successes and failures of literary research, and since the critics in particular have access to the media, more often than not university boards and governmental institutions supervising education are sensitive to the judgements of these bystanders. In spite of this not very comfortable situation, we can report on important work that is being done and we are confident that the prospects for the discipline are bright.

Deconstruction is a school in interpretation which both continued and resisted the tradition of New Criticism. Interpretation has also remained the primary goal for the deconstructionists, but instead of looking for cues which would reveal the coherence of the text (as the New Critics did), the deconstructionist critics look for what the text conceals; they rejoice in finding a trace of incoherence, a suppressed idea, an inconsistency, which would lead towards a radical re-interpretation. This reading 'against the grain' resulted in a re-evaluation of well-known, canonical texts, as well as in interpretations of marginal texts outside the canon, aiming at their 're-habilitation'.

The philosophical background of Deconstruction is complex and cannot be dealt with adequately here. Suffice to mention impulses from the 'French' Nietzsche as interpreted by Deleuze and Derrida, from psychoanalytical thinking (both Freud and Lacan), from Marxian thought, and from Bakhtinian dialogism. Yale, where once René Wellek taught, was a centre of deconstructionist interpretation and teaching for a period of about ten years, but after the death of Paul de Man in 1983, the interest in Deconstruction gradually subsided there, as elsewhere.

What is remarkable about Deconstruction is the kind of commitment it expects from its adherents – a non-scientific *engagement* which brings analysis, criticism, history and politics together in the act of rebellious interpretation. Deconstruction is professedly against theory, rejects the idea of a metalanguage, and ignores the basic rules of empirical research. From an epistemological point of view, a deconstructionist interpretation has the same status as a New Critical one – the difference, as mentioned, being mainly that the New Critics posit the unity and coherence of a text, whereas the deconstructionists assume that hints of intertextual relations can be more significant than the phrasings of the text itself. The echoes of Deconstruction have been heard as far away as India (Singh, 1984), but there it was also criticized from the point of view of traditional text-oriented research, which was never abandoned in the Anglo-Saxon world (Tripathy, 1989).

In the United States, Deconstruction has called for a reaction which is usually indicated by the name 'new historicism'. Apart from this particular interest in history with a materialist bias, there is a much wider range of historiographical work, both in North America and Europe, which must be discussed. Until recently one could hear the complaint that literary history is a neglected area. Indeed, the emphasis on narratological analysis and semiotic studies in the 1970s and early 80s had diverted talents and energy from other fields, including literary history. Moreover, the transition from narratology or semiotics to historiography was not easily made. Semiotic studies rarely included the historical point of view, except in some studies in the semiotics of culture (e.g. Uspenskij et al., 1973); and the narratological analysis of one text was often so much time-consuming that the possibility of analyzing many texts and including the historical perspective remained beyond realization.

One might surmise that the published results of these narratological and semiotic analyses would be used by other scholars in an attempt at synthesis. But this did not happen, possibly because the intersubjective value of these various analyses was less great than could have been expected on the basis of the elaborate analytical apparatus. The results of semiotic and narratological analyses were almost never presented in a way that would allow for a separation of reliable and unreliable results, for comparison and accumulation. As a result, there remained a rather sharp dividing line between semiotic and narratological analysis on the one hand, and the writing of literary history on the other.

The study of the reception of literary works – which in practice split up into a hermeneutical branch under the name reception aesthetics, focusing on the restorative enterprise of re-interpreting major texts from the canon (Hans-Robert Jauss), and an empirical branch, under the name reception research, engaging in an analysis of documents (literary criticism and other sources) reflecting the reception and significance of texts among distinct audiences (Elrud Ibsch, J.J. Kloek) – had of course closer links with historiography. The latter form of research, if directed by precise questions, indeed produced results that were intersubjectively valid and could be used in literary historiography or a history of mentalities. This kind of documentary research has proved to be of crucial value in the study of the distribution of knowledge and beliefs among certain groups, but it is still a long way from there to a literary history based on the reception point of view and exceeding the span of a literary movement or period.

The writing of a literary history indeed begins with a particular point of view, a particular interest, a question, perhaps a theory. It would be wrong, however, to assume that this insight played a primary role in the reflection on, and the practice of, literary historiography. The interest in history more often than not grew out of an interest in the particular, in individuality, rather than in questions of a more or less general nature. Many historians, including literary historians, seem to subscribe Gadamer's view in *Wahrheit und Methode* (1960), that historical knowledge should aim at understanding the individual phenomena in their unique and historical concretion ("in ihrer einmaligen und geschichtlichen Konkretion"), at understanding how this man or woman, this people, this nation has become what it is ("zu verstehen wie dieser Mensch, dieses Volk, dieser Staat ist, was er geworden ist"), or in general terms: how the present was shaped out of preceding events ("wie es kommen konnte, dass es so ist") (quoted in *Neue Technologien*, 1987: 69).

If this is considered an accurate definition of the aims of historical research and of the *geisteswissenschaftliche Methode* in general, one may question the notion of knowledge that is implied. What does Gadamer have in mind? Some intuitive almost mystical identification (indeed, a fusion of horizons!) with individual human beings, peoples and nations, or a rational, analytical view which can be communicated and discussed? From the scientific point of view only the latter possibility is of interest; knowledge in this sense means knowledge of the general aspects of things, as individual qualities can be known only by means of concepts that transcend individuality. (Even the notion of individuality is applicable to many individuals.) This point needs further elaboration, as it may help us to criticize a mistaken conception of the humanities or *Geisteswissenschaften* and to overcome the overemphasis on the difference between the humanities and the social sciences on the one hand, between the humanities and the natural sciences on the other. The German historian Reinhart Koselleck has convincingly argued that hermeneutic understanding or the 'geisteswissenschaftliche Methode' is built on the assumption of a human nature and human capacities which in all circumstances remain the same (cf. Koselleck, 1979: 177). The notions of empathy ('Einfühlung', 'Nachfühlen') and the fusion of horizons ('Horizontverschmelzung') introduce an element of identification between subject and object which obscures differences. As a *method*, hermeneutic understanding is not propitious to the discovery of historical distinctions, the detection of relations and explanations which differ from other relations and explanations. The investigation of historical sources, Koselleck argues, must be guided by questions in order to detect relations between events which lie beyond the individual sources (Koselleck, 1979: 205). This also applies to literary history, where the historian may be interested in discovering intertextual relations and characteristics of groups of texts, or may want to focus on common features in the reactions of groups of readers, or concentrate on the poetics of a number of contemporary authors. In such investigations, which look for connections – and lack of connections – between individual sources, the hermeneutic method is of no avail. It is, therefore, no mere coincidence that it is usually restricted to the understanding of a single text or a single author, isolated from the larger cultural, social and historical background.

The limitations of the hermeneutic method are clear. But it remains a question whether nevertheless the hermeneutic goal of *scientific* knowledge of individual texts, authors and events is a valid one. (Indeed, Dilthey (1900: 317) discussed "die Frage nach der *wissenschaftlichen* Erkenntnis der Einzelpersonen, ja der grossen Formen singulären menschlichen Daseins.") In answer to this question four comments can be made.

(1) There is no way of knowing uniqueness, except by means of words or instruments which are to be shared with other researchers. Unique phenomena, therefore, can be known and discussed only in non-unique terms, and thereby lose their uniqueness. One might say that that which

remains unknown constitutes the unique aspect of a particular phenomenon. One may localize and point at the unique, but cannot know it.

(2) The problem of uniqueness or unexplainable (not yet explained) coincidence is not a problem exclusive to the humanities. The social sciences and natural sciences know it as well. In fact, all historical and social phenomena are unique since they are linked up with a particular time and place, and with a particular context which is subjected to continual change. Many physical phenomena, too, such as the constitution of the atmosphere at a particular moment, meteorological conditions at a certain place and time, the particular shape of waves and vortices, not to speak of biological phenomena, from the shape of trees to the appearance of animals and human beings, are unique in the sense that there is an individual residue which cannot (yet) be explained. In some sciences (including the humanities), the unexplained remainder of individual phenomena may be greater than in others, but there is no way of knowing whether the unexplained domain has a particular value, or whether those sciences which have large domains of unexplained phenomena should be more highly or less highly regarded for that reason. The size of the unexplained domain is not a particularly convincing criterion for the trichotomy of the natural, social and human sciences, as it appears very difficult, if not impossible, to compare the dimensions of the unknown in the various sciences.

(3) In historical research, as probably in all sciences, inside and outside the humanities, we may proceed by describing and explaining unique phenomena as far as they can be analyzed in general terms. The accidental event, which must be considered unique because it cannot be explained in all of its aspects, may be considered to belong to a class of possible events conditioned by factors that are known. Historical explanation relies on the attribution of general aspects (which have been observed in other past events) to the accidental event under investigation. The historian will base his or her observation of regularities on these general aspects which leave the particularity of time and place out of consideration. It is impossible to see any regularity and to come to any law-like statement, if one does not abstract from the unique setting of the events.

(4) It follows from the preceding points that I have severe doubts about the possibility of scientific knowledge of the individual nature of texts, authors and events. In scientific, including historical, research any question can be asked, but some questions preclude an answer. One

such question is Gadamer's inquiry into the individuality of "this man or woman, this people, this nation." The goal of scientific knowledge of phenomena in their unique setting will never be reached.

Nevertheless, the hermeneutic position has remained rather strong, in spite of the fact that it has been repeatedly and convincingly criticized from a scientific point of view (e.g. Ibsch & Schram, 1987). The rational defense of hermeneutics, however, is weak and often consists of simply rejecting the claims of a scientific methodology as not being applicable to literary studies.

The tension between the general and the particular, between rational knowledge and the unknown singularity of phenomena, is far from being the only theme in reflections on literary history. Like in literary studies in general, the formation of concepts (which may serve to describe general aspects of individual phenomena) is of crucial importance in literary history. The notions of fact, event and structure, of avant-garde, canon and mass literature, of system and evolution are of crucial importance to the literary historian. What is a literary fact? What is a literary event?

In order to determine what a literary fact is, one needs criteria, and these criteria can be derived from a particular concept of what literature is. Different theories of literature generate different literary facts. The attribution of a text to a particular genre is a significant fact for E.D. Hirsch (1967: 68-126) and Horst Steinmetz (1985: 253), but not for Croce (1964: 449). Similarly, in order to trace significant events in *literary history*, one needs a theory of evolution in literature. Which factors produce change in literature? Are these factors to be sought in social and economic conditions, as Marx believed? Or are they of an aesthetic nature, as the Russian Formalists claimed? Or are there perhaps other relevant factors, inherent in the psychological and neurological conditions of writers and readers (listeners)? A decision must be made – though not necessarily a decision which excludes one of these possibilities – before an unambiguous concept of literary event can be established and used.

The final goal of literary history is not conceptualization of course, but description and explanation; generalizing concepts, however, are indispensable components of descriptive and explanatory propositions, as are the regularities they refer to, which – by means of the generalizing capacity of concepts – have been observed on previous occasions and which seem to apply also to the case under consideration. Explanations may take the form of the 'if ... then ...' formula, often including a probabilistic qualification, for instance: "If an audience has been exposed for a long time to the same literary devices, then it will be ready to accept new devices which so far were excluded from the mainstream of literary discourse" (rephrased after Tynjanov, 1924), or "When a (literary) system is defective, it is more receptive and less selective" (quoted from Even-Zohar, 1978: 52). Clearly, many of the law-like propositions in literary history can be improved and phrased more strictly (for instance, what is 'a long time' in the first proposition? and how should one measure selectiveness?), although, of course, testing by way of experiments is out of the question in historical matters. Explanations in literary history, however, which are supported by well-established theories about human behaviour or communication should be preferred over common sense intuitions about regularities (Rusch, 1987: 443). In this respect, a distinction can be made between more and less firm explanations.

These epistemological considerations lead us to a discussion of another vital trend in literary studies, the last one to be discussed in this section, viz. the empirical study of literature. Earlier, we noticed that the high degree of conceptualization in semiotics and narratology was a step forward which made a return to hermeneutics impossible. However, it remained a drawback that the results of semiotic and narratological analysis were often presented in a way which did not allow for empirical testing, i.e. testing which would either unambiguously confirm or unambiguously deny the outcome of the analysis. Indeed, in certain cases, such as establishing the mode of first person or third person narration, unambiguous results are possible, but the significance of the distinction between these two narrative modes should not be overestimated (cf. Ludwig & Faulstich, 1985). In other instances, however, such as the distinction between icon and index, or the delineation of semantic fields, the analyst has to rely so much on interpretation that it cannot be assumed that another analysis by a second researcher will yield precisely the same result, thus making testing an uncertain affair. The crucial problem which badly needed a solution was how to distinguish between valid and invalid propositions. As long as this problem was not solved, literary studies were subject to the influence of all kinds of fashionable speculations and ideologies and were likely to be reduced to what Paisley Livingston (1988) has aptly called "megaphone criticism," implying that those who have the floor and shout loudest may fancy that they are right.

Epistemological debate since the demise of positivism, in which various philosophers of science and other scholars participated – from Popper and Piaget to Lakatos, Kuhn and Von Glasersfeld – has shown that there is no simple criterion to distinguish valid from invalid propositions. Neither correspondence with the so-called facts, nor coherence with accepted theories, nor consensus among the community of scholars can guarantee the validity of propositions. As I have argued elsewhere, each of these criteria alone is insufficient (Fokkema, 1989). Combining them seems to provide a theoretical solution, but in practice each criterion will receive more or less emphasis.

Although there are no unambiguous rules for establishing the validity of a proposition, the development of the sciences (including the humanities) shows that errors can be corrected. Scientific research has certain analogies with a learning process. Both Popper and Piaget have argued that we can learn from our mistakes. Human beings have the capacity (though they do not always use it) to learn from their errors. Piaget has perhaps been the most convincing in explaining how the human mind proceeds on the basis of conjectures, frames, theories, which are held to be valid until experiences which do not fit them lead to their being corrected or abandoned (see the recent constructivist rephrasing of this position in Von Glasersfeld, 1985). The empirical study of literature bases itself on this epistemological position. Since Lakatos, the question of which experiences are capable of denying the validity of theories is no longer a naive one. Here the community of scholars has a particular responsibility, as it must handle the paradox that theory-guided observation may lead to confirmation or refutation of the theory guiding the observation. The confrontation in empirical testing with experiences which do or do not conform to the theory guiding our research may yield an operational definition of experience in opposition to theory. Experience, then, is that which allows us to say that things are or are not in conformity with a particular theory.

In many respects, the empirical study of literature is incompatible with the hermeneutic and interpretive tradition, from Dilthey's phrasing of the *geisteswissenschaftliche Methode* to New Criticism and Deconstruction.

First, interpretation is not the central preoccupation of the empirical study of literature. Empirical researchers favour examining how other readers attribute meaning to texts over providing interpretations themselves.

Second, the empirical researcher does not participate in the literary communication situation, which is what (new or deconstructionist) critics do, but studies it in all its aspects (the production, distribution, reception and processing of texts) from an outside position. As a result, a clear distinction is made between the roles of reader and researcher.

Third, the interest in the way meaning is attributed to texts leads towards the exploration of the codes, conventions, or mental frames which steer the reading of texts. These mental frames are, of course, not directly observable, but must be constructed on the basis of what can be known, such as programmatic statements by authors, reception documents, and – under certain conditions – also the texts which have been received as literature. To what extent these texts of so-called creative literature are accessible to empirical research is a point of discussion and requires further investigation. Scholars interested in stylistic and psychological problems (Norbert Groeben, Colin Martindale, Teun van Dijk, Will van Peer, Els Andringa and others) do not refrain from text-centred research, whereas sociologists of literature (Pierre Bourdieu, Hugo Verdaasdonk and others) tend to ignore textual features.

Fourth, literature is no longer a secluded, 'autonomous' field. The object of literary studies cannot be restricted to literary texts, as these are contingent entities which, as Tynjanov already knew, can be defined only in relation to the judgement of particular (groups of) readers. Empirical research, however, is focused on literary *communication*, which relies on a transaction between human beings who often have expressed themselves in plain language about the significance of the texts they consider to be literary, and who, if they are still alive, can be asked about their reading experience. The technique of interviewing, the composition of questionnaires, and statistical analysis have become important tools in the empirical study of literary communication. As far as methodology is concerned, the dividing line between the empirical study of literature and the social sciences has become completely blurred.

One of the major representatives of the empirical study of literature is Siegfried J. Schmidt. He has been predominantly interested in the conventions which steer literary production and reception, such as the aesthetic convention and the polyvalence convention (Schmidt, 1980 & 1982). The knowledge of, and the participation in, these conventions are determined by social, historical and cultural conditions as well as by psychological disposition. These variables should be taken into account when particular segments of literary communication are investigated. The empirical study of literature opens possibilities for the examination of mass literature (*Trivialliteratur*), as well as non-European literature. It also allows for a fair discussion of the problem of the literary canon – the body of texts which is considered valuable, taught at school and in the universities, and repeatedly referred to in literary criticism. Knowledge acquired through empirical research may serve as a valuable background for decisions to be taken in literary criticism and the didactics of literature.

The journals *SPIEL* (Siegener Periodicum zur Internationalen Empirischen Literaturwissenschaft), *Poetics* and *Empirical Studies of the Arts* have created an international forum for the empirical study of literature, which was further institutionalized by the founding in 1987 of the International Society for the Empirical Study of Literature or Internationale Gesellschaft für Empirische Literaturwissenschaft (IGEL), which had its second congress at the Free University, Amsterdam, in 1989.

4. Perspectives

a. The separation and complementarity of research and criticism (application)

In this essay literary studies have been conceived of as consisting both of research and criticism. This made it possible to discuss in the preceding section such different trends as Deconstruction and the empirical study of literature. I would resist the view that criticism, or literary history, or empirical research could claim the whole field of literary studies for itself, but this poses the problem of how research, criticism and history are related.

In many fields, scientific research and the application of knowledge in practice – in attempts to change or maintain the physical, social or cultural conditions of human life – are related, but distinct activities. The new field of environmental protection provides a good example. The problem of pollution may be a reason to open new fields of research, such as that of the distribution of ozone in the higher layers of the atmosphere, while the knowledge of physics can conversely be applied in the development of scenarios from which the politicians may choose their preferred line of action against the destruction of the environment.

Medical research, too, is often challenged by questions of medical practice. There are simple illnesses and simple prescriptions, but also more complex diseases, for which no certain cure (yet) exists and whose treatment depends on variable conditions. Here, the application of medical knowledge is linked to the question of what a particular patient may be prepared to be subjected to. In some cases also, the definition of what is to be considered 'healthy' or ethically permitted may become a point of discussion and may bear upon the decision whether or not to apply a particular treatment.

I cannot but see a strong analogy between literary and medical studies (and, to a lesser degree, environmental studies). In the universities, students should learn more than research alone, they must be given the knowledge necessary for intervening in undesirable practical situations (diseases, pollution, as well as blocked or poor literary communication). In literary studies, one such undesirable situation is the uncertainty about the literary canon. This problem can be examined by scientific means. It can be shown that some sort of canon is inevitable and that, throughout history, the canon has had different functions. Researchers may provide a number of scenarios for establishing a canon, from which the educators may choose the one they prefer. These proposals, which have a scientific basis, will have a contingent value only, as they are linked to different educational goals and to different beliefs regarding what should be considered important in literature. Medical doctors decide to write a particular prescription on the basis of reliable knowledge backed by research. Politicians select one of the anti-pollution scenarios that have a scientific basis. Why should literary critics and educators not follow their example and base their critical and didactic decisions on the results of the latest research? I would argue that criticism and research, far from being incompatible opposites, are complementary activities, which each has its own rules and function. Research will provide the background knowledge necessary for critical and didactic interference; criticism will formulate questions which can be answered on the basis of extant knowledge or which might be answered as a result of future research.

However much I believe that the empirical study of literature should be and will be given more emphasis, there are reasons for keeping critical activities firmly within the field of academic literary studies. In the daily and weekly press as well as in the literary magazines, criticism is preponderantly devoted to contemporary texts from the home culture, whereas the interpretation, editing and annotating of older texts and texts from distant cultures is almost completely in the hands of scholars affiliated with the universities. The writing of literary history, too, receives very little attention outside the academe and should be continued within its walls. What I would like to see, however, is that these critical and historiographical activities, which should apply insights yielded by empirical research, would indeed make more use of the results of this research.

b. Literary studies and their cultural and social context

It sounds reasonable that reliable knowledge, based on empirical research, should be used by critics and teachers of literature. But why should other people be interested in a well-founded criticism and didactics? Can knowledge of literary communication be of any interest to the public at large? Or to put it in budgetary terms, why should the taxpayer be asked to support research on literary communication and the teaching of literature?

Governmental support for literary studies can be defended very well, and from various sides attempts have been made to do so. Speaking of the humanities in general, Odo Marquard has eloquently argued that the increasing modernization of our world through the introduction of new technological inventions requires, what he called, the 'compensation' of the humanities, which have a counterbalancing role in maintaining an aesthetic sensibility, in accumulating historical knowledge and in providing philosophical orientation (quoted in *Neue Technologien*, 1987: 73-74). No one will deny that our world would be poorer if we no longer had an aesthetic sensibility, but a point of discussion might be why literature and art – without the disciplines that study them – would not be capable of keeping our aesthetic sensibility alive.

In literature, however, there is more at stake than aesthetic sensibility. The aesthetic convention enables an author to discuss matters in fiction or poetry which for political or other reasons can not be dealt with in a more straightforward way, in scholarly or journalistic discourse. The 'other reasons' mentioned can be of different kinds. There may be a taboo on the subject-matter a writer wants to deal with, or knowledge about his subject-matter may be still too intuitive or too complicated to be dealt with systematically. The aesthetic convention, which suspends to some extent the expectation that texts should be literally true, or – more accurately – that they should conform to an established world model, enables writers to discuss obliquely and metaphorically subjects which they otherwise would find impossible to write about.

Literature, then, conveys knowledge about domains which have not yet been dealt with adequately in scientific works or press reports. For example, Dostoevsky's novels were a treasure-house of psychological knowledge long before psychology was an established discipline. Science fiction, from Jules Verne onwards, explored problems in the field of space travel before scientific research in this area had begun. Utopian and dystopian fiction are similarly precursors of expository political writing. In the Netherlands, one novelist, Gerard Reve, has done more than any psychologist to create understanding for homosexuality. Writers, such as Grass and Celan, have contributed much to the mental processing of the disaster of World War II, which only recently became a central problem for German historians in the so-called *Historikerstreit*. The fiction of Pasternak and Solženitsyn preceded open political criticism in the Soviet Union of the Stalinist period, and the so-called 'scar-literature' played a similar role in China, paving the way for an open reappraisal of the Cultural Revolution. The reader, who follows the aesthetic convention, reads these texts as if they might be true, but he or she is not compelled to subscribe to their conclusions. For that reason, readers may be inclined to read about things they would refuse to be informed about in more straightforward terms.

The subject-matter of literature can perhaps be more precisely described as consisting of a discussion of the shaping, distribution and dissolution of conventions, in the sense that David Lewis (1969) has given to the term. In his view, conventions are distinguished both from natural inevitability and from logical necessity. Their main function is to provide a solution in a situation where human action is in principle free, but where it is useful or practical to establish a common pattern of behaviour. When a convention has been accepted, it provides a solution to a 'coordination-problem'. A convention, then, is a silent or explicit agreement which is arbitrary to the extent that in principle an alternative solution could also have been found. However, once a convention has been accepted by a particular population, there is a tendency to perpetuate it. As a product of habituation, this tendency is criticized in literature, which thereby performs a pre-eminently cultural function, by making us aware of alternative solutions to 'coordination-problems' affecting moral and emotional behaviour as well as social and political attitudes.

Variable solutions to coordination-problems are also discussed by the social sciences, but never in that free, non-committal, and therefore often experimental manner, which one finds in literary communication conditioned by the aesthetic convention. Of course, the decision whether or not to conform to the aesthetic convention is not a mechanical one. For instance, when it was announced in 1987 that Werner Fassbinder's *Die Stadt, der Müll und der Tod* was to be performed in Rotterdam, a large segment of the public was of the opinion that the aesthetic convention was not applicable to that play (a similar reaction was seen in Frankfurt, but not in Copenhagen). Whether or not the aesthetic convention is accepted depends on the historical, political, social and cultural context, as the conflict in 1989 over Salman Rushdie's *Satanic Verses* has once again shown. In this case, the Iranian government clearly did not accept the aesthetic convention, whereas the governments of the United Kingdom, other European countries and the United States were prepared to defend its applicability under the title of freedom of expression.

These examples show that literature is not as harmless as some people tend to believe, and cannot be reduced to its aesthetic function. Indeed, as Musil once said, it is a *Morallaboratorium*, and if we wish to continue making well-considered decisions in public as well as in private life, notably in matters where we are confronted with conflicts between conventions, we need the experimental domain of literature. In my view, the role of literature is more than 'compensation' for one-sided developments in science and technology. Literature presents an ever-increasing inventory of alternative conventions, which can be consulted by those who are engaged in building consensus for political as well as ecological decisions.

Allow me to insert an anecdote. At a recent international conference of European scholars from all disciplines and very different backgrounds, concerned with the future development of the sciences and its social implications, I was amazed to hear to what extent the frame of reference for the discussion consisted of an unexpected field of common knowledge: myth and literature. Physicists, ecologists, lawyers, psychologists, historians and others invoked Prometheus, Ovid, Don Quixote, Hamlet, *The Tempest*, Matthew Arnold and Robert Musil in support of their arguments. Apparently, as soon as scientists begin to discuss the possible applications of their work, they enter the domain of social and moral behaviour, i.e. the domain of conventions, which is the prime subject-matter of literature.

It is not enough to have creative writing; it must also be read if we wish to keep literary communication alive. But the reading of literature must be learned, and therefore must be taught, at all levels. Also, further research is needed in order to explore the communicative function of literature. It seems warranted to hypothesize that literature conveys knowledge about conventions in moral and social behaviour, in a way which we will not find in scientific or press reports. Many scientists seem to understand the need for a laboratory of moral behaviour. In general, the preparation of any political decision may profit from the treasure-house of conventional solutions to coordination-problems which is to be found in literature.

c. The relative value of the trichotomy: humanities, social and natural sciences

In § 4.a. I pointed to several analogies between physics, medicine and literary studies. All three fields of inquiry share the dichotomy of research and application (the use of scientific knowledge for interfering in a problematic practical situation). In my view, this dichotomy, which is characteristic of all sciences (including the humanities), is more relevant than the distinction between the so-called three cultures of the humanities, the social and the natural sciences.

What separates these three fields are vague boundaries between clusters of related problems. These boundaries have little to do with differences between objects of research. The human brain may be a relevant object of examination for the psychologist, the biologist interested in neurological transmission, and the student of literature interested in readers' reactions.

The distinction to be made is not between nature and spirit – as the old distinction between the natural sciences and *Geisteswissenschaften* might suggest – but between knowledge and the application of that knowledge. Following the criticism of the 'geisteswissenschaftliche Methode' invented by Dilthey in 1900, the case for a separate position for the humanities has lost much of its basis. It is, therefore, disappointing that the old distinction still lingers on in bureaucratic terminology.

I would favour to restyling the humanities as cultural sciences (Dutch: cultuurwetenschappen), whose problems are close to the social and behavioral sciences (Dutch: maatschappij- en gedragswetenschappen). The new term implies a scientific method that is similar to that of other sciences.

In one area, however, cultural sciences are different from the natural sciences. As soon as we are dealing with a historical situation, our conjectures cannot be tested in an experiment, as it will never be possible to reconstruct the original historical context. Perhaps one could adequately instruct the subjects participating in an experiment attempting to reconstruct a historical situation; those subjects might reach a level of knowledge of a particular historical period close to that of Pierre Menard, but they would not be capable of *forgetting* what has happened in modern times. For the historian, then, unlike the scientist, it is impossible to make predictions on the basis of experiments.

However, the field of the cultural sciences comprises more than history, and in the other domains experiments are quite possible, as D.E. Berlyne, Siegfried Schmidt, Dick Schram and others have shown. Reference to the psychologist Berlyne shows that the cultural sciences – in this case, aesthetics – can be close to the behavioral sciences in matters of methodology. The demise of a separate *geisteswissenschaftliche* method made possible the idea of a single scientific method (in the sense of trial and error-elimination, hypothesis and testing), which would also be applicable in the cultural sciences. The ground thus was prepared for interdisciplinary research. It is far from me to suggest that literary scholars can now freely step over the boundaries that have traditionally separated the disciplines. Of course, they must continue to specialize, to focus on a small number of problems and try to bring these to a solution. Now, however, since this specialized research is being done under comparable conditions and with compatible methods, its results can be evaluated and used by other scholars working in different fields. This new situation has expanded the methods of falsification with *interdisciplinary* testing.

5. Concluding remarks

Since the 1920s, there has been an evergrowing demand for greater scientific quality in the propositions made within the field of literary studies – so much so that the *geisteswissenschaftliche Methode* (hermeneutic understanding, literary criticism) can no longer claim to be the only valid method. It must now share the field with the empirical study of literature, and also with literary historiography which relies both on theories with empirical backing and on a particular critical position. As a corollary, so I have argued, the trichotomy of the natural sciences, social sciences, and the humanities or cultural sciences is less relevant than the dichotomy of empirical research versus hermeneutic criticism and other forms of applied science.

It is disappointing to see that in bureaucratic programmes regarding research in the cultural sciences tribute is still being paid to the *geisteswissenschaftliche Methode*, as phrased by Wilhelm Dilthey in 1900, whereas no reference is made to the empirical study of literature advocated by Siegfried J. Schmidt in his *Grundriss der empirischen Literaturwissenschaft* (1980).

The acknowledgement of empirical research in the cultural sciences opens up the possibility of interdisciplinary research between the various disciplines belonging to this cluster of sciences, i.e. between literary studies, the study of music, theatre, the visual arts, history, language, philosophy and religion. It is also a precondition for a fruitful exchange with the social and behavioral sciences, as well as with the natural sciences. For a solution to the major problems humanity has to cope with, such as the destruction of the environment, the exhaustion of natural sources, the suppression of human rights, ideological conflict, religious fundamentalism, unemployment, drug-dependence, the arms race, terrorism, insufficient education and cultural illiteracy, political will is not enough; we also need interdisciplinary research, so that political alternatives can be discussed under optimal conditions, with reference to their scientifically established consequences. It would be a serious mistake to believe that the cultural sciences, including literary studies, cannot play a part in the interdisciplinary research programmes concerning some of these issues. The general demand for interdisciplinary research will certainly strengthen empirical research into literary communication, necessitating the maintenance and expansion of facilities for both documentary and experimental research.

On the other hand, the tradition of literary criticism and literary history will also be continued. Their further development requires funding of the more traditional library facilities. An immediate problem that confronts governmental institutions in charge of education, teachers of literature, literary critics and publishing houses alike is that of the canon(s) of literary works to be studied in schools and universities, and serving as a frame of reference in literary criticism and in cultural and political life. Certainly, the increasing integration of the member-states of the European Community in the economical and political field will affect the cultural self-image of these countries and their image of their partners. It can be expected that the respective national and international literary canons will change accordingly. This process must be accompanied by both research and critical comment, in which, I assume, the idea of the contingency of values (Herrnstein Smith, 1988) will play a crucial role, but also notions such as cultural knowledge or cultural literacy (Hirsch, 1987), and its inevitable corollary, multi-cultural literacy (Simonson & Walker, 1988).

The empirical study of literature is well-equipped to deal with the problem of (multi-)cultural literacy. Much emphasis has recently been given to the study of cultural conventions. Convention, I have suggested, should be taken in its original, sociological sense, signifying explicit or implicit agreement to solve a coordination-problem in a particular way, in the awareness that it might also have been solved differently. Conventions, then, are regularities in the behaviour of human beings which are accessible to empirical research. The notion of convention has the further advantage that its use is not restricted to literary studies, but is applicable throughout the cultural and social sciences. Attempts have been made to explore culture as a system of conventions (D'haen, Grübel, Lethen, 1989).

Over the past decades, the debate within literary studies has been lively indeed. More than the natural sciences, the cultural sciences have been dependent on a favourable social and political context. In some countries, new research traditions have recently been established. I am not saying that they are fragile, but the number of universities where these new initiatives have a chance to develop is amazingly small. If we wish literary studies to play a part in interdisciplinary research geared towards the solution of major problems confronting humanity today, such as ideological conflict, religious fundamentalism, the suppression of human rights, and cultural illiteracy, these few havens of promising research should be spared budgetary restrictions and bureaucratic interference.

References

Angenot, M., J. Bessière, D. Fokkema & E. Kushner, eds., 1989. *Théorie littéraire: Problèmes et perspectives*. Paris: PUF.

Croce, B., 1964. *Aesthetic as Science of Expression and General Linguistic*. Trans. Douglas Ainslie. New York: Farrar, Strauss and Co., Noonday Press. First English edition 1909.

Dilthey, W., 1900. Die Entstehung der Hermeneutik. *Gesammelte Schriften* 5, 2nd ed. Stuttgart: Teubner, and Göttingen: Vandenhoeck and Ruprecht, 1957.

D'haen, T., R. Grübel & H. Lethen, eds., 1989. *Convention and Innovation in Literature*. Amsterdam and Philadelphia: Benjamins.

Eco, U., 1976. *A Theory of Semiotics*. Bloomington, IN and London: Indiana UP.

Ejchenbaum, B., 1926. The Theory of the Formal Method, in Matejka and Pomorska 1971: 3-38.

Erlich, V., 1955. *Russian Formalism: History, Doctrine*. The Hague: Mouton.

Even-Zohar, I., 1978. *Papers in Historical Poetics*. Tel Aviv: The Porter Institute for Poetics and Semiotics, Tel Aviv University.

Fokkema, D., 1985. The Concept of Code in the Study of Literature. *Poetics Today* 6: 643-656.

Fokkema, D., 1989. Questions épistémologiques, in Angenot et al. 1989: 325-351.

Fokkema, D. & E. Ibsch, 1978. *Theories of Literature in the Twentieth Century: Structuralism, Marxism, Aesthetics of Reception, Semiotics*. London: C. Hurst.

Gadamer, H.-G., 1960. *Wahrheit und Methode: Grundzüge einer philosophischen Hermeneutik*. Tübingen: Mohr.

Hernnstein Smith, B., 1988. *Contingencies of Value: Alternative Perspectives for Critical Theory*. Cambridge, MA and London: Harvard UP.

Hirsch jr., E.D., 1967. *Validity in Interpretation*. New Haven and London: Yale UP.

Hirsch jr., E.D., 1987. *Cultural Literacy: What Every American Needs to Know*. Boston: Houghton.

Ibsch, E. & D. Schram, eds., 1987. *Rezeptionsforschung zwischen Hermeneutik und Empirik*. Amsterdamer Beiträge zur neueren Germanistik, 23. Amsterdam: Rodopi.

Jakobson, R., 1921. Die neueste russische Poesie, erster Entwurf: Viktor Chlebnikov. *In* Stempel (1972: 19-135).

Jakobson, R., 1960. Linguistics and Poetics, in Sebeok 1960: 350-378.

Koselleck, R., 1979. *Vergangene Zukunft: Zur Semantik geschichtlicher Zeiten*. Frankfurt: Suhrkamp.

Lewis, D.K., 1969. *Convention: A Philosophical Study*. Cambridge, MA: Harvard UP.

Livingston, P., 1988. *Literary Knowledge: Humanistic Inquiry and the Philosophy of Science*. Ithaca and London: Cornell UP.

Lotman, Ju.M., 1970. *Struktura chudožestvennogo teksta*. Moscow: Izd. Iskusstvo.

Lotman, Ju.M., 1977. *The Structure of the Artistic Text*. Trans. Ronald Vroon. Ann Arbor: Dept. of Slavic Languages and Literatures, University of Michigan.

Ludwig, H.-W. & W. Faulstich, 1985. *Erzählperspektive empirisch: Untersuchungen zur Rezeptionsrelevanz narrativer Strukturen*. Tübingen: Narr.

Matejka, L. & K. Pomorska., 1971. *Readings in Russian Poetics: Formalist and Structuralist Views*. Cambridge, MA and London: M.I.T. Press.

Mukařovský, J., 1947. Zum Begriffssystem der tschechoslowakischen Kunsttheorie, in Mukařovský 1974: 7-20.

Mukařovský, J., 1974. *Studien zur strukturalistischen Ästhetik und Poetik*. Trans. Herbert Grönebaum and Gisela Riff. München: Carl Hanser.

Neue Technologien und die Herausforderung an die Geisteswissenschaften, 1987. Referate und Diskussionen eines Kolloquiums in der Villa Vigoni vom 16./17. Juni 1986. Hrsg. vom Bundesminister für Bildung und Wissenschaft. Bad Honnef: Bock.

Popper, K.R., 1973. *Objective Knowledge: An Evolutionary Approach*. Oxford: Clarendon Press. First edition 1972.

Ricoeur, P., 1969. *Le Conflit des interprétations: Essais d'herméneutique*. Paris: Seuil.

Rusch, G., 1987. *Erkenntnis, Wissenschaft, Geschichte von einem konstruktivistischen Standpunkt*. Frankfurt: Suhrkamp.

Schmidt, S.J., 1980. *Grundriss der Empirischen Literaturwissenschaft*, I: *Der gesellschaftliche Handlungsbereich Literatur*. Braunschweig and Wiesbaden: Vieweg.

Schmidt, S.J., 1982. *Foundations for the Empirical Study of Literature: The Components of a Basic Theory*. Trans. Robert de Beaugrande. Hamburg: Buske.

Sebeok, T.A., ed., 1960. *Style in Language*. New York: Technology Press of the M.I.T.

Simonson, R. & S. Walker, eds., 1988. *The Graywolf Annual Five: Multi-cultural Literacy*. Saint-Paul, MN: Graywolf Press.

Şingh, G., 1984. *Western Poetics and Eastern Thought*. Delhi: Ajanta Publications.

Šklovskij, V., 1916. Die Kunst als Verfahren, in Striedter 1969: 3-36.

Steinmetz, H., 1985. Genres and Literary History. *Proceedings of the Xth Congress of the International Comparative Literature Association* (New York and London: Garland) 1: 251-255.

Stempel, W.-D., ed., 1972. *Texte der russischen Formalisten*, II: *Texte zur Theorie des Verses und der poetischen Sprache*. München: Fink.

Striedter, J., ed., 1969. *Texte der russischen Formalisten*, I: *Texte zur allgemeinen Literaturtheorie und zur Theorie der Prosa*. München: Fink.

Todorov, T., ed., 1965. *Théorie de la littérature: Textes des formalistes russes*. Paris: Seuil.

Tripathy, B.K., 1989. I Have Lost the Text. *Jadavpur Journal of Comparative Literature* (in press).

Tynjanov, J., 1924. Das literarische Faktum, in Striedter 1969: 393-431.

Uspenskij, B.A., V.V. Ivanov, V.N. Toporov, A.M. Pjatigorskij & Ju.M. Lotman, 1973. Theses on the Semiotic Study of Cultures (as Applied to Slavic Texts), in Van der Eng and Grygar 1973: 1-19.

Van der Eng, J. & M. Grygar, eds., 1973. *Structure of Texts and Semiotics of Culture*. The Hague: Mouton.

Von Glasersfeld, E., 1985. Konstruktion der Wirklichkeit und des Begriffs der Objektivität, in *Einführung in den Konstruktivismus* (München: Oldenbourg): 1-26.

Wellek, R., 1960. Literary Theory, Criticism, and History, in Wellek 1963: 1-20.

Wellek, R., 1963. *Concepts of Criticism*, ed. Stephen G. Nichols. New Haven and London: Yale UP.

Wellek, R., 1970. *Discriminations: Further Concepts of Criticism*. New Haven and London: Yale UP.

Wellek, R., 1978. The New Criticism: Pro and Contra. *Critical Inquiry* 4: 611-624.

Marilyn Monroe meets Cassandra
Women studies in the nineties

Margret Brügmann

1. Introduction

In contrast to other disciplines within humanities, women studies is a very young discipline. This does not mean that through the ages women have not contributed substantially to the sciences, however variable circumstances of scientific acceptation and of actual opportunity for research might have been. The same observation applies to the participation of women in the field of artistic production. Depending on the spirit of the times, the representations of femininity and the tasks assigned to women accordingly, women have had – and taken – the opportunity to express themselves artistically. Considering the history of the past few centuries, one is struck by the fact that women have often been able to act on the public cultural scene in larger numbers at times of great social and political change, shifting power and identity. At such times of rupture, be it revolution or war, women all of sudden were considered capable of fulfilling, up to then, traditionally male tasks. After consolidation and stabilization of the political climate, women were called back to their traditional tasks and barred from positions previously taken by men. This tendency is noticeable not only in the social and political realm. Also at times when cultural concepts started to lose their general acceptance, womanhood could become suddenly a sort of promise of innovation. We can see this happening for instance with the French movement of Saint Simon or with the early Romanticists in Germany. Both groups joined social criticism to utopian ideas of the role and possibilities of women. As a result of the crisis of authority within cultural parameters, qualities of pure naturalness and, correspondingly, a natural intelligence, were attributed (mainly by men) to women. On the screen of this male 'hidden camera' female figures appeared who – apparently out of nothing – were endowed with intellect, sensibility, moral and emotional strength, and political vision. Even if hardly any women would have succeeded in fulfilling these instant images, it did not take long for the glamour, of those who had been successful, to fade. What is striking is not that most women failed to meet these gigantic tasks, but the fact that, the more conservative the political climate becomes, the less space there is for this type of woman. At the beginning of the 20th century we see the same kind of redistribution and revaluation of tasks. After the shock of the Russian Revolution and the First World War, all of a sudden women were given the chance – and also were taking the chance – to participate in cultural and political life. It is a rich and varied arsenal of women who were active in science and culture in the twenties and thirties. Though they had to represent a very different type of women than hundred years before, women deemed the participation in cultural life more important than the examination of the conditions underlying this sudden extension of their traditional role. The end of this prime of female talents we know: as Europe started to prepare for the Second World War, it did not take long before the 'exit' sign flashed for culturally active women. After the Second World War, women, busy polishing and straightening out male panoply, seemed to have been loosing again all rights in the process. The typical picture the fifties and sixties bring to mind is a naive, practical, Doris Day like housewife whose creativity is absorbed completely by household, raising of children and emotional support of her husband.

Reviewing this historical summary, it is easy to notice how women have been representing images of femininity that varied with the political and cultural climate of the time. This is also true of those periods in which women have been active in cultural life: even then, varying images of femininity directed the extension of artistic freedom and action. The romantic intellectual is being exchanged for the unconventional, vamp-like, Brooks imitation. What does not change however, is the argumentation based on conceptions concerning the 'nature' and 'essence' of woman, used to justify their place in cultural life. It is also remarkable how these representations change and even flip over into completely opposite images.

Another point is that representations of women and their 'essence' always follow closely the cultural patterns and tasks men have been mapping out for themselves. From this viewpoint the essence of woman can be taken as the mirror reflection of male imagination. Yet, this mirror is of a special kind: it is like the mirror of the queen in the fairy tale of Snow White, a mirror that has to affirm again and again the beauty of the queen. As we all know, this mirror is not to be trusted; as it does not do its job, the queen flies into a rage and tries to destroy the obnoxious mirror.

The reversal in this fairy tale is interesting: the mirror is male, the one mirrored female; is this a Freudian displacement?

Maybe the women's movement of the sixties and seventies in Europe and the USA can be compared with this mirror. Unequal economic opportunities at a time of increasing prosperity, and increasing dissatisfaction at incompatible role-assignments for women, certainly have contributed to the fact that women massively started to articulate the discontent they felt with respect to their life. Playfully but also militantly, they tried to capture public attention for the 'question of woman'. Though initially concrete political demands were made, the movement did not limit itself to social and political issues. In the arts and sciences as well, women started to develop an emancipatory consciousness. Slowly a discipline took shape oriented at examining the epitheton 'feminine' in the sciences and the humanities. It was named 'women studies', a name indicating as many chances as perplexities. Therefore, I will continue with a few historical notes on the idea of 'women studies'.

2. Differing roads: Women Studies

As noted before, women studies has developed within the context of the women's movement. The latter is tied up with the general atmosphere of student protests in the sixties and seventies. Both in the USA and in Europe great masses of young people took to the streets, demonstrated against their parent's ways of life and ideals which they considered unacceptable. Colonialism, capitalist exploitation, imperialist wars, and obsolete ways of life were listed again and again as reasons of discontent. The universities as well started to show signs of a crisis of authority; students refused the humanistic ideas they labelled antiquated. Inspired by classic marxist readings and the ideas of the Frankfurt School, old patters of thinking and valuation were questioned. In all this the settling of accounts with the 'fathers' got mixed with an increasing dissatisfaction at scientific paradigms. Students demanded so called 'socially relevant' science, of which personal and political interests and commitments had to be an equal part next to the regular curriculum. It is interesting to note that often the 'personal' was equated with the political, it even became a slogan. Later this equation became important in the women's movement, though in a different context. As a result of becoming more conscious of social wrongs, women started to examine critically their own position and existence, and to articulate their dissatisfaction at old patterns of behaviour between the sexes.

Within the women's movement, this type of political commitment led to a process of reflection on their identity as a group. Women and oppressed peoples were looked upon from the same perspective; the issues were: gaining an identity of one's own, liberation of imperialists and colonialists, taking over of political power, and manifestation of one's own – up to then – repressed culture.

Especially in the USA, but also in Europe, historical-materialist theories were applied to the relations of the sexes. Notions like oppression, exploitation and alienation were given new signification within the women's movement and incipient women studies. The idea of 'ideology criticism' gained a gender specific meaning. Women expressed their annoyance with the culturally imposed and ever changing images of femininity that had to be subjected to critical analysis. An atmosphere of optimism and a strong fighting spirit pervaded the women's movement. The old, early-bourgeois ideal of equality of all citizens appeared within reach. Apart from political equality, what was strived for was nothing more, nor less, than the appearance at last of the 'real' woman.

Before entering upon the implications of this strategy for women studies, I want to outline a second source of inspiration important for the women's movement and influential within women studies. With France as its base, a type of thinking evolved, mainly a criticism of culture, that is labelled nowadays, rather loosely, 'post-modernism'. Thinkers like Deleuze, Guatteri, Lacan, Foucault, Lyotard and Derrida developed a discourse of scientific criticism, fighting a battle against their scholarly legators with inherited weapons. The cultural battle of authority was fought with pens like razorblades. Cornerstones of timeless cultural self-evidence were dismantled one by one, and marked as the material of castles in the air. These French thinkers do anything but flaunt new concepts and truisms. Within the humanities they developed a style of thinking marked by ambivalence, short-circuiting any kind of truth and unequivocal meaning. The code word, by now also vogue word, of this French 'school' is Derrida's notion of deconstruction. Unlike before, at the time of the student protests, these worthy gentlemen show no interest in a regular 'parricide', they prefer the analytical razor to the axe. In a double movement of stock taking and critical editing, they acquired an attitude as radical as the students in their time but also as prudent as an executor, an attitude that was very effective in dismantling traditional scholarly authority. These 'new barbarians' were met in academia with as much reserve as the female scholars of women studies. "What is unknown is unloved" according to a Dutch saying. As in post-modernist thought, a number of truisms (or, at least, unmarketable antiques) were being exposed. Starting from the tradition of sceptics, especially Nietzsche and Freud, fundamental questions were being posed concerning Western self-consciousness. The exposition contained for instance: the rational, self-conscious subject, the idea of sovereign signifying power, of a text representing hidden truth, psycho-analytical models generating social rules, avant-garde as ultimate innovation. In France the auction resulted in an acceleration and radicalization of the process of 'genderization'. Female scholars started to examine their academic premises concerning writing practices as well as paradigms of scholarly practice. In France we see the beginning of 'écriture féminine', a feminist culture of research, critical of cultural cornerstones, that, however, never established itself as a group or a school. Inspired by contemporary intellectual discussions in France, a number of female scholars and writers have been using, in a productive and creative way, critical elements of post-modernism in women studies.

It would be an unjustified reduction to present women studies as a discussion modelled on two paradigms or schools of thought. Hereafter, the outline of the structure of paradigmatic developments within women studies should be taken as an effort to outline in exemplary fashion discussions within women studies. Apart from some general remarks, the emphasis will be on developments relevant to the art sciences.

3. Searching for a feminine aesthetics
"If women have the right to die by the guillotine, they should also have the right to public speech", thus the militant French feminist avant la lettre Olympe de Gouges. At least partly history proved her right: november 5 1793 she died by guillotine. Her amendment of human rights, the "Declaration of the rights of women and female citizens", did not conform with the aims of the French Revolution. Initially, women were accepted as political active citizens, but soon the Jacobins forbade women to establish their own revolutionary groups. Groups of women larger than five on the streets were forbidden in 1795. The bourgeois-emancipatory revolutionary

concepts of 1789, as well as those of 1830 and 1848, did not take the existence of women as citizens into account. Maybe the pressure of capitalist demands on men was too strong to give up women as sanctuary of their private emotions. Thus, it did not take long before conservatism was well established again. After the failure of the revolution, Goethe and Schiller, both close observers of the political movement in France, described the task of women as "domestic, stabilizing, harmonizing". Next is the bogey of politically active women.

In "Die Glocke" (the bell) Schiller says: "Da werden Weiber zu Hyänen" (thus women become hyenas); apparently Schiller is alluding to the enraged women who joined the storming of the Bastille. No critical comment on the public task of men however, though Schiller knew very well the course of the French Revolution.

Apart from this asymmetrical distribution of political and social tasks – or maybe rather in silent harmony with it – women were pushed more and more to the backdrop of the public platform of discussion.

It seems like a paradox: the more concrete, living women were kept away from the public scene, the more they became a topic of male art.

By the time women were silenced completely in the revolution, thé painting of the revolution, titled "Freedom leads the people", was made by Delacroix in 1831. This painting shows a woman heading a pyramid of fighting people. Up to this day, this painting is the symbol of the French Revolution – and maybe of 'revolution' in general. The woman in the painting symbolizes freedom – concrete, living women had already been domesticated to manageable companions and housewifes.

This is but one example of how the position of real women diverged from the images of her in art. In the course of late 19th century male art is dominated more and more by images of women, though now they represent menacing aspects of human existence. Pale, emaciated creatures craving for sex and blood, crowded the paintings, got voice in opera's and on stage. For several reasons, the general cultural confusion was expressed – first by intellectuals and artists – through the image of woman. Not anymore or not yet participating in public life, woman became the icon or bogey of all unfulfilled ideals. The arbitrary way in which the image of woman was used to represent emotions, resulted in widely divergent women's figures: extending from the chaste, praying farmer's wife (Leibl), to the *femme fatale* (Wedekind/Strindberg), and to the whore as menace (Birdsley). The apparent economy of the underlying pattern is quite simple: being absent from daily life, women can be used as a screen to project arbitrarily all kinds of fantasies and miraculous fictions.

In this context it is understandable that initially women studies in the art sciences have concentrated on the divergence of women's images in the arts on the one hand and the historical reconstruction of actual social-political reality on the other hand. This type of critical inquiry, weighing image against reality, did and does not lack art objects that can be used to trace the differences of reality, ideology and fantasy.

Historically, this kind of reception-research on women's images in the arts has been predominant. Widely divergent images of women – from Marilyn Monroe to Cassandra – were and are held up to historical scrutiny. The scientific framework for this kind of research is based partly on the idea of cognitive empathy, partly on the critical theory of historical materialism and ideology. The aim of reception-research is to help to put an end to the 'masquerade of femininity'.

The intention is to bring out the 'real' woman behind the masks. This presupposes a viewpoint that equates art and reality. Without further ado, fantast images are compared with social reality. In this perspective, art is perceived as a guideline for life. Knowledge of woman's 'real' identity is presupposed; in general, identity has become a catch phrase of femininity. Within the context of an analysis of the dichotomy of 'oppressor-oppressed', female identity is considered either as 'woman perishes under the pressure of society', or 'woman as a model of glorious victory, emerging all the more strongly from her battles'. Soon this opposition was to loose its simpleness. Awareness grew that the references of art are very complex and cannot be taken only in terms of (criticism of) ideology. Roland Barthes' notion of 'pleasure' became an intermediary causing all kinds of perplexities for rational-minded criticism. All of a sudden, Marilyn Monroe was not just a victim of male media politics, but a feast for the (female) eye. Everything got mixed up!

Another example is classical, stoical Cassandra, the prophetess nobody listened to, whose reputation in Western tradition was anything but pure, being domesticated as well by the conception of women as envious second-hand human beings (Christa Wolf). From this historical viewpoint, it almost does not seem to matter what women say; they are always the victim of distortion by dominant culture. But they can – and this is the feminist option – defend themselves successfully against oppression by sheer moral strength; in this way they may come out the worse for wear but still strong – a model for all those who have their doubts about female identity.

The interesting thing of this kind of research on the ideology of femininity, is the militant attitude with respect to male, bourgeois ideas of equality. At the same time however, it is confusing to see how bourgeois philosophy of equality and identity, and marxist emancipation doctrine are adopted without question. It is almost as if this kind of critical reception-aesthetics tries to recapture castles that – as almost everybody knows by now – are built on quicksands. But history shows that political utopia's, like the French Revolution, are held on to all the more persistently the more shaky they are. Thus, it is not surprising that, within feminist reception-aesthetics, often a judicial tone can be heard that is not without some new-old moralizing.

Up to now, the issue discussed was the relation of real women and their image in art, respectively, feminist reception of this relation.It was concerned in general with existent expressions of art both by men and women. Now I will continue with an outline of the innovations, discussions, and questionings taking place within a project of women studies devoted both to the arts and to the art sciences, during the last few decades when the women's movement started to influence both the arts and the sciences.

4. Crossing the USA

Let us first – also for historical reasons – turn to the USA. Adrienne Rich may not be the first critic, but she certainly combines many qualities of women studies: she is poetess, feminist, militant lesbian, female scholar, and a pioneer of black women studies. In her theoretical work she is suspicious of both established science and the women's movement becoming academic. She takes a stand against any kind of academic tradition. Her message is to 'read otherwise'.

This means: taking into account the intentions of the author, as well as the referential framework of the position of women in society, especially non-academic women. Rich distrusts academic education where women have to read literature textbooks written only by men.

She points out that there is a feminine subculture which, though not accepted by academia, might still be a source of very important information of and for women. Another thing she points out is the amalgam of social, aesthetic and scientific directives that keep women from any kind of innovation. Rich is very suspicious of the academic habit of, unwittingly, imposing its own rules, for in her opinion literary criticism forces literature into a conventional academic mould which does not reflect the reality lived by women. In this emancipatory struggle against the power of dominant discourse, a special kind of power sneaks in: moral righteousness. Rich postulates three doctrinal rules of feminist literary criticism: adequate analysis requires full knowledge of the author. The personal perspective of the one who analyses is charged with political impetus, refusing an objective, scientific attitude in favour of a 'correct' one that is not explained any further. The analysis of an oeuvre should comply with anti-capitalist class-consciousness which is equated with 'truthfulness'. This 'truthfulness' is being depicted as an 'activity in the real world'. The academic culture, being too cool, is hardly part of this real world. Referring to studies of Millett and Smith, Rich attempts to outline a politics of women studies evading stereotypes, yet expressed in stereotype marxist terms. How a feminine aesthetics or criticism should look like is expressed only in metaphorical terms as "not frozen, condescending, alienated".

Rich's criticism of prevailing practices of dominant discourses is certainly not unimportant. Yet, it is remarkable how she reverts to metaphorical language as soon as she wants to say something about 'feminine aesthetics'. I think what we see here is the central issue of women studies in the art sciences. For here, production of art joins art sciences with respect to the demand of innovating contributions by women. In other words, subject and object of analysis are entwined in a subtle, innovative movement. In order to elucidate this apparent tautology, I will take, of the many possible instances, Elaine Showalter's theoretical work as an example.

Showalter has been one of the first in comparative literature to look for the link between aesthetics and women. Inspired by historical-social models, she initially saw the specifically feminine aspect of culture in analogy with the model of subculture. Her proposition was that women's art could be compared to art developed in subcultures. However, the problem with this model is that women can not be compared with a subculture. Though almost every subculture has women as its members, not every woman is part of a subculture. For socially and culturally women are present, and partly active, at every level of society. Her quest for that which is specific of feminine culture and, related to this, feminine aesthetics, led Showalter to the field of cultural anthropology. Before she made this choice, Showalter had been reviewing, and subsequently dismissing, several models upon which a feminine aesthetics could be constructed: biological, linguistic, and psychoanalytical. According to her these models were either too restrictive or too compliant with gender-specific stereo-types concerning the possibilities of women. Showalter at last started to expect most of the cultural model of Ardener, introducing a sort of selective lunar eclipse as a gender-specific constellation: two partly overlapping full circles illustrate the constellation of the masculine and feminine cultural position. The biggest, overlapping part represents the area where men and women are both present. The left-over part, at the sides, mark the two area's that are exclusively feminine or masculine. It is not difficult to find examples for both area's in a historical-social context. In the context of aesthetics however, it is a lot more difficult to find an exclusively feminine area, as opposed to the ones marked by masculine connotations. Showalter's work shows this difficulty. In her opinion language is situated in the middle, overlapping part of the circles. Language does not have a specifically masculine or feminine mode or existence, it is an instrument at the disposal of both sexes equally. Thus, one has to conclude that there is no such thing as feminine language. Yet, where is Showalter going to find her feminine aesthetics? She looks for it in archaic expressions, for instance rituals, and matriarchal practices on the one hand, in utopian ways of writing on the other hand, meanwhile taking cover in metaphorical language. Showalter's dream is a way of writing – inspired by the French theorists of 'écriture féminine' – that is flowing and without codes. Also, she quotes existent texts depicting utopian models through which women can get their fill of cultural fantasies.

With respect to the struggle for a feminine aesthetics, Showalter is certainly not to be underestimated. Her work however, shows – maybe unwittingly – the impasse to which the quest for a model of feminine presence in culture may lead. An aesthetics of the feminine, searching for unity, presence and identity of women, turns into an utopian dream or archaic reminiscence. This does not mean that the project by itself is without value.

Toril Moi for instance, will affirm this, yet without following strictly Showalter's road. Moi was one of the first to apply psycho-analytical textual insights to feminist projects. She was also the one who introduced Julia Kristeva, a French theorist, in the USA. Moi was fascinated by Kristeva's theories for its lack of rigid social and scientific models of femininity. Kristeva is mainly interested in the process through which meaning, expressions and social configurations are created. Moi saw the crucial importance of this viewpoint for the possibility of a reflection on feminine aesthetics without moralistic – or otherwise – guidelines. Yet despite her positive valuation of Kristeva's theory, Toril Moi has some critical comments concerning this 'praxis' from a political viewpoint. She thinks Kristeva's interpretation of this 'praxis' has some feminine impetus, but is too individual. Moi herself is engaged in an amalgam of political and textual practice together with feminist commitment. According to her, women studies have to keep their guardian role, taking care that the feminine aspect is not getting lost nor fashionably incorporated in all the discussions on post-modernist avant garde.

This non exhaustive summary reviewing American theories concerning feminine aesthetics shows several consistent features: there is such a thing as an essentially female or feminine identity. Women's texts point towards a – transcendent – uni(ci)ty of female existence, related either to utopian women culture or to female subculture.

The intellectual framework as a whole is based on the presupposition that the world can be mapped and determined as a homogeneous totality of cultural layers.

In European theories concerning feminine aesthetics there are some groups or schools that show some resemblance to the American way of thinking. Especially the German writer and theorist Christa Wolf has had a lot of influence on the development of a conception of feminine aesthetics. Wolf's account of journeys made in search of the origin and reception of the mythical figure of Cassandra, are linked up with the development, in aesthetic categories, of a critical perspective on the historical-social position of women. Wolf does not have the pretention of presenting a ready-made, fully elaborated feminine aesthetics. Rather, she describes the history of a fascination. In choosing the genre of a travel account, she lets her readers participate in her discoveries. She develops an aesthetics that allows her to view already known facts in a new light and configuration. Her work is polemical with respect to the increasing specialization of various social tasks, including the arts. In the arts she sees the rise of a lifeless configuration of conventions that, in her opinion, contributes to the stifling of dissident – including feminine – ways of articulation. Referring to the oeuvre of Ingeborg Bachmann, Wolf attempts to develop a revaluation of the sensibility for commonplace, daily things, having also consequences for aesthetic practice. As noted before, Wolf does not draw up the balance or present a positive interpretation concerning models of change. Instead she describes convincingly how tiresome it is to always have to fight against an age-old cultural setting that leaves no room for the articulation of women's insights. This is important in so far as the lament of women is considered most of the time as an expression of the general dissident position of every aesthetically innovative individual, i.c. man, who initially is often underestimated. What is overlooked in this way, is the enormous, asymmetrical difference between men and women concerning the extent of possibilities both have to act in public life. In this respect, Virginia Woolf's "A Room of One's Own" still deserves to be on an obligatory reading list.

5. The French Connection

It would have been surprising if the issue of asymmetrical difference between men and women would not have been taken up by progressive dominant
discourse. The lesson of history shows that it is not the actual pariahs who
start revolutions but those, more affluent, who have the leisure to think
about the misery of mankind and articulate it theoretically. In this respect,
avant garde writers, theorists and women have something in common:
they are critical of prevailing paradigms and they are hardly listened to.
Deleuze and Guattari have formulated a theory of subversion, using the
epithet 'feminine' in a political sense. Their work on Kafka breaks new
ground with respect to ideas about aesthetics of cultural minorities. They
use Kafka's position to illustrate a complex of diverging motives of power:
Kafka as a German in Czechoslovakia, as a protagonist of Imperial Austria,
Kafka as a jew, as a second-hand citizen within this context. And Kafka as
a writer, as a non-citizen within both domains of bourgeois identity.

In this aporetical state Kafka works at an oeuvre that in some aspects can
be compared to the work of many female artists finding themselves in a
deadlock. The Kafka study shows a position elaborated in another work by
Deleuze and Guattari on the notion of 'being small' related to that of
'woman' in literature. They introduce the notion of power in literature,
signifying – like Wolf later – the rules and directives that determine the
aesthetic commercial worth of art. Naturally, these vary according to the
spirit of the time. Their model of 'small literature' is in no way intended as
an issue of genre or form. It refers to a type of literature that is not yet
incorporated by the establishment and that critically comments on cultural
configurations.

Deleuze and Guatteri compare the position of this type of marginal art with
the one women have in society. Quantitatively, women make up half of the
world's population. However, as far as their cultural contribution goes,
they are marginal. Based on this fact is the statement of the two theorists
that every artist really should become 'woman'. That is, he should take up
the feminine cultural position in order to deconstruct conventions. The
Hamlet question is: to be woman or to become woman, that is the difference!

This question is taken up by the theorists of so called 'écriture féminine'.
Hélène Cixous starts with the first part of the question: "what does it mean
for a woman to be a woman in this culture?" – and continues with the
question: "what does this constellation mean for aesthetic practice?" Cixous'
starting point is that, historically speaking, women have been squeezed

into a tight corselet of representations of femininity, stifling them physically. This restriction and repression should be abolished, not only through historical analysis but also by a-historical annexation of cultural heritage. Cixous' aim is that woman should find and take back their voice. She introduces the notion of *voler* as a strategy; it means both 'flying' and 'stealing'. This terminological invention indicates on the one hand the licence of an unhistorical approach, on the other hand the fact that existent cultural forms are owned by 'others'. In aesthetic practice this results in a post-modern amalgam, mixing analysis, criticism, agitation, poetry and utopia in one text.

Apart from these political-strategically inspired theoretical reflections, Cixous takes part in the discussion on the process-character of aesthetic texts. Based on the linguistic ideas of psychoanalysis and its duality of a masculine and feminine economy, Cixous develops a theory about sexe-biased aesthetics. She starts from the idea that every individual is fundamentally bi-sexual. She maintains that the castration complex, the fear to loose something precious and to become a cripple, is an important motive explaining the tendency of many people to collect goods, also art objects, namely as prevention for potential lack. This, according to Cixous, is masculine economy. With respect to the other, feminine cultural economy, Cixous states – politically provoking – that it is without castration anxiety; implying that women are without fear of 'lack' and therefore without any tendency to accumulate. This hypothesis leads to the supposition that the body could be of influence in aesthetic economy.

With bi-sexuality as starting point, Cixous views aesthetics as a changing play of masculine economy of accumulation and feminine economy of spending, flowing. She situates this practice in the context of innovative artists, hardly distinguishing between males and females. Though Cixous does encourage women to take this feminine economy as a challenge and to use it as a way to produce self-willed texts.

The latter seems to have happened already: in the case of Julia Kristeva, literature theorist and psychoanalyst of Bulgarian origin. She represents several positions: originally trained in marxist structuralism, she grew to be one of the most radical critics of established culture sciences and its paradigms in her second homeland France. As a woman in a male dominated field, she soon started to articulate "the discontent of womanhood", becoming, before long, one of the sharpest critics of the women's movement. In her work Kristeva joins conservatism to *avant garde*: on the one hand she revolutionized conceptions of aesthetic practices, on the other hand she remained a relatively orthodox Freudian. In the context of this essay, I will discuss Kristeva's ideas about the relation of women to aesthetic production.

Inspired by the Lacanian model of the subject, Kristeva developed a theory concerning aesthetic praxis, the way an expression of art comes about, using the notion of 'femininity'. Kristeva starts with the observation that the production mechanisms of signs should be looked at, rather than the ready-made grammatical/syntactical tableaux that most scholars take as starting point of analysis. For in the latter case, it is precisely the interesting deviants, for instance the language of lunatics and artists, that are being excluded. Engaged in the literature of 19th century *avant garde*, she tried to theorize linguistic deviations and innovations. She soon reached the conclusion that every individual is, in a small way, a linguistic innovator. The underlying argumentation is as follows: in the first stage of life (the imaginary stage) when mastery of grammatical language is still lacking, the child experiences a lot of important bodily sensations like sound, colour, rhythm, temperature, and smell. These experiences are made mostly in close contact with the mother. At the point where this duality is extended to include a third one, the father, the child reaches the stage of learning to articulate its demands in language. The child enters the symbolical order which Kristeva, following Lacan, describes as "the law of the father". The early sensations of the child are not 'forgotten', they make their appearance in the symbolical order as bodily language, pitch and rhythm of speech on the one hand, and as slips of the tongue, grammatical and lexical innovations on the other hand. Chronologically, these components of language – of any kind of sign practice – are to be situated in the early stage of development, yet they remain an essential part of symbolical articulation. These components are called by Kristeva the 'semiotic', or , with reference to the dominant person of the early stage, the 'feminine'. She localizes the semiotic-feminine aspect in social and aesthetic practice. What she calls the "effect of woman" is what she sees happening in the social-political field: women being the silent support of authority in power. Here, I think, Kristeva points out the conservative aspect of the semiotic. In aesthetical context however, the semiotic has a prominent place: it is the driving force behind any innovation. The artist has to leave partly the symbolical order by 'diving into the semiotic' in order to reach an innovative (re)arrangement of the symbolical order. Sometimes Kristeva calls the dive into the semiotic the 'mother-function' of aesthetic practice. Kristeva does not advocate a new language nor a return to non-language, she always emphasizes that every experiment should result in symbolical articulation. In this respect, she has her doubts about the innovative value of feminist art. Kristeva reproaches feminist artists for wanting to introduce a notion of femininity in aesthetics in either a too chaotic or too simplistic way. Analyzing former *female avant garde* writers, Kristeva points out that, because of their position in society, these women often had to fight hard to escape madness and to return to the symbolical order. One is struck in this analysis by Kristeva's strictly psychoanalytical and individualistic argumentation. She does not refer at all to socially dominant discourses and representation practices that cannot have failed to influence the emotional balance and aesthetic practice of female artists.

Reviewing the various French theories concerned with the positioning and the application of the notion of 'femininity', one can see several general resemblances. Femininity is not, at least not unqualifiedly, equated with specific female identity. Insight in discourses of power and psychoanalytical models prevents the unambiguous presenting of the feminine in culture. It is an unhappy combination of circumstances that exactly at the moment when women start to develop an emancipatory discourse, philosophers start to deconstruct theoretically notions like identity, power, and consciousness. This does not make reflection on the ferment 'femininity' in culture any easier, but, reversely, for that very reason it may be more of a challenge. For, as the preceding discussion made clear, femininity is not anymore considered as referring exclusively to a specific social or biological group. On the one hand, it is accorded the quality of general cultural subversion, on the other hand it is seen as part of every individual. Thirdly, and partly as a result of these two positions, it appears to be taken as a necessary element of creativity in contemporary theories on aesthetic innovations.

6. In search of the future
Naturally, the intention to predict the future of women studies in the art sciences on the basis of this rough sketch, cannot involve methodological or thematic directives. In general, predictions are accompanied by the same unpleasant feeling as burial rituals: with a lot of ceremony something is called to symbolical presence in virtue of its absence. Thus, instead of outlining guidelines and directives, I prefer to finish this discussion with some questions inciting reflection on possibilities of further research.

First, it might be helpful to look again at the place of women studies. As a new discipline women studies has attempted to gain a foothold within the

institutional bulwark of the universities. That has required, and still requires, the surmounting of several obstacles. In sheer quantity, the presence of female faculty at the universities is below any standard. However,
being a woman – like being a man – is by itself no qualification for practising
science or being a scholar. In the context of a policy of positive action, it
nowadays almost appears as a sign of enlightenment if women are allowed
to become faculty members. As she probably had to fight hard to reach this
position, it is by no means a matter-of-course that a female scholar will be
notable for a critical attitude with respect to her institution. Therefore,
there is nothing to be taken for granted in the relation between women
studies and being a woman scholar. Mostly a woman scholar will prefer to
keep a low profile with respect to her being a woman, in order to enhance
her so called scientific objectivity. On a larger scale, the whole discipline
of women studies has the same problem. Up to now, women studies is
mostly an affair of women, as they still have the most extensive and thorough knowledge of the, rapidly expanding, literature of the field. This
women's enclave mostly is looked at with suspicion and from afar. Lack of
knowledge and representations of social roles join together in making up a
judgement that is more emotional than scientific. Universities in general
have three strategies in dealing with women studies: it tries to create a
modern profile for itself by financing fashionable (women studies) research. Or it puts up with women studies for a time, but does not support it
anymore in case of lacking finances or positional assistance. Or, last but
not least, it takes women studies serious, meaning most of the time that
women studies are being subjected and judged according to traditional
standards of scholarship and management. In this way, new publishing
channels, changed didactic and research practices, and different social
connections are approved only on the condition that they do not fail to
meet the more narrowly defined regular university standards. But, of course,
that is exactly where the trouble starts. Women studies is not intended to be
merely a catching up strategy devised for underprivileged female students,
nor a supplement filling gaps in established fields of research. Having a
critical attitude towards prevailing and established practices of scholarship,
women studies challenge, and incite reflection on methodological issues
and paradigms that are taken for granted. If this aspect of women studies is
taken seriously – and I think that this is the point where women studies
presents a challenge – the result will be a paradoxical situation: the institutions
that are being criticized have to allow their own undoing, or, at least, the
fact that they are going to be changed. For this reason it is understandable
that the attitude towards women studies is ambivalent: stimulation on the

one hand, negation on the other hand. Recent variations on this strategy are the neutralizing of women studies by labelling it 'gender studies' (USA), or the concentration of women studies in a few 'centres of excellence' (the Netherlands). In both cases, the range, the diversity, and the critical innovative aspect of women studies is threatened in the long run.

With this institutional balance act of women studies in mind, it might be worthwhile to think about its potential, its further developments, if given a chance. First, it is important to point out that the critical attitude of women studies is always in relation to existent disciplines. This does not mean however, that critical revisions and innovations do not take place within feminist theory itself. On the basis of Kristeva's theory, one can distinguish between the function of the semiotic and the critical practice of women studies.

If the 'effect of woman' signifies the silent, invisible support of dominant scientific discourse, then one could devise an emancipatory strategy to help minorities, and in particular women, to become more visible and audible within this discourse. Apart from numerical visibility, one can opt for perspectives and ideas for research that, historically speaking, have been attributed to women. A drawback is that this could lead to confirmation of traditional patterns and restrictions. On the other hand, this strategy would allow women to contribute to all fields of science and scholarship without negating their own, sexe-specific experience. If this strategy is to succeed, the institutions have to be open, and also prepared, for plurality in thematic, paradigmatic, and methodical respect. I would welcome such course of events for its innovative potential. Though willingness to do away with the still prevalent equation male = man = human being, is a first precondition; a willingness that also might result in breaking down the stereotype bogey of the frustrated bluestocking and in making possible cooperation on equal terms. Being still very far removed from the ideal of non-repressive science and research, I would still applaud this vision of a desirable future.

Returning to Kristeva's theory of the semiotic, we have seen that she also attributes a positive quality – apart from the more conservative 'effect of woman' – to the semiotic: its creative 'mother-effect'. Especially in the art sciences where aesthetic production is the central theme, the notion of 'the semiotic' can be used to signify future research perspectives. Since the end of the last century, the criterion of quality in art, and by extension the art sciences, is its innovative, avant garde aspect. Kristeva characterizes the semiotic as the element of disturbance of order and innovation within practices of signification. In the analysis of art, it would be interesting to examine how exactly the semiotic element functions within a specifically historical, physiological, and aesthetic praxis. It may require adaptations of the framework and instruments of analysis, as the framework and method of existent theories is not adequate in this case. Down the line it could mean the challenge to leave the meta-theoretical discourse without lapsing into incomprehensible subjectivism that allows no dialogue nor criticism. Deleuze and Guattari acclaimed the qualities marginal discourse can have under the title of "becoming-woman". Taking up this point, it is not impossible that – because of their marginal position in academia – actual, concrete women are able to develop perspectives leading to a more pluralistic academic discourse. Implying a way of thinking that tries to minimize the hierarchizing of differences, this type of emancipation requires a self-critical attitude of all those who set the tone of academic discourse. Apart from that, it also requires that one is allowed to use insights from other disciplines for one's own research. And finally, of utmost importance in general are the reciprocal interweaving and cross-fertilization of separate disciplines, the passing on of detailed knowledge, and an old-fashioned, broadly ranged, (post-)humanistic learning.

Translating these general perspectives into possibilities of further research in humanities, the following accentuation of complementary themes results:
An area of research in which women studies has gained already some prominence is the uncovering of 'forgotten' female artists. In general, artists are – following the spirit of the times – fairly often rediscovered and revaluated. The same is true of female artists. It would be interesting to inquire further into the reasons why female artists have fallen into oblivion. Which social-cultural discourses have played their part in their disappearance and reappearance? And how do historians deal with this phenomenon?
Closely connected to this question is the problem of aesthetics being canonized. Roughly speaking: did female artists only produce second-rate art or did the things they made fail to comply with the aesthetic conceptions of their time? The question is, how does the dissident, forgotten art of women relate to the spirit of the times?
Is it a matter of perspective, point of view, stylistic innovation, deviation of content, causing the disappearance? And, in order to be able to compare: which maybe more adjusted female artists did succeed? How do forgotten female artists fit into the whole spectrum of artistic production of their

time? How do art critics then and now relate to the aesthetic products of women? At this point analyses of style and content entwine with analyses of social-historical representations of femininity. Cooperation of history, art and social sciences in this field of research probably would be productive.

The above mentioned issues are tied up with the question how, in general, femininity is being represented culturally. Which andro-centric features are playing a consistent role in the cultural perception of femininity? Further inquiry into this question will lead to a kind of foundational research where the presuppositions of Western dominant categories of thinking are analyzed. Notions like visibility, unity, duality, consistency, permanence are the foundation of the type of thinking that – as mentioned earlier – is being questioned by post-modernity. As a practical result of such questioning, also ideas like identity, power and morality seem to have been robbed of their traditional unequivocal meaning. It would be a challenge if women studies of the art sciences, closely cooperating with philosophy, would take part in these discussions, not only to refine paradigms or as a manifestation of otherness. Rather the challenge is: is women studies, with its (sexe-)specific originality, able to contribute to the extension and change of systems of thought as instruments of knowledge? Which methodical-theoretical contributions can be developed here? This type of research certainly requires the contribution of several disciplines. It is not unlikely that a so called marginal discipline can come up with enlightening new perspective on old paradigms. Such research will be productive in at least two fields of women studies in the art sciences which will be sketched below.

Often the innovative element in processes of aesthetic production is thought to be found in the unconscious. As discussed above under the heading of 'écriture féminine', the notion of femininity is being used here in relation to aesthetic innovation and the creative process. Theoretical work in this field is for a large part inspired by psychoanalysis. The latter however, is based on a couple of traditional Western presuppositions. Within women studies research the question can be posed: what are the possibilities to renew systematically and remove the restrictions of psychoanalytical theory with the help of critical notions concerning femininity? And on the other hand: with the help of a psychoanalytical theory thus changed, how can theories concerning aesthetics be developed further in such manner that they are able to describe and situate systematically the way creative processes and its products are sexed? Research that is already being done in this field certainly deserves more attention in the future.

Apart from the field of aesthetics where the epitheton feminine is used frequently, it is important that research will be done in all cultural domains concerning models and theories that work, for whatever reason, with notions of femininity. The question is: in which social and scientific fields notions concerning femininity are being cited as metaphor, allegory, or analogy? The issue of interest here is the fact that theories are 'ontologized' and legitimized with the help of the notion of femininity. Only apparently contradicting this are statements focusing on womanhood and declaring, on the basis of existent andro/homocentric theorizing, women and femininity deviant with respect to any origin. It would be of importance to track down such descriptive models. What is at stake here is the question if any underlying structures can be analyzed, how paradoxical ways of reasoning can be deconstructed, and how they can be explained (and changed).What kind of interaction is there between such kind of theorizing and cultural expressions of femininity, and – last but not least – what effects do these ways of thinking have on the total panorama of society?

Women studies already has, to a large extent, an interdisciplinary practice and tradition. It is necessary not only in order to be able to analyze the complex, asymmetrical relation of the sexes. Interdisciplinarity has also created the space in which criticism, ethics and innovation can be thought and practised together. Within women studies of the art sciences, the awareness of social wrongs has resulted in an increasing awareness of rigidity and cliché's on the one hand, and possibilities of change on the other hand. One could call it a mixture of deconstructive practices and an 'aesthetics of commitment'. Both in the arts and in the art sciences, there are discrete attempts to understand the combination of deconstruction and identity, not anymore as destroying, but as intensifying the latter. This would allow numerous and, as yet, unheard-of possibilities to generate new links and connections. And maybe then it will be the time that a Marilyn Monroe can be both beautiful ánd intelligent, that a Cassandra not only will foresee the future but will be heard as well. Inevitably, time will teach us.

References

Barrett, Michèle (ed.), 1979. *Virginia Woolf: Women and Writing*. London.
Bovenschen, Silvia, 1979. *Die imaginierte Weiblichkeit*. Exemplarische Untersuchungen zu kulturgeschichtlichen und literarischen Präsentationsformen des Weiblichen. Frankfurt am Main.
Braun, Christina von, 1985. *Nicht ich. Ich nicht: Logik, Lüge, Libido*. Frankfurt am Main.
Brügmann, Margret, 1986. *Amazonen der Literatur*. Studien zur deutsch-sprachigen Frauenliteratur der 70er Jahre. Amsterdam.
Cixous, Hélène, 1975. Le rire de la Méduse. *L'Arc* 61.
Cixous, Hélène, 1976. Schreiben, Feminität, Veränderung. *Alternative* (108)9.
Deleuze, Gilles & Felix Guatteri, 1975. *Kafka. Pour une littérature mineure*. Paris.
Friedan, Betty, 1963. *The Feminine Mystique*. New York.
Irigaray, Luce, 1974. *Speculum de l'autre femme*. Paris.
Kristeva, Julia, 1974 *La révolution du language poétique*. Paris.
Kristeva, Julia, 1980. *Desire in Language*. New York.
Moi, Toril, 1985. *Sexual/Texual Politics. Feminist Literary Theory*. London/New York.
Rich, Adrienne, 1986. Toward a More Feminist Criticism. In: *Blood, Bread, and Poetry: Selected Prose 1979-1983*. New York.
Wolf, Christa, 1983. *Kassandra*. Darmstadt/Neuwied.
Wolf, Christa, 1983. *Voraussetzungen einer Erzählung: Kassandra*. Frankfurter Poetik-Vorlesungen. Darmstadt/Neuwied
Woolf, Virginia, 1981. *A Room of One's Own (1928)*. New York.

Part 5

History

History

P. den Boer

1. Is innovation predictable?

Fundamental innovation in scholarship is basically unpredictable. However, when one takes into account information gleaned from the past and present, it is possible to point out certain issues, fields of research, methods, and techniques, on which many scholars will be apt to focus. It does not follow that it is in particular these areas which will yield the greatest scholarly progress. It is merely to be expected that research institutes will spend on such projects that part of their budgets which has not been tied down in advance.

The position of the study of history is ambiguous, like that of many other social sciences. A vast professional scholarship in history does exist; many people are able to earn a living as historians in the fields of research and teaching. In professional historiography considerable financial resources are available and these are handled in accordance with official procedures, as is the case with other sciences. Alongside there exists a non-professional study of history, not regulated by money and official routine – this kind of historiography is able to command a wide audience and in the past it has repeatedly initiated new directions among professional historians. History is a very accessible field of study, where the self-taught amateur has played, and presumably will continue to play, an important role. Naturally, this unofficial, uncontrolled historical output is in no way predictable. My comment on the study of history in the nineties will therefore mainly refer to trends in professional historical research, regulated by money and official rules.

2. Innovation in an age-old discipline

General trends cannot be prognosticated merely on the basis of recent information. One needs a historical perspective for sketching a diachronic development. In the case of the study of history this must go far back in time, for historiography is a very ancient discipline.

It is an innate human characteristic to give an account of the past. Putting down such accounts into writing is almost coeval with the invention of the art of writing. Centuries of historical study have preceded the writing of the first history book transmitted to us in its entirety, the *Histories* of Herodotus of Halicarnassus. Can one expect a discipline with such an age-old tradition to be in any way capable of innovation? Can we seriously, without seeming ridiculously conceited, raise the question of possible changes in the study of history in the last decade of the second millennium of the Christian era? Isn't every kind of historiography in the perspective of such a vast span of time a repeat performance? Is it not mainly a lack of historical knowledge and erudition which enables us to fool colleagues and authorities, so as to make them believe that we are doing some really innovatory work? To summarize: is there ever anything new under the sun?
Such questions originate in a wisdom which has overtones of the Old Testament and which undeniably contains a grain of essential truth. This philosophical modesty could perhaps be defended in the perspective of intellectual abstraction, but on the other hand it should not be denied either that the actual conditions under which historians are to work have radically changed. There exists a world of institutional differences between the classical historiographers and professional historians of today. It could be added that even parallels between the old and new are basically a matter of the level of abstraction. The further we move away from the earth, the

more human beings come to resemble one another. Only when considered at close range it is the differences which stand out.

3. A triple perspective
When we focus on the changes in the study of history, these can be highlighted in various ways. Let us opt for a three-fold approach. We may distinguish three temporal categories with regard to institutional change: the long-term perspective, the medium length and the short-term one. With the 'long-term' we shall refer to the many centuries which separate us from the classical historiographers. The institutional differences between, say, the situation of roughly 2500 years ago, the time of Herodotus or Thucydides, and that of early nineteenth-century historians. With the perspective of medium length we shall refer to the last hundred and fifty years, roughly from the beginning of the nineteenth century onward. With the 'short term' we refer to the last twenty-five years, from the sixties onward. Each of these spans of time requires further consideration.

4. The long-term perspective
Viewed in our perspective the study of history up to the beginning of the nineteenth century displays four conspicuous changes. The differences relate in the first place to the social position of the historian, in the second place to the availability of historical sources, in the third place to technical equipment and in the fourth place to history's function.

With regard to the first point one ought to realize that from time immemorial the study of history depended on one's own financial resources. Professional historians did not exist, that is to say, historians who earned their living by means of the study of history. From the beginning of the Western educational tradition, which goes back to ancient Greece, the teaching of history had no more than a subordinate position. Leaving aside a few exceptions, it was only in the nineteenth century that teaching history in a separate course gained a firm footing. For more than two thousand years history was no institutionalized and independent subject in teaching.

With regard to the second point we can hardly imagine what historical research was like when almost no written sources were available. Even so, for many centuries the historian gained 'knowledge by asking questions'. Actually, that is the original meaning of the Greek word 'historiai': enquiries. When later on repositories of written sources are set up, in temples and palaces, this does not yet entail that such archives are accessible for historical research workers. The archives, deposit of government and repository for proofs of antiquity, and so providing legal sanction of power and rights of property, were secret. Public access to archives is alien to a government which does not allow for participation or for people having a say.

In a society without the printing-press, where vellum is scarce and each copy has to be made by hand, historiographers will be rare and have a very special status. Consequently, history has a very different function. Classical historiography had a very exclusive reading public. In that kind of mainly pragmatic history the acts and motives of princes, generals, and authorities were central. It was only useful to become acquainted with their history for such people as were to assume comparable social offices. Classical historiography is an elitist historiography.

By and large Christianity preserved this secular historiography, but something was added to the school programme: Biblical history with the aim of edifying. Here we have a contrast with the pragmatic and elitist classical historiography: this Biblical history was fundamentally intended for everyone, without exception.

In the special field of ecclesiastical history, history of the monasteries, and lives of the saints some congregations developed an unrivalled critical expertise. The *De re diplomatica* (1681) of the Benedictine monk Jean Mabillon, for instance, is generally considered to be the fundamental work on palaeography and diplomatic studies. Yet the influence of this erudite monastic scholarship was confined to a relatively small group of scholars.

5. The medium-length perspective

In the first half of the nineteenth century some fundamental changes took place in the age-old study of history.[1] State power increased and historiography was 'nationalized'. In preceding centuries there had been no government which gave employment to historians on a generous scale. The increase of state activities gave rise to a growing number of professional historians. Promoting the study of history as a matter of national importance came about in various ways and at different times. Germany was in the lead, France followed, and the Netherlands trudged behind. When compared to the present situation the professional community of historians was still small and specialization in its infancy. Specialist periodicals played as yet a very insignificant role. The most prominent historians of the first half of the nineteenth century were still in touch with a wide and informed reading public. The social position of the academic historian was not yet reduced to the marginal status of the average modern specialist.

---

[1] For a further development of this institutional approach see P. den Boer, 1987.

Historical sources became far more accessible consequent upon the French Revolution. In the history of public records three important developments can be distinguished: centralization/nationalization, making the records public, and the making of inventories. These developments did not happen simultaneously. Centralization of historical documents was of old a favourite aim of many governments. During the Revolution in France and afterwards elsewhere the records of the Royal Household, of the noble families, and of old monasteries were confiscated and gathered together. The public character of the archives was a revolutionary principle. Access to the records was to be free for everyone. The proclamation of the so-called archival human rights was mainly due to the activity of the first administrator of the *Archives Nationales*, Armand Gaston Camus. This public character, which was then limited with regard to the most recent records, is the foundation for modern historical research. Making inventories of the archives was an immense task which was begun only in the middle of the nineteenth century.

The technical equipment available to historical research workers at the beginning of the nineteenth century had already increased, but it was still limited. Historians could consult various printed publications of sources in large libraries, but he must still make do without photostat, computer, or microfilm. These aids came only much later in use. Fernand Braudel tells us that in 1927 in the castle of Simancas, repository of the Spanish archives, he aroused jealousy and admiration owing to his use of a film camera for reproducing historical documents. (Braudel, 1972) How much quicker, easier, and better can the average student of history nowadays become acquainted with material in the archives.

History acquired a national function. Teaching history and historical research in the nineteenth century were put into the service of national governments. Large editions of sources were published to highlight the origins of the fatherland. Numerous chairs for national history were established. Innumerable new schoolbooks were made for primary and secondary schools which were geared to the cultivation of patriotism. This national function has significantly contributed to the flourishing of the discipline and the sincere interest of a wide audience. Up to the sixties of our century this national function of history remained a matter of course, rarely to be queried.

6. The short-term perspective
The study of history has evolved from 'little science' to 'big science'. The number of professional historians has multiplied, the mass of historical

publications in books and periodicals is booming, and the degree of specialization begins to be disquieting.

An overwhelming amount of historical sources is available. Even ultra-
modern technical equipment cannot prevent the historian from a recurrent
feeling, especially with regard to modern history, that he will be swamped
by his material.

With regard to the function of history feelings of uncertainty prevail. According to a recent report of the UNESCO (1988: 305) the first aim of the
historian ought to be to gain an understanding of the inheritance bequeathed
by preceding generations. This insight ought to focus on one's own native
country as well as on the inheritances of other cultures. It is the function of
history, according to this report, to teach man to become aware of his own
place and to be tolerant towards others. Also named are items like fostering a critical attitude and becoming aware of relativity. It sounds well, and
it is also crucially relevant for our multiform society with its many migrants.
Even so, can one seriously maintain, when surveying the annual harvest of
historical publications, that the aims named just now played a significant
role in historical research? The professional study of history hardly ac-
knowledges such a high-flown social and moral function. In the community of professionals the urge to publish is present, but this arises mostly
from a routine performance of one's duty, self-preservation, career planning,
and disinterested interest. By far the largest part of professional studies are
written by specialists and for specialists.

7. Institutional prospects

Taking this very brief bird's eye view as a starting-point, is it possible to
formulate some expectations with regard to the study of history in the
nineties? As far as the availability of historical sources goes, the progress
of inventory-making, publication of sources, and cheap reproduction techniques will continue to facilitate the historian's access to source material.
Computerizing, when it has survived its growing pains, will also facilitate
bibliographical research. The personal computer will speed up the assimi-
lation of data, replace (for some people) the card-index box, simplify the
composition of written documents, and facilitate the exchange of data. The
booming development of computer science will have its impact on the
research worker in the field of history as well. Here a problem will certainly emerge, to wit that the increase of historical information in itself
does not guarantee a gain of historical knowledge. In the world of history
(as elsewhere) the growing availability of data in many cases will result in
actual ignorance. Whereas in the old handbooks on methods of historical

research the lack of historical data was continually emphasized, it is at present and in the future the abundance of information which will create great problems for the historian.

Uncertainties with regard to the function of history have already been pointed out. Consequent upon the political and economical unification of Europe it is now the national cultural identity which is emphasized in influential quarters. It is to be expected that in the immediate future more financial resources will be made available for studies of national history, of one's own language and culture. Doubtlessly historiography here will not regain its old national function of the nineteenth century. National ideals are lacking, and in any case they do not anymore play a crucial role in a society in which political and economical power with regard to vital aspects is exerted on a supranational level.

A substantial growth of the number of professional historians is not to be expected. In secondary education, which from the nineteenth century onwards has been the job market for graduates in history, the subject of history has lost ground to other subjects. Although at present many people acknowledge that it is important to be well-grounded in history in school, and a further encroachment on our subject need not be envisaged, yet the situation will be one of stabilization on the present low level, rather than regaining the strong position of old with regard to the number of hours in the timetable and jobs for teachers.

8. The historical output

Up to now we have confined ourselves to the general institutional aspects of the study of history. Let us now attempt to add some remarks on the results of the historians' exertion, historical publications.

There exist no precise data on the amount of the historical output of the past. Yet some comments can be made. In the nineteenth century the number of historical publications grows conspicuously. It is estimated that the historical output has been multiplied by ten. The increase of printed matter was a general social phenomenon which also benefited the study of history. This increase of annual publications was in the nineteenth century particularly noticeable in the field of national history, in accordance with the institutional developments already mentioned. (Den Boer, 1987: 26)

9. Innovation around 1900

Around the turn of the century one can signal an evident disagreement with regard to the ways and means of historical research in several countries.[2]

---

[2] For a general survey see G. Iggers, 1975.

The advocates of innovations blamed the preceding generation of historians for a one-sided political interest with far too much attention being given to the actions of prominent persons. Added to this was the fact that far too much importance had been attached to source-criticism and that an open mind with regard to other disciplines was lacking. A more economic and social approach was advocated, with attention being given to large social groups and using concepts deriving from other disciplines. Naturally, such innovations related to the rise of a more democratized and industrialized society, in which other ideals and interest prevailed than before. These general historical developments became noticeable in historiography. Historians are also children of their time.

In Germany, the country which in the nineteenth century had been regarded as the Mecca of the study of history, the controversy focused on the person of Karl Lamprecht (1856-1915) who had initiated a real crusade against the old trend in studies of history. (Lamprecht, 1988) The work of Leopold von Ranke (1795-1886) had been cherished as a paradigm by traditional historians. In this mainly political kind of history national states were central – they were even defined as 'Gedanken Gottes'. Attention mainly focused on the actions of leading personalities in diplomacy and war. Lamprecht championed a modern alternative, namely a historiography which was to focus on social groups, without metaphysical notions. In his view it was the historian's task to reveal the laws of social development. In his own country Lamprecht managed to rouse so much resistance that it was partly due to this that economic and social history came somewhat under a cloud or, in any case, did not manage to gain the position afterwards acquired by the discipline in France.

Around 1900 comparable discussions about the innovation of the study of history were held in France. In that country, however, the controversy did not focus on a single individual and nobody was anathematized or execrated. Polemics remained pragmatic, and tradition and innovation coexisted in peace, as for instance in the case of the older *Revue historique* of Gabriel Monod (1844-1912) and the young *Revue de Synthèse historique* of Henri Berr (1863-1954). Be that as it may, in the course of the twentieth century France gradually came to be regarded as the country of historical innovation. In a process of what one could label as epic concentration many innovations, although also present elsewhere, came to be more and more ascribed to the French. The term 'Annales-paradigm' was coined (called after the periodical set up in 1929, *Annales d'histoire économique et sociale*), offering an alternative for the traditional paradigm ascribed to Germany, which focused on politics and statecraft.

Generalizing characterizations like the German or the French vein of historiography may be careless and unjustified, yet it is beyond doubt that in our country towards the end of the 1960's the historiography of the Annales was set up as a model with a great fanfare, and that it was used to stage an attack on other more traditional trends in the study of history.[3] It was in accordance with the spirit of the turbulent sixties that on the authority of this 'nouvelle histoire' (itself heir to the reforming movement around 1900) a study of history was advocated in which large sections of the populace, the 'underdog classes', were to be central and not the establishment. 'Social relevance' and 'collective' were the slogans. Public characters, among the preceding generation of historians still praised to the skies, must yield their place to the common man. The historians' attention ought to focus on social tensions, strikes, and inequality. Social and economic history was brought to the fore and political history was waived aside as being unimportant and old-fashioned. With regard to methods quantification was strongly advocated. History could become a 'hard' science if parochial registers and the archives of notaries were now studied instead of the 'unreliable' literary sources.

In the same way as traditional historiography was personified by Ranke, the name of Fernand Braudel (1902-1985) came to be linked to this 'nouvelle histoire'.[4] In the Braudellian paradigm geographical conditions, economical processes, and social groups were given primacy. Historical developments were gauged according to famines, mortality rates, economical expansion, and trading figures. In the preceding period, in their history of the political and military vicissitudes of the European states, Ranke and the 'Neo-Rankeaner' had adopted success in foreign policy as the crucial criterium for the verdict of history.

Braudel strongly emphasized the famous 'longue durée': long-term historical developments. He may have been the first to use the complementary pair of concepts, structure and conjuncture, and set his face against the so-called 'histoire événementielle'. The exhaustive study of vicissitudes in war and diplomacy in a short-term perspective blinded the historian, according to Braudel, for fundamental large-scale processes and permanent patterns. Statistics was considered to be an essential aid; historical source-criticism, from Ranke onward the foundation of historical methodology, was pushed into the background. Series of figures, diagrams and charts made their entry as illustrations in historical works. The art of narration, of

---

[3] Formulated in an arresting style by Kees Bertels, 1973.
[4] For the apotheosis of Braudel see a.o. Review 1 (1978), 'The impact of the Annales school on the social sciences'.

old the secret of a historian's success, came to be neglected and even to be regarded with suspicion.

The reaction of the 1980's: historical anthropology

Whereas the Braudellian paradigm triumphs among the fraternity of professionals, a reaction is already noticeable among the avant-garde. In 1975 the most brilliant pupil of Braudel, Emmanuel Le Roy Ladurie publishes a book, which was to become a bestseller in many languages, on a tiny village in the Pyrenees around 1300. With the file of an inquisitor as his starting-point the author attempts to reconstruct the life, thought and feeling of villagers and herdsmen. (Le Roy Ladurie, 1975) In 1976 the Italian historian Carlo Ginzburg publishes a book on the world-picture of a sixteenth-century miller, again based on the reports of the Inquisition. (Ginzburg, 1976) Both works are regarded as specimens of 'micro-histoire'. Instead of a 'histoire globale' with long lines and quantitative surveys one tries to go deeply into a single point, a single detail on which a large amount of documentation exists. In order to illustrate the different approaches Le Roy Ladurie at one time spoke of the historian as either a parachutist or as someone who seeks truffles. Even so, he tries to combine these two approaches. Carlo Ginzburg, however, in a well-known article has sharply distanced himself from the quantitative and generalizing approach which stems from the sciences. (Ginzburg, 1979) Ginzburg compares the historian to a hunter who needs no more that the slightest clues and trusts his intuition. According to this author the historian ought to be like someone who follows a trail and who is guided by seemingly trivial details toward crucial and far-reaching conclusions. In order to support his view Ginzburg even goes so far as to fall back on the Stone Age, the period when man could only be guided by instinct and intuition in order to survive.

In the 1980's this new 'nouvelle histoire' has reached full maturity, and has even become a dominant trend in historical research. It clearly distances itself from the old 'nouvelle histoire' in three ways.

In the first place the field of study is deliberately very much restricted, often focusing on a single individual. The idea behind this is that a thorough study of a microcosm yields a better historical insight than a necessarily more superficial analysis of the macrocosm. At times research workers even go so far as to regard the macrocosm as being mirrored in the microcosm. But even when one leaves this unprovable and metaphysical principle aside it ought to be clear that by means of the microscope the historical insight is sharpened. The representative character of the specimens of 'micro-histoire' remains a problem, however.

In the second place there has been a perceptible shift from socio-economical history to mental and cultural aspects of the past. Often the focus of this interest is so narrow that, for instance, the reports of the Inquisition and other records of repression are used for the single purpose of reconstructing a world-picture of ideas and of emotional life in general. Not a trace remains, then, of the harsh reality of heretics and Inquisition: of the violence, the suffering, and the inequality.

This should be related to the third point. It is anthropology which is the primary auxiliary science of the new 'nouvelle histoire'. As 'maîtres à penser' Karl Marx, Friedrich Engels, and Lenin have had to yield place to Claude Lévi-Strauss, Edmund Leach, and Clifford Geertz.

In the reflection on the study of history little attention has been paid so far to this development.

10. Narrative logic and the history of concepts

In recent years the small world of historical philosophers has focused on the theme of the so-called 'linguistic turn'. This term, which, for that matter, was already in use in philosophical circles in the 1960's (Rorty, 1967), but was only afterwards adopted by philosophers of history, put the art of narration again central for historians, with a concomitant interest in the status of historical concepts. The small circle of professional philosophers of history produced theoretical treatises on the nature of narration, yet these yielded few fundamentally new insights. One cannot deny that the philosophy of history is a hybrid specialism in which an extract, diluted or strong, but in any case an extract, of the great philosophical problems is served after several reheatings. The really fundamental issues of the historicity of interpretation, reconstruction, and the forming of concepts have already been analyzed in the nineteenth century by Johan Gustav Droysen (1808-1886), William Dilthey (1833-1911) and later representatives of historism. The counter-arguments brought forward by (neo-)positivists focused mainly on the problem of the historical explanation.

A short article by the philosopher of German origin Carl G. Hempel, first published in 1942, was often quoted. (Hempel, 1959: 344-56) In this Hempel argued that general laws are followed in historical descriptions as well. Yet the historian is unaware of these laws, according to Hempel. In his view the study of history should not be regarded as a special discipline with its own separate methodology. The historical explanation which lies hidden in many descriptions actually has a logical structure wholly identical with an explanation in other disciplines. Whenever a historical explanation is carefully analyzed it will always become clear that a general law is used, albeit not made explicit. These general laws cover, as it were, causes and consequences or, in other words, initial conditions and final results. That is why they are called 'covering laws'. This term has been coined by William Dray who in *Laws and explanation in history* (1957) conclusively argued against Hempel that the 'covering law paradigm' is not a satisfactory account of what historians consider to be an explanation. Even so, in the 1960's the scientific way of forming concepts in the manner of Hempel became popular. Various historians drew the radical conclusion that what had so far been regarded as an explanation, was no good according to scientific norms, and that the study of history ought to be methodologically purified. Cogent arguments were brought forward for an intensive methodological training of historians in order to gear the study of history to other disciplines and so to help achieve the unity of the sciences.

This neo-positivistic urge in methodology and philosophy of history was the counterpart of the wish of practical historians, referred to above, to remould the study of history into a hard science by means of quantification and historical statistics. But whereas the quantitative approach produced a concrete gain of knowledge – crucially modifying, for instance, the picture of the age of the Sun King Louis XIV by a careful study of the enormous mortality rate (Goubert, 1966) -, in the methodological and theoretical discussions of the advocates of neo-positivism fundamentally new insights were wholly lacking. In this respect the theory of history resembles perpetual check: an endless repetition of identical moves.

What did emerge under the influence of the controversy, where historians with a literary outlook were in the defensive, was a sharpened consciousness as to the function of the historical narrative and the conceptual apparatus of the historian. In the early 1970's a 'tropological' analysis of some of the great nineteenth-century historians by the literary theoretician Hayden White was published, in which the author tried to prove that each variety of historical consciousness may be reduced to a specific linguistic protocol. (White, 1973) White's argument is a specimen of reductionism – in this case, rhetorical reductionism – but whatever criticism one is tempted to voice, it was proof of a renewed interest in the historical narrative and the art of narrating.

Historical concepts in particular were subjected to an innovatory and penetrating analysis. In a splendid introduction to the philosophy of history and afterwards in some articles H.W. Walsh focused on the concepts used by historians. (Walsh, 1951 & 1967) Walsh pointed out that historians are apt greatly to value 'colligatory concepts' which yield historical insight and reveal links between historical phenomena.

In the Netherlands in 1981 a doctoral thesis, written in English, on the subject of historical philosophy was defended which focused on this issue. (Ankersmit, 1981) The author, Frank Ankersmit, rechristened the 'colligatory concepts' as 'narrative substances' and radicalized the meaning of the term. According to Walsh the colligatory concepts do indeed refer, in one way or another, to a historical reality. According to Ankersmit the narrative substance does not denote a historical reality but is a reality in itself, to be compared to the monads of Leibniz. Just like Hayden White Ankersmit exaggerates his initial thesis with gusto. In a provoking manner the entire historiography is reduced to narration. It was once more an anti-positivistic sign of the times.

It is worth noting that it is mostly non-historians who engage in such theoretical polemics. Even so, a renewed preoccupation with language and concepts was also perceptible among the fraternity of professional historians. Naturally, the history of concepts and the use of language had already been researched before. It is in particular Lucien Febvre who had advocated interdisciplinary cooperation with, among others, linguists. He himself had produced masterly dissertations on the use of words in the sixteenth century with far-reaching conclusions on the 'outillage mental'. (Febvre, 1942) According to Febvre thinking and feeling in sixteenth-century France was characterized by a 'mentalité primitive'. This view flatly contradicts that of the nineteenth-century liberal historians who regarded that century as the cradle of modern man. Febvre's conclusions could be queried. Just suppose that he had put Montaigne instead of Rabelais central in his study...? And just suppose that he had taken the language of science and scholarship, neo-Latin, as his starting-point instead of sixteenth-century French...? Yet in any case there remains a brilliant lecture on historical method and an inspiring example of the interdisciplinary approach.

In Germany the 'Begriffsgeschichte' has developed into a mature branch of scholarship. Under the direction of Reinhart Koselleck a monumental lexicon of historical key concepts was published, focusing on the socio-political terminology in Germany. (Brunner, Conze, Koselleck, 1972) In France another large-scale project of the history of concepts is going on, under German direction. (Reichardt, Schmitt, 1985) There are signs that in other countries and languages comparable research is being launched.

11. Crystal gazing

Will the reaction of the 1980's gain further ground in the Dutch historical world? Historical-anthropological research is the fashion in the Netherlands as well. It does not seem likely that this trend will be cut short in the immediate future. This kind of history fits in with the interest of a wide audience. There is no saying whether this research will still produce much that is new. With regard to the history of concepts hardly anything has been done so far in the Netherlands. It is to be expected that Dutch historians also will go into this field of study.

The weak point of the new anthropological history is to be found in its trivializing tendency. Money and power are factors which a historian cannot neglect with impunity. Perhaps a revival of economical history will occur among a new generation of historians, when one has one's fill of 'petite histoire'. The same conclusion is valid with regard to studies of political and military history.

New directions for historical research can be found through serious interdisciplinary cooperation and comparatism. Sadly, both issues have become somewhat tarnished in the eyes of historians because programmatic treatises have been piling it on. It is furthermore to the point that up to now interdisciplinary projects have yielded few results as to increase of knowledge, and in some rare cases which have benefited from large government grants the perspectives are not very promising.

Even so, an interdisciplinary approach, if well thought-out and supported by good specialists from various disciplines (and not by bunglers venturing into alien territory) could be very stimulating and reveal unthought-of relationships of historical phenomena.

Comparative history in a single stroke has been enriched with a masterpiece, *The Low Countries* (1978) by E.H. Kossmann, although no tradition of this kind of research was to be found in our country. It demonstrates again how much depends on individual talent in the study of history. Naturally, the splendidly cool and ironic style of Kossmann cannot be plagiarized, but the idea of such comparative research deserves to be imitated. The mainly political perspective of Kossmann ought to be a stimulus and challenge for other starting-points in coordinating the historical development of the Netherlands and Belgium, for more detailed comparisons, for charting regional and local differences.

Not only bilateral comparisons, but multilateral ones are also a possibility. Europeanization could perhaps become a stimulus to study our national history in a comparatist perspective. The success of such obvious research projects will, as with the interdisciplinary ones, wholly depend on a very carefully thought-out approach and on the concrete support of eminent specialists from home and abroad.

However, could one call these remarks predictions? As often, the wish is father to the expectation.

References

Ankersmit, F.R., 1981. *Narrative logic. A semantic analysis of the historian's language*. Meppel.

Bertels, K., 1973. *Geschiedenis tussen structuur en evenement* (doctoral thesis). Amsterdam.

Boer, P. den, 1987. *Geschiedenis als beroep. De professionalisering van de geschiedbeoefening in Frankrijk (1818-1914)*. Nijmegen.

Braudel, F., 1972. "Personal testimony", *Journal of modern history*, 44.

Brunner, O, W. Conze, R. Koselleck (Hrsg.), 1972. *Geschichtliche Grundbegriffe. Historisches Lexicon zur politisch-sozialen Sprache in Deutschland*, Band I-V. Stuttgart.

Febvre, L., 1942. *Le problème de l'incroyance au XVIe siècle. La religion de Rabelais*. Paris.

Ginzburg, C., 1976. *Il formaggio e i vermi. Il cosmo di un magnaio del '500*. Turin.

Ginzburg, C., 1979. "Spie. Radici di un paradigma indiziario". In A. Gargani (ed.), *Crisi della ragione* Turin.

Goubert, P., 1966. *Louis XIV et vingt millions de Français*. Paris.

Hempel, C.G., 1959. "The function of general laws in history" (1942). repr. In P. Gardiner (ed.) *Theories of history*. London-New York: 344-56.

Iggers, G., 1975. *New directions in European historiography*. Middletown, Conn.

Lamprecht, K., 1988. *Alternative zu Ranke. Schriften zur Geschichtstheorie*. Leipzig.

Reichardt, R., E. Schmitt (Hrsg.), 1985. *Handbuch politisch-sozialer Grundbegriffe in Frankreich 1680-1820*, 10 Vols. München.

Rorty, R., 1967. *The linguistic turn. Recent essays in philosophical method*. Chicago.

Roy Ladurie, E. Le, 1975. *Montaillou, village occitan de 1294 à 1324*. Paris.

UNESCO, R. Rémond (red.), 1988. *Etre historien aujourd'hui*. Paris-Toulouse.

Walsh, W.H., 1951. *An introduction to Philosophy of history*. London.

Walsh, W.H., 1967. "Colligatory Concepts in History". In W.H. Burston and D. Thompson (eds.), *Studies in the nature and teaching of history*. London.

White, H., 1973. *Metahistory. The historical imagination in nineteenth-Europe*. Baltimore-London.

Archaeology
in the modern world*

H.T. Waterbolk

"The public, faced with a somewhat dehumanized modern world, makes new demands on archaeology"
(freely rendered from W.J. Mayer-Oakes, 1989)

1. Subject, methods and aims of archaeology

According to Webster's dictionary, archaeology is "the scientific study of material remains of past human life and activity". Archaeologists deal with what has been called both the 'residues of human behaviour' (Salmon, 1982) and the 'soil archive' (Van Es *et al.,* 1988): with the physical remains of man himself, with movable artefacts such as tools, weapons, pottery and ornaments, with immovable remains such as earthworks, field systems, temples, roads and house sites, with the remains of food, food-procuring and food-processing, and with the relations of man to his natural environment and the changes in flora, fauna and landscape he brought about.

Most of the movable study material has passed some time in the soil, from which it is recovered by chance or by deliberate excavation. In the soil the material has been subject to weathering, displacement or damage resulting from all sorts of natural processes or human activities. These 'site formation processes' (Schiffer, 1976) have to be studied carefully before one can define the nature of the site and distinguish human activities from phenomena of natural origin, and before one can proceed to the description and ordering in time and space of the artefacts by the traditional methods of archaeology: typology, chronology and chorology.

Typology comprises the sorting of objects, their description and the distinction of types on the basis of stylistic, technological or functional considerations or quantitative properties. Chemical, physical, biological or geological analysis can be of great help in identifying the nature and source of the raw material and the mode of production of the artefacts. For the classification on the basis of quantitative properties, various mathematical techniques are used.

Chronology is the ordering in time of the objects, types and assemblages.

A distinction has to be made between absolute and relative chronology. Dendrochronology and radiocarbon dating are methods of direct absolute dating. Indirect indications for absolute age can be given by associated materials imported from areas with an established historical calendar, such as Roman coins in northern Europe. The major direct method of relative dating is stratigraphy. Indirect relative dates can be obtained through geology or palaeobotany. *Seriation* is an important technique for the relative ordering in time of assemblages. *Typochronology* is the combined result of typological and chronological analysis.

Chorology is the study of the distribution in space – on any scale – of the types distinguished. The resulting distribution patterns may exclude each other or either completely or partially overlap, and they may show correlations with immovable archaeological structures or with features of physical geography, such as soil types or contour lines. For these correlations explanations have to be proposed. Chorology is a powerful tool in archaeology. Much interpretation is done on the basis of distribution maps.

These three, basically independent methods provide a mutual check on the usability of individual objects and assemblages for interpretation, for their typological attribution, the chronological assessment and the localisation may be uncertain.

On the basis of analogy with the historical past or the ethnographic present, functions (often multiple) can be ascribed to individual objects. By analyzing context and association (the 'find circumstances') they can be grouped and meaningfully interpreted as, for example, the contents of a grave, a votive deposit, a working-floor or a household refuse dump. On this level, too, analogies play an important part. Theoretical archaeologists have been battling against the subjective element which analogy brings into their field, but there is no way out. An archaeology that restricts itself purely to a science of material remains from the past, cannot satisfy.

Excavation is a means, not so much to obtain more material, as to obtain stratigraphically and situationally well-separated assemblages, so-called 'closed finds', which form the backbone of archaeological analysis.

Surveying (Landesaufnahme) is the collecting of the maximum amount of archaeological data from a certain area without excavating: by field- walking, study of private or museum collections, by scanning the existing archaeological publications, air photography and modern techniques of remote sensing.

To the basic activities of archaeology can be added those systematic procedures that help in establishing the probable function of individual items

or assemblages: *experimental archaeology* (experiments in the production
and/or use of replicated tools) and *ethnoarchaeology* (the study of the activity, abandonment and waste disposal patterns of living primitive communities).

In the procedures mentioned we recognize elements derived from the natural sciences (physics, chemistry, biology, geology), from the social sciences (cultural anthropology, ethnography) and from the humanities (history, history of art). Basic archaeology is a truly interdisciplinary undertaking.
What is actually done with the data that result from these basic activities
depends on the archaeologist. There is an enormously wide spectrum of
archaeological interests, as I shall demonstrate in the next paragraph. The
diversity is so wide that it seriously affects the cohesion of the discipline
and leads to ambiguity as to its academic position. Indeed, one can wonder
whether archaeology is a truly independent discipline, or merely a body of
procedures with a little theory, serving other disciplines (Waterbolk, 1980).
I shall come back to this problem later.

As to the goals of archaeology, one finds different formulations, corresponding to the theoretical position of the archaeologist and the demands
of society. I find myself best represented by Thompson (1978), who after
having formulated five areas of responsibility of the archaeologist (to the
archaeological resources, to the archaeologist himself, to his colleagues, to
the citizen and to society) lists eight goals for archaeology, which may be
used singly or in combination. The list should not be considered exhaustive.

1. To identify, record, and protect the non-renewable sources of archaeology.
2. To develop and maintain the highest professional standards for archaeological research.
3. To delineate culture history.
4. To reconstruct past cultures and lifeways.
5. To formulate cultural processes.
6. To provide the citizens with the best archaeological interpretations possible.
7. To assist in the making of policy for the archaeological resources and in
   making decisions about them.
8. To interact in general with the non-archaeological world in a way that
   will promote the best use of both our limited and dwindling resources
   and the results of our research on them.

In the vein of Thompson, I should like to add as Goal no. 9 (or as an extension of Goal no. 4):
9. To reconstruct past human environments and landscapes.

Most authors would restrict themselves to Goals 3, 4 and 5, and formulate them in a different way, often emphasizing understanding and even explanation of the archaeological phenomena as the main purpose of archaeology. To Ucko, for example, archaeology is "the investigation not only of how people lived in the past, but also of how and why changes took place resulting in the forms of society and culture which exist today" (Ucko, 1989). In view of the many different kinds and schools of archaeology and of the different positions archaeologists occupy in society – at universities, museums and government agencies – a many-sided, but not too pretentious formulation of objectives is to be preferred.

2. The many subdivisions of archaeology
There are at least five major criteria according to which archaeology and archaeologists can be classified: geography, chronology, theoretical position, theme, and physical context.

Geography
Most archaeologists work in their own country, and very often concentrate on an area which in the course of history or by virtue of its geographical position has acquired some sort of regional identity. Their subject is the archaeology of that region: the archaeology of Drenthe, of Denmark, of the South-West (of the United States), of Palestine, etc. Archaeological remains are felt to be part of the national or regional heritage, to which the nation bears a sense of collective ownership and responsibility. In many countries these sentiments have found expression in laws prohibiting the export of antiquities and making excavation subject to government permission. We should realize, however, that such feelings exist at all levels. When in 1955 at Beilen a gold-hoard comprising a bracelet, five neckrings and 22 Roman coins from c. 400 AD turned up, it was the wish of the local authorities that it should be kept and exhibited in a local museum (which only existed in a rudimentary form). In this case the provincial forces were stronger and the gold-hoard is now in the Provincial Museum of Drenthe at Assen. That the provincial government acted promptly – part of the hoard had to be bought – was certainly caused by the fear that the National Museum of Antiquities at Leiden would get hold of the hoard. Recently a

hoard of Early Medieval gold coins was discovered at Rhenen (province of Utrecht) and partly excavated by the State Service for Archaeological Investigations (ROB) at Amersfoort. The find is now on show in the Leiden museum, but in the province of Utrecht people want to know whether the legally prescribed formalities with regard to the destination of excavated objects have been applied correctly – hoping, of course, that the finds can be 'brought home' to Utrecht. If such sentiments play a role in a small country such as the Netherlands, this will be even more so in larger states like France or Spain, where regional feelings are very strong.

An occupant of the chair of Danish archaeology at the University of Copenhagen, now retired, told me that he felt obliged to deal with the archaeology not only of present-day Denmark, but also of Scania and Schleswig-Holstein, former parts of the Danish kingdom. It is evident that problems can arise when there are territorial disputes or when under former regimes or colonial rule important archaeological finds have been transferred to other countries. The question of the Elgin marbles from Greece in the British Museum is well-known. Much to the regret of the majority of British archaeologists, Britain still refuses to be bound by the 1970 UNESCO convention on the transfer of ownership of cultural property (Shaw, 1989). In 1987, on the occasion of the 150th anniversary of the Schleswig-Holsteinian Museum, founded under Danish rule by the Danish National Museum, an important stone with a runic inscription from a findspot north of the present German-Danish border and acquired when Prussia occupied the area, was presented to the Danish National Museum. But the famous Nydam ship from the same general area remains firmly in German possession at the Museum of Schleswig, where any Danish citizen can easily visit it. Both Danes and Germans know that a much larger area once was Danish territory, but neither side wants to change the present border. Though mainly illustrating present good relations, the handing-over of the rune stone was a gesture heavily charged with history, and so it was understood on both sides.

As is the case with the Danish-German border, present national frontiers hardly ever coincide with boundaries that are archaeologically relevant. Every regional archaeologist has to compare his material with that of neighbouring areas. He then faces the problem of gaining access to the relevant publications, which are often hidden in regional journals and written in another language. If he wants to include in his work an as yet unpublished find, which he discovers in a museum exhibition or a store room, he may suddenly come up against some reluctance and find that the museum curator feels that he would rather 'publish the find himself'. That peculiar possessiveness which I mentioned on the national and regional level thus manifests itself also in the policy of some museums. In Western Europe such an attitude has become rare. But in new countries and in countries with an ethnic minority such feelings can be very strong and be supported by considerations of presumed better qualification. To quote a Bolivian archaeologist: "An Indian archaeology, under our control and systematized *according to our concepts of time and space* (my italics), should perhaps form part of our enterprise of winning back our own history and freeing it from the centuries of colonial subjugation" (Condory, 1989). Sami students in Norway find that "there should be no further archaeological excavations before the Sami archaeologists can take over and perform this invaluable work" (M. & P. Aikio, 1989). A 'world archaeology' in which all the archaeological data are open for examination to all archaeologists, is still very far away.

Extreme feelings of possessiveness have been encountered by American and Australian archaeologists when they were excavating human skeletons in aboriginal cemeteries and were confronted with fierce and even violent opposition from the side of those who claimed to be the living descendants of the buried. They demanded that the remains should not be displayed to the public or stored in laboratories and museums, but be handed over for proper reburial, thus bringing peace to the ancestors (Hubert, 1989). The question of 'who owns the past' is a really important issue. The earliest settlement of Australia is a problem of interest to the whole of mankind. Australian aborigines, however, insisted that all excavated skeletal remains, even those older than 25,000 years, be reburied! As a compromise, they are now being put in an underground 'Keeping Place', where they can be studied if permission is obtained from aboriginal custodians.

Even in Western Europe the subject is of importance, as the events at Stonehenge and its surroundings in recent years have demonstrated. In 1985 conflicts broke out in which the parties were the legal owners (English Heritage and National Trust), the general public (a million visitors per year), the Druids (allegedly continuing ancient summer-solstice ceremonies), the participants in an annual festival (originally a ritual gathering of countercultural archaeologists, who see Stonehenge as a focus of ancient knowledge and cosmic power, a group grown in number beyond control) and of course the police, who broke up the festival with force. Damage to the site in general, but also to visible archaeological monuments such as barrows had become unacceptable. In a penetrating way Chippindale (1986) describes the difficulties in finding a workable compromise between the interests of the monument, the general public, and the fringe groups. Addyman

(1989) suggests a solution which would include a subterranean life-size replica of Stonehenge in its presumed original form.

Another group of archaeologists choose to work in other countries than their own. But in most cases old ties of a cultural, political or religious nature connect these countries with the home country. Classical archaeologists thus turn to Italy, Greece and other Mediterranean regions to study the material remains of the ancient Greek and Roman civilizations, their respective Mycenean and Etruscan precursors and Byzantine and early Christian successors. In fact, the earliest archaeology in Europe was classical archaeology: it goes back to 15th-century Italy, where Ciriaco de Pizzicola of Ancona (1391-1452) copied inscriptions and documented antique sculptures and buildings (Rowe, 1978). Much archaeology in the Mediterranean countries still conforms to the old definition of archaeology as the art history of the classical world, being part of classical studies together with ancient history and the study of the Greek and Latin languages, and emphasizing religion, art and handicrafts. But an increasing number of people free themselves of these old ties and preoccupations and study also other aspects of what is now being called 'Mediterranean archaeology'.

Egyptologists, Assyriologists and Palestinian archaeologists go to do fieldwork in their respective areas. Their source of inspiration, directly or indirectly, is the Bible, and they often have their institutional basis in faculties of theology. In recent decades, interest has shifted from the biblical world in the narrow sense to the general cultural developments in SW Asia, to which Europe owes so much. But one still hears of expeditions sent out to find Noah's Ark on Mount Ararat.

Other archaeologists work in former colonies, such as the Dutch in Indonesia and the Caribbean and the Belgians in tropical Africa, always in close cooperation with the archaeologists of the new countries. In this respect some former colonizing countries are more active than others. France stands out in a positive sense. In that country the Ministry of Foreign Affairs is financially involved in excavations abroad.

For the organization of field work in the Mediterranean countries and SW Asia many countries maintain local research units. In the Federal Republic of Germany national archaeology is largely a matter of the *Länder*. Archaeology abroad falls under the federal *Deutsches Archäologisches Institut* in Berlin which has auxiliary branches in Madrid, Lisbon, Rome, Athens, Istanbul, Cairo, Damascus and San'a. Temporarily closed are the German schools in Baghdad and Teheran. Many other countries in Western Europe have schools in one or more of these cities. The Netherlands maintain small schools in Rome, Athens, Istanbul and Cairo. In some countries permits for archaeological fieldwork are granted only to these schools.

Archaeological activities in other countries entail prestige, both in the home country and abroad. When a country like Japan starts archaeological activities in e.g. Iran, Indonesia and Polynesia, there certainly is an element of foreign policy involved.

Chronology

A second criterium for subdividing archaeology is chronology. Prehistoric archaeology studies the material remains from before the time for which written sources are available. Often there is a transitional period with some documents written by outsiders, such as the Romans on Western Europe or the Chinese on Japan. The term 'protohistory' is then used. In France 'protohistoire' covers everything between the Neolithic and the Roman period. In practice, few archaeologists call themselves protohistorians. A much clearer division is between those prehistorians who deal with the Palaeolithic, Mesolithic and part of the Neolithic period (primarily documented by flint and stone artefacts) and those dealing with other facets of the Neolithic, with the Bronze Age and with the Iron Age (documented mainly by pottery and metal). In Western Europe, 'flint' people and 'pottery' people pretty well exclude each other.

In recent years the term 'historical archaeology' has become popular. The term is used with various meanings. In SW Asia it is the archaeology of the Bronze and Iron Ages. In America it includes all archaeology dealing with historical periods (Schuyler, 1978b); in Europe the term is mostly used in the restricted sense of the archaeology of the post-medieval period (mainly 16th-18th century AD). It is preceded by medieval archaeology and provincial-Roman archaeology (in those countries outside Italy that were part of the Roman empire). It is only in recent years that historical archaeology (in the restricted sense) developed into a subdiscipline, parallel with urban archaeology. The study of mass craft products such as clay pipes, which can give valuable information on social status and trade routes, is an example of a specialization within historical archaeology.

Industrial archaeology concludes the chronological sequence of archaeologies.

At the very end we might add the 'archaeology of us', as it has recently been defined and practised in the U.S.A. and India: the study of garbage disposal in modern society, as a form of ethnoarchaeology (Gould & Schiffer, 1981).

Theoretical position

A very fundamental distinction can be made among archaeologists as to the philosophical position they hold with regard to the nature of their discipline. On this basis one can distinguish anthropological archaeologists, cultural archaeologists, and human palaeontologists or ecological archaeologists.

For most white North-American archaeologists "archaeology is anthropology or it is nothing" (Willey & Phillips, 1958). This attitude is understandable. Living Indian and Eskimo communities still exist in the U.S.A.; their prehistory locally lasted well into the 19th century. In teaching, terminology and scientific approach, American archaeology is closely associated with cultural anthropology. Most American archaeologists thus see archaeology just as a part of anthropology, pursuing the same aims of understanding human behaviour and formulating laws of human behaviour. Even historical archaeology in the U.S.A. is seen as a subarea of general anthropology (Schuyler, 1978a). A minority see archaeology as an independent science of past material culture, which should play its own role in the social sciences along with anthropology, psychology, etc.

By contrast, a Mexican archaeologist, representing the countries 'south of the Rio Grande' states: "to us, archaeology must be history" (Lorenzo, 1981). Mexico was colonized much earlier than the U.S.A. The colonists used the local infrastructure and much intermarriage took place. All archaeology, whether prehistoric or protohistoric, should be incorporated into history. "The Mexicans must be given the idea of a past of their own".

In Western Europe, where most nations are older, and language and traditional culture provide a strong sense of identity, such positions are easily labelled as '19th-century', or 'romantic' – with the 20th-century 'hervorragend nationale Wissenschaft' ('eminently national science') practised by Kossinna in Germany as a reminder of the potential dangers of an archaeology turned into a justification of political expansion and racism. What does, however, unite the old countries of Western Europe with the new countries, is the collectively felt ownership of the archaeological heritage which I already mentioned, with the resulting self-evident position of archaeology as part of the humanities, beside the other culture studies.

A considerable part of archaeology studies early man in his physical frame and origin, in his role in the natural ecosystem, in his dietary habits, in the way he has changed the face of the earth. Research of the Palaeolithic period especially is often based in science faculties, linking up with geology, palaeontology and biology. Traditionally this approach is particularly strong in France and Italy, but as a phenomenon it is widely encountered. Many human palaeontologists and ecological archaeologists are, by training and habit, natural-science people. In section 6 I shall come back to the various theoretical positions.

Thematic specialization
For some forms of archaeological research a highly specialized training is necessary. This applies particularly to the specializations based in the natural sciences, such as palaeoethnobotany, archaeozoology, archaeometry (the application of physical and chemical methods in archaeology) and human biology, which I have just mentioned, but the same holds good for specializations based in the social sciences and humanities. Ethno-archaeologists need to be trained as cultural anthropologists. Epigraphers must of necessity be trained in the respective languages.
Glancing through the titles of recent library acquisitions one finds a large number of specialized archaeologies that have already acquired some status, or may do so in the future: Christian archaeology, Islamic archaeology, Hindu archaeology, social archaeology, archaeology of colonization, archaeology of slavery, historic-sites archaeology, archaeoastronomy, etc.

Context
A final distinction can be made as to the natural or man-made environment in which archaeologists work, and which very much determines and/or limits the sort of evidence that can be retrieved. So one can speak of desert archaeology, arctic archaeology, urban archaeology and maritime or nautical archaeology.

3. The position of archaeology in relation to other branches of learning
From the foregoing it may be clear that beyond the basic activities of archaeology – typology, chronology, chorology, study of closed finds, analysis of find circumstances, excavation, surveying and functional attribution – there is little that unites all archaeologists.
A palynologist, identifying in his peat sample the pollen grains of rye and associated weeds such as cornflower, is dealing with biological data. If he uses these data for dating his pollen diagram in the framework of a geological or phytogeographical study, he is a geologist or a palaeobotanist. But if he uses these data in a study of the origin and spread of winter-grain cultivation – an important element in the reconstruction of past ways of life – he is an archaeologist, though a very specialized one, for the identifi-

cation of these pollen types requires mastering various techniques: that of drilling peat samples, chemical preparation of the samples, microscopic analysis and the use of a reference collection. Further he must be a field botanist, who is acquainted with the ecological requirements of these plants. He should also know about soil cultivation, sowing and harvesting. His position is ambiguous – or rather, he is both an archaeologist and a natural scientist. To do his job well as an ecological archaeologist, he must be a fully trained botanist. In addition, early agriculture is of interest not only to archaeologists and palaeobotanists, but also to the agricultural scientist who needs the data of archaeology and palaeobotany to understand the present distribution of grain species and varieties.

Comparable relations prevail in many other subareas of archaeology, such as archaeozoology with regard to zoology and veterinary sciences, Palaeolithic archaeology with regard to quaternary geology and palaeontology, radiocarbon dating with regard to physics, chemistry and hydrology, the study of human bones with regard to physical anthropology and pathology, the study of prehistoric bronzes with regard to metallurgy, the study of early houses to architecture, the study of pottery to ceramology.

The situation is not fundamentally different if we turn to the humanities. Any historical archaeologist must at the same time be an historian, or, as the case may be, a linguist or a theologian – at least if he wants to contribute to what is one of the main goals of archaeology, the history of culture. Prehistoric archaeology, in particular the archaeology of the Neolithic, Bronze and Iron Ages, is perhaps the most 'archaeological' archaeology, at least with regard to the aim of writing cultural history. Although the prehistorian cannot do without the help of environmental specialists, metallurgists, architects and ceramologists, he has to write cultural history largely by himself. To my mind, he can only achieve results by using 'archaeological cultures' in the original Childean sense and studying their development and interrelations. Childe used the term 'archaeological cultures' for "recurrent assemblages of types or groups of types repeatedly found associated" "provided the assemblages illustrate more than one aspect of human behaviour" (Childe, 1956). I shall come back to the concept of 'archaeological culture' in one of the following paragraphs.

It has already been said that for a large group of archaeologists, archaeology simply is a social science. In a more detached view, one can say that for reconstructing certain aspects of past ways of life and for formulating cultural processes a basic training and specialization in cultural anthropology is a necessity – just as for the reconstruction of other aspects of past ways of life and for other archaeological goals, a training in biology or history is a prerequisite. The many subareas of anthropological archaeology have relations with such fields as psychology and sociology and in these cases we meet with the same sort of overlaps as were described for the humanities and the natural sciences.

There is one other field with an interdisciplinary character comparable to that of archaeology. It is geography. Its subareas show the same sort of overlaps with other branches of learning which in this case include not only the natural sciences, humanities and social sciences, but also economics and political science. Geography has the chorological method in common with archaeology, but has developed it much further.

Some subareas of geography come very close to subareas of archaeology. Physical geography and environmental archaeology often deal with the same field situations. In the reconstruction of the occupation history of the Low Countries, physical geography plays a decisive role. Historical geography bridges the time span between the pre- and protohistoric settlement of an area and the present. When it comes to the Middle Ages, archaeologists and historical geographers meet and often do similar work with the same objectives.

In the Dutch university system, geography and prehistory were for some decades united in an 'interfaculty of geography and prehistory'. With a recent reform, interfaculties have been abolished and geography has acquired faculty status. At the University of Amsterdam prehistory has been incorporated in this new faculty; at the University of Groningen prehistory has been transferred to the faculty of humanities. Both positions have their practical advantages: the proximity of physical and historical geography at Amsterdam, the proximity of history and other archaeologies at Groningen. Academically, archaeology may perhaps with equal right be incorporated in the natural sciences, the social sciences, the humanities or the geographical sciences. In modern society at large, however, it is the humanities side of archaeology which is of greatest weight, as we shall also see in the next paragraph.

4. The role of archaeology in modern society

Archaeology and identity

As I remarked above, archaeology is very much a matter of regional and national concern. Once more to quote Thompson (1978): "Today, when so many new nations, and some old ones, are invoking past glories as revealed by archaeology, to instill a sense of national identity in their populations ..." or the Israelis Bar-Yosef & Mazar (1981): "For the Israeli, archaeology provides a means by which he can expose the past of his nation and country". "The appeal of archaeology to the Israeli public is in its strengthening of the link between the nation and the land." The Swede Moberg (1981) noted the danger of archaeology being turned into "a vehicle for national and cultural boasting". He refers to the large international archaeological exhibitions from Bulgaria, China, Hungary and the U.S.S.R., and to what he calls the "Viking syndrome" in Scandinavia (and other countries!). He sees "a tendency among the general public to regard archaeologists as a sort of national clergy, the guardians of the sacred paraphernalia, the (pre-royal) crown jewels". According to Grahame Clark (1980), "one of the keys to archaeology's appeal lies in what it has to tell us about our identity".

Earlier I already quoted Lorenzo, Condory and Aikio on the identity issue, and it would be easy to increase the number of quotations of this kind. In view of the political aspects of the search for cultural identity, both among the young states, and among minorities within established states, "archaeological approaches to cultural identity" (the title of a recently published book, ed. S.J. Shennan, 1989) is a topic of great interest.

The legal situation

Most countries have laws governing the ownership of treasures of unknown provenance, the classification and protection of ancient monuments, the right to excavate, the ownership of excavated objects and the export of antiquities. Some laws include the obligation for any private person, company or government agency to pay for the archaeological rescue excavations necessitated by their proposed construction works. Such laws exist in such countries as Norway, Japan, U.S.S.R. and Mexico. Unfortunately, the recently changed legislation regarding monuments in the Netherlands does not contain such a rule, which would have received wide public support. Yet it must be said that in many cases requests for financial support directed at the destroying companies and agencies are granted.

As a research worker, the archaeologist finds his academic freedom limited by the legal restrictions. In his own country he is not allowed to dig in a protected archaeological monument without permission from the responsible cabinet minister. Working abroad, he will have to file a request for a permit for a survey or an excavation, often waiting long before it is granted (or refused), and must comply with all sorts of conditions. These may include the obligation to include a representative of the government in the team (and to pay him), relate to the specialist composition of the team, and contain rules about the handling and storing of the finds and the way of reporting. Often one of the conditions is the consolidation of building fragments subsequent to excavation. Permits are sometimes granted only to the foreign schools which have a permanent base in the country.

In detail, the antiquities or monuments laws are very different. In former Spanish and Portuguese colonies, for example, the state is the successor of the Crown, which at one time – by papal decree – owned all the overseas lands. In these states, archaeology is now a state monopoly. In areas such as the United States, which were settled later, colonization was largely a matter of private individuals, whose rights were not in any way restricted by their home governments. In such countries archaeological state monopolies do not exist. Ancient Crown rights to treasures of unknown provenance exist in some countries: Treasure Trove in Great Britain, *Danefae* in Denmark. In countries with laws based on the Napoleonic legal system, such as France and the Netherlands, finder and landowner share the ownership of treasures in the soil. Whilst in most countries excavation permits are granted to persons, they are in the Netherlands only given to professional institutions, with adequate technical facilities at their disposal.

We must realize that when archaeologists from Western Europe and North America pursue archaeological studies in the Mediterranean and Near Eastern countries, they are looking for the deeper roots of their civilization. But in these areas they meet with local colleagues in search of their national identity. Here is a potential area of difficulties, which can be avoided by seeking close cooperation with the local archaeologists or by avoiding their major spheres of interest, which mostly concentrate on the more recent archaeological periods, such as the medieval 'Arabic' period in the Arab countries, or on the more spectacular monuments, such as the classical and Mycenean towns in Greece.

Museums, field monuments and archaeological parks
It is mainly through the museums, the archaeological field monuments and the consolidated excavation sites that archaeology presents itself to the general public. It is here that people can see the objects made and used by their forbears and touch the stones that were brought from afar to be used for the building of temples, palaces and houses. Stories about the past told at home, at school or in public writings appear to find confirmation in the direct confrontation with the ancient objects, though in reality they can only serve as a background for these stories.

The multiple origins of archaeology are nicely illustrated in the variety of museums where archaeological finds are exhibited: in museums of natural

history, such as the Naturhistorisches Museum in Vienna, in anthropological museums, such as the Musée de l'Homme in Paris, in cultural-histori-
cal museums, such as Nationalmuseet in Copenhagen and the provincial
museums in most Dutch provinces, and in museums specifically devoted to
archaeology, such as the National Museum of Antiquities in Leiden.

There is a wide consensus that the museums should not only exhibit the
finds, but also give 'the best archaeological interpretations possible'. In
view of the great variety in archaeological approaches, there cannot be
only one interpretation. It is the multitude of questions that can be asked of
the archaeological record, which is one of the attractions of archaeological
museums.

Increasingly, archaeological monuments are included among the adver-
tised tourist attractions of a region. They are provided with explanatory
panels, and printed guides on the local, regional or national level give
further information.

In recent years archaeological parks have become popular. They consist of
assemblages of reconstructed buildings either from one period or from a
succession of periods. They may be built *in situ,* close to the original site,
or in an area selected for the purpose. The idea of presenting the results of
archaeological interpretation to the public in the form of full-scale reconstructions is just one step beyond the consolidation of the foundations and
the partial rebuilding of ancient stone buildings from their ruined remains
lying scattered around, which has been practised since the beginning of
scientific archaeology.

In-situ reconstructions are a minority. A spectacular example is the work
done at Nara, the birth-town of the unified Japanese state, where the site of
a huge wooden palace complex from the 8th century AD, after expropri-
ation of modern houses and fields, is being completely excavated and
transformed into a public park. The results of the excavations are shown in
reconstructed buildings, in layouts of concrete, pseudo-wooden post stumps,
in cylindrically trimmed shrubs resembling columns, in artificial elevations of the terrain and in explanatory panels. A museum with the finds and
further information on the site completes this highly prestigious, nationally funded project. Education is its main purpose.

Closer at home, Xanten on the Lower Rhine in Germany is another instance. Here the site of a Roman colonial town is being excavated and
partially reconstructed with the primary aim of attracting tourists from the
neighbouring industrial areas. The waters of the Rhine, now flowing at
some distance of the site, will be brought back to the site by extending

gravel pits to form a large recreational lake. In this way, reconstructed Roman harbour installations can be placed on the waterfront and reconstructed walls will rise out of the water. Here archaeology primarily serves recreation and tourism, though education is not forgotten. The local authorities aim at "eine bildungsbezogene Erholungsmöglichkeit populärwissenschaftlichen Charakters" (an educative recreational facility of a nonspecialist nature).

Both at Nara and Xanten the archaeological work is of high quality, but the reconstructions only reflect today's personal views, some of which will soon be outdated. Verification will never be possible, for excavation always means destruction. Though we cannot deny the educational value of these projects, it is equally true that locally the soil archive is prematurely exhausted. An interesting single-period park has been established at Kasora in Japan. In an area with a number of crescent-shaped shell mounds from the Jomon period, a section through one of the mounds was covered by a small building; two excavated house sites were also covered by a building that forms part of a museum devoted to the Jomon culture in general, and a full-size reconstructed hut was erected on the terrain. Here with a minimum of excavation and destruction, a maximum of information has been made available to the public.

Multi-period reconstructions are often placed in areas with varied natural environments, so that each building can be placed in its proper setting. Examples of archaeological parks with a more or less successful ecological component are the Irish Heritage Park at Wexford, and Samara near Amiens, France. In both parks the reconstructions are based on excavated evidence in the general area (Ireland and Picardy, respectively). In the Netherlands a large archaeological park project (Archeon) has recently been started. It will be realized near Alphen, province of South-Holland.

The reason why professional archaeologists like to be involved in reconstruction work is the element of experiment. At Xanten the stone-built Roman baths, which were preserved in great detail, have been reconstructed and their heating system successfully brought into function. In most cases, however, the archaeological documentation is very meagre. For solving problems of, for instance, roof construction of excavated wooden buildings, one has to rely on indirect evidence, of which the excavated plan of postholes is only a part. Evidence from existing historical buildings, and the general technological level of the period in question should also be considered. Here is reason for great concern. For economic reasons many constructions are carried out in a hurry, and often present a much too primitive view of the past. The full scientific potential of the reconstructions remains unused. A notable exception is the Viking-period hall built at Fyrkat in Denmark.

There is little doubt that archaeological parks will be a major asset of archaeology in the nineties, but it will be a hard job for professional archaeologists to keep them under control and to ensure that no concessions are made to prestige, quick profit and unjustified ideas of past primitiveness.

Amateur archaeology

A clear indication of the growing public interest in archaeology – at least in the Western countries – is the increasing number of people that make archaeology their major pastime. In the history of archaeology the amateur has always played an important part. New, however, is the wish to be directly involved in field-work: in excavating, sieving, cleaning, sorting, restoring. It is new also that this interest is widely spread over all levels of society, and not restricted to the upper classes.

Four, often overlapping categories of amateur archaeologists can be distinguished. Every summer, hundreds of volunteers gather at professional digs, where they provide the main workforce, are given food and shelter and perhaps some pocket money, and are taken out on one or two excursions. Experienced volunteers are in high regard and demand.

A second group of amateur archaeologists operate locally in their home areas. They form flying squads, running from one rescue excavation to the next, with their bare hands salvaging flints and potsherds from the mud, noting depth and coordinates, before the machines roaring over their heads dump the whole lot onto trucks. In the larger towns there may be a 'town archaeologist', paid by the local authorities, but he is always in need of volunteer assistance.

A third group of amateurs form regional or national societies. They organize lectures, courses and excursions to field monuments and museums, and instigate research and measures to protect monuments.

There also are a large number of – often unorganized – private persons who go out walking over recently ploughed fields, inspecting sand, clay or gravel quarries and sorting the stone dumps of potato-harvesting machines. The tense expectation of a sudden spectacular encounter unites these people with the angler, the bird-watcher and the field botanist or entomologist. Many an amateur archaeologist turns hunter when the hunting season starts. Often people take an interest both in the natural and the cultural history of their region. In the course of years, amateurs may assemble important collections.

Just as there are poachers besides hunters, so are there people that try to make money out of illegal excavations and selling the finds to private collectors or antique dealers. Many people with metal detectors operate in the twilight zone between legality and illegality. Some town archaeologists have to hire professional security guards to prevent the looting of their excavations at night or during the weekends.

Relations between the amateur and professional archaeologists are not always easy. The amateur collector likes to keep his sources secret until they are exhausted. The temptation to start a small, private dig is great. He is eager to keep the finds to himself, but he may be tempted to exchange finds with a colleague or even to sell them to a passing visitor. Cases are known of archaeological finds being used as payment for medical or dental services. On the other side, the professional archaeologist prefers to see them safe in a public museum, so that they can be shown and are available for scientific study. Often, the amateur needs the expertise of the professional for the identification of his finds. But if he decides to mention his site to the professional, hoping it will be excavated, he may find that the professional has other priorities, and appears not to attach to the site the measure of importance that the amateur is convinced it has. All in all, the regional museum archaeologist is well advised to be careful and patient in his relations with the amateur collectors in his area. In the long run he may be rewarded with the collection being bequeathed to the museum.

In sum, present-day archaeology is heavily dependent on the amateur contribution, whether as a workforce in scientific excavations, as flying squads for rescue work, as field inspectors or as collectors. In Britain the 'independent archaeologists' have their own conferences. With full support of the British Academy they have formed an umbrella organization "to ensure that proper recognition is given to the aspirations and interests of amateur archaeologists". In other countries, too, the status of amateur archaeology will have to be raised, if archaeology is to fulfil the task society demands of it.

Archaeology and environment
One of the goals of archaeology is the reconstruction of environmental developments. Since the introduction of agriculture man's influence on his environment has been steadily increasing. The modern cultural landscape is the product of a long development. The study of its most recent centuries is the domain of the historical geographer. For those landscapes that in origin are older than the earliest existing maps and other historical documents, archaeology comes to the fore. In some recent studies of regions in

the Netherlands (Veluwe; Drenthe) (Heidinga, 1987; Waterbolk, 1985) and Denmark (parts of Jutland) (Hvass, 1988) the distribution patterns of settlement finds from the Early Medieval and Roman periods are related to historical rural occupation patterns. The settlements might have shifted their location over small distances, but the territorial structure of the area remained intact. Other elements in the landscape that lend themselves to archaeological study (by excavation and air photography) are the roads connecting the villages, the field boundaries and the layout of the villages themselves (parcelling, roads).

In this way, the archaeological information may help to identify the basic structure of a landscape, so that this can be retained when the use of the land in detail is to be changed through reallotment schemes, afforestation, house-building and new roads. By keeping the main structure intact, the cultural landscape may maintain its regional identity. The archaeology of the cultural landscape could develop into a valuable aid in land-use planning (Waterbolk, 1984; Cleere, 1989).

The information contained in the soil archive can be of great use in modern environmental studies. Since the beginning of the 20th century, archaeological data have played a prominent role in the study of changes of climate and sea level since the last glaciation. These data gain more weight now that anthropogenic carbon dioxide in the atmosphere is interfering with the natural processes on a world-wide scale. Another case in point is the deforestation that has taken place in Europe since the introduction of agriculture. Climatologists expect the climate to have been affected, and in the framework of a project of the European Science Foundation archaeologists and palaeobotanists are now asked to present quantitative estimates of the degree of deforestation for a small number of 'time slices' after the last glaciation. A further example is given by ancient agricultural methods. In the Negev desert a sophisticated Byzantine irrigation system, reconstructed from archaeological evidence, is being successfully brought into modern use. It may well be that in the near future other questions of practical relevance will be asked of archaeology.

Environmental archaeology has great potential in education, for it lends itself both to demonstration and explanation of the results of archaeological research, and to enhancing the awareness of the dangers of environmental overexploitation. In addition, it is an archaeology that is much less liable to nationalistic lapses than the presentation of the treasures of a glorious past which so often is the explicit or implicit content of archaeological exhibits.

Archaeology and women's studies

Since women's studies are the subject of a special chapter in this book, I can restrict myself to the contribution archaeology can make in this field. The scientific contribution of women archaeologists has been considerable. Mention can be made of Johanna Mestorf, director of the Schleswig-Holsteinian Museum from 1891-1909 and professor of prehistory at the University of Kiel, of Dame Kathleen Kenyon, who in the years 1952-1958 directed large excavations at Jericho in Palestine, where she found spectacular remains of a very early 'pre-pottery Neolithic' culture, of Denise de Sonneville-Bordes who is an authority on the Upper Palaeolithic of Western Europe and the American Marija Gimbutas, who wrote a much-discussed book, entitled *Goddesses and Gods of Old Europe*. In Sweden, Margaretha Björnstad has recently been called to the prestigious position of *riksantikvarie* (State antiquarian). In the Netherlands (and in many other countries) classical archaeology has always attracted many women scholars. In recent years, however, prehistoric archaeology has become equally popular. At the moment three Dutch university chairs in archaeology are occupied by women.

Of special interest in women's studies are the religion and social structure of prehistoric societies, and, in particular, the role of matriarchism and the Great Mother Goddess. Gimbutas advocates the view that in Neolithic Europe an indigenous matriarchal society was replaced by an intrusive patriarchal society of people speaking an Indo-European language. She bases her theory mainly on a study of the many clay figurines which are found in graves and settlement sites in Central and Southeast Europe. Her conclusions can be criticized, but this should not mask the fact that archaeological objects such as figurines, votive deposits, cult shrines as well as data on the burial ritual are highly relevant, together with data from linguistics, ancient history and cultural anthropology, for the reconstruction of the position women occupied in ancient societies. In view of what has been said on the role of identity in archaeology, it is obvious that among the present generation of women archaeologists many are attracted to this particular theme.

5. Developments in archaeological methods and techniques

The past decades have given us a wealth of new methods and techniques that have changed the character of the discipline considerably. This development will certainly continue in the nineties and will be one reason why archaeology is becoming increasingly expensive. Space permits only a very schematic treatment of the trends that can be observed.

Classification

The computer has greatly facilitated the use of mathematical classification methods, such as various forms of cluster analysis, factor analysis and multidimensional scaling. An early appraisal of the potential of computer use in archaeology is given by Whallon (1972).

Analytical techniques

For the determination of the chemical composition of archaeological materials various techniques are available. They all serve to identify the nature of the object, the way it was produced and/or the source of the raw material, so that the object can be better described typologically. Some methods are destructive, but need only a very small sample, others are non-destructive. Trace elements and their relative quantities are of great importance for the identification of metals. For identifying stone and potters' clay the mineral composition can be studied. Methods regularly used in archaeometry are atomic absorption spectroscopy, X-ray fluorescence spectrometry, neutron activation analysis, scanning electron microscopy, and X-ray diffraction analysis. Various other methods are being developed (Parker, 1986).

Dating techniques

Radiocarbon dating is without doubt the most spectacular development in archaeology since 1950. In prehistoric archaeology it has solved all the major dating problems for the last 40,000 years. Recently a new technique is being developed, whereby the sample size can be reduced from c. 5 grams to c. 0.05 gram. Only organic material can be used for the radiocarbon dating technique.

The precision of radiocarbon dating for the last 7000 years has been greatly improved by the possibility of calibrating the data with the aid of radiocarbon dates made on wood samples that are independently dated by dendrochronology. In Europe there is now a continuous sequence of oak tree rings covering 7200 years, and with some 'floating' sequences that are older, there is good hope that a few more millennia will become available for precision dating.

Beyond the time range of radiocarbon dating, two techniques, equally based on radioactivity, can be used: Uranium-series dating for the time range 30,000-100,000 years, and Potassium-Argon dating for yet earlier periods. The applicability of these two techniques is much more restricted. Other dating techniques of limited applicability and precision are thermoluminescence dating, archaeomagnetism, fission-track dating, obsidian hydration dating, aminoacid-racemization dating and nitrogen, fluorine and uranium content dating (for bone) (Parker, 1986).

Chorological techniques
The plotting of find-spots on maps can be greatly facilitated if the coordinates are fed into a computer. If the total known soil archive of an area is computerized, one can, with the appropriate software, easily produce distribution maps on any chosen scale and compare them with each other or with maps showing natural features. In the Netherlands the ARCHIS project of the leading archaeological institutes aims at such a complete data-base, in combination with a geographical information system (GIS) (Burrough, 1986). Other European countries where such systems operate are Britain and Denmark. When it is ready, the new possibilities will without doubt give a quite new direction to archaeological research.
The analysis of distribution patterns often poses complicated problems. *Spatial analysis in archaeology* (Hodder & Orton, 1976) has become a specialist subject, in which archaeology links up with mathematics and geography. In this respect, too, the computer has created new possibilities.

Excavating
Excavation will remain a major activity of archaeology, but, clearly, no longer as a means to satisfy primitive curiosity, as a form of treasure hunting or to enlarge museum collections as it used to be, but only as a method to solve distinct problems. Excavation means destruction of unique evidence and should be done with the utmost care. Excavation is also expensive, and should be done efficiently, with the combined use of excavating machinery, shovel, trowel, brush and sieve.
Excavations prompted merely by scientific questions will become increasingly rare. In practice, so much of the soil archive is destroyed by building activities and public works, that one can pursue a scientific program by making a selection from sites that are threatened. Excavation technique in itself is simple. What counts are (1) the logistics – the layout of trenches, levels, and sections, the division of work between staff, assistants and hired or volunteer labour, (2) the experience of the machine operator, the man with the shovel and the volunteer with the trowel and the brush, (3) the precision of recording by drawing and photography, and (4) the staff's capability to compromise between the smooth running of the project as a whole and the improvising which is needed as unexpected finds or problems turn up.
Recent technical developments include the systematic use of metal detec-

tors, devices for recording field data by stereo-photogrammetry and drawing machines, computer storage of field drawings, machinery for sieving
the soil in order to collect small archaeological items and animal and plant
remains, and, in waterlogged situations, the use of drainage pumps.

Surveying

Since excavation means destruction, non-destructive methods of analyzing
the subsoil have been and are being developed. They are based on physical
principles, such as earth magnetism, electrical resistivity and radar. Chemical
methods, too, are being used, in particular the phosphate method. Although
spectacular results have been obtained in individual cases, the interpretation of the data is often difficult. This is due to the complicated interaction
of natural soil processes with the human activities that took place at a site,
and which in themselves may have been cumulative and complex in an
unpredictable way. Often, two or more independent techniques have to be
applied conjunctively.

On the whole, progress in the development and use of these surveying
methods is slow but good, and it is certainly to be expected that specialized
teams, availing themselves of a variety of equipment, will play an increasingly important role in the planning and monitoring of excavation projects
and in the extrapolation of the results.
On a wider geographical level, air photography will continue to play an
important part in the reconnaissance of non-natural phenomena in a landscape. In recent years infrared photography has added new details. False-
colour photographs by satellites are beginning to be used in archaeology.
For a regional archaeological survey the basis will always be the use of
ancient topographical maps in combination with the traditional method of
field-walking: the systematic inspection of ploughed fields, road and ditch
cuttings, molehills, rabbit and fox burrows and blown-out sand areas for
any indication of human activity – burnt earth, charcoal, potsherds, flint
chips – in combination with a close inspection of any topographical irregu-
larities that might be man-made. The problems in surveying should not be
underestimated: scrubby or tropical vegetation may make walking impossible, ancient surface layers may be covered by later natural deposits, modern exploitation forms may either enhance or impair the visibility of archaeological remains.
A major goal of surveying is the ability to predict the presence and nature
of early human activity in the study area and to estimate its archaeological
potential.

Association

One of the basic activities of archaeology is the study of find associations. The analysis of the local context and the find circumstances constitutes the first step. Associations become really important when they recur. Comparison of associations used to be done rather intuitively with little regard for the quantitative and statistical aspects involved. In recent years various mathematical techniques have been developed – or rather, been introduced into archaeology (Shennan, 1988) -, which help to assess correlations between find associations. In most university curricula statistics and computer use are now an obligatory element. Though archaeology can never do without qualitative judgment, quantitative data will play an increasingly important role and these data should be well-founded so that they can be brought together in an expert system. The computer can serve archaeology well also as a calculator.

Archaeobiology

Biological methods and techniques pervade the whole field of archaeology. This is not surprising, for man is a living creature himself. He collects plants and animals for food, uses organic materials for making tools and building shelter and interacts continuously with the biological environment in a highly complex way. Developments in biology will sooner or later be of relevance in archaeology.

At the typological level, botanical and zoological methods help in identifying the nature and species of biological materials used for making artefacts (wood, bone, shell, horn, skin). In chronology, dendrochronology, based on the differential annual growth of tree rings, is becoming increasingly important, both directly as a means to determine exactly the felling year of a tree used for building a house, a well or a fence, and indirectly for the calibration of radiocarbon dates. The spectacular extension of the oak dendrochronology for certain European regions has made it possible, for example, to exactly date lake-side dwellings in Switzerland from the fourth millennium BC. The method works only if a number of parallel tree-ring sequences of sufficient length are available. Plant and animal chorology (phytogeography, zoogeography) provides data on modern and ancient plant and animal distributions, and thus, indirectly, on past climates, which were decisively important to man.

Archaeobiological methods are particularly important for studying the environmental context in which human society evolved. In recent years new categories of animal and plant groups have been added to the traditionally studied mammals and trees. On the zoological side, birds, fishes, insects and mites are now used, on the botanical side the number of identifiable taxa of pollen, spores, seeds, fruits and wood is steadily increasing. On the technical side, sampling and collecting have received special attention.

A major task of archaeobiology is the study of domesticated plants and animals, including their origins, spread and differentiation and the reconstruction of agricultural methods. In these fields, too, quantitative analyses are becoming increasingly important.

The heading of experimental archaeology covers for instance the experiments in cultivation of crops on the unprotected salt marshes, as an aid to understanding the occurrence of these crops in Iron-Age marsh settlements. These experiments have been conducted both in the Netherlands and North Germany. In Denmark cultivation experiments have been done in natural oak forests that were opened up by the slash-and-burn technique. Well-known is the Butser experimental farm in England, where experiments are done such as crop growing, harvesting and storage, along with experiments in house reconstruction, building of earthworks, etc. Experimental archaeobiology is a promising line for future research.

Anthropobiology studies the biology of man himself. Along with the traditional morphological data on age, sex and physical type, archaeologists now learn that the isotope composition of bones (human and animal) can reflect ancient diet (marine versus terrestrial, animal versus vegetable foods). Reconstruction of past ways of life being one of the major goals of archaeology, archaeobiology will always play a vital part in archaeology. Yet, progress can only be achieved by further specialization. I foresee the emergence of specialized groups, possessing reference collections and long experience, together with whom excavations are planned and monitored. They will be regarded as partners with equal rights in a team, and not as 'auxiliary scientists' as they often have been called (and locally still are called, with treatment to match).

At a more general theoretical level I foresee an intensified application in archaeology of the results of modern ecological and ethological studies on such themes as predator-prey relations, energy budget, optimal foraging, territorial behaviour, etc.

6. Theoretical discussions

The past 25 years have brought an explosive increase of interest in the theoretical aspects of archaeology. It started independently in the U.S.A. and Britain in the beginning of the sixties, spread in stages over western continental Europe – first the Scandinavian countries, then Holland, later again in France and Germany – and it is now nearly a world-wide phenomenon. The countries of Eastern Europe long had their own discussions, but have in the last decades joined the general discussions. As early as 1977, the Russian archaeologist Leo Klejn undertook the meritorious task of producing a global "panorama of theoretical archaeology".

One of the complicating factors is the difference in archaeological tradition in the various countries and regions. In 1981 the journal World Archaeology devoted two issues to the theme of 'Regional traditions of archaeological research' and invited specialists on the archaeology of the U.S.A., Great Britain, Germany, France, Scandinavia, the Netherlands (Waterbolk, 1981), the Soviet Union, Israel, the Near East, India and Pakistan, China, Australia, Japan, Africa, Mexico and Peru, and asked them to "delineate as clearly and dispassionately as possible the special characteristics, achievements, and (where appropriate) the current problems of individual regional traditions" (Trigger & Glover, 1981). Only the German archaeologist failed to contribute. The differences proved to be enormous indeed – often within the areas as well. Whilst in some countries, like the U.S.A. and Australia, archaeology is an offspring of the interest in the indigenous population of the country, in many others, such as France or India, it has a polyphyletic origin: in natural history, in particular the study of paaeontology, and in the antiquarian interest in relics from the ancient, historically documented peoples living in the area. The antiquarian interest may be very old: in China it goes back to the 11th century AD. American archaeology had to free itself from a colonialist attitude towards primitive people, who were not considered capable of developing any culture of their own. German post-war archaeology, on the other hand, had to free itself from an exaggerated nationalistic view of a glorious past. Archaeology in Eastern Europe had to find ways to comply with the fundamental principles of historical materialism. The new countries had to develop traditions of their own, and as I noted earlier, made a start with a national archaeology to enhance their national identity. Realizing further the multiple goals of archaeology, so eloquently formulated by Thompson (1976), it is clear that no single theory can serve the whole field of archaeology. His view that archaeology as a whole is best served by a variety of theories, and that for the solution of a particular problem the formulation of multiple hypotheses gives the best results, strongly appeals to me.

This is not the place for a lengthy treatment of the discussions. I will restrict myself to some main themes. A major issue was whether archaeology should be a nomothetic discipline like the natural sciences or an ideographic discipline, such as history. The American L. Binford (1972, 1989) is the eloquent proponent of what has come to be called 'processual archaeology'. Archaeologists' main concern should be cultural processes and the laws that govern these processes. The general principles are of interest, not the particular situations and their interpretations. Only by deductive reasoning and using the 'covering-law model' can truly scientific explanations be obtained. In the research of Binford and that of his many followers there is no chronological or geographical limitation. They hold a 'systemic' and 'adaptive' view of culture, and for analyzing the various subsystems of culture they insist on quantification of archaeological data. They have done a great job in developing methods for the analysis of these data (Watson, Leblanc and Redman, 1984). Ecological information is extensively used. In Britain a bright young archaeologist from Cambridge, D.L. Clarke (1968), who died much too young, wrote a book entitled *Analytical Archaeology* which also made a great impact. Archaeology should "aim at the identification of patterns or regularities in the functioning of cultural systems, which would ultimately lead to a higher category of knowledge in the form of models and hypotheses" (Paddayya, 1985). It is a plea for archaeology as a science of material culture. In the theoretical writings of Clarke, man himself is only remotely present.

Young archaeologists all over the world were fascinated by the ideas of this 'New Archaeology' and it was some time before a reaction came. A major spokesman of what already is called the 'post-processual' archaeology is another Cambridge scholar, I. Hodder (1982, 1987b). He states that "processual, behaviourial and systems theory archaeology have accompanied a massive fragmentation and compartmentalization of archaeological research". He advocates a 'symbolic' or 'contextual' archaeology and emphasizes the fact – based on his ethnoarchaeological studies – that the meaning of material culture traits varies from context to context, and that beliefs and ideologies play an important role in social and economic strategies. Whereas Binford's and Clarke's systemic and adaptive view of culture may have led to an overemphasis on the role of external factors in the development of culture, Hodder draws attention to the importance of internal factors (Paddayya, 1986). His interest is more with cultures than with culture. The unique, the exceptional and the deviating in human behaviour once more come to the fore. In a recent book, *Archaeology as long-term history*, Hodder (1987a) speaks of the natural links between history and archaeology, which had been despised by many anthropological archaeologists within the New Archaeology, but are now being reappraised. Of course, this reassessment is taking place only among those archaeologists who had turned away from history in the great years of the New Archaeology.

In Germany there has been very little response to the New Archaeology. At the same time there has been a reluctance to continue the discussion about the ethnic interpretation of archaeological data, which in that country had a long tradition and which even went on during the Nazi period, with people like Wahle, Reinecke and Jacob-Friesen very much opposing the views of Reinerth and other Kossinna followers. After all, the idea of 'archaeological cultures' had originated in Germany, to be taken over by such influential people as Gordon Childe. It is the misuse of this concept in the Nazi period which explains the reluctance. In the immediate post-war period German archaeologists would claim that ethnic interpretation on the basis of archaeological sources alone was impossible. They much preferred to turn to the early historical period, where one could speak with confidence of Germans, Slavs, Romans, Goths, Saxons, etc. Their archaeology can in a sense be described as 'neo-antiquarianism'. According to Klejn (1977) this term would also apply to the work of many post-war British archaeologists, such as S. Piggott and G. Daniel. In an important paper, Veit (1989) remarks that the old ethnic concepts continued to survive in research practice: "the term 'archaeological culture' became a quasi ideology-free substitute for the term 'ethnic unit'". Rightly Veit states that Lüning's view that the term archaeological culture should only be used in the chronological sense, undervalues its potential. We cannot know what group of people consciously belonged to an archaeological culture, but we can be sure that it was a group of people sharing, perhaps unconsciously, common behavioral elements and traditions resulting in a uniformity of their material culture. I agree with Veit that as a heuristic device, the 'archaeological culture' is indispensable for delineating culture history for the prehistoric period. I also believe that the concepts of 'adaptation group' and 'adaptive area' or 'nuclear area' (*kerngewest*) as developed in the Netherlands (Waterbolk, 1974, 1979; Heidinga, 1987) do provide the regional building stones of the archaeological cultures, at a primary level of abstraction above the individual settlements. Although 'archaeological cultures' in the Childean sense still are in bad repute among younger archaeologists – Shennan (1989) finds them "positively misleading as the basis of an approach to prehistory" – I foresee a revival of them in the nineties. What is urgently needed, however, are clearer, more disciplined definitions of these cultures than the often intuitive labels which in the past have been given to observed similarities in the archaeological record.

In a recent paper Härke (1989) draws attention to the utter lack of communication between Anglo-American and German archaeologists with regard to the investigation of cemeteries from the early historical period. For more than two decades, parallel methodological discussions took place, without the two nationalities taking notice of each other. "Die Erklärung dürfte im 'Auseinanderleben' der deutschen und anglo-amerikanischen Archäologie seit der Entstehung der 'new archaeology' in den sechziger Jahren zu suchen sein, in dem dabei ständig gewachsenen Unverständnis für die Ansätze der jeweils anderer Seite und der von vornherein niedriger Erwartung anderen Ergebnisse" (The explanation may have to be sought in the drifting apart of German and Anglo-American archaeology since the rise of the 'New Archaeology' in the sixties, in the growing misapprehension of the other side's points of departure and in the *a priori* low expectations of their results).

Soviet archaeology is very little known outside the U.S.S.R. and its direct neighbours. This applies particularly to the theoretical discussions in that country. In their contribution in World Archaeology, Bulkin, Klejn and Lebedev (1982) distinguish as many as seven trends within present Soviet archaeology, all based on the principles of historical materialism: archaeological history, archaeological ethnogenetics, archaeological sociology, descriptive archaeology, archaeotechnology, archaeological ecology and sequential investigation of the past (including theoretical archaeology). The authors "do not approve of the alienation of archaeology from history". It is very promising that Soviet archaeologists are now joining the international debate, which can only be of mutual benefit.

In an interesting essay Trigger (1981) has demonstrated that the major paradigmatic shifts in archaeology have not occurred independently of changes in the way archaeologists perceive the societies in which they live. "The unilinear evolution of the nineteenth century was an optimistic expression of faith in a new economic order that had brought prosperity and political power to the middle class". As at the end of the 19th century "the growing power of the working class produced growing doubts about cultural progress", "an evolutionary approach gave way to a historical one". "In the optimistic period immediately after World War II, American archaeologists turned again to evolutionary theories", but "following the political and economic crises that began in the 1960's" they "continued to employ evolutionary concepts but saw development as tending in a negative and perhaps catastrophic direction". Looking forward, Trigger recently summarized (1986): "archaeology is neither simply a reflection of society nor fully independent of it. Archaeology is influenced by the inherent limitations of the archaeological record, and the interpretation of this record is influenced in major ways by social processes. Yet the data of archaeology are not entirely a construction of our own mind even if their recording and analyses are coloured by our presuppositions".

To an outsider much of the theoretical discussions in archaeology may look provincial and reminiscent of earlier discussions in other disciplines, such as history (Ankersmit, 1986), which had been largely ignored. As Hodder remarks, "archaeologists hung on to positivism long after serious scepticism had been established elsewhere. Functionalism and systems theory were adopted as if the critique of functionalism and the notion of structure did not exist". He speaks of a "general pattern of retarded borrowing".

We find Hodder's remarks in the foreword of an original, highly critical and provocative analysis of all contemporary archaeology by Shanks and Tilley (1987). One of the elements they have brought into the discussion is the fact that archaeologists produce texts. Whatever theoretical position they adhere to, they tell stories about the past that reflect the present and include the narrator's point of view, his judgement. There is no primary truth in the past; the past *requires* interpretation. Such views have much in common with the narrativism in historical research as opposed to historicism (Ankersmit, 1986).

The theoretical debate in archaeology is continuing. As I complete this paper, I find on my desk Binford's latest book (Binford, 1989), and a discussion paper by Shanks and Tilley called *Archaeology into the 1990's*, with critical comments by Bender, Hodder, B. Olsen, Herschend, Nordbladh, Trigger, Wenke and Renfrew (Shanks & Tilley, 1989).

7. Dutch archaeology in the nineties

The Netherlands
At home, the main task for Dutch archaeologists will be the management of the national archaeological heritage, the 'soil archive' as it has recently been called (Van Es *et al.,* 1988). In this respect much is already being done, but the process of registration and protection of archaeological field monuments must be accelerated and receive greater priority in the State Service for Archaeological Investigations. We should realize that the Netherlands is one of the most densely populated and affluent countries in the world, and its archaeological heritage is therefore more severely threatened than that of other countries.

Dutch archaeology will be increasingly involved in rescue excavations, in documentation and in planning procedures. I already mentioned the ARCHIS project, which should lead to a complete archaeological data bank, from which it will be possible to retrieve information on the geographical distribution of any find category or site type. It will not only be of great help in archaeological heritage management, but also open up new possibilities for research. We shall certainly see an increase in 'contract archaeology': archaeological surveys requested by various government agencies involved in land-use planning, contracted out to university institutes. The University of Amsterdam has already set up a special foundation for the purpose (R.A.A.P.)

Regional archaeology has been a major issue in Dutch archaeology in the 1980s, with emphasis on the regions of Drenthe, the Veluwe, the Campine, the Eastern River Area, the Meuse estuary, and Waterland. As has been said, these regional studies may gain an extra dimension and practical application if a link is sought with historical geography and the origin of the historical cultural landscape is set as a research goal.

Urban archaeology has equally been an expanding element in Dutch archaeology in the past decade. Even though the economic situation makes it difficult for many local governments to create permanent positions for town archaeologists, popular interest in archaeology is increasing and new forms of collective archaeological activity will have to be found to meet the demand. The situation in Groningen may be taken as an example. The museum, the society of amateur archaeologists and the university joined forces with other local groups, and have formed a foundation which raised money from industry, private individuals, the local authorities and cultural and scientific foundations. In this way the means were found for excavating and studying in an interdisciplinary way a site that occupies a key position in the town's evolution from a strategically situated rural settlement of the Roman and early medieval period.

The present generation of Dutch archaeologists are much impressed by the new perspectives for research opened up by the theoretical discussions in the Anglo-Saxon countries. They try to apply them to the familiar archaeological materials with varying success. These efforts will certainly continue in the nineties. They are one way to separate the few fruitful ideas from the many that look good theoretically but are doomed to failure because the basic archaeological data lack the required quality or quantity. With increasing knowledge of regional developments at home, the need will be felt to widen the geographical scope and to tackle problems on an interregional scale. With the southern Netherlands as a basis, a group of archaeologists are now studying the protohistoric development of adjacent parts of Belgium, Luxemburg, France and Germany, forming the homeland of the Carolingian empire (Austrasia). Emphasis is put on early state-formation (Rowlands *et al.*, 1987) and centre-periphery relations (Renfrew & Shennan, 1982). In this project archaeologists from all the countries mentioned cooperate. Other areas suitable for such an interregional approach are the coastal districts of the northern Netherlands with the adjacent North German coastland, and the uplands between the rivers IJssel and Ems in the northern and eastern Netherlands and adjacent parts of Lower Saxony and Westphalia. In both areas archaeologists already cooperate closely. Interesting research perspectives are also offered by the comparison of adjacent areas with different physical properties, such as the Holocene coastal and fluviatile marshes with their Pleistocene hinterland.

Such projects can indeed only be successful when friendly relations exist across the present borders, and when financial support is obtained from the central research-funding organizations in the respective states. With the opening-up of the borders in 1992, the increased tendency to cross them for research purposes should be accompanied by greater scope for international funding. The European Science Foundation can play a key role. In the Netherlands the Royal Netherlands Academy has recently created wider possibilities for financial support of international contacts among established research workers.

One of the best radiocarbon dating laboratories in the world is situated in Groningen. Dutch archaeologists have profited very much from it, both passively, by using the dates in their archaeological research, and actively by developing methods for the interpretation of radiocarbon dates in archaeology. It is hoped that the laboratory will be able to realize a unit for accelerator dating, a technique which bears great promise for the future, for it permits samples to be dated that are 100 times as small as those needed for conventional dating.

In other sectors of archaeometry the Netherlands have a backlog. The Foundation for Archaeological Research in the Netherlands (ARCHON), a branch of the Netherlands Organization for Scientific Research (NWO) realizes this and has formed an archaeometry committee which will actively promote research along promising lines, the aims of course being twofold: both development research and application – the formula which has been so successful with radiocarbon dating.

As to archaeobiology, the Netherlands have occupied a front position in the past decades, both in development and application. The possible use of new categories of organisms, such as mites and insects, is being explored, and the existing techniques are used in new areas, such as Southeast Asia.

Yet the situation is a stressful one, for the number of permanent positions for this type of work is decreasing, while with the newly-developed possibilities the demand, both national and international, is increasing. As I indicated before, the formation of specialist teams outside the traditional museums and university institutes may be an answer to this challenge.

Another forte of Dutch archaeology is settlement archaeology, in the restricted sense of the archaeology of houses and settlements. Progress has been spectacular, but only for particular areas and periods. Only for Drenthe has a reasonably complete picture been obtained of the typochronology of house-plans for the last 3000 years. In other areas such schemes still have to be completed. The comparative study of house-plans and settlement patterns bears great promise for the study of the structure of society in the various periods. Internationally, settlement archaeology is being actively practised, e.g. in Denmark, parts of northern Germany and England. Elsewhere, e.g. in Belgium, it has hardly begun.

The past decades have seen a great advance in our knowledge of the early occupation history of the delta, for example in such areas as the Alblasserwaard, West-Friesland and the IJsselmeer polders. Yet the picture is far from complete. A major problem is that of separating the role of the marine and fluviatile environments from the cultural development which took place during these periods (Neolithic and Bronze Age). In any case, the delta sites, though often waterlogged and difficult of access, produce a wealth of environmental data, the interpretation of which is both of regional and international interest.

For the study of the Palaeolithic and Mesolithic periods the Netherlands do not seem to be particularly well situated. In large parts of the country the ancient surfaces are deeply buried under younger sediments; Mesolithic bog habitation was much less frequent than in Scandinavia, and there are no natural caves as in France. Yet sites such as Oldeholtwolde in Friesland and Maastricht-Belvédère in Limburg are producing highly interesting data, and the regional working-over of all available material is a widely-felt necessity. A problem with such studies is that much material has been collected in the thirties and fourties by private persons and its documentation is often meagre. Private collections are often not easily accessible.

Along with these special lines of research, traditional archaeological activities will certainly be carried on. The archaeological field monuments in the Dutch landscape, such as megalithic tombs, barrows, Celtic fields, ancient dwelling mounds (*terpen*) and castle mounds, will continue to attract attention. There are no signs that the age-old fascination with the

Romans is going to dwindle. Nijmegen, where efforts to protect the rich soil archive have been a complete failure, will be the scene of major rescue excavations – though all archaeologists feel that the working-over of existing materials should have priority. The Limes forts along the Rhine, the *villae* with their baths and wall paintings, the cemeteries in Noord-Brabant and Limburg with their rich finds, all strongly appeal to the public; and, more professionally, the process of romanization of the area south of the Rhine and the Roman influence on the area north of the river are a challenge to archaeologists.

And certainly the rich finds in the museums will continue to be studied. New finds may suddenly offer unexpected perspectives. There is no doubt that on the home scene Dutch archaeology in the nineties will present a lively picture.

The Mediterranean countries

For a long time Dutch classical archaeologists have concentrated on the works of art of the Greeks and Romans: temples, wall paintings, sculptures, vases. Such studies will certainly continue during the nineties. But in the past decade other interests have become manifest, in two new directions: the layout, siting and interrelations of the settlements, and the periods preceding the classical ones. Intensive surveying in combination with limited excavations and a new analysis of the historical data yields settlement data which lend themselves to interpretations in terms of social, economic or political structure at the local and regional level. Such studies can be pursued with relatively limited financial means. Projects along these lines are conducted in Latium, Apulia, Thessaly and on the Peleponnesus. Studies of the periods preceding the classical period, such as those of protohistoric Latium (1000-500 BC), are equally rewarding. They do, however, require more excavations alongside of surveying, and the application of the methods, techniques and theoretical view-points of prehistory.

Both types of activity are welcome additions to the activities of the archaeologists of the host countries and those of the Schools of the larger countries, which tend to concentrate on the actual classical monuments.

SW Asia and Egypt

Dutch field activities in SW Asia and Egypt will certainly continue during the nineties. In the last two decades a young generation of capable, internationally oriented field workers has been trained. Emphasis in SW Asia (mainly Syria, Jordan and Turkey) is on the early food-producing stages (early Neolithic) and on those later Neolithic and Bronze Age cultures that are contemporary with, or form part of, the early Mesopotamian cultures. The work in Syria and Turkey comprises both surveying and excavations. Archaeology in SW Asia is still in its pioneer stage, and progress is slow. Many areas still need to be surveyed. Every excavation can change the existing picture. Political restrictions are rigorous. A fact which should not be forgotten is the enormous length of time requiring detailed study. The earliest evidence of food production goes back to 8000 BC! Yet through the concerted activities of many countries so much is already known that good research proposals can be formulated – of which the filling-in of gaps may well be a part. The problems in this general area are fascinating. For it is here that basic elements of Western society such as agriculture and animal husbandry, organized settled life, towns, writing and Christianity originated and spread.

In Egypt surveying in the Nile delta is coupled with excavations in the classical cemeteries of Saqqara – a traditional activity of the Leiden National Museum, whose Egyptology department is of international importance.

Other parts of the world
The independence of former colonial countries has sometimes resulted in a complete break in the tradition of archaeological research. Often, however, the organizational structure has been maintained, and where relations between the new country and its former ruling power have become or remained relaxed, it is possible for European archaeologists to work again in these countries, albeit on a new footing, as partners of the local archaeologists. It is not only a matter of continued scientific interest, but also of obligation and responsibility, as T. Shaw, the president of the Prehistoric Society, recently put it with regard to Africa. "It is we in this country who have introduced the practice of archaeology into the anglophone countries of Africa; we have been responsible, directly or indirectly, for the creation of jobs – but now the holders of these jobs often find themselves deprived of many of the tools of their trade". He laments that Britain does so little, compared to France, in providing funds and exchange programmes (Shaw, 1989).

The Netherlands thus have a responsibility to archaeology in Indonesia and Surinam. With Indonesia there is a good cooperation in prehistoric archaeology, but on the Dutch side the expertise in historical archaeology is dwindling, and there is no longer a university chair for the archaeology of SE Asia. Dutch archaeological activities in Surinam and in the – not yet independent – Dutch Caribbean islands have been of a limited nature. They must continue in the nineties.

8. Epilogue

Archaeology has developed enormously in the last two decades. On the basis of a careful analysis of the soil archive, stories can be told about a wide variety of subjects: on the origin of man himself, his changing dietary habits, the development of settlements and towns and burial customs. More ambitious archaeologists talk about subjects such as state-formation, class formation, commercial networks, ceremonial exchange and levels of social complexity. But archaeology also relates of the simple things that people living here before us used as tools in their daily efforts to obtain food and to build shelter.

The relation of archaeology to the modern world is very direct: wherever we build our new roads, houses, offices and factories, we are destroying the soil archive. Up to the beginning of this century new buildings in the medieval towns were constructed upon the foundations of earlier buildings. In the centre of Utrecht the Roman level is 4 metres below the present street level. Now underground parking garages mean a sudden and complete destruction of everything that was left of these earlier constructions, including wells, cesspools and the accumulated layers of household refuse. In the rural landscape the intensification of agriculture and animal husbandry is equally disastrous. After the large-scale destructions through heathland reclamation and afforestation in the 19th and early 20th century, modern reallotment schemes now erase ancient parcel boundaries, deep drainage destroys the organic component of cultural deposits, surface levelling wipes out the microrelief that originated from earlier human activities, deep ploughing damages sub-surface culture deposits. Quarries for sand, clay, gravel, limestone, peat and brown coal play their part in the destruction of what is not only our natural environment but also our cultural environment.

If Marquard (1985, quoted after Wild, 1987) is right in saying that the main task of the humanities is to compensate for the increasing colourlessness, estrangement and disorientation of the modern world, by relating *Sensibilisierungsgeschichten, Bewahrungsgeschichten* and *Orientierungsgeschichten* (stories of sensibility, perpetuation and orientation), there is a job to do for archaeology in the nineties. Archaeology quite often deals with objects of aesthetic value (as *Sensibilisierungsgeschichten*). It is of great importance in providing regional and national identity (thus offerring *Orientierungsgeschichten*). Above all, it tells about the past and about

things worth preserving: objects in museums, monuments in the urban and rural landscape, and the landscape itself (*Bewahrungsgeschichten*).
Interestingly, Marquard's compensation theory finds support across the Atlantic, where Mayer-Oakes also connects the increasing interest in archaeology with the dehumanization of modern society. The Englishman Cleere sees the "revulsion against materialism" as an explanation for the appeal of archaeological monuments. In the compensatory task of the humanities, archaeology must take its full share.

* An early version was read by A.C. Bardet, R.W. Brandt, H.F. Fokkens, O.H. Harsema, M. Maaskant-Kleibrink, K. Randsborg, H.H. van Regteren Altena, D. Stapert, R. Whallon and M.H. Wijnen. The author is grateful for their comments. The English text was improved by A.C. Bardet.

References

Addyman, P.V., 1989. The Stonehenge we deserve. In: H.F. Cleere (ed.), *Archaeological heritage management in the modern world*. London, Unwin Hyman.
Aikio, M. & P., 1989. A chapter in the history of the colonization of Sami lands: the forced migration of Norwegian reindeer Sami to Finland in the 1800's. In: R. Layton (ed.), *Conflict in the archaeology of living traditions*. London, Unwin Hyman.
Ankersmit, F.R., 1986. *Denken over geschiedenis. Een overzicht van moderne geschiedfilosofische opvattingen* (tweede druk). Groningen, Wolters-Noordhoff.
Bar-Yosef, O & A. Mazar, 1981. Israeli archaeology. *World Archaeology* 13: 310-325.
Binford, L.R., 1972. *An archaeological perspective*. New York/London, Seminar Press.
Binford, L.R., 1989. *Debating archaeology*. San Diego, Academic Press.
Bulkin, V.A., L.S. Klejn & G.S. Lebedev, 1982. Attainments and problems of Soviet archeology. *World Archaeology* 13: 272-295.
Burrough, P.A., 1986. *Principles of geographical information systems*. Oxford, Clarendon Press.
Childe, V.G., 1956. *Piecing together the past*. London, Routledge and Kegan Paul.
Chippindale, C., 1986. Stoned Henge: events and issues at the summer solstice, 1985. *World Archaeology* 18: 38-58.
Clark, J.G.D., 1980. World prehistory and natural science. *Det Kongelige Danske Videnskabernes Selskab historisk-filosofiske Meddelelser* (50) 1: 3-40.
Clarke, D.L., 1968. *Analytical archaeology*. London, Methuen.
Cleere, H.F., 1989. Introduction: the rationale of archaeological heritage management. In: H.F. Cleere (ed.), *Archaeological heritage management in the modern world*. London, Unwin Hyman.
Condori, C.A., 1989. History and prehistory in Bolivia: what about the Indians? In: R. Layton (ed.), *Conflict in the archaeology of living traditions*. London, Unwin Hyman.
Es, W.A. van, H. Sarfatij & P.J. Woltering, 1988. *Archaeologie in Nederland. De rijkdom van het bodemarchief*. Amsterdam, Meulenhoff.
Gimbutas, M.J., *Goddesses and Gods of Old Europe*.
Gould R. & M. Schiffer (eds), 1981. *Modern material culture, the archaeology of us*. Academic Press.

Heidinga, H.A., 1987. *Medieval settlement and economy north of the Lower Rhine*. Assen, Van Gorcum.
Hodder, I. & C. Orton, 1976. *Spatial analysis in archaeology*. Cambridge, Cambridge University Press.
Hodder, I., 1982. *Symbols in action*. Cambridge, Cambridge University Press.
Hodder, I., 1987a. Preface, in I. Hodder (ed.), *Archaeology as long term history*. Cambridge, Cambridge University Press.
Hodder, I., 1987b. *The archaeology of contextual meanings*. Cambridge University Press.
Hubert, J., 1989. A proper place for the dead: a critical review of the 'reburial' issue. In: R. Layton (ed.), *Conflict in the archaeology of living traditions*. London, Unwin Hyman.
Hvass, S., 1988. The status of the Iron Age settlement in Denmark. In: M. Bierma et al., (eds), *Archeologie en landschap*. Groningen, Universiteitsdrukkerij.
Härke, H., 1989. Die anglo-amerikanische Diskussion zur Gräberanalyse. *Archäologisches Korrespondenzblatt* 19: 185-194.
Independent archeologists, 1989. Outline Programme Third Congress York.
Klejn, L.S., 1977. A panorama of theoretical archaeology. *Current Anthropology* 18: 1-42.
Lorenzo, J.L., 1981. Archaeology South of the Rio Grande. *World Archaeology* 13: 138-155.
Marquard, O., 1985. *Über die Unvermeidlichkeit der Geisteswissenschaften*. Vortrag bei der Jahresversammlung der westdeutschen Rektorenkonferenz.
Mayer-Oakes, W.J., 1989. Science, service and stewardship – a basis for the ideal archaeology of the future. In: M. Cleere (ed.), *Archaeological heritage management in the modern world*. London, Unwin Hyman.
Moberg, C.A., 1981. From artefacts to time tables to maps (to mankind?): regional traditions in archaeological research in Scandinavia. *World Archaeology* 13: 209-221.
Paddayya, K., 1985. Theoretical archaeology. A review. In: S.B. Deo and K. Paddayya (eds), *Recent advances in Indian archaeology*. Proceedings of a seminar held in Poona in 1985. Poona.
Paddayya, K., 1986. The epistemology of archaeology: a postscript to the new archaeology. *Bulletin of the Deccan College Postgraduate and Research Institute* 45: 89-115.
Parker, P.A., 1986. *Current scientific techniques in archaeology*. London/Sydney, Croom Helen.
Renfrew, C. & S.J. Shennan (eds), 1982. *Ranking, resource and exchange. Aspects of the archaeology of early European society*. Cambridge, Cambridge University Press.
Rowe, J.H., 1978. The Renaissance foundation of archaeology. In: R.L. Schuyler (ed.), *Historical archaeology: a guide to substantive and theoretical contributions*. Farmingdale, New York, Baywood Publishing Company.
Rowlands, M., M. Larsen & K. Kristiansen (eds), 1987. *Center and periphery in the ancient world*. Cambridge, Cambridge University Press.
Salmon, M.H., 1982. *Philosophy and archaeology*. New York, Academic Press.
Schuyler, R.L., 1978a. Emergence and definition of a new discipline. In: R.L. Schuyler (ed.), *Historical archaeology: a guide to substantive and theoretical contributions*: 1-2. Farmingdale, New York, Baywood Publishing Company.
Schuyler, R.L., 1978b. Subfields of historical archaeology. In: R.L. Schuyler (ed.), *Historical archaeology: a guide to substantive and theoretical contributions*: 33-34. Farmingdale, New York, Baywood Publishing Company.
Shanks, M. & C. Tilley, 1987. *Pre-constructing archaeology. Theory and practice*. Cambridge, Cambridge University Press.
Shanks, M. & C. Tilley, 1989. Archaeology into the 1990's. *Norwegian Archaeological Review* 22: 1-54.
Shaw, T., 1989. Presidential address, quoted in: *Past, the newsletter of the Prehistoric Society* 7: 1-2.
Shennan, S.J., 1988. *Quantifying archaeology*. Edinburgh, University Press.

Shennan, S.J., 1989. Introduction: archaeological approaches to cultural identity. In: S.J. Shennan (ed.), *Archaeological approaches to cultural identity*. London, Unwin Hyman.

Schiffer, M.B., 1976. *Behavioural archaeology*. New York.

Thompson, R.H., 1978. *Mesoamerica and the goals of archaeology*. Vierde Kroon-voordracht. Amsterdam.

Trigger, B.G., 1981. Anglo-American archaeology. *World Archaeology* 13: 138-155.

Trigger, B.G. & J.C. Glover, 1981. Editorial. *World Archaeology* 13: 133-137.

Trigger, B.G., 1986. Prospects for a world archaeology. *World Archaeology* 18: 1-20.

Ucko, P.J., 1989. Foreword. In: R. Layton (ed.), *Conflict in the archaeology of living traditions*. London, Unwin Hyman.

Veit, U., 1989. Ethnic concepts in German prehistory: a case study on the relationship between cultural identity and archaeological objectivity. In: S.J. Shennan (ed.), *Archaeological approaches to cultural identity*: 35-36. London, Unwin Hyman.

Waterbolk, H.T., 1974. l'Archéologie en Europe, une réaction contre le 'new archeology', *Helinium* 14: 135-162.

Waterbolk, H.T., 1979. Siedlungskontinuität im Küstengebiet der Nordsee zwischen Rhein und Elbe, *Probleme der Küstenforschung im südlichen Nordseegebiet* 13: 1-21.

Waterbolk, H.T., 1980. Het vak prehistorie. Karakter, doel en werkwijze. In: M. Chamalaun and H.T. Waterbolk (eds), *Voltooid verleden tijd? Een hedendaagse kijk op de prehistorie*: 9-20. Amsterdam, Intermediair.

Waterbolk, H.T., 1981. Archaeology in the Netherlands: delta archaeology. *World archaeology* 13: 240-254.

Waterbolk, H.T., 1984. *Archeologie en landschap.* Zevende Kroon-voordracht, gehouden voor de Stichting Ned. Museum voor Anthropologie en Prehistorie te Amsterdam op 23 maart 1984. Haarlem.

Waterbolk, H.T., 1985. Archeologie. In: J. Heringa et al., *Geschiedenis van Drenthe*. Meppel, Boom.

Watson, P.J., S.A. Leblanc & C.L. Redman, 1984. *Archeological explanation. The scientific method in archeology*. Columbia University Press.

Whallon, R., 1972. The computer in archaeology. *Computers and the humanities* (7) 1: 29-45.

Wild, W., 1987. Naturwissenschaften und Geisteswissenschaften: immer noch zwei getrennte Kulturen? In: *Neue Technologien und die Herausforderung an die Geisteswissenschaften*. Referate und Diskussionen eines Kolloquiums in der Villa Vigori vom 16./17. Juni 1986. Bundesminister für Bildung und Wissenschaft, Bonn.

Willey, G.R. & P. Phillips, 1958. *Method and theory in American archaeology*. Chicago, University of Chicago Press.

Area studies in the 1990's: prima donna or member of the chorus

Wilt L. Idema

1. Area studies in the Netherlands: past and present

Gustav Schlegel, who in 1876 became the first Dutch professor of Chinese language and literature, displayed in his publications an omnivorous range of interests. His *Uranographie chinoise* (1875) is still used as a manual for identifying the traditional Chinese names of stars, and he was the first to describe the rituals of the Chinese secret societies. In addition, he wrote about Chinese *kongsi*s, prostitution in China, and children's games. Of course he worked enthusiastically in comparative linguistics as well, and also devoted a monograph to parallelism in Chinese literature. Along the way he compiled a Dutch-Chinese dictionary for the Amoy dialect.

Schlegel's successor, J.J.M. de Groot, could perhaps best be characterized as an ethnographer – he put in a long stint as professor of the ethnography of the Dutch East Indies – but his unfinished magnum opus, *The Religious System of China* (1892-1910), describes not only contemporary religious beliefs and practices but also the historical origins of Chinese religion and ritual; and after leaving Leiden, he accepted a professorship in Berlin and became a specialist on the history of Central Asia.

The third Dutch professor of Chinese language and literature, J.J.L. Duyvendak, was equally at home in classical Chinese philosophy and in the history of early Sino-Western contacts; besides that, he published regu-

larly on contemporary developments in China. The first occupant of the
chair of Chinese language and literature to have had a well-defined research
specialty was the fourth professor, my predecessor, A.F.P. Hulsewé, who
is internationally recognized for his publications on China's early legal
history.

The above survey may serve to demonstrate that professors of Chinese
language and literature in the past seldom restricted their scholarly efforts
to the fields encompassed by the title of their chair. The principal requirement for a Sinologist was a thorough mastery of Chinese source material,
both written and oral, together with a broad knowledge of Chinese society
and culture, preferably reinforced by a lengthy stay in China. On the grounds
of these qualifications, every aspect of Chinese society, past and present,
was considered to be the rightful domain of the Sinologist; and this preten-
sion was shared by the scholars themselves and their audiences.

Sinology is not unique with regard to this situation. It was true in the past
and still is true today of such fields as Japanology, Javanology, Arabic
studies, and Egyptology. It should be pointed out that in many of these
fields philological text criticism plays a very important, even central role.
It is not that Sinologists and Japanologists are too lazy to prepare text
editions, but rather that in East Asia, philology at an early date – presumably due to the invention of printing – developed into a well-established
discipline and veritable industry, leaving not much work of this sort for
Westerners to do.

Today, such wide-ranging interests as those shown by Sinologists of the
nineteenth century are not usually found united in a single individual, but
are spread over several scholars within a department. In the Netherlands,
although the traditional names of the chairs have been retained, the departments are usually named 'Languages and Cultures of ...', in order to distinguish them from departments dealing with the modern Western languages, which genuinely restrict themselves to language and literature.
Through their choice of name, departments of non-Western studies indicate clearly that in their view, not only language and literature, but also
history, art, religion, and philosophy – in short the whole culture of the
area in question, both past and present – are included in their domain. In
such cases, where it is not a discipline but rather a geographical area that
constitutes the common denominator of a department, one could appropriately
refer to non-Western studies in the Netherlands as 'area studies'.

The way non-Western studies have been structured in the Netherlands is
certainly not the only valid way. Within the target countries, non-Western
studies have no counterpart. Sinology does not exist inside China: the

universities there carry out this research in departments arranged along disciplinary lines – Chinese language and literature, Chinese history, Chinese art history, and so on. In the United States as well, the case most commonly encountered is a department of Chinese language and literature that indeed restricts its attention to language and literature, whereas historians involved with China are found in the department of history, economists in the department of economics, and so forth. One can hardly make the claim that the quality of American scholarship on China has suffered from this. Is the structuring of non-Western studies in the Netherlands then no more than a cherished relic from the past, one that has some practical use for the purposes of the instruction of lower-level students but that only hinders scholarly efforts? It is true that the present structure results partially from a certain inertia. However, I will argue that it offers special opportunities for meeting the challenges of new developments in the academic world.

In masochistic moments, Orientalists must admit that their calling does not have a methodology of its own. The Orient as a homogeneous cultural area stretching from the Bosporus to the Bering Strait does not exist, and there certainly is no single method for studying it. Non-Western studies deal with a great many widely varying cultures, which both in the past and in the present differ from each other as much as they differ from European Christian culture. The mastery of the language or languages in which the culture in question finds expression is ultimately, however indispensable, only a means and not an end in itself. For any given aspect of a culture, the methodology for studying it must be borrowed from the disciplines of linguistics, literature, or history, anthropology, sociology, or political science, which each claim universal validity for their own methodology.

The realization that Orientalists must combine their area specialization with one or another disciplinary specialization has long been commonplace among non-Western scholars. However, as E.M. Uhlenbeck (1986) argued, area studies serve an important purpose. In fact, area studies are gaining ground now that the balance is shifting within much of the humanities away from structure and towards function.

As long as scholars approach their objects of study exclusively along disciplinary lines and focus primarily on the internal structure of a phenomenon, they can afford to disregard the cultural and social context. Under this approach, however, differences can be described but not explained. As soon as one seeks to explain a phenomenon, one must look at its function within a wider cultural context, and to do so, one must rely on the help of area specialists in relevant disciplines. At this point, the boundary between the humanities and the social sciences becomes meaningless. Culture and society, after all, are two sides of a coin. Developments within language, literature, religion, philosophy, and art are intimately tied to social developments, just as social behaviour can only be understood against a background of cultural assumptions that we can come to know through language and image.

If disciplinary specialists want to make use of the fruits of research from other fields, then they will be well advised to work closely with them in order to be certain of having access to the most recent advances in the field. This multidisciplinary cooperation is of course not a monopoly of non-Western studies. Research on a foreign culture can in many respects be usefully compared with the study of earlier phases in the development of one's own culture. In this regard, recent years have seen a strong tendency towards multidisciplinary groupings set up according to time period, for the simple reason that the practical requirements of research dictate a cross-disciplinary approach. Examples of this in the Netherlands are multidisciplinary networks for the medieval period and for the seventeenth century. The integration of social science methodology in historiography is taken for granted today, and the social sciences have long ago left behind their static functionalism and gone in the direction of examining the role of historical factors in social processes. Intermediate disciplines such as sociolinguistics and intellectual history are proliferating like toadstools.

It should surprise no one that in the United States of the 1950's – among other things the high tide of the New Criticism – people opted for structuring non-Western studies along disciplinary lines. Recent developments in the humanities and the social sciences, however, have resulted in equally valuable multidisciplinary groupings set up along area lines; even in the United States, American studies is now being taught, while in Amsterdam, European studies is offered; apparently these umbrellas offer useful possibilities for research.

But however useful they are, these multidisciplinary groupings are not sufficient in and of themselves: in order to guarantee the methodological quality of the research, a continual linking back to the relevant core discipline is necessary. Often, Orientalists follow the discussions within the discipline of their choice at a certain distance, in the hope of staying out of reach of the extreme cyclical shifts in methodological fashions that seem to attack the humanities periodically. Maintaining a certain distance is perhaps healthy, given the limitations of the human mind, but Orientalists must not retreat behind the walls of an exotic philology in order to relax in the company of a handful of initiates. Let us be honest: it has seldom happened that Oriental studies have generated important methodological advances that have had an impact on other fields. Rejecting intensive contact with the relevant core disciplines can only lead to a spontaneous mummification of area studies. What is needed for this contact to be fruitful, though, is that scholars in the various core disciplines be continually involved with the language, culture, and societies of the various non-Western areas. In this regard, scholarship in the Netherlands is somewhat lacking.

2. Outsiders and insiders: advantages and disadvantages

Those who study some aspect of a living culture other than their own must deal not only with the Western academic tradition in that field, but also with the academic tradition in the target culture. Under normal conditions (I mean here those conditions considered normal in the West), scholars working on topics within their own culture enjoy certain advantages with which 'outside scholars' cannot hope to compete. To begin with, the subject being researched is close at hand. Those raised and educated in the culture that is the object of their study, simply by virtue of having the local language as their mother tongue, will have readier access to oral and written material, and both primary and secondary sources. Many of the details of local history, and the ins and outs of the manners and customs of the country have been learned by osmosis during childhood. Sarcasm, allusions, and other subtleties that puzzle outsiders, or escape their notice altogether, are transparent to the insider.

Furthermore, under normal conditions, the number of people within a culture that are studying that culture will be far greater than the number of 'outside scholars'. One would assume that this numerical superiority would lead to greater specialization and keener competition, and thus to publications of a higher quality. Under normal conditions, then, outside scholars could be expected to be able to do no more than struggle along in the wake of academic work produced in the target country. Certainly we would expect any foreign scholar intending to do a study on Dutch language, history, art, or law to start out by becoming familiar with related work being done in the Netherlands. An important task of outside scholars, perhaps even the most important task, under normal circumstances, is to follow carefully the progress of research in the target country in order to give a critical presentation of the results to an audience within their own culture. Seen in this way, area specialists are mediators between two cultures, and translation in the broadest sense is one of their principal functions.

Unfortunately, the conditions for research in many non-Western countries are much less favourable than those in the West. While some cultures have a long and distinguished academic tradition and have been able to link up with the international academic world with little problem, in other cultures academic research is a comparatively new phenomenon, and not only is the number and quality of the scholars less than optimal, but the necessary infrastructure is often largely absent. In many non-Western countries the economic situation hinders the development of academic research because there are no funds to equip scholars to do their work; even the most devoted scholar cannot work without access to the relevant literature. Furthermore, the Netherlands is not the only country where the humanities stand low on the list of priorities when it comes time to apportion funds for education and research. Even more devastating to the development of the humanities is the political climate in many non-Western countries. Authoritarian regimes frequently subject education and research in the humanities to strict censorship. Many subjects then become exceedingly dangerous, and even those subjects considered suitable for study must be treated in such a stereotypical manner that the results hardly deserve to be called scholarship. How far-reaching the political effects can be on academic pursuits is exemplified by the case of the People's Republic of China: during the ten years of the Cultural Revolution (1966-1976) almost no academic literature worthy of the name was published in that country.

Because of such factors as these, the centre of academic study of a given culture has in some cases come to lie partially or entirely outside of that region – usually in Europe, North America or Australia. The geographical distribution of these centres reflects to a high degree former colonial ties and current economic interests, as well as long-standing national academic traditions. However unnatural these processes have been, the result is that extensive library and museum collections and high levels of expertise are located in places far removed from the target country. This entails certain responsibilities: not only to maintain and expand existing expertise and collections, but also to promote the development of such expertise within the target country. Certainly in the case of living cultures, it seems to me self-evident that these studies can flourish, and finally can survive at all, only through close contact with scholars who study the country from the inside out, as one might say. The situation in which the study of a culture takes place primarily outside that culture is not one that can last forever, and it is fitting that we contribute towards hastening the end of such a situation.

This responsibility is one of the reasons that wideranging international contacts are essential to area studies. Non-Western studies have a strongly international orientation; research results are directed not primarily to a national audience but rather to an international forum of colleagues. Academic contacts often extend over the whole world. In addition, scholars must maintain close relations with the area of their research specialty; regular visits to the region are essential to keep abreast of social and cultural changes and to carry out research projects. Not infrequently, requests originate from the target country to draw on Western expertise for help in developing internal academic research and education. This sort of cooperation can take many forms, from international projects for the upgrading of university staff to individual participation in local research projects. The more successful such cooperation is, the sooner the leading role of Western expertise can fade away.

Does this mean that sooner or later the role of non-Western studies in the West will be reduced to a marginal one academically? Certainly not. In the first place, there is more than one audience to be addressed. The 'outside scholar' can speak either to an academic audience in the target country, or to a well-educated audience within his or her own culture. Each choice has advantages and disadvantages. Those who aim at an audience in the target country will need to specialize to the same degree as native scholars; although this may not harm their international standing, the impact on the outside scholars' own culture will be greatly reduced, especially in the case that they publish their work in the language of the target country. Those who, on the other hand, decide to present their research results to a Western audience are required to provide a great deal of background information, whether methodological or thematic, in order to equip readers to understand the cultural context of whatever is being discussed. If this is not done convincingly, the results can hardly be of interest to scholars in the target country. But when the author develops an original viewpoint, such publications can contribute significantly to academic debate in the target country as well. The gap between textbooks and specialized monographs is a wide one in most countries; readable synthesizing studies that speak to a wider public are few and far between. The phenomenal success in the Netherlands of Simon Schama's *The Embarrassment of Riches* (1987) illustrates how a study directed primarily at a well-educated foreign lay audience can stimulate debate in the target country as well.

The success of such studies is not unrelated to the strongly normative self-image that most cultures have, not only in terms of their present cultural identity but also in terms of the country's history. Because this idealized self-image is instilled during childhood, the adult scholar is rarely entirely conscious of the extent to which it influences his or her perception. Outsiders, while having an equally normative image concerning their own country, can cast a fresh, unprejudiced eye on aspects of a foreign society and culture that escape the notice of insiders; this can compensate for the outsider's lack of knowledge of some details of the culture. In academic circles in the humanities, the normative self-image has been elevated to an academic tradition, and dictates both the subjects of research as well as the questions posed; the greater the difference between the cultures, the more easily this phenomenon can be perceived. Where these academic circles consider themselves as having exclusive claim to being the thinkers of the nation, this can mean that large parts of their own culture will not be studied at all but will be dismissed as silly nonsense or superstition.

Attention paid by outside scholars to neglected parts of a culture can sometimes lead to a re-evaluation of those parts by native scholars. Examples of this from the field of Sinology are the history of science and the study of Taoism. Since the middle of the nineteenth century, China's intellectuals have been proclaiming that China's backwardness in technology is due to her consistent neglect of the hard sciences; under these circumstances it is hardly surprising that the development of the history of science within China was hampered. Then along came Joseph Needham with his monumental, still unfinished series *Science and Civilization* (1954-), showing convincingly that in nearly all areas of science and technology China once enjoyed a substantial headstart with respect to the West. Needham's work has been an important stimulus in fostering the history of science within China, where scholars are now asking how it came about that China lost her technological lead. Similarly, whereas Buddhism still enjoyed a certain status in the eyes of twentieth century Chinese intellectuals, Taoism, in spite of its long and extensive written tradition, was long looked down upon as superstition. Research findings by such foreign scholars as K.M. Schipper, who clarified the connection between the Taoist written tradition and the living religion with its lavish ritual, have led to an enhanced consciousness not only among believers and priests but also in Chinese university circles, where people are slowly but surely beginning to accept religious Taoism as a subject worthy of academic study.

For other areas and cultures, comparable examples can undoubtedly be found. Even when academic life is not subjected to heavy and explicit external ideological pressures (as unfortunately is all too often the case), the constraints on the academic tradition imposed by a normative self-image are so strong that many topics of study are left unexplored. Scholars from the outside thus have an opportunity to develop these topics and to show how productive they can be. Because a normative selfimage changes over time, alert scholars from the outside will always have a role to play, often to the advantage of minority groups and their cultures. If we continue this line of reasoning, the study of one's own language and culture will benefit greatly from the interest shown by scholars from other cultures, at least if one is willing to read their work. However, focusing on topics that are neglected by the native academic tradition and the dissident viewpoints of the outside scholar will often mean that he or she is regarded as a troublesome guest or even a persona non grata within the target country. So be it.

One area in which outside scholars will always enjoy a lead is that of intercultural relations. This field requires knowledge of at least two cultures and access to the sources in two languages, where one of the two languages and cultures will usually be native to the scholar. In the many areas of the world where the Netherlands has played a role in history, Dutch scholars have an advantage over foreigners when it comes to knowledge of Dutch language and culture, since these are little known outside of the Netherlands and Flanders. Thanks to the recordkeeping instincts of past generations of Dutch, the archives of the Dutch East India Company form one of the most important sources for the history of many areas bordering on the Indian Ocean and beyond, while the colonial archives have an obvious significance for Indonesian history. In light of the extremely rich source materials in the colonial archives in the Netherlands, it is not surprising that recent years have seen rapid growth in the history of European expansion and its repercussions. Due to mutual interests and interdependence, intercultural relations is a field where international academic cooperation has been carried out with quite some success. Since intercultural contact can only increase in the future, one can predict that the study of cultural borrowing will steadily gain ground within non-Western studies.

The study of how a culture borrows elements from other cultures and assimilates them, leads us automatically to a branch of research that will necessarily be one of the main tasks of non-Western studies: intercultural comparison. Western Orientalists are obliged to make their research findings understandable and relevant to a Western audience. In order to do this, it is necessary to translate the phenomena under study into phenomena familiar to the audience. Orientalists are therefore obliged to do intercultural comparison, since their Western audiences nearly always lack the necessary background knowledge. Unfortunately, this sort of cultural translation is too often performed implicitly, and all too often takes the normative self-image of the Western culture as the yardstick by which to measure the perceived shortcomings of the non-Western culture. In an ideal situation, Orientalists would be constantly aware of the problems of intercultural comparison. In research with the explicit goal of comparing different cultures, scholars would try to treat the ideals and the reality of the two cultures in comparable ways; not only would these scholars translate the foreign culture into their own, but also try to observe their own culture and all its peculiarities from the outside.

Such systematic comparison of widely differing cultures can uncover those basic premises of each of the cultures that are so taken for granted as to be invisible to insiders. In Gernet's analysis of the mutual and deep misunderstandings between the Jesuits and the Chinese literati in the seventeenth century (*Chine et le christianisme. Action et réaction* (1982)), he extracts the basic premises of the highly developed scholastic traditions of each of these groups and then explicitly compares them and points out their limitations. Gernet's student, François Jullien, used a similar method to compare the premises of traditional Western and Chinese literature in his *La valeur allusive* (1985).

Intercultural comparison makes almost superhuman demands on individual scholars. Not only must they acquire a broad and deep familiarity with a foreign culture, they need to have a similarly deep and broad knowledge of their own culture. Few scholars are intellectually and emotionally equipped to achieve this. But a successfully executed intercultural comparison not only enriches our knowledge of the foreign culture, but also contributes to our insight into our own culture. Only through a foreign culture can we fully become aware of the peculiarities of our own: the strong points and weak points, the possibilities exploited and the chances missed. Because of this, the study of other cultures is a precondition for the continuing growth of the study of our own culture. Explicit intercultural comparison prevents area studies from an exotic obscurantism; it equally saves the study of our own culture from a smug ethnocentrism.

3. Oriental studies in the Netherlands: between past and future

The study of non-Western languages and cultures in the Netherlands has a long tradition, primarily associated with the University of Leiden. Right from the founding of the university in 1575, Hebrew and Arabic were taught, and some scholars occasionally devoted attention to more distant lands. Foundations were laid in the seventeenth century for the university library's unique collection of Middle Eastern manuscripts.

Oriental studies expanded in the second half of the nineteenth century, a development closely associated with the expansionist colonial policies of that period. In particular, Japanese, Chinese, Indonesian, and Arabic studies grew. Aims that would now be deemed irreconcilable were then believed to be compatible: the first professor of Chinese language and literature,

Gustav Schlegel, viewed his work as contributing not only to scholarship, but also to improving the welfare of the Chinese population in the Dutch East Indies and augmenting the Dutch national treasury. Colonial policy was not the only factor in the rising interest in non-Western cultures, as the study of Sanskrit and South Asian cultures grew during the same period. The nineteenth century also saw foundations laid for collections still important today, such as the Egyptian collection of the National Museum of Antiquities and the collection of Japanese ethnography and art in the National Museum of Ethnology. A significant development for Indonesian studies was the founding of the Royal Institute of Linguistics and Anthropology (Koninklijk Instituut voor Taal-, Land- en Volkenkunde), with a library that has grown to be one of the largest in the world on Southeast Asia.

Oriental studies continued to grow during the first half of the twentieth century. The paradoxical interweaving of Oriental studies with colonial policy, combined with scholarly efforts of high quality, are nowhere better personified than by C. Snouck Hurgronje (1857-1936), Arabist and Islamicist, as well as advisor to the colonial government. Collections on non-Western cultures continued to grow during this period. The university library of Leiden acquired a unique collection of manuscripts in various Indonesian languages, and the library of the Sinological Institute, founded in 1930, was to become one of the most important Chinese collections in Europe. This period, in which Oriental studies in the Netherlands came to enjoy world renown, is described, with suitable respect and a touch of nostalgia, by a great number of authors in a collection of essays edited by W. Otterspeer, entitled *Leiden Oriental Connections* (1988).

After a time of hesitation and consolidation in the 1950's, non-Western studies enjoyed a period of strong growth in the 1960's and 1970's. Single chairs grew into fully staffed departments, new chairs were created, and what previously had been optional subjects or side disciplines became full-fledged programs of study. In Leiden, departments of Egyptology and Assyriology took their place beside the Hebrew department; the existing chair for Hebrew was augmented by one for Aramaic. Within the Department of Languages and Cultures of the Middle East, Arabic, Turkish, Persian, and comparative Semitics became separate study programs. The South Asian and Southeast Asian departments grew dramatically, while the East Asian Department split in two, resulting in the Department of Languages and Cultures of China and the Department of Languages and Cultures of Japan and Korea. Growing academic interest in Africa was manifested within the Faculty of Letters by the founding of the Department of African Linguistics.

This boom in non-Western studies within the humanities, while most pronounced in Leiden, also occurred elsewhere. Nearly all the Dutch universities did more in the area of Semitic and South Asian studies than ever before. Even though the pace slowed down in the late 1970's, the biggest obstacle to continuing growth was formed by the budget cuts of the early 1980's. These budgets cuts, and the concomitant need to apportion scarcer funds so as to maintain the stronger departments, resulted in the reduction or even elimination of a number of smaller departments throughout the country. The University of Leiden was not immune to these budget-cutting pressures; the Department of Languages and Cultures of South and Central Asia was especially hard-hit. Some departments were able to escape mutilation because of explosive increases in the number of students (in the Chinese and Japanese departments) or because of being granted special preference by the Ministry of Education (the Southeast Asian department). The expansion of Oriental studies within the humanities during the 1960's and 1970's was remarkable; however, it was dwarfed by the explosive growth in the study of the non-Western world within the social sciences, such as cultural anthropology and development studies.

While it was the rapid expansion of Dutch higher education that made the growth of non-Western studies possible in the 1960's and 1970's, this growth was made inevitable by independent developments in the approach to the study of these fields. Academic study of foreign cultures, before World War II, was usually carried out by a handful of individuals; professors had almost no academic staff to aid them in their work. The quality of the academic work of these individuals was buttressed by long stays in the country of study and a thorough control of the primary sources. Secondary literature was scarce; disciplinary specialization was not required. In early scholarship, the term 'linguistics' seems often to mean simply 'fluency in the language', while 'literature' seems to mean 'the ability to read works written in the language'. Because of the scarcity of people with any knowledge at all of far-away lands, anything these professors said was treated as the final word on the subject. This situation changed rapidly after the Second World War. Up to 1940, the Netherlands was one of only a very few countries that had strong, multifaceted Oriental studies at all. Since the 1950's, non-Western studies, both in the humanities and the social sciences, have expanded all over the world. Decolonization and other political and economic trends led to the development of academic activities within the target countries themselves. In the Anglo-Saxon world, at first primarily the United States but later also Canada, Australia, and New Zealand became important centres of study. Oriental studies in Europe (and also in the Netherlands) in many cases lost the leading role they had previously enjoyed – partly due to lack of competition – and were forced to make renewed efforts just to stay in the race. Explosive growth in the number of scholars worldwide, greater accessibility of primary sources, a flood of secondary works, and developments within the disciplines of linguistics, literature, history, and others – all these changes have created a situation in which the scholar is forced to specialize increasingly as to discipline, region, theme, and time period. The territory confidently covered by a single individual in the nineteenth century now requires a number of specialists, none of whom enjoy the unquestioned authority of their early predecessors. What has been won in terms of academic depth and quality has been lost in terms of public visibility.

Turning now to an evaluation of the Netherlands' place in non-Western studies internationally, one must realize how small the number of Dutch scholars is. Simply from a numerical point of view, the Netherlands is at a great disadvantage. Let us take Chinese studies as an example. In China itself, nearly all of the more than one thousand universities has its own department of Chinese language and literature and of Chinese history. At least a score of these universities operate at an internationally competitive level. Since the end (in 1978) of the repression of intellectual activities during the Cultural Revolution, scholars at these universities have made up for lost time by a staggering productivity. Looking to other countries, West Germany now has nearly thirty universities with at least one chair in Chinese studies. In France, where academic disciplines are concentrated rather than being spread out over many universities, Chinese studies is taught in at least ten places, and a recent bibliography refers to publications by more than sixty established scholars. In the United States, the Association of Asian Studies has several thousand members, and at least twenty universities offer full-fledged Ph.D. programs in the area of Chinese language and linguistics and Chinese history, while Modern China studies is offered at almost every university of any size. In contrast, in the Netherlands, where Chinese studies is concentrated in one university, the Department of Languages and Culture of China has an academic staff of twenty, some of whom are non-tenured and others of whom have only teaching duties. One should have realistic expectations of the effectiveness such a Light Brigade can have in the international academic race. In Indonesian studies, in which the Netherlands rightly feels a strong international responsibility, each individual branch of study, whether Indonesian linguistics or Javanese philology, is covered by only a tiny number of scholars. How indeed can

one expect of so few people that they continue to uphold the special responsibility of the Netherlands in Indonesian studies?

Another factor which will make it harder for the Netherlands to compete
internationally in non-Western studies in the future is related to recent
reforms in Dutch secondary and tertiary education. Motivated primarily by
good intentions or attempts to reduce the budget, these reforms have seldom taken into account the needs of the numerically marginal 'exotic'
fields. These days beginning university students only rarely come equipped
with competence in the three modern languages, English, French, and
German, whereas formerly such competence could almost be taken for
granted. Students who lacked one of these languages formerly could take
the time to learn it during their university years, but due to the recent
shortening of the university study program to four years, this is no longer
possible. And because so many students do not have a sufficient level of
reading competence in French and German, university teachers can hardly
assign compulsory reading in those languages.

This eliminates what used to be a great advantage of Dutch scholars: they
not only had a thorough control of their primary sources but also of the
secondary sources in English, French, and German. Within the humanities,
these three language communities constitute, to a certain degree, self-
contained academic traditions. On the one hand, this tendency towards
isolation is being lessened by increased knowledge of foreign languages;
on the other hand, it is being strengthened because of the growing number
of scholars within each of these language communities. Dutch scholars in
the past, who published mostly in English, have had the fascinating role of
bridging the gap between continental European traditions and the Anglo-
Saxon countries. Because of the impoverished language requirements of
the secondary school curriculum today, future Dutch scholars will no longer
have the advantage they used to have over the rest of the world's scholars,
an advantage that compensated to some extent for the numerical inferiority
of Dutch academia.

Another former advantage of Dutch university training was the length of
its study programs. Many non-Western studies departments used to have
study programs of six years, which students often stretched out to seven or
eight years. And there was no limit on the number of years one could spend
writing a doctoral dissertation. Since 1982, university study is limited to
four years, with negative financial consequences for students who take
longer to complete the program. The few students lucky enough to obtain a
fellowship for writing a dissertation must complete it within four years.

One cannot deny that the shortened program of study has certain advantages for practically oriented students aiming at careers in government or business. But four years is a very short time in which to lay the foundations for doing independent research. In the Faculty of Letters at Leiden, fully one quarter of the four-year program must be reserved for electives. This leaves only three years in which to acquire a thorough control of listening, speaking, reading, and (if possible) writing skills in a foreign language, and often this language has a writing system that is very time-consuming to master. The same three years must equip the student with an acquaintance with the historical development of the culture and the rudiments of some discipline such as linguistics, literature, history, or a social science. Unless one wants to reduce programs of non-Western studies to intensive practical language courses, the present program of study is simply too short to do everything that needs to be done; the result is that departments have been forced to cut out essential elements of the curriculum. The current program of study can no longer require a second language, as Japanese was formerly required for Sinology students and Sanskrit for Javanologists. The broad and philologically sound knowledge of the languages of the sources and of the relevant secondary literature, once the pride of Dutch Oriental studies, has been severely weakened.

Many students of non-Western studies graduate from university having acquired knowledge of no more than one modern non-Western language and only a rudimentary acquaintance with its older stages; although this may be sufficient for a job with government or business, it certainly is not enough for doing competent research. The possibility of remedying this deficiency during the four years of postgraduate work is small. How can a Sinologist take the time to build up an adequate reading competence of Japanese and still produce a finished dissertation in four years? Again, there are undeniably advantages to completing a dissertation in four years, but the consequences for future generations of scholars are unfavourable. Those lucky enough to win university posts upon completion of their Ph.D. need not expect to have the opportunity to learn another language or steep themselves in a new discipline, because of increasing pressure to publish. The end result cannot but be a weakening of some very exciting areas of research that require not only a sound grasp of the modern languages of the target country but also a sound philological command of the earlier phases of the language, and of equally exciting areas of research that require command of two or more non-Western languages. In other words, especially 'classical' Oriental studies and the study of intercultural contacts within the non-Western world will decline in the Netherlands, unless drastic measures are taken to support them.

Does all this mean that the Netherlands had better simply leave non-Western studies to other countries, whether the target countries or Western countries? Of course not. Dutch society, government, and business and industry all need reliable and thorough information on non-Western countries. Political, economic, and cultural developments in these countries influence our society in a great many ways, and it is very much to our advantage to know what happens there, how, and why. Universities play a crucial role in providing this information through the training of specialists and the maintenance of collections. That there is a great demand for such 'intercultural brokers' is evidenced by the low unemployment figures for graduates of non-Western studies programs.

Essential to upholding the quality of education in foreign languages and cultures is that it be continually nourished by research of an international calibre. Much of this research will be in fields where scholars must compete with work done in countries where more people and more money are invested in the field. This makes it doubly important that future academic research in the Netherlands be structured in such a way as to allow scholars enough freedom to link up with larger research centres abroad, within as well as outside of Europe.

Although the modern language and culture of a country will be increasingly emphasized in university study programs, it is essential that advanced academic work continue to cover pre-modern periods as well. Not only does knowledge of the historical roots of living cultures contribute to an understanding of the present situation; academically speaking, such study is equally important as a goal in itself. Linguistic and cultural differences both between one culture and another as well as between one time period and another are worthy of study in order to deepen our insight into the phenomena of language and culture as such. Directly and indirectly, this insight contributes to reducing chauvinism and discrimination against people of different backgrounds.

The unique collections maintained in the Netherlands will make it possible for the Netherlands to continue to play a leading role internationally in certain fields. These special collections should be viewed not only as a privilege but also as a responsibility. Non-Western studies in the Netherlands have the duty to make the unique materials held in this country accessible to foreign scholars, so that this Dutch prerogative is voluntarily given up as soon as possible. One does not have to sing a solo part in order to be useful in the chorus. Personally, I prefer to be a lasting, valued member of the chorus rather than a prima donna on the decline.

References

Gernet, J., 1982. *Chine et le christianisme. Action et réaction.* Paris: Gallimard.
Groot, J.J.M. de, 1892-1910. *The Religious System of China.* Leiden: E.J. Brill.
Jullien, F., 1985. *La valeur allusive, des catégories originales de l'interprétation poétique, dans la tradition chinoise (Contribution à une reflexion sur l'altérité interculturelle).* Paris: École Française d'Extrême Orient.
Needham, J., 1954-. *Science and Civilization.* Cambridge University Press (15 vol. published so far).
Otterspeer, W., 1988. *Leiden Oriental Connections.* Leiden: E.J. Brill.
Schlegel, G., 1875. *Uranographie chinoise.* The Hague: Nijhoff.
Schama, S., 1987. *The Embarrassment of Riches.* London: Collins.
Uhlenbeck. E.M., 1986. *De niet-westerse studies in Nederland; Een verkenning* (Non-Western Studies in the Netherlands: A Survey).

Summing up

E. Zürcher

The areas of science dealt with in this volume constitute a motley collection which at first sight displays very little coherence. This is partly the result of the selection made, which concentrated on a number of broad areas of research. Consequently, little attention was of necessity paid to the dozens of areas that to a great extent fill up the open spaces: specialisms that form bridges between the sciences of art and history, between theology and philosophy, and between area studies and linguistics. The total picture of the humanities displays more internal cohesion than is apparent from this bundle. The collection may be motley but it is held together by a common focus on manifestations of human culture and, moreover, as the contributions show, by a number of shared aspirations and expectations of the future.

In this epilogue I shall attempt to define these common elements. Some of them are of a *fundamental* nature: they deal with the identity of the humanities themselves and the question of the viability of this concept in the nineties; with the applicability of one generally accepted scientific method such as has been developed in the natural sciences, and with the problems arising from the unprecedented complexity of cultural phenomena. A different complex of common elements is a trend that emerges clearly in almost every contribution: a *changing attitude with respect to the subjects of research*, a tendency to shift the accent from the object (the linguistic utterance, the work of art, the text) itself to the way in which it functions in its social context, arouses responses, and is interpreted. It is a trend that I, for want of a better word, shall call "actualization". Finally, there are a few shared aspirations as regards the *practice of research*, such as expansion and inter- disciplinary cooperation, internationalization, and the impact of automation and informatics. I shall make a few comments, which can only be of an impressionist nature, on each of these three topics. They are generalizations which I think roughly apply to most areas of research, although it would be possible to name areas in respect of every point where this is not or is hardly the case.

1. Identity: from "humanities" to "cultural sciences"
Academic terminology has a tough life, and this certainly applies to the term "humanities", which is burdened with a centuries-old heritage. Originally it referred to a group of sciences dealing with the most prestigious manifestations of civilized man, the *literae humaniores*, as earthly counterpart to the *literae divinae*, theology. They were linked by a pre-eminently elitist ideal based on classical models, and they retained this character for a long time. As late as the end of the last century Webster defines the humanities as "the branches of polite and elegant learning, as language, rhetoric, poetry, and the ancient classics; belles-lettres". The study of texts was central; the face of the humanities was primarily determined by a thorough study of the written word, philological skill and literary erudition. All this implied a focus on the past as a source of inspiration, and a minor interest in contemporary phenomena. For a long time the tempestuous rise of the natural sciences had little effect on the classical, "hard-core" humanities: scientists had no business in the world of scholarship. Science concerned itself in principle with the measurable, the quantifiable, whereas the humanities concentrated by preference on quality: great historical events, exemplary works of art, prominent writers and thinkers – and it is by definition impossible to quantify quality.

Meanwhile, however, developments had occurred which undermined the traditional edifice of the humanities. For example, linguistics broke away from philology; it concentrated to a considerable extent on studying living language and speech, and in doing so developed methods and techniques that leaned heavily towards those of the natural and life sciences. The most striking – and for the classical humanities most undermining – process was the emancipation of the social sciences as a complex of fields that specifically did not concern itself with the exemplary and unique but with large-scale processes and collective behaviour, and not with the heritage of the past but with contemporary social phenomena. They made extensive use of statistical methods and quantitative analysis, studied processes and problems of undeniably public interest, and thought – in their most optimistic moments – they could have a substantial affect on the course of social development.

The rapprochement with the natural sciences was unmistakable – no social scientist will ever call himself a "scholar".

This fission had disastrous consequences for the humanities. Looked at from the point of view of the social sciences their departure was totally justified because emancipation was a pre-requisite for their free development. But as a result of this schism the humanities ran the risk of being reduced to a residual category of more or less "non-social" subjects withdrawn from concrete reality. In the sixties various developments contributed towards confirming this image: due to their close relationship with technology, which affected every sphere of daily life, the natural sciences increasingly demonstrated their social interest; the movement for democracy turned against everything that was or was said to be elitist, and the accompanying general belief in the "makeability of society" resulted in an explosive growth in the social sciences. The contrast between the humanities and the social sciences was consequently further accentuated, and it seemed as though the humanities were predestined to live on as a vaguely defined residual category.

But since the late sixties this picture has changed profoundly. As a result of developments on both sides of the dividing line – the rise of new specialisms, the discovery of new possibilities for joint research – the borders are becoming less distinct, and in some areas have in fact already disappeared. Some overlapping occurs in the fringe areas, and (as so often in the science business) these are the very areas in which new activities get their chance. The contributions in this bundle give examples galore of this blurring of the borders, seen from the point of view of the humanities. But similar developments are occurring in the social sciences, where people have realized that social phenomena cannot be taken as a momentary snapshot, but that they need to be placed in their cultural and historical context. The communication sciences cannot be dissociated from linguistic utterances: cultural anthropology is no longer confined to "cultures with no written heritage"; women's studies have an important historical dimension. Just as oriental studies (which have started to focus more and more on the present day) cannot manage without the input of social scientists, so the study of ethnic minorities depends on the knowledge of the relevant non-western languages provided by the humanities.

The same situation has arisen in the sphere of "development studies", which deal with the current problems of the Third World, because in the last two decades people have become more and more interested in the cultural dimension of development. There is an increasing blurring of borders in all manner of fields, and the phenomenon has grown to such an extent that the rationale of the existence of the concepts "humanities" and "social sciences" must be called into question.

Consequently, several calls are made for the two groups to be combined under the common denominator of "cultural studies", a broad field of sciences dealing with the totality of human behaviour not given by nature but acquired. It is primarily a question of a conceptual framework in which all constituents of the (former) humanities and social sciences are given their place, without the artificial distribution of roles that results from the partition of an estate. We shall have to wait and see to what extent this conceptual reunification results in joint programs of action, and ultimately in an organizational reshuffle. But a clear formulation of the concept "cultural studies" is in itself a significant step: a broadening of the perspective that can clear away mental barriers that still exist, and an opportunity for finally doing away with a hopelessly outdated and misleading terminology.

2. Complexity

Goudsblom gives the initial impetus to this clear formulation, continuing to build on (and adopting a stand against) R. Dawkins' outline of the study of science at two levels of complexity: dead matter (the natural sciences) and living matter (the life sciences), with the humanities and social sciences as marginal table companions to biology and the medical sciences. Goudsblom rightly postulates the cultural sciences as a third category, focusing on the study of phenomena at a third level of complexity and specificity: man as a social being and as a participant in a culture. There is every reason to speak, together with Goudsblom, of a *higher* level of complexity, if only on account of the collective and communicative dimension of the phenomena studied. The natural and most of the life sciences can concentrate on one individual, or even a minuscule part of that individual, but the cultural sciences cannot: acquired human behaviour can only be studied in its cultural context and in the social relationships in which man functions. A comparison with those branches of biology dealing with collective animal behaviour does not hold true because in the first place human behaviour, precisely because it has been acquired, displays an infinitely greater individualization and variability, but also and primarily because man, unlike animals, functions in a "cultural environment" which he himself has largely created, which is extremely complicated in structure and, moreover, which is subject to continual change. We can therefore certainly speak of a *higher* level of complexity and variability.

But furthermore, the cultural sciences deal with a complexity of *a different order*. The cultural sciences are in essence always reflective: a cultural element themselves, they study culture and can only do so using the means their own culture gives them. As a totality they are affected by the same dilemma in which the linguist finds himself in his own field: he thinks *in* language *about* language, and will never be able to escape from this. This problem is characteristic of the cultural sciences. Physics and biology are, of course, also components of culture, but the phenomena they focus on are not, which makes it possible for the researcher to distance himself more from the subject of research. It is not a question of a feeling of personal involvement on the part of the researcher – the tendency to identify oneself with the subject because one "is dealing with people". This problem also occurs, sometimes even to an extreme degree, but that is not the problem in this case. Subjectivity of this kind is individual and can largely be neutralized. The dilemma that is responsible for this "complexity of a different order" is more of a cognitive nature: we can only see cultural phenomena (apart from those of our own culture at this time) through the spectacles our own culture has placed on our noses. Our choice of subjects, observations and judgements are charged with contemporary western values and preferences. More so than with other sciences, scientific trends are influenced by social developments and ideological factors; both de Boer and Waterbolk have focused on this correlation where the historical sciences and archaeology and prehistory are concerned.

Areas of preference are to a substantial degree determined by fashions of our own age and environment. The sudden interest in Japanese printing in the west was a by-product of impressionism; industrial archaeology is largely a reaction to precipitate modernization. The critical re-interpretation of the bases of Christianity undertaken by theologians is, as Wegman says, taking place within the context of contemporary social and political trends (e.g. women's liberation and the role of churches in the Third World), and one wonders whether the special interest shown by religious scholars and anthropologists in rituals is not a reaction to the deritualization of our own society. Our particular interest in oppositional literature is fed by the aversion we have to totalitarian systems. Obviously, the "existential situation" is substantially different in the case of the natural and life sciences. When selecting his field of research, the chemist can allow himself to be guided by practical and social considerations, as a conscious choice, but this will have no appreciable influence on his perception of the subject of research. No post-modernist fashion for debunking will cause a biologist to deny the existence of elephants, and no wave of democratization will induce a special preference for star clusters in the astronomer.

But no matter how great the influence of one's own contemporary cultural perception may be, it is obvious that the scholar cannot give in to it limit-lessly. For the ultimate consequence would be that we would only be able to understand elements from the past or from a different culture if they were fully absorbed into our own current world of experience, irrespective of their original essence, message and context: an empty Zen painting is minimal art; Stonehenge is landscape architecture: a Shakespeare play is what the audience makes of it. A comparison of language is instructive because if our own culture were completely dominant, we would not be able to learn a second language in addition to our mother tongue. We know from practice that we can do so. But at the same time we know that using this second language, acquired with difficulty, is no easy matter precisely because our mother tongue continues to function as a frame of reference and is consequently a source of errors and distortions.

Up to a certain level it is possible to place cultural phenomena and cultural products in their original context and so to do justice to their authenticity. At the same time we have to assume that the interpretation we attach to them is to a great extent the product of our own current conceptual universe. And in the third place a continuing critical contemplation of ourselves is necessary in order to account for the degree to which this distortion takes place – we cannot escape our cultural cell, but we can continue to endeav-our to make its walls transparent. This need to work at three levels means a permanent challenge for the cultural sciences, but it also means that the entire undertaking is of an unimaginable complexity.

3. Method and formulation of theory

The question is to what extent there is one universal method of research that can be applied in every science, including that of culture. The question receives a positive answer from Cohen and Fokkema, who point out that research in the cultural sciences too follows the accepted scientific method: choice of theme, hypothesis, isolation of the subject of research, verifica-tion (or falsification) and, if necessary, adjustment of the hypothesis. This sounds encouraging as it suggests that there is in essence an underlying unity of method in all scientific research, and that the pessimistic picture of two separate cultures painted by C.P. Snow should be taken with a pinch of salt. The differences between natural and cultural sciences arise from the nature of the subjects of research, not from the method used.

Is this optimism justified? On the basis of what has just been said about the special nature and complexity of the phenomena the cultural sciences deal with, I fear that consistent application of this method is a far-removed ideal, theoretically not impossible, but not feasible in practice. The method as summarized here in a few catchwords certainly also applies to the cultural sciences – but it is nothing more than a vague description, so generalized that some of its most essential elements have disappeared. The most striking is the elimination of the quantitative aspect. It should be possible to test a hypothesis in quantitative terms; it should be possible to simplify the subject of research to such an extent that it is suitable for exact measurement under laboratory conditions.

Obviously, cultural phenomena can only to a limited extent be forced to comply with this requirement. As in the natural sciences the hypothesis will generally be based on the supposition that there is a correlation between certain phenomena or complexes of phenomena, e.g. between economic recession, the presence of migrant workers, and emergent racism. Only certain elements of these three complexes can be quantified, for example the number of unemployed, the amount of income that can be freely spent, and the size and distribution of the minorities. But the most essential element – racism – is by definition immeasurable because it cannot be expressed in numerical quantities. It will never be possible to "count" phenomena of this kind in pre-agreed units, one "rac" being the "racist energy" needed to shout one slogan.

The misunderstanding is, I think, based on the fact that in each of the cultural sciences it is possible to find certain areas and specialisms that can successfully be quantified, and that are capable of reducing their subject of research to a simplified model, free of interfering factors. Phonetics finds itself in this exceptional position, and art history and archaeology make extensive use of chemical analysis. Insofar as the material permits, certain historical hypotheses can be examined against quantitative data. But, contrary to the natural sciences, the role of measurement remains restricted; in most cases it is an additional aid and not the basis of the method itself. Even in linguistics the "measurement of meaning" has proved an illusion; a play cannot be reduced to an isolated test model, and the chemical composition of the paint only says something about the painting as such in a very restricted sense. It is possible that all those imponderable factors that currently form an obstacle to the application of scientific methods will one day be removed, by a gigantic increase in available data, views and advanced equipment, combined, for example, with the method of "complexity studies" mentioned by Cohen. Dik showed us what this entails in his description of the model of the "integrated language user" – an inspiring perspective, but for the time being a fata morgana.

What applies to the first steps in the procedure of the scientific method – a quantifiable hypothesis and reduced test model – applies to an even greater extent to the experiment, the most essential part of the programme. This will make or break the method; not without reason did the burgeoning natural sciences announce themselves as "the New, or Experimental, Philosophy". Again, it is obvious that in certain very specific fields (we keep, in fact, returning to the area of linguistics) the experiment plays its part as it should: in quarantine, out of context, under controlled conditions, quantifying, repeatable, and with results that can be generalized. By and large, manifestations of culture do not lend themselves to this type of experiment. In the historical sciences the hypothesis is examined against the material available to us; the material cannot be manipulated. The responses and interpretations evoked by a literary text among the reading public can be challenged in the "empirical study of literature" with interviews and questionnaires, but "measuring" such responses among human informants is, of course, something entirely different from counting the number of salmonella bacteria per cubic centimetre of protein at different temperatures. Such empirical methods are certainly useful, as a brake on utterances of an all too impressionistic nature, but their exactness goes no further than that of the multiple-choice test for grading written exams. The predictive value of their conclusions is consequently minimal. No Islamic scholar foresaw modern muslim fundamentalism; no art historian can make reliable statements about future developments in style; no historian, Slavist or political scientist predicted the dramatic fall of the communist empire. The big stumbling block remains the unprecedented complexity and intertwining of human manifestations of culture which stand in the way of the application of a truly exact method of research and which will continue to do so in the foreseeable future.

The specific character of the cultural sciences, and in particular the way in which they are influenced by general social and ideological trends, also has consequences for the formulation of theory. The reader schooled in the natural sciences will have noted that nowhere is there actually mention of very stable, fundamental and very comprehensive theories comparable with the theory of evolution in biology, the theory of relativity in physics, or the heliocentric view of the world in astronomy. Neither will it have escaped this reader that what presents itself as a theory frequently lasts a remarkably short time – so short that it can be stated in years: "Structural Linguistics 1922-1957", "Russian Formalism, approx. 1915-1930". And, finally, it is striking that however influential they were in their day, they are not generally accepted but always accompany the formation of a school. The succession of theories is consequently not linear and accumulative: one theory does not incorporate the previous one by standing on its shoulders, it takes over from its predecessor, as a new start.

It cannot be denied that the absence of durable and generally accepted theories is a weak point in the cultural sciences. In fact, we are not dealing with theories, but with "styles". Everything that has been mentioned above – the briefness, the sectarianism, the discontinuity – is characteristic of the sequence of styles in graphic art, architecture, music and the belles-lettres. Someone, or a group, finds new means of expression, a new approach, a new genre, which are then "tried out", generally as a reaction to a preceding trend that has become conventional, until the style has exhausted its possibilities and in its turn fossilizes into convention. "Theory" in the cultural sciences has a primarily heuristic function. It announces "a new way of looking at things", and so opens peoples eyes to study phenomena, relationships and structures that until then had not received much attention. So developments in most fields have been rather fickle, and it cannot be assumed that this will change. It is also very doubtful whether it would be of any service to the cultural sciences. The cautionary example is obvious, in those countries where the cultural sciences in particular have suffered severely because they have been studied for more than half a century within the framework of a rigid Marxist theory with universal pretensions. Big, revolutionary "breakthroughs" such as the natural and life sciences have produced cannot therefore be expected in the theoretical field, and the cultural sciences should be extremely cautious and modest when using the term "theory".

4. *"Actualization" : from structure to perception*

In his contribution on area studies Idema notes a general shift of emphasis from structure to function. He does this, in the context of his subject, to make it clear that a multilateral approach and a bundling of disciplines is necessary in the field of non-western studies specifically. As long as attention was focused on the unique object *per se*, this necessity did not exist. A Westerner specializing in Chinese art could study a Chinese landscape painting as an independent entity, and describe it in every detail. If in doing so he aired aesthetic value judgements, these were largely based on current western standards.

A functional approach to the same painting is more multilateral and more demanding. It is no longer just a question of the structure, the formal characteristics of the object itself, but of the role (or roles) it plays in the culture in question. All manner of aspects then come up for discussion: the monochrome landscape as a pre-eminently elitist genre; the painter of such works as a cultivated "gentleman artist" working for a like-minded audience; the status of connoisseurship as part of "the gentleman's way of life"; the judgement of the piece by contemporaries ("unspoiled Nature as a symbol of the greatest Truth; lofty ideas combined with virtuoso brush technique"). But contemporary aspects are expressly included, e.g. the painting as a museum object, modern Chinese perception – in different varieties: modernistic ("no longer of this era"); synchretistic ("a source of inspiration, but not something to be copied indiscriminately"); traditionalist ("an example to follow"); nationalistic ("our great national heritage"); isolationist ("antidote to western bourgeois influences"); Marxist ("a manifestation of feudal escapism"). And, finally, modern western perception with all its distortions, formal ("a watercolour on silk, with inscription, and elements of both impressionism and expressionism") as well as regards content ("exotic culture"; "a demonstration of Eastern Wisdom").

This example shows how complicated it is to study a visual work of art by the new approach. The work is no longer an object in itself, but a multifaceted "sign" that can be interpreted in all manner of ways, depending on the situation, the period and the nature of the *actores*. The advantage of a semiotic, communicative approach of this kind lies in the enormous enrichment and expansion of the research, the greater depth of insight, and the opportunities it opens for interdisciplinary cooperation. The disadvantage lies in the obvious expansion of the theme of research, which can easily result in "the subject being drowned". But the advantage weighs heavier: one could say that exactly because of this approach the cultural sciences have become fully aware of the complexity of the phenomena they are dealing with.

The contributions in this volume show how general the trend is. The key words that crop up again and again are reception and perception, interpretation, semiotics and communication, function and social context. Reinink defines the study of the visual arts concisely as the "study of ways of seeing (of the artist, and of the audience)", and the world of artifacts as "a system of communication". Wegman advocates a new approach in theological studies, "literary theology", which makes a freer interpretation of canonical texts possible: the texts as metaphoric images of truth which are open to various interpretations. Christianity has lost its monopoly position in the western world and should therefore be studied above all as a complex of cultural manifestations in their social context. In the field of linguistics Dik stresses the character of language as "discourse", a communicative system, interactive and situational. The historical sciences have for a long time been convinced of the fact that they are topical, however early the period they are dealing with. The past no longer exists because it is past time. The written sources and material remains do not constitute a part of the past: they exist now, before our eyes, as part of our current world of experience. They are interpreted by archaeologists and historians who do not resurrect the past (because that's a false metaphor), but who "tell stories about the past" (Waterbolk). That applies not only to the perception of the researcher, but also to those of his or her audience. The response to a figure like Bismark is irrevocably coloured by association with Hitler's Third Reich, which he had nothing at all to do with. Certain aspects of the history of western colonial expansion appeal in the western reader, consciously or unconsciously, to feelings of national pride and Eurocentrism, while non-western readers react quite differently to it. *Montaillou* moves the modern reader with modern feelings of sympathy and pity: a small, innocent community as victim of a merciless Inquisition. A hypothetical medieval reader would probably have observed with satisfaction that heretics had got what they deserved.

And, finally, the shift from structure to perception is very evident in the studies dealing with literature and the performing arts (music and theatre): "a shift of research goals from an exclusive focus on the text to an emphasis on the communication situation" (Fokkema); an emphasis of the essential role that perception and interpretation need to play in the analysis of musical activities (Op de Coul/de Haen); the attention that needs to be paid to the performance as a communicative process, hence to the relationship between theatrical expressions and the response of the audience (Schoenmaker).

Seldom will one find in so diverse a group of sciences a trend that is so unanimous. One might speak of the creation of a "new paradigm" were it not for the fact that we need to be very careful when using this pretentious term too. The trend is unmistakable and general but, as always, we do not know how long it will last and where it will ultimately lead. The same applies, incidentally, to the much broader concept of "holism", to which this trend displays a certain resemblance. As it is frequently a question of reaction against an earlier formalistic and structural approach, there is a danger that people will swing to the other extreme, and that excessive attention to reception and communication will result in a neglect of the production side, and the object's own identity. Reception and interpretation are variable, but bound by limits: a Petrarchan sonnet is, after all, a sonnet by Petrarch, and not just some literary linguistic sign that anyone can read anything into. The three components I listed above under the heading "complexity" should continue to go hand in hand: the discovery (no matter how inadequate) of the original context and authenticity, the current reception, and the attempt to define why this reception is as it is – critical self-reflection.

5. Expansion and interdisciplinary collaboration

Actualization results in a great number of new activities, partly in areas of research still to be explored. But that should not result in such a re-orientation that the traditional, "established" fields of research are sacrificed to it: new plantings should be made without clearing the old forest entirely. In every study based on texts philological work will continue to feature predominantly; the patient inventorying of the past continues without taking much notice of cognitive reflections and semiotic theories. Even our Chinese mountain landscape first has to be identified, examined for authenticity, dated and described in detail as a "material object" before it can be subjected as an "aesthetic object" to a multifaceted, functional analysis.

The process is therefore cumulative; it should result in an expansion of research in every field of study. Whether this will actually happen depends largely on external factors that not even the researchers have any hold over. In general, what de Boer says concerning professional historians, namely that in the next few years the number of researchers will not increase so sharply, applies to the cultural sciences as a whole. This therefore creates a dilemma that is noticeable in all the fields concerned and acts as a break on the enthusiasm for big new undertakings: if people want something new, they'll have to cut back somewhere else. This in itself creates tension between the "innovators" and the "continuers", a difference inevitably coloured, but generally not expressed, by personal interests and career considerations. Representatives of the established fields of research accuse the innovators frequently of superficiality, fashionable opportunism, and a tendency towards vain theorizing; in their turn they are told that they have got into a rut and are only producing "more of the same".

Such discussions are, of course, fruitless. Under current circumstances only two solutions to the dilemma are conceivable: either far-reaching concentration per field on a national scale, with the result that all researchers are gathered at one point (the most obvious example being France, where the majority of resources available for cultural studies is concentrated in Paris), or a clear division of tasks per speciality, both traditional and new, in a network of institutions that work together (on the model of the University of California).

I prefer the first alternative because it is essential for close and regular cooperation between specialisms within one field that the researchers be in the immediate vicinity of one another. Long-distance cooperation is always a perilous undertaking. The latter applies to an even greater degree to the distribution of tasks and research networks on an international (e.g. West European) scale. It is true that in the natural and life sciences such very large associations with internal distribution of tasks have been created in fields like nuclear physics, space travel and cancer research, but no matter how tempting it is, there is no point for the time being in emulating such mammoth projects because the situation cannot be compared. They work with very costly equipment, which necessitates international cooperation; as far as social relevance is concerned they are very highly regarded and consequently have ample funds, and they can rely on a tradition of internal organization and science management, contrary to the cultural sciences which are habitually characterized by a very low degree of organization. For the time being, the concentration of resources and formation of networks in the cultural sciences will take place primarily on a national scale, and that in itself would be a first step towards dispersing the tension that exists between developing new and keeping up old activities.

In every contribution the development of new areas of research is related to interdisciplinary cooperation, both within the cultural sciences (or, in the terminology I prefer not to use, between the humanities and the social sciences), and once or twice, particulary in linguistics and archaeology, with the natural and life sciences as well. The need for inter-disciplinarity is evident in every case, and it has already started in a number of fields. The question that arises is not so much whether interdisciplinarity is desirable and necessary, but what one understands by "cooperation" – a term open to various interpretations. In its minimal meaning it means nothing more than that researchers schooled in various disciplines take note of each others methods and techniques and benefit from them because they learn to apply them in their own field of research. This process of mutual enrichment is unstructured and continuous. It does not take place within any organizational framework, and can even take place through perusal of each other's publications. This is the most general form of interdisciplinary influence, and its importance should not be underestimated. Many "accelerations" in the cultural sciences were started by researchers who worked in this way: not by starting or participating in interdisciplinary activities, but by "staying in touch" with what is going on in other disciplines. It is a process that should be part of normal practice in the science business, and where this is not yet the case, it should be effectively stimulated. One of the obstacles in this field is formed by the specialist nature of the professional literature, which is quite frequently written in impenetrable jargon, making it difficult for people to orientate themselves in a discipline other than their own without having to resort to popular generalizations and first-year "readers". I would advocate producing methodological, explanatory publications aimed at non- colleagues, at a level between popularization and professional literature. The occasional meetings of disciplines at "mixed" symposia and workshops are useful, but still too fleeting for the appointed goal.

A more intense and more structured form of cooperation takes place within the framework of specific interdisciplinary projects. Under current circumstances, in which it is difficult to maintain permanent research groups, this should be the most obvious form of interdisciplinary cooperation. Nevertheless, they are thin on the ground in the cultural sciences. Each field has its own big, ambitious projects which sometimes produce collective publications of encyclopedic size, but they are for the most part based on cooperation between colleagues. Only seldom do the contributions in this volume speak of actual current interdisciplinary projects; they generally only point to the pre-eminently interdisciplinary character of new developments. The next step should be to actively give shape to this in the form of mixed projects. The stimulation of such structured cooperation, aimed at specific subjects, is one of the primary tasks for the cultural sciences in the next decade, and should therefore play an important part in the science policy of every national government.

The most intense form of interdisciplinary cooperation is achieved by a permanent research team with an internal distribution of tasks. It is the type of integrated research that has been developed in the natural and life sciences and in industrial research, using very advanced equipment. This phenomenon occurs only seldom in the cultural sciences; archaeology and prehistory, where the unlocking and interpretation of the soil archive is indeed the joint work of scientists from a whole range of disciplines, come closest to it. Another example of such permanent interdisciplinary teamwork in which advanced computer equipment plays an essential role is provided by Cohen in his description of acoustic research and of the experiments aimed at automated simulation and recognition of natural language.

Here, in the fringe area between cultural science and informatics, we encounter phenomena that for various reasons can fulfil the role of advance guard and example: in the first place because they are evidently part of the most vital developments of our time, in science and society, but also because one can see here the first attempts to use information science to explore entirely new possibilities that involve the essence of the field, with its own questions and its own method, itself. There is little talk of this in most of the specialist fields dealt with here. The computer has made its entry everywhere, but the use made of it is still at an elementary level. The functions of automation generally remain confined to those of an upgraded card index: storage, retrieval and combining data. The principal advantage of this is a saving in time because much more data can be processed in the research much faster, and correlations between data can be detected much swifter. Without doubt this increases the "solidity" of the research because it is based on a larger store of material, and pronouncements can be examined against it much faster. But in essence it is no different from the more laborious manual methods that used to be applied.

It would indeed be impossible to carry out some investigations without a computer for practical reasons, because the number of data and correlations is so large that the project, if carried out in the traditional manner, would take a hundred years. But, in principle, nothing new has happened: in most cases the computer has made existing paths better accessible, and has enabled us to travel farther and faster, but it has not blazed any new trails. Where this has happened, the authors detect great difficulties. Reinink stresses the inadequacy of existing software in recognizing visual figurations, a problem that reminds us very much of the difficulties described by Cohen experienced by the computer in its attempts at automatic speech recognition. These problems are still far from being solved in either field. Automatic pattern recognition in the visual arts is still in its earliest infancy, and for the moment no computer is a match for the almost infinite complexity and variability of spoken language (and we would do well to remind ourselves that speech recognition is still only the first of the eleven skills that Dik's integrated model of the natural language user should possess!). But in spite of these formidable problems, we are in fact confronted with new developments, which are so fascinating for the very reason that we have no idea of their consequences. Whether they will be able to expand depends not only on the inventiveness and goodwill of the researchers, but also on the question to what extent society will be prepared to give them a chance. Why should it?

6. Social relevance

It is striking that none of the authors asked, let alone answered, the question of the social relevance, the "useful effect", of the cultural sciences. They rightly assumed that the research in their field is worthwhile because it is aimed at acquiring an understanding of important areas of our world of experience. Man is naturally curious not only about his physical and biological environment but also about other things close to him: the cultural environment he himself has created. Research into cultural phenomena has a domain of its own – that of Goudsblom's "third level of complexity" – and it is neither more nor less worthwhile than studying the behaviour of elementary particles or the sense of direction of migratory birds. This providing-a-purpose has nothing to do with the useful spin-off principle. From the point of view of the researcher each fundamental research is in the first place justified in itself as a small contribution to the question that has occupied man, a curious being, ever since time began: the question of why things are as they are. If, in addition, it has a useful effect, that's a welcome bonus.

We should be happy that the essays in this bundle reflect this attitude and that the authors have not given in to the temptation to demonstrate the social use of their specialist fields using all those arguments that have been thought up in the course of the last decades. These arguments as a whole constitute a reaction to a utilitarian way of thinking that is very much alive among governments and other agencies on whom the study of science depends in a material sense; and because that utilitarian way of thinking, as far as the cultural sciences is concerned, is based on an incorrect pattern of expectation, the apologetic responses are equally contrived and forced. The expectations are generally based on a false analogy between the cultural sciences on the one hand and the natural and life sciences on the other. Just as the latter result in concrete applications in technology, health care, nutrition, care for the environment and economic prosperity that everyone can see, so people expect the cultural sciences also to contribute visibly to "the welfare of society". A whole series of forced arguments have been thought up to meet this requirement.

For example, we have for a long time had the educational argument. Society not only needs engineers and medical specialists, but language and history teachers, curators and translators as well. The cultural sciences that concern themselves with our current society can add sociologists of all kinds to this list; diplomats are required for external relations, and the legal sciences provide top level civil servants. The argument is weak because it is based on a mixture of two essentially different sectors: scientific research and higher education. It is very doubtful whether the close ties people are in the habit of making between the two is really realistic, and whether workers would not be better served by courses of higher education focusing on practical use, largely outside the circuit of scientific research. The latter point does indeed have an educational aspect, but that relates expressly to the education of researchers. The importance and the level of scientific research should be evidenced by the quality of the research results themselves and cannot be determined on the basis of branches of education. They are two different sectors which in the future will probably grow further apart. A second utilitarian argument, mentioned by Waterbolk (with reference to Marquard), is based on the idea of "compensation". The humanities should form a counterbalance to materialism, the alienation and de-humanization of modern post-industrial society. At first sight this is an attractive theory: man versus machine, emotion versus realism; the artistic dimension as antidote to dullness, contemplation of the past as a remedy to the obsession with the present. But on closer consideration the theory of compensation is illusory reasoning because it is based on an incorrect – and highly exaggerated – conception of the role the cultural sciences can play in this context. I shall not go into the question of whether this pessimistic image of dullness and de-humanization is correct here. Even if it is correct, the cultural sciences are not the panacea some think they are. Those that can form a counterweight are not the scientists, no matter how elevating the material they are dealing with might be, but the workers who produce cultural values in practice: writers and thinkers, visual artists, architects, musicians, and surrounding them the entire world of organizations in which they work: theatres, exhibitions, concerts and galleries. The counterbalance does not lie in the history scholar who studies documents from the archives and generally writes for colleagues, but in the enthusiasm of history teachers. Writers are generally not academics, and the art of painting flourished for centuries before art historians ever came into existence. Linguistics may indirectly increase the effectiveness of learning foreign languages, but it does not result in a more refined use of language. The cultural sciences contribute as little directly to the "higher things of life" as aerodynamics does to popularizing flying as a sport, or as astronomy does to the beauty of the stars in the sky.

The supposition that those who study culture should also be pre-eminent producers of cultural values does not do the cultural sciences any good because, especially in a period of utilitarian thinking, it can easily lead to further marginalization: the cultural sciences as a beautiful but ultimately not indispensable decoration. The expectations that arise from this are sometimes absurd. Not so long ago the opinion was expressed in a serious document that the humanities should contribute to a high degree to solving the problem of "too much leisure time" (as a result of shorter working hours, earlier retirement, and an ageing population). The argument was meant well because it was intended to demonstrate the right of these sciences to exist, but the marginalization contained in it is ominous: philosophy as a purposeful leisure-time activity, linguistics as a substitute for fishing and collecting stamps. Because the theory of substitution is essentially based on the wrong premises, it can result in such absurd conclusions. It is not very helpful to scholars when such false arguments are used, because in the long run they are counterproductive.

In the end the question of how much the cultural sciences produces socially cannot be answered from the point of view of the sciences themselves. "Usefulness" is a question of social demand; each culture and each era formulates in its own way what is considered socially useful. Scholars are convinced that their field of research – the behaviour of man in the cultural environment he has created, now and in past – is legitimized by the importance of the subject itself, and that this importance is of a different order to that of the natural and life sciences. It would be a good thing if they were to stand by this point of view without dragging in false arguments. Whether society shares this point of view depends on its total system of values, and the evolution of that system is a global process that cannot be steered, whatever politicians and other policy-makers might think. Even those who doubt the point of these sciences do so because our current culture has programmed them to do so. There's no escape: marginalization of the cultural sciences is itself a manifestation of culture – and as such is an interesting subject of cultural study.

About the authors

Pim den Boer (1950) studied history in Leiden and Paris. He took his doctoral degree in 1987 in Leiden with the thesis Geschiedenis als beroep. De professionalisering van de geschiedbeoefening in Frankrijk 1818-1914 (Nijmegen, 1987). From 1978-88 he held a post at the Institute for History of the University of Utrecht. In 1988 he was appointed Professor in the history of European culture at the University of Amsterdam. Recent publication: Europese cultuur: geschiedenis van een bewustwording (Nijmegen, 1989).

Dr. Margret Brügmann (Hamburg, 1948) is associate professor at the Centre of Women Studies and the Department of Comparative Literature of the University of Nijmegen, the Netherlands. Main interests of research: postmodernism, feminine aesthetics, literature of the 19th and 20th century.
Books written and/or edited:
- Amazonen der Literatur. Studien zur deutschsprachigen Frauenliteratur der 70er Jahre (Amazons of Literature. Studies of German Women's Literature of the Seventies), Amsterdam 1986.
- Vrouwen in opspraak. Vrouwenstudies als cultuurkritiek (Women get themselves talked about. Women Studies as Criticism of Culture), Nijmegen 1987.
- Verstilde verhalen – sprekende beelden. Mythen, vrouwelijkheid en het postmoderne (Silenced Stories – Talking Images. Myths, femininity and Post-Modernism), Amsterdam 1990.

A. Cohen (1922). Doctorate in General Linguistics (1952) on dissertation "The phonemes of English".
1954-55: Rockefeller Fellow, M.I.T., Mass.

Started in 1959 speech research at Institute of Perception Research (IPO), Eindhoven, The Netherlands. From 1967 till retirement Professor of English and Phonetics, Utrecht University. Chairman of 10th Int. Congress of Phonetic Sciences (since 1983). Since 1985 Director of national research programme on Analysis and Synthesis of Speech.

Paul Op de Coul (1940) studied violoncello with Tibor de Machula and musicology at the University of Utrecht and at the Free University of West-Berlin. From 1973 to 1985 he was lecturer in the theory and history of music at the University of Groningen. In 1983 he completed his doctoral thesis on Ferruccio Busoni's opera *Doktor Faust* and was awarded his FHD. In 1985 he was appointed to the chair of Professor of Music History (post 1600) at the University of Utrecht. His special area of interest is the theory and history of the opera in the 19th and 20th centuries.
Co-author Frits de Haen (1955) studied guitar at the Arnhem Conservatory of Music and musicology at the University of Utrecht. Besides his activities at this university he is working both as a publicist and as a radio broadcaster.

Simon C. Dik (1940) is professor of General Linguistics in the University of Amsterdam since 1969. After studies in Classics and General Linguistics he obtained his Ph.D. in 1968 (Coordination; its implications for the theory of general linguistics). His main subsequent publications are Algemene Taalwetenschap (1970, with J.G. Kooij), Functional Grammar (1978), Studies in Functional Grammar (1980), The theory of Functional Grammar (1989), and PROFGLOT: and English-French-Dutch PROLOG implementation of Functional Grammar (forthcoming). Prof. Dik was chairman of the Linguistic Foundation of the Dutch Research Council (NWO) and Dean of the Faculty of Arts of the University of Amsterdam. Currently he represents NWO and the Royal Dutch Academy of Sciences in the European Science Foundation, and chairs the Committee for the Humanities of the Academy. He is a founding member of the Academia Europaea.

Prof. dr. Wim van Dooren (1934), teaches philosophy at the universities of Delft and Utrecht.
His main publications concern the philosophy of Hegel, dialectic philosophy, the history of philosophy in the Netherlands and the philosophy of the Renaissance.
He is now editing the work of the Italian Renaissance philosopher Pietro Pomponazzi.

Douwe Wessel Fokkema (1931) is Professor of Comparative Literature and Director of the Research Institute for History and Culture, University of Utrecht. His recent books are Theories of Literature in the Twentieth Century (1977, 1986) and Modernist Conjectures: A Mainstream in European Literature, 1910-1940 (1987), both written in collaboration with Elrud Ibsch. He also wrote Literary History, Modernism and Postmodernism (1984) and co-edited Approaching Postmodernism (1986), Exploring Postmodernism (1987) and Théorie littéraire: Problèmes et perspectives (1989). He was secretary and vice-president (1973-1982) and later president (1985-1988) of the International Comparative Literature Association.

J. Goudsblom is Professor of Sociology at the University of Amsterdam. His publications in English include Dutch Society (Random House, 1967), Sociology in the Balance (Basil Blackwell, 1977), Nihilism and Culture (Basil Blackwell, 1980) and (with E.L. Jones en Stephen Mennell) Human History and Social Process (University of Exeter Press, 1989). His current research is focused on the domestication of fire as a long-term socio-cultural process.

A.W. Grootendorst was born in 1924. During the years 1942-1946 he devoted himself to the study of Greek and Latin. From 1946-1952 he studied Mathematics and Physics at the University of Leiden, where he obtained in 1959 his doctorate with a thesis on theta-series in relative-quadratic number fields; his supervisor was Prof. Dr. H.D. Kloosterman.
From 1956-1989 he worked at Delft University of Technology, first as a scientific collaborator, subsequently as a lecturer, and finally as a full professor.
With his colleague Prof.Dr. B. Meulenbeld he wrote a textbook on Analysis in 3 volumes. Further he published several articles, a.o. on the history of mathematics, and translations of a number of Latin mathematical texts; some of them are brought together in a booklet with the title "Grepen uit de Geschiedenis van de Wiskunde" (Selected topics from the History of Mathematics).
In 1989 he retired from the University *propter aetatem immunis*.

Wilt L. Idema (1944) studied Chinese and Non-Western Sociology at Leiden, Sapporo and Kyoto. Obtained his doctorate at Leiden University in 1974. Since 1976 Professor of Chinese Literature in the Department of Chinese Language and Culture, Leiden University. Visiting Professor at the University of Hawaii at Manoa (1977); first Grotius Fellow of the Netherlands-America

Commission for Educational Exchange (1987).

Since September 1988 Director of the Centre for Non-Western Studies at Leiden University.

Publications: Chinese Vernacular Fiction, the Formative Period (1974); Chinese Theater 1100-1450, A Source Book (1982, together with Stephen H. West); The Dramatic Oeuvre of Chu Yu-tun 1379-1439 (1985); The Moon and the Zither, the Story of the Western Wing (1990, together with Stephen H. West).

Ton Langendorff (1950) is the only non-scholar among the authors. After he graduated in clothing engineering he studied social anthropology and sociology at the University of Amsterdam. He published several reports on science indicators. As a staff member of the Dutch Advisory Council for Science Policy (RAWB) he recently finished a statistical and policy oriented report on the present situation of the humanities in the Netherlands.

Adriaan Wessel Reinink (1933) studied Law and History of Art at the University of Leiden. PhD Dissertation on *K.P.C. de Bazel, Architect* (Leiden University Press 1965). Professor of Architectural History at the University of Utrecht since 1969.

Further publications: Amsterdam and Berlage's Exchange (Staatsuitgeverij, The Hague 1975); Rom: Spanish Treppe (with Roland and Janne Günter, VSA Hamburg, 1979); IJskelders. Koeltechnieken van weleer (Ice Houses; Heuff, Nieuwkoop 1981).

His next book will be a monograph on the architect Herman Hertzberger (010 Publishers, Rotterdam) and a German translation of Ice Houses (Böhlau, Vienna).

He is Chairman of the Dutch Association of Art Historians and Secrétaire Scientifique of the Comité International d'Histoire de l'Art (CIHA).

H. Schoenmakers (1944) studied Theatre Studies at the University of Amsterdam. From 1971 – 1984 he was lecturer at the Theatre Department of this University. Since 1984 he has been professor of Theatre Studies and Head of the Theatre, Film and Television Department of the Faculty of Arts and Literature of the University of Utrecht. As a visiting professor he lectured at the theatre departments of the Universities of Bologna (1986), Stockholm (1988), Antwerp (1988/1989), and Munich (1989).

He wrote a dissertation on performance theory and reception research (1983: Zeven Manieren om de Zevende Hemel te Bezoeken: Van receptie-onderzoek in het theater naar een voorstellingstheorie; Seven Ways to Visit Cloud

Cuckooland: From reception research to a performance theory). Other publications are mainly in the field of reception research, performance theory, and theatre semiotics. In 1989 he published a book, Filosofie van de Theaterwetenschappen (Philosophy of Theatre Studies) (Martinus Nijhoff, Leiden).

H.T. Waterbolk (1924) read biology and archaeology at the University of Groningen. From 1951-1954 he was a palynologist with the Bataafsche Petroleum Maatschappij (Royal Dutch/Shell Group) in the Hague. From 1954-1987 he occupied the chair of Prehistory and Germanic Archaeology at the Biologisch-Archaeologisch Instituut, University of Groningen. He was a member of both the Netherlands Monuments Board (1956-1974) and the Nature Conservancy Board (1962-1982).In 1970 he became a member of the Royal Netherlands Academy of Sciences. From 1981-1986 he served as President of the Board of ARCHON (Foundation for Archaeological Research in the Netherlands, a branch of NWO, the Netherlands Organization for Scientific Research).

H.A.J. Wegman was born in 1930 and studied theology (History of liturgy and theology) in Rome and Paris. He received his doctorate (Pàques du premier jour au huitième) in 1959. Since 1970 he has occupied the chair of the history of liturgy and theology at the Catholic Theological University Utrecht (Netherlands) in association with the theological faculty of the University of Utrecht. His publications include Geschiedenis van de Christelijke eredienst in het Westen en in het Oosten, 2nd ed., Hilversum 1983 (English translation: Christian Worship in East and West: A study Guide to Liturgical History, New York 1985). From 1980 to 1986 he was chairman of STEGON (Dutch Research Foundation for Theology and Religious Studies) and of the Research Commission of the Section Theology of the Council of Universities of the Netherlands.

Prof.dr. Erik Zürcher studied Chinese language at Leiden University, with additional training in various branches of pre-modern Chinese studies at Stockholm (Chinese art) and Paris (Chinese Buddhism). Since 1962 he is professor of East Asian History at Leiden University. His special field of interest is the history of intercultural relations, and the Chinese reaction to complex systems of thought imported from abroad. In this context he has published studies on Chinese Buddhism and on early Sino-European contacts. Since 1975 he is general director of the Sinological Institute of Leiden University.